TAKING A STAND

TAKING A STAND

Contemporary US Stand-Up Comedians as Public Intellectuals

Edited by Jared N. Champion and Peter C. Kunze

University Press of Mississippi / Jackson

The University Press of Mississippi is the scholarly publishing agency of
the Mississippi Institutions of Higher Learning: Alcorn State University,
Delta State University, Jackson State University, Mississippi State University,
Mississippi University for Women, Mississippi Valley State University,
University of Mississippi, and University of Southern Mississippi.

www.upress.state.ms.us

The University Press of Mississippi is a member
of the Association of University Presses.

Any discriminatory or derogatory language or hate speech regarding race,
ethnicity, religion, sex, gender, class, national origin, age, or disability that
has been retained or appears in elided form is in no way an endorsement
of the use of such language outside a scholarly context.

Copyright © 2021 by University Press of Mississippi
All rights reserved

First printing 2021
∞

Library of Congress Cataloging-in-Publication Data

Names: Champion, Jared N., editor. | Kunze, Peter C. (Peter Christopher), editor.
Title: Taking a stand : contemporary US stand-up comedians as public intellectuals / edited by Jared N. Champion and Peter C. Kunze.
Description: Jackson : University Press of Mississippi, 2021. | Includes bibliographical references and index.
Identifiers: LCCN 2021036662 (print) | LCCN 2021036663 (ebook) | ISBN 9781496835482 (hardback) | ISBN 9781496835499 (trade paperback) | ISBN 9781496835505 (epub) | ISBN 9781496835512 (epub) | ISBN 9781496835529 (pdf) | ISBN 9781496835536 (pdf)
Subjects: LCSH: Stand-up comedy—United States—History and criticism. | United States—Intellectual life—20th century. | United States—Intellectual life—21st century.
Classification: LCC PN1969.C65 T35 2021 (print) | LCC PN1969.C65 (ebook) | DDC 792.7/6028092—dc23
LC record available at https://lccn.loc.gov/2021036662
LC ebook record available at https://lccn.loc.gov/2021036663

British Library Cataloging-in-Publication Data available

CONTENTS

ACKNOWLEDGMENTS
ix

INTRODUCTION. LAUGHING OUT LOUD
Stand-Up Comedians in the Public Sphere
Jared N. Champion and Peter C. Kunze
3

1. MO'NIQUE
Con Woman and Sister Citizen in *I Coulda Been Your Cellmate*
Linda Mizejewski
16

2. SCORCHED-EARTH COMEDY
Laughing Off Wounded Warriors with the Humor of Bobby Henline
Christopher J. Gilbert
32

3. MARIA BAMFORD
A/Way with Words
Rebecca Krefting
52

4. AWKWARD EMBRACE
Tig Notaro and the Humor of Social Discomfort
Kathryn Kein
70

5. COMEDY FROM THE INTERSECTIONS
Chris Rock on Class and Race
Philip Scepanski
86

6. WHITE COMEDIANS, STRATEGIC RACIST HUMOR, AND THE (RE)NORMALIZATION OF RACISM
Lisa Lampanelli as a Case Study
Raúl Pérez
103

7. LEGUIZAMO'S COMIC FRAME
Identity and the Art of Impersonation
Miriam M. Chirico
123

8. "OF COURSE, BUT MAYBE"
Louis C.K. and the Contradictory Politics of Privilege
David Gillota
139

9. JERRY SEINFELD VERSUS PC SOCIAL MEDIA
Professional Dissonance and the Public Intellectual as Gatekeeper
Timothy J. Viator
154

10. STANDING FLAT-FOOTED AND TALKING
W. Kamau Bell Talks Race in an Age of "Post-Race"
Monique Taylor
168

11. SMARTPHONE SOCIOLOGY
Aziz Ansari on Intimacy in the Twenty-First Century
Ila Tyagi
184

12. STEWART HUFF, P.I.
Intellectual at Large
Susan Seizer and Aviva Orenstein
199

13. LARRY THE CABLE GUY
The Anti-Political Correctness Public Intellectual
David R. Dewberry
219

14. "KILLER CLOSER"
Doug Stanhope and the White Libertarian Stand-Up Tradition
Thomas Clark
237

15. THE COMEDIAN AS PREACHER
Bill Hicks and the Rhetoric of Fundamentalism
Rob King
252

ABOUT THE CONTRIBUTORS
267

INDEX
272

ACKNOWLEDGMENTS

First and foremost, we want to thank our contributors for their expertise, scholarly excellence, and patience. This process was unusually long, and they continued to support our efforts to produce this book with grace and kindness.

We would like to thank Katie Keene for stewarding this project through review and publication, and Mary Heath for her adept editorial assistance. Their professionalism, encouragement, and good humor were appreciated throughout the process. We also appreciate Valerie Jones, Evan Young, and Todd Lape for their assistance in seeing the book through production.

Jared would like to thank Mercer University for their continued support of his research and work in gender and popular culture. In particular he wishes to thank Rebecca Krefting for encouragement throughout the anthology's completion. Peter would like to thank Rebekah Fitzsimmons, Naomi Hamer, Derritt Mason, Angel Daniel Matos, Kate Slater, and Victoria Ford Smith for their suggestions and support. Peter would also like to thank the library support staff at the University of Texas at Austin and at Eckerd, especially Cristina Juska; the dedicated professionals in each institution helped locate much of the research needed to complete this project. Finally, love and gratitude to Kimberly Feldman, who always makes me laugh.

TAKING A STAND

Introduction

LAUGHING OUT LOUD
Stand-Up Comedians in the Public Sphere

Jared N. Champion and Peter C. Kunze

In 2015, the journalist Megan Garber proposed in *The Atlantic* that comedians had harnessed the power of social media to become public intellectuals. "Comedians are fashioning themselves not just as joke-tellers," she observed, "but as truth-tellers—as intellectual and moral guides through the cultural debates of the moment."[1] Holding up the recent television success of Amy Schumer (*Inside Amy Schumer* [2013–2016]), Keegan-Michael Key and Jordan Peele (*Key and Peele* [2012–2015]), Abby Jacobson and Ilana Glazer (*Broad City* [2014–2019]), and such seasoned stand-up comedians as Patton Oswalt, Sarah Silverman, and Nick Kroll as examples, Garber argued that comedians' jokes double as arguments. In so doing, she said, they insert themselves into the national dialogue as voices of reason dedicated to social change.

These claims undoubtedly amused scholars of comedy and humor, who have long explored how comedians operate as spokespeople for and commentators on society. In US culture, one need only look to the wisdom of the crackerbox philosophers, the varied works of Mark Twain, the Semple stories of Langston Hughes, the newspaper columns of Will Rogers, or the poetry of Dorothy Parker for a nuanced balance of cultural criticism and humor.[2] Garber's argument, in fact, depends on a blatant straw man that pigeonholes contemporary comedy as the onetime "province of angsty and possibly drug-addled white guys making jokes about their needy girlfriends and airplane food"—a bold swipe at the likes of Bill Hicks, Marc Maron, and Jerry Seinfeld. Garber not only dismisses the complexity of these performers' comedy, but she also neglects a wealth of comedians of color and women comedians who perform much of the same intellectual labor as those more recent comedians she exalts. The work of Moms Mabley, Dick Gregory, Joan Rivers, Phyllis Diller, and Lily Tomlin engaged with the social politics of their time while also imagining radical futures where political power would be redistributed and cultural citizenship would be guaranteed. Indeed, Rebecca Krefting's influential work on "charged humor"—that is, politically engaged humor that contests social injustice and the marginalization of minoritized citizens—clearly demonstrates how comedians see themselves not just as entertainers, but very often as advocates, gadflies, and even moral authorities.[3] While Garber admits that Carlin, Pryor, and Rivers were engaged in "productive subversion," she hesitates to elevate them to the public intellectual status she so readily affords to Schumer and company.

But Garber does make one point that even scholars of humor and comedy might build upon in their own work: the reception of these comedians as intellectuals. While we can find intellectualism in the work of humorists and comedians dating back to the earliest days of American humor, we would be well served to examine not just what these individuals said, but the power they were afforded in the public sphere as knowledgeable, credible articulators of these ideas. Late-night television was long been a forum for this kind of intellectual performance, as shows such as *Politically Incorrect* (1993–2002) gave stand-up comedians equal footing with academics, activists, and politicians. When Janeane Garofalo decried Tea Partiers as racists to Keith Olbermann on MSNBC or Dennis Miller railed against liberal "snowflakes" on Fox News's *The O'Reilly Factor* (1996–2017), they were mobilizing their public status as prominent comedians to vocalize their personal political investments. Similarly, when Sarah Silverman appeared at the Democratic National Convention, she channeled her popularity as a comedian to draw attention to the need for unity among Democrats after a tense showdown between the party's nominee, Hillary Clinton, and her primary opponent, Vermont Senator Bernie Sanders, whom Silverman had publicly supported throughout the primary. Garofalo, Miller, and Silverman demonstrate stand-up comedians' long-standing commitment to engaging with the major issues and ideas of their times. In fact, one might rightly argue that such engagement is essential to what comedians do. Comedians are rare as entertainers in that their acts are in a constant state of flux, as jokes may be tweaked depending on the venue, the audience, or the day's events. They must be rhetorically sophisticated about assessing and understanding the context they are entering into in any given performance to ensure maximum comedic effectiveness. Furthermore, the very art of stand-up comedy requires performers to assume an upright posture and to address (and respond to) the audience in front of them; this essential posturing conveys "status and power as well as qualities of aggression and authority."[4] By necessity, they are very often astute observers of the sociopolitical moment in which we live, prepared to comment on it and defend their point of view against potentially unresponsive or hostile audiences.

The public roles that comedians have assumed over time warrants our continuing attention, and this collection draws attention to recent endeavors along these lines. Our focus on the present has two goals. First, we want to direct scholarly consideration to both emerging and established comedians, some of whom are being discussed here at length by academics for the first time. Second, we want to consider the current social and cultural moment as one of change—technologically, politically, and intellectually. To this end, we continue the critical conversation around stand-up comedy as a cultural form that is, in the words of Matthew R. Meier and Casey R. Schmitt, "uniquely rhetorical and capable of engaging discourses of social change by calling into question dominant cultural practices and assumptions."[5] Discussing stand-up comedians as public intellectuals allows the writers included here to consider the enduring importance of both comedians and intellectuals to US culture and the national discourse around social and political issues. We hope that this work furthers the ongoing public and scholarly conversation of the sociopolitical *and* intellectual significance of comedy in the United States.

Before proceeding any further, we need to unpack the term "public intellectual," a concept that is seemingly self-evident in the naming and yet takes on many meanings depending on who is using it. Most discussions of intellectualism rightfully return to Antonio Gramsci's foundational work on traditional and organic intellectuals. Whereas traditional intellectuals continue the long-standing convention of learned individuals being trained within the academy for lives of institutional service and administration, the organic intellectual emerges from within the group itself to inspire, organize, and lead her people. Gramsci proposed that "All men are intellectuals, one could therefore say: but not all men have in society the function of intellectuals."[6] Edward Said largely supports this notion, noting how both radical and reactionary movements have found leadership through the labor of intellectuals.[7] Said importantly adds:

> The central fact for me is, I think, that the intellectual is an individual endowed with a faculty for representing, embodying, articulating a message, a view, an attitude, philosophy or opinion to, as well as for, a public. And this role has an edge to it, and cannot be played without a sense of being someone whose place it is publicly to raise embarrassing questions, to confront orthodoxy and dogma (rather than to produce them), to be someone who cannot easily be co-opted by gov-

ernments or corporations, and whose *raison d'être* is to represent all those people and issues that are routinely forgotten or swept under the rug.[8]

We can see in Said's words an affinity with Rebecca Krefting's aforementioned proposal that charged humor serves to empower the marginalized through a direct confrontation with power structures that perpetuate inequality and disenfranchisement. Especially important here is the idea of the public intellectual as a communicator both of and for these people. Megan Garber herself admits that "laughter [serves] as a lubricant for cultural conversations—to help us to talk about the things that needed to be talked about,"[9] an idea often articulated by humor scholars. Regina Barreca, for instance, contends that humor and comedy have "always been the most effective way to put abstract impressions into specific and precise language: to reduce experience, emotion, or thought into its essence—without misrepresenting it—is a kind of alchemy."[10] Stand-up comedians must be able to build intimate relationships with their audiences, and their ability to do so allows them to push against established worldviews, thereby prompting laughter.[11] The artfulness of stand-up comedy lies in the careful combination of complex ideas, accessible communication, and engaging performance. If comedians falter on any of these fronts, they risk alienating their audience.

This is not to say that all comedians assert themselves as public intellectuals; rather, understanding comedians as such requires us to give credit to the arduous task of translating nuanced concepts, theories, or positions in a way that is succinct, understandable, and captivating. In his study of public intellectuals, Richard A. Posner observes that most intellectuals remain in the academy because their role as specialists rarely prepares them for a life of public intellectualism, in which they have to serve occasionally as a "critical commentator addressing a nonspecialist audience on matters of broad public concern."[12] Much of that labor, Posner argues, rests on journalists, who explain the ideas for a general audience.[13] Posner's definition, therefore, distinguishes between a scenario in which the intellectual works within their academic discipline to develop sophisticated ideas and the journalist who translates that intellectual's ideas for a reading public, and a second scenario in which the public intellectual translates his or her ideas directly for the public through editorials, talk show appearances, and trade books. According to Posner, then, stand-up comedians may be translators, but they are rarely public intellectuals.

In his recent book, *The Ideas Industry*, Daniel W. Drezner separates public intellectuals from thought leaders. While he acknowledges that both groups engage in "acts of intellectual creation," public intellectuals have a broad knowledge they can use to critique and even expose "intellectual charlatans," whereas "thought leaders" tend to become cheerleaders for a single, game-changing idea.[14] Boiling it down to a series of oppositions, Drezner sees public intellectuals generally to be critics, skeptics, and pessimists by trade, and thought leaders as creators, evangelists, and optimists.[15] In reading this list, one can see how stand-up comedians can move among these categories. Like public intellectuals, stand-up comedians benefit from a certain status, wherein they develop an outsider personality that allows them to present themselves as uncompromised individuals who can comment on their society without being tainted by its influence.[16] John Limon has gone so far as to suggest that stand-up comedians are compelled to channel their abjection into their art, which allows them to escape it precisely by "living it as an act."[17] Similarly, Jessyka Finley explores how Black women comics have employed stand-up comedy "from the position of their own marginality . . . as an attempt to equalize the duties and responsibilities of citizenship and everyday life."[18] On the other hand, stand-up comedy is a commercial endeavor that requires participants to satisfy their customers in order to achieve a livable income, let alone popularity and prestige.

For the latter reason, Elizabeth Bruenig of *The New Republic* dismissed Garber's argument because the Jon Stewarts and Stephen Colberts of the comedy world possess a "special motivation to flatter their audiences . . . win some laughs and get good ratings."[19] This rather facile response echoes a vulgar Marxism that fails to acknowledge the sophistication of stand-up comedy as an artform, preferring instead to dismiss it out of hand as commercial dreck. Again, we might return to Said, who argued that rather than dismissing, for example, the philosopher Jean-Paul Sartre for his friendships and rivalries, one should embrace "these complications [to] give texture and tension to what he said, expos[ing] him as a fallible human being, not a dreary and moralistic preacher."[20] Indeed, comedians are very often what Lawrence E. Mintz has called "*negative exemplars*" whose numerous defects allow us not only to find them amusing, but to identify with them.[21] It is here, with our guard down, that we may become open to new ideas through suggestion or musing rather than overbearing didacticism. Bambi Haggins proposes this very notion at the end of her influential study of post-soul African American stand-up comedians:

> Although the black comedy of both the civil rights era comics and post-soul comics, like the entertainment-based moments of philanthropy discussed earlier, might seem unlikely repositories for serious

discourse on race and class, it is within spaces not marked as necessarily pedantic or particularly threatening that folks might actually become open to questioning their ideological presuppositions—whether during their spectatorial experience or in their postviewing musing. And the comic messenger makes a difference.[22]

In a culture long criticized for its anti-intellectualism, stand-up comedians in the United States have become one avenue for the exploration and promotion of a range of ideas, whether one is discussing gender roles, immigration, post-racialism, or mental illness. Even if the idea is not originally their own, it is rather hard to dismiss completely the valuable work being performed by such comedians in rendering these ideas public, accessible, and (perhaps most impressively) funny.

With this observation in mind, we might be better served by shifting our understanding of "public intellectual" from an identity in society to a type of labor one can perform for the public. Discounting the social and cultural value of comedians who introduce, repackage, and endorse these ideas because they do so in a shorter form, in a commercial context, or on the backs of "real" intellectuals is an arbitrary distinction. Both labors are important, and just as journalists provide a valuable service in translating ideas for their readers, so too do comedians, although they provide that valuable service in a different medium and context. Both "services" are intellectual in nature; they are simply different in the kind of intellectual labor that they perform compared to the specialist based in a university setting. Considering stand-up comedians as public intellectuals, therefore, allows us to examine different roles that comedians play within our national discourse while also re-examining the oft-cited presumption that the United States has long been afflicted by anti-intellectualism—at least, periodically.[23] In a political moment when a president attempts to enact authoritarian measures and the very concept of truth is called into question, comedy becomes an invaluable weapon for interrogating the powers that be. At the same time, comedy can empower the same individuals, and as the #MeToo movement has shown, some comedians misuse the power to demoralize and subjugate others rather than directing it toward defusing oppressive officials and power structures. The Australian comedian Hannah Gadsby's 2018 special *Nanette*, for example, powerfully addresses how comedy can reinforce the domination it claims to resist. Scholars of comedy have the opportunity and obligation to reveal how comedy and laughter both can undermine and reinforce the hegemony.[24]

We should also make clear that we are not claiming that scholars have not considered stand-up comedians as intellectuals before. They most certainly have done so, though they have rarely used that term. Rather, by focusing our attention here on recent stand-up comedians we seek to explore how stand-up comedians have expanded into other media, including books, television shows, social media, and film, to exalt their various intellectual priorities. In so doing, they do not so much give up their reputation as stand-up comedians as leverage themselves into the role of public intellectual, very often of the organic variety theorized by Gramsci. This framing builds on foundational and emerging scholarship on stand-up comedians as anthropologists (Koziski), social and cultural mediators (Mintz), cultural critics (Gilbert), activists (Krefting), and rhetoricians (Meier and Schmitt) to explore how the enduring and changing significance of stand-up comedians impacts our social, cultural, and intellectual life in the United States.[25] In the chapters that follow, scholars (much like their subjects) adapt an accessible approach to analyze, understand, and even critique how stand-up comedians present complex ideas to their public. They complicate Garber's presumptions while conscientiously avoiding simple explanations of how these comedians balance politics, comedy, and commentary. Through these nuanced explorations, *Taking a Stand* reveals that quite often the most pleasurable comedy in fact offers a forceful, even radical stance that deserves more attention and analysis than those outside of comedy are willing to give it.

No edited collection is either complete or without flaws, and we want to acknowledge the deficits of this collection. We had commissioned chapters on more women comedians, for example, but various circumstances led those authors to withdraw. The absence of those contributions is made even more lamentable by the volume of excellent feminist scholarship, both historically and recently, on women's stand-up comedy. We hope this present collection will continue the discussion on stand-up comedians as public figures, including articles and books that will address the gaps herein.

The chapters have been clustered thematically, starting with chapters that focus on the local perception of bodies, broadening to works that address the interactions between subjectivities and audiences, and finishing with pieces about comedians working with broad national themes ranging from religion to politics. As with any organizational approach, many of the chapters could fit seamlessly in other sections, but the current groupings bring order to an otherwise often unwieldy topic.

COMEDIC BODIES AND THE BODY POLITIC

Comedians' bodies are as much a part of their performance as the words they speak: Robin Williams used his as a prop, Moms Mabley used hers to seem innocent while her humor very rarely was, and Joan Rivers grounded her "failures" as a woman in jokes about her physical appearance. In this spirit, *Taking a Stand* opens with Linda Mizejewski's chapter on Mo'Nique, an appropriate starting point given Mizejewski's influential work on comedy and femininity, *Pretty/Funny: Women Comedians and Body Politics*. Mizejewski focuses her argument here largely on Mo'Nique's special, *I Coulda Been Your Cellmate* (Binkow, 2007), to demonstrate not only how the performance creates a sisterhood between the performer and audience, but also how the stage, the set, and the costuming all reinforce a hierarchical relationship between the speaker and her immediate audience that carries over to the television audience (home viewers) and the live audience (women in prison). The section then turns to Christopher J. Gilbert's chapter, which makes a similar argument about the politics of visibility present in the work of Bobby Henline, a war veteran who became a comedian after being severely injured by a roadside bomb during a military tour in Iraq. Henline forces audiences to confront the physical horrors of war, but Gilbert adds that Henline's upbeat and positive approach to life creates the parallel risk of erasure, specifically of psychological trauma. As a proxy for injured soldiers, Henline creates in his performance a situation wherein audiences cannot look at him and simultaneously ignore his burns or missing limbs and ears. He makes the corporeal costs of war real, but the audience might also leave with a sense that mental toughness and positivity alone can overcome PTSD and other mental illnesses.

Rebecca Krefting continues the examination of mental illness in her chapter, which approaches the potential of comedy to provoke empathy to combat social stigma in her appropriately titled chapter, "Maria Bamford: A/Way with Words." Indeed, Krefting argues that Bamford pushes audiences to consider mental illness and its effect on gender equality and social hierarchies. She acknowledges that Bamford seems an unlikely candidate for the status of public intellectual, given her small stature and self-acknowledged childlike voice, but these only render her consistent and focused reworking of stereotypes of mental illness all the more powerful, especially given Bamford's ability to avoid "preachy" material.

Kathryn Kein's chapter on Tig Notaro continues the consideration of bodies and threat. For Kein, Tig Notaro's use of discomfort opens up the possibility of cultural citizenship for cancer patients (and others who have fallen ill) as well as people who identify as androgynous. Kein argues that Notaro creates productively uncomfortable pauses that capitalize on cringy material and, in doing so, walks audiences through a revision of stigma. Kein argues that Notaro's hyperbolic awkwardness uses humor to undermine previous associations of awkwardness with shame, replacing them with positive associations. Likewise, Notaro creates a number of jokes about the ways people understand her androgyny, a topic that is front and center in Notaro's comedy—especially in her second special, titled *Boyish Girl Interrupted* (Karas and Notaro, 2015). Most importantly, Kein argues that Notaro's contribution to public intellectualism rests in her new representation of abject bodies.

COMPLICATED SUBJECTIVITIES

The next cluster of chapters interrogates complications that arise when comedians, their subject positions, and their comic material create complicated, if not outright paradoxical, ideological positions. This section opens with a chapter by Philip Scepanski, who raises questions about the ways race and class do (and do not) intersect in Chris Rock's stand-up material. While some critics have challenged Rock's treatment of race, arguing that he confuses or conflates race and class in problematic ways, Scepanski draws upon both Rock's work and the outside criticisms of his work to show that Rock's perspectives on class and class mobility are infused with and defined by race.

Raúl Pérez continues the intersectional analysis of stand-up comedy in his thoughtful discussion of Lisa Lampanelli's most racially problematic material. Here, Pérez addresses the almost paradoxical nature of Lampanelli's success: many of her jokes depend on an outright racist conceit, yet she remains successful in a hypersensitive environment especially concerning racial matters. Pérez argues that Lampanelli skirts claims of "serious racism" by articulating a post-racial fantasy, defined by an imagined world devoid of racism's historical importance. The ethical dilemma, Pérez argues, is that Lampanelli's work creates a model for racist jokes. Miriam M. Chirico considers a parallel complication between subjectivity and ethics in John Leguizamo's work. Chirico asks where the line is between challenging and reifying cultural stereotypes of ethnic identity in Leguizamo's dramatic monologues about identity formation and presentation. The difficulty Chirico highlights is that the audience determines many of the ways stereotypes are made, reinforced, or deconstructed. A Latinx audience would be unlikely to receive the material in quite the same way as mostly white audiences, so Chirico tests Leguizamo's thesis that he creates "prototypes" rather than exploiting stereotypes—a claim Chirico finds complicated by the audience's ability to recognize and understand the jokes' cultural valence.

David Gillota's examination of Louis C.K. tracks an equally problematic tethering of progressive politics to white privilege. Gillota examines C.K.'s inability to move fully outside his own privileged position in order to create a cohesive criticism of that same privileged position. Gillota contends that C.K.'s work critiques American capitalism from a privileged position. But, Gillota points out, C.K.'s positions remain largely inconsistent and often contradictory, as we learned from recent revelations of his sexual misconduct. Timothy J. Viator offers a related assessment of Jerry Seinfeld's challenge of political correctness. Viator points to Seinfeld's criticism of political correctness as a valid metric for assessing comedy and instead insists that comedy only be judged by the laughter it produces (or does not produce). Viator notes, however, that Seinfeld's web series, *Comedians in Cars Getting Coffee* (2012–), steers away from humor to instead grapple with questions of social politics, ironically often returning to political correctness. More simply, Seinfeld's later work depends on a contradictory position where he calls for comedy to be apolitical while simultaneously asserting his power as a comedian to make such arguments.

CHANGING VALUES IN A CHANGING AMERICA

Seinfeld's contradictory take on political correctness reveals a broader trend: as the United States changes, for better or worse, new cultural anxieties emerge, and these tensions become more pronounced as digital media accelerate information dissemination. Some comedians embrace digital technologies and shifting social values, while other comedians remain steadfast in their embrace of tradition. Still, comedians who address national politics, social or governmental, are united in their ability to respond to wide cultural shifts. To open this conversation, this group of chapters begins with Monique Taylor analyzing W. Kamau Bell's articulation of a social justice vision that utilizes the potential of digital media platforms. Bell, who has gained national attention through his CNN docuseries, *United Shades of America* (2016–), cut his teeth on podcasts and other digital projects. Rather than considering social mores in a changing media landscape, as Aziz Ansari does, Bell utilizes emergent technologies to "harness the power of the hashtag" (169). Taylor shows how Bell fits squarely into a tradition of Black intellectualism that speaks to an audience specifically interested in matters of race, whether because they belong to that group (i.e., Black public intellectuals speaking to Black audiences) or because they care about the topic (i.e., white audiences interested in social justice). Bell's power, argues Taylor, rests in his and other Black public intellectuals' ability to appeal to demographically diverse audiences in a way that opens difficult conversations about race in America.

Ila Tyagi's chapter addresses Aziz Ansari's engagement with pro-feminist masculinity in the digital age through what Tyagi terms "smartphone sociology." Ansari's comedy, which often utilizes his cell phone and social media accounts as props, raises questions about social mores and feminism in the digital age. Moreover, Tyagi argues, Ansari's oeuvre includes characters like Tom Haverford (*Parks and Recreation* [2009–2015]), a character who utilizes social media to hyperbolic proportions, or Dev Shah on *Master of None* (2015–), an up-and-coming millennial professional who constantly seeks clarity about evolving social mores in the digital age. Tyagi draws upon Ansari's many comedic registers to show that his engagement with love and heartbreak in the digital age works to challenge binary views of technology's potential harm and benefits.

Susan Seizer and Aviva Orenstein examine the relationship between the audience and the performer through the work of regional road comic, Stewart Huff, using a clear and accessible ethnographic approach. They argue that Huff deserves the status of "Intellectual at Large," despite his small following and geographical limitations, because he has an openness to new ideas that many other comics (and audience members) do not. Huff pairs this openness with an almost incantatory use of tropes that "encourages the audience to *make the show with him*" (emphasis added), a dynamic that creates opportunities for audiences to enter into self-reflection that leads to empathy. In a related address of how comedians respond to their audiences' ideological dispositions, David R. Dewberry argues that Dan Whitney's character "Larry the Cable Guy" can be understood as a "postmodern intellectual," as defined by Zygmunt Bauman. Rather than accept a limited definition of the public intellectual, Dewberry reframes the public intellectual as a sort of social liaison between a specific community and other communities. Dewberry contends that Larry the Cable Guy's anti-intellectualism, especially his attack on political correctness, presents an alternative to the "aristocratic legitimation" and "social superiority" of the "intellectual in a tweed jacket" (224). Dewberry argues that Larry the Cable Guy's broad public reach and consistent antipathy to political correctness render him an unusual public intellectual, but no less a shaper of public thought.

Thomas Clark moves back to race and social politics by suggesting that Doug Stanhope also connects race and class through what Clark terms "the white libertarian stand-up tradition" (237). Clark suggests that Stanhope provides a "work of total criticism" that addresses the social anxieties "of humanity as a species, of society, nation, and family" (238). The inherent shortcoming of Stanhope's existentialist lens, argues Clark, is the reliance on nihilism that leaves humans resigned to a world without objectivity, a dynamic that safeguards white privilege. Clark argues that Stanhope represents the modern-day embodiment of Emerson's "man thinking" or even Thoreau's "majority of one," all while maintaining "the troubling segregation of American society into disconnected filter bubbles of closed discourses" (238). Rob King also advances the discussion of national social politics in his chapter exploring Bill Hicks's attempt to reclaim "comedy's 'healing' promise" as a response to an increasingly disenchanted America. Drawing on comic form and biography, King argues that we can view Hicks's comedy as a sort of "holy mission" that confronts capitalism's corrosion of American ethics. King suggests that Hicks offers less of a diatribe against American culture and more of a church sermon that provides both comprehensive assessment of social problems and an imagined alternative world to which rationalism can retreat. Though he died in 1994, Hicks's approach and influence continue to resonate within the world of stand-up comedy.

Taken together, the chapters in *Taking a Stand* consider a wide array of comedians, intellectual traditions, and sociopolitical complications. Whether a comedian serves as a comic shaman, cultural anthropologist, organic intellectual, or any other of the myriad roles available to comedians generally, one point remains clear: comics respond to and seek to reconcile contemporary anxieties. This collection examines how comedians navigate, understand, and even exploit those ongoing rifts and tensions to position themselves as essential contributors to our national conversation.

Notes

1. Megan Garber, "How Comedians Became Public Intellectuals," *The Atlantic*, May 28, 2015.
2. See, for example, Jennette Tandy, *Crackerbox Philosophers in American Humor and Satire* (Port Washington, NY: Kennikat, 1964); Tracy Wuster, *Mark Twain, American Humorist* (Columbia: University of Missouri Press, 2016); Richard D. White Jr., *Will Rogers: A Political Life* (Lubbock: Texas Tech University Press, 2011); and Sean Zwagerman, *Wit's End: Women's Humor as Rhetorical & Performative Strategy* (Pittsburgh: University of Pittsburgh Press, 2010).
3. Rebecca Krefting, *All Joking Aside: American Humor and Its Discontents* (Baltimore, MD: Johns Hopkins University Press, 2014), 2–5.
4. Linda Mizejewski, *Pretty/Funny: Women Comedians and Body Politics* (Austin: University of Texas Press, 2014), 15.

5. Matthew R. Meier and Casey R. Schmitt, "Introduction: Standing Up, Speaking Out," in *Standing Up, Speaking Out: Stand-Up Comedy and the Rhetoric of Social Change*, ed. Matthew R. Meier and Casey R. Schmitt (New York: Routledge, 2017), xxii.

6. Antonio Gramsci, *Selections from the Prison Notebooks of Antonio Gramsci*, ed. Quintin Hoare and Geoffrey Nowell-Smith (London: Lawrence and Wishart, 1971), 9.

7. Edward W. Said, *Representations of the Intellectual* (New York: Pantheon, 1994), 10–11.

8. Said, *Representations*, 11.

9. Garber, "How Comedians Became Public Intellectuals."

10. Regina Barreca, "Preface," in *Women and Comedy: History, Theory, Practice*, ed. Peter Dickinson, Anne Higgins, Paul Matthew St. Pierre, Diana Solomon, and Sean Zwagerman (Lanham, MD: Fairleigh Dickinson University Press, 2013), xv.

11. Ian Brodie, *A Vulgar Art: A New Approach to Stand-up Comedy* (Jackson: University Press of Mississippi, 2014), 218.

12. Richard A. Posner, *Public Intellectuals: A Study of Decline* (Cambridge: Harvard University Press, 2003), 5.

13. Posner, *Public Intellectuals*, 161.

14. Daniel Drezner, *The Ideas Industry: How Pessimists, Partisans, and Plutocrats Are Transforming the Marketplace of Ideas* (New York: Oxford University Press, 2017), 9.

15. Drezner, *The Ideas Industry*, 10.

16. David Gillota, "Stand-Up Nation: Humor and American Identity," *Journal of American Culture* 38, no. 2 (June 2015): 105.

17. John Limon, *Stand-up Comedy in Theory, or, Abjection in America* (Durham, NC: Duke University Press, 2000), 6.

18. Jessyka Finley, "Raunch and Redress: Interrogating Pleasure in Black Women's Stand-up Comedy," *Journal of Popular Culture* 49, no. 4 (2016): 794.

19. Elizabeth Bruenig, "Comedians Are Funny, Not Public Intellectuals," *The New Republic*, June 3, 2015.

20. Said, *Representations*, 14.

21. Lawrence E. Mintz, "Standup Comedy as Social and Cultural Mediation," *American Quarterly* 37, no. 1 (Spring 1985): 75.

22. Bambi Haggins, *Laughing Mad: The Black Comic Persona in Post-Soul America* (New Brunswick, NJ: Rutgers University Press, 2007), 243.

23. Richard Hofstadter, *Anti-intellectualism in American Life* (New York: Vintage, 1966), 6.

24. For example, Raúl Pérez has demonstrated how comedy can reinforce harmful social scripts around race and ethnicity that it claims to be using playfully or ironically. See Raúl Pérez, "Rhetoric of Racial Ridicule in an Era of Racial Protest: Don Rickles, the 'Equal Opportunity Offender' Strategy, and the Civil Rights Movement," in *Standing Up, Speaking Out: Stand-Up Comedy and the Rhetoric of Social Change* (Abingdon, UK: Routledge, 2017), 71–91.

25. In addition to earlier citations of Mintz, Krefting, and Meier and Schmitt, see Stephanie Koziski, "The Standup Comedian as Anthropologist: Intentional Culture Critic," *Journal of Popular Culture* 18, no. 2 (September 1984): 57–76; and Joanne R. Gilbert, *Performing Marginality: Humor, Gender, and Cultural Critique* (Detroit, MI: Wayne State University Press, 2004).

MO'NIQUE
Con Woman and Sister Citizen in *I Coulda Been Your Cellmate*

Linda Mizejewski

"A BIG FAT MOTHERFUCKING SEX SYMBOL"

The incarcerated girls I met at a juvenile detention center several years ago were crazy about Mo'Nique. "Pretty! Hot! And Thick!" they yelled. They were cheering the anagram P.H.A.T. in the Mo'Nique movie *Phat Girlz* (Likké, 2006), a comedy that hijacks fatness into fabulousness and rewards large-bodied women with sex, romance, and an upscale wardrobe. Not many of these girls were actually fat or "thick." But P.H.A.T. was the movie's catchphrase, celebrating female bodies not often seen in romantic comedies—Black bodies most of all, and bodies that don't fit runway measurements of femininity. The girls especially loved the sex scene in which Mo'Nique insists the lights stay on so she can better see her naked Nigerian hunk—and be seen by him as well. *Phat Girlz* was almost universally panned by critics, who rolled their eyes at its predictable one-joke structure. But that one joke—large Black women claiming acknowledgment and desirability—spoke to those girls.

They were at the Scioto Juvenile Correction Facility in Delaware County, Ohio, about an hour's drive from Columbus. A colleague in Women's Studies who was working with the girls had arranged to bring in speakers for presentations in the spring of 2011. Driving the rural roads through the increasingly isolated countryside to get to the bleak spill of buildings there, I used to think of the phrase "put away," and about how far away these girls had been put. They were often noisy and disruptive, and my colleague pointed out that they were anxious to get attention from any adult who wasn't a corrections officer.

The Mo'Nique film I'd originally planned for them was her comedy special/documentary *I Coulda Been Your Cellmate*, filmed just fifty miles away at the Ohio Reformatory for Women, which houses women serving sentences for felonies and violent crimes. The show stirred up some controversy when it was aired on television because Mo'Nique presents the women sympathetically in interviews in the first few minutes of the special, and because during her stand-up routine she expresses admiration for their strength and endurance.[1] Performing for them in the prison yard, she calls out, "You are all some beautiful fucking women! ... We live in a society that will throw you the fuck away, like you no longer exist, and like you're not valuable or worthy." She was filming at the prison, she tells them, because she wants people to *look* at them, and the camera often comes in for close-ups of the women assembled for her performance. "You could be their mother, their daughter, their cousin, their aunt, their sister, their wife. I want people to see you still exist," she says. Because of the sexually explicit comedy in other parts of the show, *I Coulda Been Your Cellmate* was deemed too raunchy for the girls at Scioto, but as it turned out, they found in *Phat Girlz* the same message Mo'Nique had pushed at the women's prison—that they were not throwaways, that even stigmatized and reviled bodies could be given visibility and respect.

This agenda syncs with decades of work by feminist criminologists concerned with the social invisibility of incarcerated women, despite appalling conditions in many prisons including sexual abuse, lack of sanitation, and inadequate access to healthcare, legal counsel, and education. "Like homeless and mentally ill women," writes Joanne Belknap, "women prisoners are among the most neglected and oppressed groups in society."[2] Racism compounds the problem of neglect because prison is regarded as "a fate reserved for 'evildoers' ... fantasized as people of color," Angela Davis points out, so that prison becomes an "abstract site into which undesirables are deposited," making it possible to ignore the role of race in the conditions that got them there.[3] Increasingly, prison reformists and abolitionists focus on declining incomes, the war on drugs, and the cutbacks to social services that have resulted in a 700 percent increase in imprisoned women from 1977 to 2010. The growth of prisons as a profitable industry depends on this population deemed "expendable," as Kay Whitlock puts it—"overwhelmingly people of color, poor people, women, youth, and people with mental illness," a roster that makes even more resonant Mo'Nique's declaration, "I want people to see you still exist."[4]

I Coulda Been Your Cellmate is sometimes compared to Johnny Cash's famous live albums *At Folsom Prison* (1968) and *At San Quentin* (1969), recorded at a time when Cash was making a turnaround after years of drug abuse. All three of these performances are unique in their double address—on the one hand, to a live audience with whom the performers show empathy, and on the other hand, to a general audience which is asked to share that empathy. In turn, the histories, personas, and bodies of the performers are positioned as both abject and privileged, triumphant but also humble. Cash's dark history of substance abuse was well known at the time of his prison performances, and Mo'Nique repeatedly presents herself to the imprisoned women as a sister and equal, someone who came within inches of making a bad decision that would have landed her there among them.

Three years later, she revealed another point of identification: early in *I Coulda Been Your Cellmate*, a title shot tells us that 80 percent of the women at the Ohio Reformatory for Women had been victims of "psychological, sexual, or physical abuse," a statistic that's true of incarcerated women nationwide, and in 2010 Mo'Nique revealed that her older brother had abused her when she was a child. Her fiercely personal investment in this performance is evident in her bond with her audience; she had spent the previous day meeting with many of them individually and in groups, so she brings to her stand-up act her concern with the details of their lives, making them howl with glee at every single thing she says. In turn, in the deeply didactic tone that predominates in this performance, she exhorts the larger, nondiegetic audience to engage in the bond as well: "We are all one decision away, one bad decision, from being right here," she says toward the end of the act. "I am one bad decision away from being your motherfucking cellmate." Throughout the performance, her refrain about being "your cellmate" was addressed to the incarcerated women, but this final declaration sweeps up both audiences in a more radical act of identification.

Marketed as both comedy special and documentary, *I Coulda Been Your Cellmate* deserves critical attention not only for this unique rhetorical agenda, but also for the complexity of its comic sleight of hand, which gradually switches our focus from the performer to the women in front of her in the prison yard. Making this switch and talking us into seeing these women differently, Mo'Nique draws on the tradition of the con woman or female trickster, an approach that further aligns her with criminality. Presenting herself as a lush, outsize diva, taking up all the space on the stage, Mo'Nique wears a jazzed-up version of an orange prison jumpsuit, studded with rhinestones and embellished with fringe, telling the women it's the Mo'Nique-style fabulousness she would bring with her if she were one of them. Doubling as would-be cellmate and star, she flaunts her glamour but constantly emphasizes her proximity and identification with bodies that are restricted, disciplined, and under constant surveillance. Central to this empathy is Mo'Nique's identity as a "sister citizen," to use Melissa V. Harris-Perry's term—a Black woman who understands abjection and shame and stands up against it to claim space in the public sphere. "Dream the impossible dream, baby. Dream as big as you can," Mo'Nique tells the women in her closing manifesto. "They told me I was too fat, they told me I was too Black, they told me I would never be a sex symbol. But right now I'm a big fat motherfucking sex symbol. So fuck what you heard. I love you, baby." Tellingly, it's unclear if her instruction to "fuck what you heard" refers to the voices that had disparaged the incarcerated women or those that disparaged Mo'Nique herself; it works both ways because she has positioned herself among disciplined bodies as a body both disciplined by and in defiance of a critical cultural gaze.

REVOLUTIONARY, REACTIONARY

Mo'Nique brings to *I Coulda Been Your Cellmate* the theme of marginalized bodies that dominated her comedy career from 1989 until 2010, after which she veered toward dramatic roles. Born Mo'Nique Imes in 1967, she developed a following in comedy clubs in the 1980s with her outrageous routines on "life as a BIG girl," as she puts it in her memoir.[5] A number of television guest spots in the ensuing decade led to her breakthrough role on the sitcom *The Parkers* (1999–2004), for which she earned three NAACP awards for Outstanding Lead Actress in a Comedy Series. Her stand-up performances and two comedy specials during that time showcased her explicit sexual bravado about large-bodied women. "Once you go fat, you never go back," she proclaims in *Queens of Comedy* (Purcell, 2001), and asks the "fat-assed girls" in the audience to stand up and take a bow. In *Mo'Nique: One Night Stand* (Small, 2004) she brags that "big girls," with their ample folds of flesh, can offer sexual pleasures that "frail" women can't even imagine. Her campaign for large-bodied female sexuality and attractiveness continues in her books *Skinny Women Are Evil* (2003) and *Skinny Cooks Can't Be Trusted* (2006), as well as in her reality-show beauty pageant for large women, *F.A.T. Chance* (2005–2007)—which, echoing the hijacking of the word "fat" in *Phat Girlz*, defines F.A.T. as "Fabulous And Thick."

When she names herself a sex symbol in *I Coulda Been Your Cellmate*, Mo'Nique affronts the history of that figure not just as grudgingly measured in inches but as overwhelmingly blonde and if not white, then light-skinned with Caucasian features—Mae West through Marilyn Monroe through Kim Kardashian. As DoVeanna S. Fulton points out, Mo'Nique's celebration of large-bodied Black female sexuality inverts the mammy stereotype and disempowers it.[6] The audiences seen in *Queens of Comedy* and *One Night Stand* are predominantly Black, and the camera often catches the women screaming with delight as Mo'Nique describes her sex life, imitates sex acts onstage, and exclaims about the power and awesomeness of Black women. Rebecca Krefting names Mo'Nique as one of the Black female comics whose work is "proactively anti-racist and antisexist" because it "contests the terms by which Black women are defined by the dominant culture."[7] Along the same lines, Shayne Lee names Mo'Nique as one of the "erotic revolutionaries" of contemporary female Black culture, claiming that her "imposing physicality, brash pronouncements about sexual pleasure, and aggressive sexual imagery wield a tremendous impact on black sexual politics."[8] Lee is referring to the politics of respectability that have pressured Black women to "behave" under the critical white gaze because of the Jezebel stereotype that characterizes Black female sexuality as primitive and dangerous.

Yet Mo'Nique's performances in *The Queens of Comedy* and *One Night Stand* illustrate far more conservative and even reactionary impulses as well. For one thing, in celebrating large-bodied women and exposing sexist norms, she attacks other women—"evil skinny bitches"—rather than sexism. Far from blaming men for some of the problems women face, she urges women to do whatever it takes to keep a man. Also, her hypersexualized persona, intended to refute respectability politics, can "reinforce stereotypes of black female sexuality," as one critic puts it.[9] And finally, these performances are laced with homophobic slurs, so that liberating Black women often comes at the expense of gay men.

Seven years after *I Coulda Been Your Cellmate*, in the context of drama rather than comedy, Mo'Nique began making serious appeals for acceptance of gays in relation to her indie film *Blackbird* (Polk, 2014), in which she stars as a religious woman struggling to accept her son's gay identity.[10] *I Coulda Been Your Cellmate* is the pivot between the earlier comic routines and the tolerance message of *Blackbird*, in that Mo'Nique goes for some easy homophobic laughs and dismisses lesbianism as a survival mechanism in prison, but also admits that her biases are wrong and reproaches those who condemn homosexuality on religious grounds. "Who are we to do that bullshit to another human being?" she chides. Her reproof is part of the didactic thrust of this performance that sets it apart from her other comedy specials, in which she performs her homophobic routines without the backpedaling. But her rebukes of homophobia in *I Coulda Been Your Cellmate* are less passionately delivered than the comic bits in which she acts out her distaste for anal sex, sympathizes about it with gay men, and worries about her son being more interested in ice-skating than in football. In this way, Mo'Nique resembles other contemporary Black comedians whose "progressive critiques in the realm of race relations are undermined by a regressive gender politics," as David Gillota puts it, citing *The Queens of Comedy* as evidence that it's a problem not limited to Black male comedians.[11]

The conservative slant of Mo'Nique's comedy is evident in the rhetoric of individual autonomy that structures *I Coulda Been Your Cellmate*. Claiming that all of us are "one bad decision" away from prison is a humbling platitude, but it effaces the social and economic structures that make crime and punishment more likely within some populations. The documentary framing device of this film actually works against the individualist ideology of the stand-up performance. *I Coulda Been Your Cellmate* begins with an introductory sequence filmed in documentary style, with film clips and photo stills accompanied by captions and titles. We're given a brief history of the prison—"one of the toughest in the system," we're told—and we see clips of Mo'Nique interacting with incarcerated women and speaking with several of them one on one. The women speak of making bad decisions, adhering to the overall theme of Mo'Nique's performance; but interspersed with these interviews are title shots that offer a different perspective on what propels a person into serious crime. I mentioned earlier the title shot stating 80 percent of the women had suffered abuse; others report the repeated pattern of substance abuse at an early age and patterns of mothers who were in "abusive or destructive relationships, and that is the legacy they have inherited." These are markers of what criminologists call the "gendered pathways to crime."[12]

Mo'Nique's comic routine, in contrast, is grounded in the rhetoric of personal choice. And despite its radical political positioning—its argument for the dignity and visibility of convicted criminals—it glosses over the political issues of incarceration. It doesn't critique the racism and institutional failures of the criminal justice system, or the human rights violations in the prison system. So it doesn't fall into the category of social satire usually associated with comedians-as-public-intellectuals, the topic of this anthology. In a widely circulated *Atlantic* essay on the subject, Megan Garber focuses on comedians whose political biases tilt left—Jon Stewart, Amy Schumer, Sarah Silverman, Stephen Colbert, Larry Wilmore—and whose work is grounded in wit, satire, and parody. "They're exploring and wrestling with important ideas," she writes. "They're providing fodder for discussion, not just of the minutiae of everyday experience, but of the biggest questions of the day."[13] I want to return to this notion of "everyday experience" and its implications for race, but my point here is that in important ways, *I Coulda Been Your Cellmate* tests the concept of the public intellectual in its ideological slant—its mix of progressive politics and conservative bias—and also in its style, which favors connection and empathy over wit.

In fact, the performance's emotional pitch is its key strategy. Mo'Nique brings anecdotes rather than one-liners to her performance, and though her set is heavily didactic in its appeal to the wider audience, she prioritizes personal identification with the women sitting in front of her. As Mo'Nique performs, the reaction shots show the women's palpable excitement—they are clearly thrilled that a comedy star has not only come into their space but seems to understand who they are. Mo'Nique mentions that it's Mother's Day weekend, acknowledges how many of the women are mothers, and talks extensively about her own experiences as a mother and the recent birth of her twins. For the larger audience watching this, the interactions between Mo'Nique and the women are often touching; she calls a number of them by name as the camera comes in for close-ups, and she ends her performance by inviting one of them up on stage with her to sing a hymn. There's emotional power, too, in a Black woman bringing both her history of marginalization ("too Black") and her stardom to a marginalized audience. Mo'Nique plays the rowdy, loud-mouthed glamour queen who relates to her incarcerated audience because she understands the abjection of Black female experience.

Writing about her "sister citizens," Harris-Perry argues for the importance of emotion in racial politics, claiming that "the internal, psychological, emotional, and personal experiences of black women are inherently political . . . because black women in America have always had to wrestle with derogatory assumptions about their character and identity." Harris-Perry likewise emphasizes *what it feels like* to be misrecognized and shamed because of race, as well as the material and political impact of those feelings; asking to be publicly acknowledged as a citizen and subject, she says, is "nearly impossible" for those who feel ashamed.[14] Harris-Perry is particularly relevant here because when journalist Ta-Nehisi Coates described her as "America's foremost public intellectual," he was met with the objection that she could not compare with Noam Chomsky, E. O. Wilson, Susan Sontag, and Paul Krugman—an argument which, he points out, stakes out public intellectualism as the space of whites who don't write about race.[15]

These racialized assumptions about public intellectualism are reflected in the exclusions evident in Garber, who praises the "newfound diversity" of contemporary comedy even though her own roster of comedians is overwhelmingly white.[16] So it's crucial to contextualize Mo'Nique within the larger history of critical Black comedy, a distinct tradition complicated by its origins, its relationships to white audiences, and its mandate to represent Black experience. Garber glosses over this distinction when, in describing the roots of political comedy, she names the Black comedian Dick Gregory as coming from the same tradition as Joan Rivers and George Carlin, bracketing them as "people who used laughter as a lubricant for cultural conversations—to help us talk about the things that needed to be talked about." But unlike Rivers and Carlin, Gregory was an engaged social activist, often jailed for his participation in civil rights protests, and this was reflected in the political edge of his comedy as well. Gerald Nachman notes in his history of the "rebel" comedians of early stand-up that Gregory was "one of the toughest sociopolitical comedians of the 1960s" who "used his comic tools to build a playing field much larger than comedy."[17] That is, he brought his ironic commentaries on segregation and racism to mainstream audiences on television talk shows and variety shows, and he eventually moved out of the entertainment world completely so that he could focus on civil rights activism. Gregory tapped a long tradition of Black social satire seen not only in venues such as the Black vaudeville Chitlin' Circuit and the Apollo Theater but in street humor and folk humor—a tradition with an "insistent impious thrust," as Mel Watkins puts it in his history of African American humor. This humor, responding to the everyday hypocrisies and biases of American life, is "bitingly satirical . . . an outlet for grievances and a vehicle for critical expression" of "an underlying ironic vision shared by most African Americans."[18]

So while Garber contrasts a comedy of "ideas" to a comedy of "everyday experience," Watkins reminds us that this distinction falters for comedy animated by the political and ideological ironies and absurdities of everyday life for Black people. Bambi Haggins breaks down this distinction in her eloquent analysis of Black comic stars since the civil rights era, from Gregory and Richard Pryor to Dave Chappelle, Martin Lawrence, Whoopi Goldberg, and Chris Rock. Borrowing from Antonio Gramsci, she describes these comedians as "black organic intellectuals" who emerge from the community to express its social and political issues and problems. She also emphasizes how their comedy, crossing over to white audiences, negotiates "the insider's knowledge of the community and the outsider's objective view" in representing the problems and "internal contradictions" of Black culture.[19] Given this context, the contradictory politics of *I Coulda Been Your Cellmate* become legible as an expression of organic Black experience and its mixing of conservative religious attitudes—which includes the mandate of individual choice for redemption—with a progressive sense of collective grievance. We see the Black comic tradition too in the specific "impious thrust" of Mo'Nique's performance: its ironic embrace of criminality as a liminal identity, given that mainstream culture characterizes all Blacks as criminal. Mo'Nique's recognition of the incarcerated women—talking about their living conditions, calling them by name—is linked to her own everyday, organic experience, and this is the emotional charge, the political power, and the controversial contention of *I Coulda Been Your Cellmate*.

CON WOMAN

When Mo'Nique redefines "fat" as F.A.T. ("Fabulous and Thick") or P.H.A.T. ("Pretty, Hot, and Thick"), she uses wordplay in the tradition of the female trickster, who outwits the authorities by manipulating language for her own advantage. In her eloquent work tracing the female trickster from nineteenth-century novels through screwball comedy and sitcoms, Lori Landay describes how this character uses "linguistic trickery and ironic layering of resistance and dominant meanings" as one of her strategies.[20] Landay emphasizes this comic character's antecedents in African American fiction and folklore, where the trickster figure has been a recurrent trope for cunning and survival since the era of slavery. In *I Coulda Been Your Cellmate*, Mo'Nique taps this tradition of subversion under surveillance when, learning that one of the prison rules forbids masturbation in public, she advises the women to find new places on their bodies to pleasure, which she demonstrates by vigorously masturbating a spot on her neck. Then she uses the gesture throughout the performance as a code for duplicitous self-care.

In moments like this, Mo'Nique plays the female trickster for the benefit of the prison audience, but the trickster strategy is evident, too, in the overall trajectory of this comedy special. Her agenda, like the switching of F.A.T. for fat, is to make us see abject bodies differently. *I Coulda Been Your Cellmate* begins with Mo'Nique's trademark raucous comedy but gradually shifts attention to the incarcerated women themselves. It's a classic bait and switch. When Mo'Nique concludes by bringing one of the women onstage with her to sing, we realize the shift in focus was the point all along.

This dynamic is all the more compelling—and tricky—because it involves a shift in how we see Mo'Nique as well. The title *I Coulda Been Your Cellmate* openly invites us to do this; as Landay points out, the trickster character in comedy performs in the "subjunctive," acting out what *could* or *would* happen in the liminal space of fantasy or play.[21] Mo'Nique creates this liminal space by introducing herself as the would-be cellmate with rhinestones on her clothes, appearing on a stage that has been set up as an upscale prison cell, with a toilet in plain view but also a bidet, flowers, a brass lamp, and a silver telephone. Mo'Nique tells the women that she'd toured their cells the day before, "out of respect, to see how y'all living," so she's giving them a chance to look at her space, too. "This is what my shit would look like!" she exclaims, telling them she'd have a comfy bed "with linens on that shit that I done stole from Walmart." As part of the comic fantasy, this joke impels us to imagine Mo'Nique as a small-time con artist pulling a fast one at Walmart, but the joke also lays bare the real-life links among crime, class, and domestic life. It's a detail that shows someone imagining what these women's lives were like. Equally important is the prominent toilet onstage. Even if Mo'Nique had visited and viewed their living quarters as a sign of "respect" for their lives, she was, without their permission, looking at their intimate spaces, which are in fact defined by their lack of privacy, whether or not the toilets are in plain view. So Mo'Nique's subjunctive act, asking her audience to imagine the toilet on stage as hers, is a humbling gesture of empathy through abjection: "This is what my shit would look like."

The female trickster as "bad girl" is always associated with doubleness and duality, Landay tells us, because she's the shadow figure of the "good girl," and thus deeply implicated in the binary stereotypes that anchor Western femininity—the good girl versus the bad girl, the madonna versus the whore.[22] The bad girl has long been Mo'Nique's stand-up persona—highly sexualized, aggressive, quarrelsome—so picturing her as a cellmate is not a stretch. But the point of this performance is the doubleness of the criminal she *could* have been and the glamorous star that she *is*. Her toilet is onstage behind her, but so is her bidet, which she explains to the women is a feel-good way to "clean your figgy pudding." Her stardom is the perfect foil for criminality, in fact, because the latter is imagined here in individualist terms as "one bad decision" away. The ideology of stardom likewise posits extraordinary individualism as the key to success and fame. As a result, Mo'Nique can pull off a set heavily peppered with didactic messages because both her identities—star and would-be criminal—are a matter of good decisions vs. bad decisions: No fighting! she cautions them. Follow the rules! Don't pull any racial "shit!" Be good to each other! The crack in this rhetoric appears at two moments when she tells the women they need to listen to the corrections officers, and there's some muffled booing from the crowd. The booing is clearly for the staff, not for Mo'Nique, but as a brief interruption of her routine, it's a reminder of the power dynamic lurking in the comic doubling of cellmate and star: in the comic subjunctive, she could be there as one of them, but in real life, she's on the side of the institution, which never comes under critique.

Emphasizing her likeness to her audience, Mo'Nique repeats her refrain "I coulda been your cellmate" throughout the performance, sometimes capping various stories about herself. She tells of being angry to the point of violence with an ex-husband and with an irritating nurse during her caesarean section, and she imagines the violence she'd inflict on anyone messing with her sons. Mo'Nique also jokes about her own life in petty crime—writing the occasional bad check and, more creatively, ripping off Popeye's, the fast-food chain, when she worked there in high school. She needed money for a prom dress, she explains, so she stole chickens from the restaurant kitchen, brought them home, fried them up herself, and sold them. With its exchange of pilfered chickens for a party dress, this is a story that rings with the sly humor of trickster folklore. It also reveals the trickster's criminal slant: one of the women shouts to the stage that Mo'Nique shouldn't tell more stories like that, or she really will be a cellmate.

The Popeye's anecdote also demonstrates the smarts and resourcefulness of the con woman (or confidence woman)—the version of the female trickster most characterized by "controlled calculation," as Landay points out.[23] The larger calculations of *I Coulda Been Your Cellmate* are evident in the way Mo'Nique works this anecdote into the act. After telling this story, she calls out by name some of the women she'd met and interviewed the day before, while the camera closes in on their faces in the crowd: "Deborah, it's okay to laugh, baby. How you doing? Hey, Heather. Hey, Mindy. Hey, Julie. Miss Catherine. Nikita, Danielle, Laura. I remember you bitches, baby." In the first half of the performance, Mo'Nique had repeatedly told the cheering audience that they're beautiful and special, a bonding device commonly used by stand-up performers to warm up a crowd. Calling the women by name is a gimmick, too, with calculated effects on her two audiences. It's a surprise move, for one thing, because stand-up performers often pick out audience members to tease or invite into collusion, but they don't call them out by name. For the incarcerated women, the personal acknowledgments come in the wake of a true story about not having money and conning the system; it's not a playful fantasy like the bidet and flowers in the prison cell. So after a moment of honest confession, Mo'Nique comes across as authentically caring when she calls the women by name and tells them she remembers them.

The shout-outs to the individual women occur halfway through Mo'Nique's routine, a clue to the carefully calculated structure of this performance. The interview clips at the beginning had been captioned with information about each woman's crime and sentence: "Aggravated Murder/Robbery, 145 years," "Burglary, 9 years," "Aggravated Murder, 182 years." The scenes portray the women sympathetically—one of them talks emotionally about realizing she'll die in prison, alone—but they also admit their guilt ("Yes, I killed him"), so there's a distance set up between the film's spectators and the documentary subjects who are labeled with captions. However, when we see the same women again, they're the laughing spectators positioned alongside us as the audience for an unruly stand-up performance. Laughter is a powerful bonding device. We're suddenly on the same side in this experience, in not quite the same place as we'd been at the beginning of the film.

Mo'Nique's finale makes an even bolder switch in tone and focus, moving out of comedy into pathos. She invites onstage "the sister that can sing," a young black woman wearing the pink shirt that's the code for a maximum-security prisoner. In a powerful alto voice, she sings *a cappella* the first two verses of the Christian hymn "I Know Who Holds Tomorrow," a song about hope in the face of an uncertain future, which gets a standing ovation from the prisoners and a long, tearful hug from Mo'Nique. It takes Mo'Nique a few moments to compose herself enough to do her wrap-up, in which she praises the singer, lovingly admonishes her not to "fuck up again," and moves into the rousing closing manifesto encouraging the women to "dream," reminding them that she herself was judged "too black" and "too fat" to succeed. So the performance ends on the high-energy note of a traditional stand-up act, but it's a closure that also makes us realize the comedy act was a red herring of sorts. Mo'Nique admits as much after the hymn. Still holding hands with the singer, tears streaming down both their faces, she confesses that although she was "here for a comedy show . . . that's why I thought I came here," she ended up making connections and being touched in ways she hadn't expected. It's an apt summary of the trajectory of this performance.

SISTER CITIZEN

Of Mo'Nique's three comedy specials from this era, *I Coulda Been Your Cellmate* is the only one with a racially diverse diegetic audience, and Mo'Nique's stand-up pitch reflects this change; gone are her routines about large-bodied women and sexy Black sisters, and her appeals of identification are on the basis of gender and class. However, in the second half of the performance, she explicitly identifies herself as part of an historical line of Black female "jump starters" who make trouble but also distinguish themselves in the public sphere. Mo'Nique begins by cautioning the women about racial conflicts and fights at the prison: "All that racial shit, cut that shit out," she chides, but then adds, "Black women, we know we crazy as shit sometimes. We know who the fuck we are. We do. We are jump-starters."

In the context of prison fights, this description of Black women as troublemakers is risky, but in a sly reversal—like the switch from "fat" to

F.A.T.—Mo'Nique includes Harriet Tubman and entrepreneur/activist Madam C. J. Walker as Black women who succeeded precisely because they fall into this category. "Black women like to jump shit off, and it started with Harriet Tubman," she says. "To have to free slaves, that bitch was a jump-starter." She impersonates Walker and Tubman as cussing, bad-tempered women, with Tubman using her sharp tongue to shepherd slaves to freedom: "Buck, get your black ass in the line, n----r! You're gonna fuck it up for everybody!" The historical references are a startling departure from Mo'Nique's usual comedy topics and from this performance's frame of reference, which up to now has encompassed Mo'Nique's personal life and the world of the prison—the bad food, the "tickets" for bad behavior, the prohibition on masturbation. Suddenly opening the world of her comedy routine to Black women's history, Mo'Nique most pointedly makes her move as sister citizen: asserting her right to voice and visibility, connecting it to gender and race, and refusing to be shamed by compounded stereotypes—the Sapphire, the Angry Black Woman, the ghetto Black, the Black violent woman—which, Harris-Perry argues, discourage women from citizenship and participation in politics.

Pausing to identify herself and also the incarcerated Black women in this genealogy ("We know who the fuck we are"), Mo'Nique reveals how much race matters in the rhetorical argument of this performance. Not all of the women in her prison audience are Black, but as a Black woman, Mo'Nique understands the stigma and shame of incarceration. When she uses the word "sister" to describe the singer who joins her later on stage—"right now she's my sister, and we hand in hand"—she's claiming the "Black fictive kinship" of sisterhood that Harris-Perry calls the "voluntary sense of shared identity that maps onto the historical construction of race."[24] The image of the two women hand in hand on the stage powerfully conveys the racial connection but also symbolizes the "fictive kinship" of Mo'Nique with the incarcerated women as a larger group.

With its emotional appeal to humanize and make visible the women at the Ohio Reformatory, *I Coulda Been Your Cellmate* is a powerful demonstration of stand-up comedy as a civic act and manifesto. The question remains, however, as to what kind of cultural and political work she does, exactly, through a performance inside a prison, geared for an emotional impact, distributed and circulated to spectators who will most likely never themselves set foot in such a space nor see in person the women incarcerated there. As with all minority representation, visibility is a charged issue, complicated in this case by the logistics and politics of incarceration. The film begins with Mo'Nique entering the prison as both tourist and tour guide, with the camera following her through the security check. "I'm going to walk through these doors, okay?" she says dramatically. "This is where it begins." Writing about the visual dynamics of the prison tour, Michelle Brown argues that "This kind of looking is fundamentally voyeuristic, distracting, and yet authoritative," giving the spectator "the convenience of the highly mediated, fleeting gaze, looking in on the world of punishment in a manner that does not force or ask observers to speak back or engage in a dialogue."[25] The voyeurism is evident in the close-up shots of the women in the prison yard laughing at the performance; while these shots bond them to us as fellow spectators, they also position us to look at them in a different way than we would look at the spectators in Mo'Nique's other comedy specials because we see a population not usually accessible to us. A title shot at the beginning specifically invites a voyeuristic gaze by explaining the color coding of the women's shirts that indicates which inmates are in maximum or minimum security.

As an especially privileged tourist the day before her performance, Mo'Nique was, in fact, able to "speak back or engage in dialogue" with the women, though we hear only the briefest clips from those conversations; in effect, her stand-up performance is her speaking *for* them, based on what she saw and heard. When she invites the young singer onto the stage at the end of the performance, the woman whispers something into Mo'Nique's ear but doesn't speak a single word of her own for the crowd; instead, she sings a hymn that vocalizes Christian acceptance: "I don't worry about my future/ For I know what Jesus said." Her song is the emotional climax of *I Coulda Been Your Cellmate*, and though it focuses the spotlight entirely on an incarcerated woman and away from Mo'Nique, it's also a carefully scripted moment. As Brown points out regarding prison films and stories, "it is incredibly difficult to find a popular, mainstream representation" that enables "the kinds of complex narratives necessary to challenge our presumptions about prisons."[26] To what extent can the unruliness of comedy resist or erode those presumptions? Does it happen in Mo'Nique's invitation for the women to view her own "shit," for example, or in her repeated self-identification with the women as a mother, a Black woman, and a potential cellmate? And the larger issue is whether or not this performance pushes "questions about power dynamics and privilege and cultural authority," as Garber puts it, or simply makes us feel better about an abject population far far away from most of our lives, like the girls I met at Scioto.

Notes

My thanks to Mary Thomas for her commitment to incarcerated girls and women, which led me to this topic, and for her expertise, which enabled me to write this essay.

1. An angry Dayton newspaper article criticized Mo'Nique for being "overly sympathetic," in her prison interviews and in her performance, to two women convicted of multiple murders in that city. See Mary McCarty, "Comedian Praises Dayton's Christmas Killers in Tasteless TV Special," *The Dayton Daily News*, February 4, 2007.

2. Joanne Belknap, *The Invisible Woman: Gender, Crime, and Justice* (Belmont, CA: Wadsworth International, 1996), 91.

3. Angela Davis, *Are Prisons Obsolete?* (New York: Seven Stories Press, 2003), 5.

4. Kay Whitlock, "The Long Shadow of Prison: My Messy Journey through Fear, Silence, and Racism toward Abolition," in *Interrupted Life: Experiences of Incarcerated Women in the United States*, ed. Rickie Solinger et al. (Berkeley: University of California Press, 2010), 28.

5. Mo'Nique and Sherri A. McGee, *Skinny Women Are Evil: Notes of a Big Girl in a Small-Minded World* (New York: Atria, 2003), 47.

6. DoVeanna S. Fulton, "Comic Views and Metaphysical Dilemmas: Shattering Cultural Images through Self-Definition and Representation by Black Comediennes," *Journal of American Folklore* 117 (463): 84. See Richard Dyer's analysis of the importance of the whiteness of the sex symbol, given the prized value in patriarchal culture that makes the white woman "part of the symbolism of sexuality itself." *Heavenly Bodies: Film Stars and Society*, 2nd ed. (London and New York: Routledge, 2004), 42.

7. Rebecca Krefting, *All Joking Aside: American Humor and Its Discontents* (Baltimore, MD: Johns Hopkins University Press, 2014), 92.

8. Shayne Lee, *Erotic Revolutionaries: Black Women, Sexuality, and Popular Culture* (Lanham, MD: Hamilton, 2010), 96.

9. Glenda Carpio, "Black Women, Black Humor," *Bulletin of the American Academy* (Summer 2010): 34. Following her Academy Award for Best Supporting Actress for *Precious* (Daniels, 2009), Mo'Nique was again embroiled in controversies about Black female stereotypes, with similar questions about the usage and political impact of negative images.

10. In these interviews and promotional stories, Mo'Nique claims a long-standing affinity for gay men and repeatedly professes her belief that Black culture is no more biased about homosexuality than other cultures are. These interviews also allude to her gay following, certainly likely given her performances of over-the-top sexuality, though the routines about anal sex and effeminate behavior are also likely to be interpreted by straight audiences as flat-out contempt for gay sexuality. See "Mo'Nique on Playing Mom to a Gay Teen," *New/Now/Next*, February 2014; Daniel Reynolds, "Mo'Nique: *Blackbird* is My 'Love Letter' to the Gay Community," *The Advocate* 24 (April 2015); Michael Musto, "Mo'Nique: 'Listen, Honey, I Hung Out with the Gay Babies,'" *Out Magazine* 4 (April 2015).

11. David Gillota, *Ethnic Comedy in Multiethnic America* (New Brunswick, NJ: Rutgers University Press, 2013), 21.

12. Joanne Belknap, Sandra B. Simkins, et al., "The School to Prison Pipeline for Girls: The Role of Physical and Sexual Abuse," *Children's Legal Rights Journal* 24, no. 3 (October 24, 2004): 56–72.

13. Megan Garber, "How Comedians Became Public Intellectuals," *The Atlantic*, May 28, 2015.

14. Melissa V. Harris-Perry, *Sister Citizen: Shame, Stereotypes, and Black Women in America* (New Haven and London: Yale University Press, 2011), 5 and 122.

15. Ta-Nehisi Coates, "What It Means to Be a Public Intellectual," *The Atlantic*, January 8, 2014. "Here is the machinery of racism," he concludes, "the privilege of being oblivious to questions, of never having to grapple with the everywhere; the right of false naming."

16. The African American comedians Garber lists are the duo Key and Peele and Larry Wilmore, whose style of social satire is similar to the white comedians who headline her story. She also mentions Richard Pryor as one of the comedians who began to stir up social questions in his comedy in an earlier era.

17. Gerald Nachman, *Seriously Funny: The Rebel Comedians of the 1950s and 1960s* (New York: Pantheon, 2003), 481.

18. Mel Watkins, *On the Real Side: Laughing, Lying, and Signifying, the Underground Tradition of African-American Humor that Transformed American Culture* (New York: Touchstone, 1994), 476.

19. Bambi Haggins, *Laughing Mad: The Black Comic Persona in Post-Soul America* (New Brunswick, NJ and London: Rutgers University Press, 2007), 243, 246–7.

20. Lori Landay, *Madcaps, Screwballs, and Con Women: The Female Trickster in American Culture* (Philadelphia: University of Pennsylvania Press, 1998), 16–18.

21. Landay, *Madcaps*, 25.

22. Landay, *Madcaps*, 10–11.

23. Landay, *Madcaps*, 26.

24. Harris-Perry, *Sister Citizen*, 102.

25. Michelle Brown, *The Culture of Punishment: Prison, Society, and Spectacle* (New York: New York University Press, 2009), 13.

26. Brown, *Culture of Punishment*, 80.

2

SCORCHED-EARTH COMEDY
Laughing Off Wounded Warriors with the Humor of Bobby Henline

Christopher J. Gilbert

When one refers to bodies of knowledge, rarely does one mean *actual* human bodies. A body of knowledge, after all, is a shareable set of ideas, impressions, activities, and principles in a particular domain of understanding. This is hardly the case when it comes to the body itself as a site of knowledge transfer, and even less so when that body belongs to a combat veteran who exhibits his disfigurements as part of an effort to help citizens understand the consequences of twenty-first-century US American warfare.

Nearly 40 percent of former Staff Sergeant Bobby Henline's body was burned after his Humvee was struck by a roadside bomb in 2007. At the time, Henline was on his fourth tour of duty in Iraq. He was the only survivor; four of his fellow servicemen were killed by the explosion. Despite countless surgeries and innumerable hours of occupational therapy, Henline is what the journalist Howard Chua-Eoan calls a "phrenological nightmare." His head is now "an amalgam of his entire body," writes Chua-Eoan, "with skin from his arms, his belly, his crotch. One eye is lidless. He is almost earless: half a lobe on one side, a large hole on the other. His mouth, without an upper lip, is in permanent scowl—or smile, depending on the angle you look at it. His left arm ends in a bulbous stump."[1] But rather than follow a Hemingwayesque logic and proclaim that there is nothing more revolting than armed conflict, Henline has since made a career as a stand-up comedian, motivational speaker, and veteran advocate who acts like there is nothing more risible than exhibiting the (in)visible wounds of war. After revealing the extent of his burns, for instance, he is quick to tell both civic and military audiences of his comedy routine that he expects a discount on his cremation. His mission is sure enough: on one hand, to make our soldiers' returns home matters of concern for fellow citizens, and on the other, to materialize the literal bodily matter that makes the soldier a civic other.[2] Comedy is Henline's main line of defense against the challenges of reentry, not to mention the psychic pain of combat trauma. It is also his resource for turning himself from a "cultural outsider" into a public figure with inside knowledge of war.[3]

Henline uses the ostensive healing power of humor to coach people on what it means to welcome returning soldiers back as citizens. In this way, Henline conveys his combat-related knowledge as if he were a public intellectual, raising critical awareness about the plight of wounded warriors and the truth of war's aftermath, but also expressing how lay publics might deal with the serious civic problems that stem from armed conflict. He does this by rendering combat trauma ridiculous with a mash-up of observational comedy and odd wordplay that betrays what the rhetorical scholar Debra Hawhee might call a "corporeal intellect."[4] Of course, he is no intellectual per se, and his advocacy is often as crude as it is clear-sighted. When joking about how to avoid the same mistakes he made, for instance, Henline might advise civic audiences to enunciate when praying to God. "I distinctly remember . . . praying for a blowjob in a Hummer," Henline says in one joke. But his poignant (if occasionally perverse) jokes are expressions of the individual body helping the body politic to think differently. Returning soldiers—especially those with severe physical wounds—advertise their new identities when they step back into the public frays of civilian life. They are "citizen strangers."[5] Henline makes the strangeness of war and its aftermath, and the peculiarities of civic selfhood, more familiar by variously identifying and disidentifying with his abject body, and then again transforming combat traumas into comic spaces for negotiating normative ways of seeing nonnormative individuals. He does this by goading audiences to at once avow and disavow abjection.[6] Furthermore, Henline's humor kindles a public discourse of civic responsibilities to returning soldiers. His comic routine relies upon the unstated assumption that any despoilment of soldier identities is largely the result of a populace that proclaims support for its troops while upholding an expectation for them to survive subjugation, brutality, and pain at war and at home.[7] The soldier body is a civic body. Henline thus enjoins his spectators to rhetorically stand in his shoes. For laypersons, this means identifying with visibly defective embodiment and disidentifying with the marginalization of damaged selves. For veterans, it means identifying with the subjective hybridity that accompanies a return home. It also means disidentifying with the notion that soldiering somehow disempowers an individual to be an ordinary citizen who looks like a domestic stranger.

The upside to Henline's humor is evident in its accumulation of artifacts that demonstrate how comic intellectualism can expose the "hidden wounds" of war that so often emerge as stigmas around physical disfigurements and emotional sufferance. Henline's comical corruption of his own body evinces a certain license gleaned from the "loss of corporal and moral control."[8] Henline folds this license into a rational basis for (and logical outcome of) "excess and revelry" as performative resources for making fun of the follies of war.[9] This chapter examines the contents of some of Henline's stand-up performances,[10] as well as the implications of his appearances in short biopics, documentary films, interviews, and other public communications. Comedy relies "on shared experience, attitudes, and values" that enable mockeries of "aberrations from the norm or the norm itself."[11] I argue that Henline's comic acts of (dis)identification scramble and reconstruct normative ways of seeing and being in the world. By resisting the aversion to sufferance and stigma, and by embracing the anxiety that comes with exposing one's nonnormative, war-torn body to public scrutiny, Henline unfolds the mystery of his pain in its unusual virtue.

Then again, even if his comedy inflames ideas about the civic burdens of a soldier's return home, there is a chance that Henline's humor is not the spark or the light at all—it is the abject shadow, the snuff, the shady backing of a phantom *hoi polloi*. In other words, making fun of combat trauma might actually reassert the cultural privilege of militarism, never mind machoism and masculinity. The popular press documents the "body horrors" that follow from tragedies of war, particularly in "our contemporary age of abject publicity."[12] This makes Henline's apparent marginality a direct result of the odd prestige assigned to those who experience the sublimity of battle and then return to all the ridiculousness of ordinary living—the relationship woes, familial quirks, bureaucratic nuisances, and more. If Henline's comic intellectualism collapses images of civic life into war culture while conflating the "pity pots" of personal ordeals with combat traumas as evidence of a "new normal," then it actually leaves the returning soldier routinely abject. It also makes Henline's jokes the artillery for something like scorched-earth comedy, disturbing a rhetorical storehouse for advancing our understanding of some manic commitments to normativity, which seem to demand that the fallout from war is not felt in the body politic. The comedy of war is a smoke signal when it draws audiences deeper into war culture and keeps the consequences thereof at a distance.

OF IMPACT AREAS AND MILITARY INTELLECTUALISM

Servicemen are "dumb, stupid animals."[13] This, at any rate, was the opinion of the statesman and national security expert Henry Kissinger. It is conventional wisdom that the military has its knowledgeable brass and its intelligence officers, and then its rank and file. In addition, at least since the Vietnam era, there has been an image of a "military-intellectual complex" that fashions friend–enemy relations alongside a need-to-know public ethic. Returning soldiers betray a general lack of intelligence about what it means to manage combat trauma in a war culture.[14] Very often, mental fortitude is identified as that which allows some to stomach warfare and stave off post-traumatic stress. A key problem is that this is also how returning soldiers tend to be portrayed publicly, leaving those who suffer as the wreckage of battle in a society that is out of step with their experience.[15] Yet, returning soldiers are in a breakoff position insofar as they can serve as agents of knowledge about the burdens of coming home.

The knowledge I am imagining here is not simply about personal battles waged against enemies within. It is also a "social knowledge," or a structure of (unstated) assumptions that "gives *form* to information" and is exhibited by the "functional characteristics" of interactions between, say, citizens and soldiers.[16] As Cara A. Finnegan points out, this is precisely "the shared knowledge of public life that we all use to 'get by.'"[17] Elsewhere I have argued that our contemporary war culture is buttressed by images of wounded soldiers tormented by *their* combat injuries, and that this circumstance is a *fait accompli*.[18] I have also argued that Henline in particular "embodies a crisis of returning soldiers," exhibiting his all too visible pains of war while simultaneously wounding the sensibilities of his audiences."[19] By and large, "few Americans encounter the real burdens of fighting and life after military conflict."[20] Henline's comedy performs such an encounter. The difficult task, though, is to couple social knowledge of war and its aftermath with an acknowledgment of the practical implications of this form of layperson's military intelligence for civic relations involving returning soldiers.

To situate returning soldiers in discourses of military intelligence is to suggest that they operate in milieus of public (anti-)intellectualism.[21] A few important factors stand out here. First, hidden wounds of returning soldiers are not actually unknown. There is "a steady stream of magazine articles, Internet videos, public pronouncements, and television newscasts dedicated to honoring their injuries and assuaging Americans' fears about the bodily toll of military intervention overseas."[22] But there is an undercurrent of both acceptance and shame that makes combat trauma incomprehensible. What we do not know about "the person inside" cannot hurt us. Yet we fear what we do not know. Coupled to this is the fraught position of the public intellectual. Those who publicize their cogitations have long faced a generalized climate of American anti-intellectualism. Henline is a wounded warrior turned stand-up comedian. So-called intellectual humor notwithstanding, comedy is not usually known for high-mindedness. Comedians are granted comic license because their performances are rarely acknowledged for their real-world consequences.[23] They are given leeway to laugh at themselves and others, but usually only insofar as they preserve their function as fools throwing metaphorical rocks through the windows of majoritarian culture. Perhaps ironically, "the more marginal the performer, the greater the comic 'capital' available to him or her."[24] Greater abjection means greater comic license, at least in houses of good humor. The soldier therefore has a license to kill in multiple senses. A soldier embodies an unthinking "nonhuman animal" that follows orders like a dutiful dog of war. A soldier also sacrifices conscious presence and self-control in the wake of warfare.[25] This is what gives a comedian like Henline cultural privilege: he demonstrates his expertise about combat trauma based on his experience with it, thus enabling a sort of "intellectual superiority" that might otherwise attract scorn for the intellectual elite.[26] Furthermore, there is a popular opinion that many of today's comedians are in fact "comedic intellectuals," occupying "an echelonic place" in public culture.[27] Henline exploits "the knowledge that the dominant [war] culture itself has endowed his marginal position with,"[28] and so complicates the very notion of expertise by revising what it is to be in the know. He activates his comic license to be a spokesperson not just for himself or for the damaged soldier body, but also for the body politic.

Hence a third consideration: public intellectuals need not be "specialists" or "agents of reason and progress."[29] Instead, they can be persons of principle and correspondents of authentic experience. In this way, Henline combats anti-intellectualism by honing a civic intellect around the consequences of warfare (despite his self-deprecatory comments about being "just" an Army truck driver and a high school dropout). This has to do with his sense that informed judgments in wartime are the responsibility of citizens both in and out of uniform. In one joke, for instance, Henline suggests that those who are stupid enough to drink and drive should enlist in the army and actually do some good for society, especially since substantially more people who drive under the influence die as a result than do those who go to war. His illogic relates directly to the long-standing idea that, amongst the citizenry, there is "widespread ignorance about national affairs,"[30] which is reinforced by a "reverent but disengaged attitude toward the military—we love the troops, but we'd rather not think about them."³¹ It also has to do with what Andrew J. Bacevich calls "action intellectualism," or the efforts of someone like Henline to publicly confront the stigma of coming home from war.³² This combination of experiential expertise and gross embodiment enables Henline to get away with a "comically styled" mode of public advocacy that unifies disparate communities via shared perspectives on the struggles of public life.³³ Fourth and finally, then, it is important to consider how Henline's comic intellectualism disrupts conventional wisdom about returning soldiers.

To some extent, Henline utilizes his interest in breaking down barriers between citizens and soldiers to his advantage, such as when he quips about the social privilege of bodily disability. "Being burnt is like being an old person," Henline joked in one performance at the Laugh Out Loud comedy club in San Antonio, Texas. "I can say what I want and get away with it." Such an allusion to public discomfort with human embodiments of warfare bespeaks how "the disabled figure operates as a code for insufficiency, contingency, and abjection," and yet simultaneously fosters "sympathetic, grotesque, wondrous, or pathological" identification.³⁴ Additionally, it exhibits the collective activity of what Jane Gallop dubs "thinking through the body,"³⁵ a process that is provoked by Henline's comedy as the voice lent to visible scars, wounds, and pain. Wounded bodies can mediate knowledge not only about the bodily fallout from armed conflict, but also about the fact that returning soldiers must reinvent their civic selves. The knowledge that comes from these bodies morphs into *métis*, or "embodied intelligence," that can aid negotiations of self and otherness when one's body is mired in the "normative matrix" of war discourses.³⁶ One problem, though, is that returning soldiers are almost inherently abject insofar as they occupy "a domain of excluded sensibilities and excluded Others,"³⁷ making them the anti-bodies of a body politic.

It is therefore fitting that *therapeia*, or therapy, has ancient connotations of "service."³⁸ This goes for rhetorical responses that can function as remedies for social, political, and cultural ills. Tellingly, a *pharmakos* was the name applied to unwitting victims—in comedies, the scapegoats; in tragedies, those condemned to death and/or sacrificed for the sake of a community. The *pharmakon*, in a related sense, connotes both remedies and poisons expressed in discourse. Henline's self-laughter is a form of civic therapy. Humor heals. In displaying his own abjection as a subject of ridicule, Henline turns tragic comedy into a discursive "antidote to trauma."³⁹ Too many skin grafts have made it impossible for Henline to tell his ass from his elbow—or so he says. He also has a "butt face," "taint lips," and a "crotch eye." But if comedic self-deprecation demonstrates the opinions of dominant culture and not just, well, the butt of a joke,⁴⁰ then Henline's self-laughter also travesties common responses of horror and even disgust that get cast upon wounded veterans. Put differently, Henline allies his body with the body politic as a collaborative site for the abjection of the intellect. He therefore informs audiences of *their* judgments about *his* corporeal deviance.[41] As Rebecca Krefting says, stand-up comedy succeeds inasmuch as an audience identifies with the comic.[42] Henline's comedy deals with the identifications and divisions between soldiers and citizens because it harnesses the "raw materials for representing a disempowered politics or positionality that has been rendered unthinkable by the dominant culture" to make abjection more recognizable.[43] One reason is that the comedian, in this case, is responsible for dematerializing the soldier body *as* an abject body. On stage, Henline is a Daniel come to public judgment, acknowledging an audience's laughter for its manifestation of anxiety and awkwardness as opposed to straightforward affirmation. As such, his comic intellectualism is to self-laughter as *therapeia* is to mutual sufferance.

Perhaps most importantly, Henline's comedy engages the complex forms of trauma that exist *between* soldiers and citizens. Such an engagement can function as a normative posture that makes an already hyper-visible body even more explicit through, in this instance, "shared laughter."[44] Laughter here lets citizens suffer through support for the troops. Henline's comic intellectualism articulates bodies in tension, à la Freud, and demonstrates abjection itself as the way "to see ourselves as others see us, or to see the other as we see ourselves."[45] This is the good news. The bad news is that, even as Henline disrupts "the tyranny of the normal,"[46] his comedy also risks contributing to the normalization of combat trauma in civic culture. What follows is an examination of his ongoing veteran advocacy as a sort of parody of C. Wright Mills in its generalized expression of a wartime continuum (if not a universal experience of private embattlements) interrupted by moments of levity about war (or personal struggle) itself.

OF ACTIVIST DUTY AND COMEDY CAMPAIGNS

"I'm trying to give back."[47] This is Henline's reason for wanting to open a restaurant in San Antonio that would employ—and so empower—other veterans.[48] Of course, this is the same answer he offers when asked about his stand-up comedy, motivational speaking, and veteran advocacy. During the countless hours he spent in rehabilitation after being blown up by an Improvised Explosive Device (IED) in Iraq, Henline used humor as a coping mechanism. He has since gone public with his comic ethos, exposing the mutual discomfort that grew out of his interactions with others by cracking jokes to force an interface. Comedy remains his go-to for reconciling the tensions between citizens and soldiers by helping himself and others "to look at life differently."[49] For Henline, this means recovering his civic selfhood "by living it as an act,"[50] and urging audiences to reconsider ways of seeing returning soldiers. All of this begins when a disfigured veteran walks into a comedy club....

STAGE

If there is a core truth of Henline's stand-up comedy, it is that laughter is a battleground *in situ*.[51] That is, to laugh at jokes about his wounded body is to participate in the conversion of a comic stage into a theater of homegrown war. A secondary truth is that Henline's comedy engages how lay audiences are "trained" to see the cultural problems of war sufferance and the bodies that bear it.

Henline fosters a "self-image of the citizen-subject as a stoic *defender* of the outcast."[52] For example, Henline might call attention to his embarrassment about being in public, but by suggesting that his disfigurement is the result of horrifying acne, or that it came from a rare birth defect caused by his mother's role as a fire-eater in the circus while Henline was in utero. Either case is ridiculous. However, this "comic vision" of combat and its aftereffects reorients the public gaze away from the returning soldier and toward the broader culture of war by compelling people to stare "back at the toll war can take on a veteran."[53] It is therefore not only the comedy but also the tragedy of Henline's circumstances that inspires an active engagement with the chasms between citizens and soldiers. When soldiers are portrayed as objects of pity, the hard work of healing is left to them alone. Because Henline operates on a comic ethos of don't-pity-me, he subjects audiences to an alternative framework for imagining the particularly public health of wounded warriors.

Henline builds a good deal of this framework on his imbrication of military with civic life. Henline often proclaims how much he loved his job—until it became a "real blast." Also, when referencing his recovery, he regularly alludes to the familiar quarrels of family life. In one joke, his doctors inform him that his wife has arrived at the hospital. Henline exclaims, "don't you think I've been through enough?" Another develops this image of the burdensome wife by relating that, if the nagging and yelling were not enough, certainly Henline has had enough of the "third degree." Importantly, though, Henline transitions from the private space of the home to more public spaces, such as convenience stores. In a joke that takes up the awkwardness that can come from interactions with a cashier (say, when one is reluctant to purchase a particular product for fear of judgment), Henline portrays a scene with him at CVS filling a handcart with bottles of scar removal products. The punchline has Henline asking the cashier whether he is purchasing the right quantity to do the trick. To drive his point home, Henline will either preface or conclude a bit about his deformities with an even more explicit insult: "I'm mooning you all right now." (His face now includes skin that doctors grafted from his rear end.)

Most compelling about Henline's stand-up routines is that, even as the aura of the wounded warrior is always present, the matter of war itself seems to fade away into jokes about generalized problems of pain or suffering. Joanne R. Gilbert argues that "some form of identification (or disidentification) must occur" if a routine is to retain its critical edge.[54] Although Henline enlivens combat trauma by opening up "possibilities for identification *through shared experience*,"[55] he keeps the horrors of battle at a distance. This makes it easier for lay audiences to disidentify with the particularities of war wounds. It also makes it harder for veteran audiences to align themselves with Henline if the goal is to keep the discrepancies between audience and performer (which is to say, civilians and soldiers) on display. Here familiarity risks breeding contempt—or worse, neglect. My intent is not to say that Henline is not transgressive. In fact, with some of his more obscene jokes he is able to "heighten and intensify the expression" of his complicated "perspective, affect, and experience."[56] Obscenity, in this way, reinforces the "offensiveness" of Henline's body, reminding audiences that combat trauma—and not a butt-face—instigates "the transgressive interruption of the flesh into our minds."[57] But comic licenses can be renewed or revoked depending on how reception is calibrated by the recognition and/or revulsion that follows from perceptions about the shareability of activities, feelings, and conventional wisdoms. Since Henline ultimately assumes that wounded veterans are not the only ones with (in)visible scars or mutilated bodies, his stand-up moves the plight of returning soldiers from obscurity to ordinariness, and maybe to better judgment.

FILM

A problem remains if a hero's welcome cannot offset the reality of unwelcome responses that wounded warriors often receive when they introduce damage and disorder to civic spaces. A particularly jarring part of Henline's comic routines comes when he announces his four tours and his audiences respond with perfunctory applause—for which he sometimes waits, expectantly. He may be an "Abject Hero," in Michael André Bernstein's terms, but both his abjectness and his heroism are bittersweet if they cannot close "the enormous chasm between military and civilian society."[58] That is, insofar as Henline's comedy inflames the tensions between "good soldiering" and "good citizenship," it occasionally makes the stage into a scorched earth.

At least one reason for the indiscriminate "alienation of experience" that underlies Henline's message is the pervasiveness of tragic stories about soldier sufferance.[59] Within two years of the initiation of Operation Iraqi Freedom in 2003, numerous accounts began referencing the trauma haunting combat veterans, most of them with a single message: "They can't relate to anyone."[60] Particularly poignant are the documentary films. "The Soldier's Heart" (Aronson and Navasky, 2005), part of PBS's *Frontline* series, profiles the lives of service members who discover that their homecoming is as harrowing as being in a battle zone. In 2010, HBO aired *Wartorn: 1861–2010* (Alpert, Kent, and O'Neill, 2010) to expose the enduring effects of combat trauma "on military personnel and their families throughout American history."[61] The film's release came amidst what seemed like daily bombings in Iraq, talk of a US drawdown of troops, and growing public commentary about the disabling physical and psychic pain caused by war injuries. Even more recently, CNN released *The War Comes Home* (O'Brien, 2014), one of the more overt expressions of war's impacts on the home front. Yet another is Laurent Bécue-Renard's *Of Men and War* (2014). The "after-war" discourse promulgated by these documentaries is reinforced by journalistic reports, including "Couch," a psychotherapy series published by *The New York Times*, plus those by former infantry officers like David J. Morris and military correspondents like David Wood.[62] Put simply, there is a glut of public images and ideas that portray the personal struggles of returning soldiers, variously pegging them as victims, as agents of their own recovery, and as broken citizens.

The best-known documentaries about Henline offer alternatives because his story is about the "healing power" of humor as a *communal* enterprise. *Healing Bobby* (van Agtmael, 2013), a production of *Time* magazine's Red Border Films, tells a "remarkable, sometimes-funny" tale that is driven by Henline's motivation "to make people laugh" in order *to help others*.[63] Henline has his "bad days." But he uses his survivor's guilt (never mind PTSD) as the impetus to discern a higher calling to empower others to overcome obstacles. In many ways, this calling is underwritten by an ethic of revenge: "What I want to do is to help more people than the guy that blew me up can hurt,"[64] says Henline. So he does stand-up comedy. He visits child burn victims. He drops in on those who survived the deaths of their military family members. He addresses students at schools. These activities flout the conventional wisdom of soldier returns because they advertise a responsibility of the body politic to actively engage in a wounded warrior's efforts at reintegration. Henline therefore serves as a metonym for the "travails of American society as a whole,"[65] burdening a citizenry to cure its dis-ease with combat veterans. A similar orientation is apparent in the PBS *Stories of Service* series, "Coming Back with Wes Moore" (2014), which organizes a soldier's return in stages that go from "Coming Home" through "Fitting In" to "Moving Forward." The gist is that a body politic does a monstrous disservice when it cannot recognize itself in the bodies and minds of those who live through war.

Importantly, these films perpetuate Henline's identity as a "comedy warrior." This identity was codified in the full-length feature documentary *Comedy Warriors: Healing Through Humor* (Wager, 2013), which was originally broadcast on Showtime and supported by the Wounded Warrior Project.[66] The film follows five war-torn comedians who work with comic greats (such as Lewis Black, Zach Galifianakis, B. J. Novak, and Bob Saget) to hone their individual routines before performing at the LA Improv in Hollywood. The prima facie point is to help the soldiers address the monstrosities and turmoil of their own bodies. However, because it bears public witness of "laughter-filled rehabilitation sessions,"[67] the film (and each performance) establishes partnerships in the preparation, practice, and support for social interface. To be funny is to feel better, but it is also to increase public awareness of what it means to help a wounded soldier recover. When the comedy warriors combat cultural anxiety by "killing it" onstage, audiences participate in their rehabilitation. In so doing, audience members animate their "participation in the collective artifact" of war culture itself.[68] They also enable a view of the humanity of combat veterans, thereby bringing a sense of humor to everyday engagements with all disabled citizens.

These filmic portrayals of the comedy of combat trauma garner "extraordinary public attention" to after-war matters.[69] But the rhetoric of betterment is not necessarily the best route to recovery, inasmuch as it risks treating war as just one of many life challenges that can lead a person to get down in the dumps. Before concluding, then, it is worth considering how Henline's comic intellectualism simplifies the consequences of combat even as he activates a complex form of empathy that acknowledges the vulnerability, and fallibility, of human being—aspects that are most obvious in some of Henline's interviews, photo shoots, and social media communications.

TALK, PHOTOGRAPHY/EROTICA, EPHEMERA

At his best, Henline converts combat trauma into civic education with tales of the battles fought by soldiers who wage ongoing wars against so-called enemies within. He is less impactful when he diminishes his rationale with Pollyannish boilerplates about positive thinking and silver linings.

Henline has done many interviews since 2007, and has been profiled by numerous military publications and news outlets. Perhaps most impressive is the consistency of his public reflection on his *raison d'être*. In nearly every interview, Henline offers some variation on the theme that he does comedy to honor the memories of his fallen compatriots, to get revenge on enemy combatants, and to help anyone who is suffering to be more visible and accepted. As he said back in 2011: "I'm just being positive and realizing the good things in life," which has also "helped others to look at life differently."[70] Or, in reference to his comedic objective: "If I can do this, I can break that barrier down for burn survivors. A lot of them don't like to go out and show their scars. I'm proud. This is who I am. I earned these scars. They're like tattoos with better stories."[71] Even further, Henline proclaims his obligation to "live on" for those soldiers who died and who would "rather be in pain and look funny and be here."[72] While promoting *Comedy Warriors* at the Gold Coast International Film Festival in 2013, Henline announced during a panel discussion that his comedy is meant to put publics at ease so that he can eventually break from his warrior ethos and adopt a more civic orientation that allows him to laugh at, and laugh off, the hard times of "normal" life. A January 2013 interview with the life coach and online TV/radio host Marilyn Sharon exemplifies this inspiration to improve his fitness for public existence.

In his interview with Shannon, Henline comes close to treating combat trauma like a clownish encumbrance. That is, when he talks about transforming what the social justice activist Angela Davis might call the "radical work of healing" into the *ridiculous* work of healing, he does so in accordance with our common sense of the clown: "Barump! If the clown falls, it's comedy; if he doesn't get up again, it's tragedy."[73] So Henline gets up. In the interview, he even claims to have been a clown not unlike the do-not-try-this-at-home goofballs of *Jackass* (2000–2007) fame, exemplified by the self-injuring and coarse tricksters Steve-O and Johnny Knoxville.[74] Furthermore, he relates this to something like the pride "that goeth before a Fall." In other words, if war made Henline an atheist, recovery made him find God. This discovery is what drives him to "get out there" and make publics more comfortable with bodily deformity and embodiments of warfare, so that life might be easier for other burn victims, disabled individuals, and despondent persons in general. As much reflects a Bakhtinian concept of the comic body, converting singularly embodied incapacities and disfigurements into a comedy of the body politic. This is precisely how Henline approaches his more visual spiritual-survival activism: photography.

It is beyond the scope of this chapter to address the various implications of combat veteran imagery. However, relative to Henline's promotion of knowledge about war injuries, photographic iterations offer a show-and-tell experience of (in)visible wounds. "If I can say, 'look at me,'" Henline asserts, "then it'll make it easier for other people. The more we see in the media, the easier it'll be."[75] Such a sentiment flies in the face of stock journalistic photos featuring a dejected, solitary soldier slumped over his own body with his head in his hands. It also accommodates what Bakhtin might call the "comic gesture" of putting the grotesque body on display. With the aid of photographers like David Jay (and the "Unknown Soldiers" series), the graphic nature of war wounds is making severely maimed veterans like Henline less subject to either ignorance or aversion.[76] Stacey Pearsall, too—herself a veteran (who appeared in Wes Moore's above-mentioned biopic), military photographer, and founder of the Veterans Portrait Project—has contributed to Henline's public image as the "Burnt Comedian."[77] Add to these Michael Stokes's glamour photos of wounded vets. Stokes is known for his male erotica. In 2015, he published a hardcover coffee table book entitled *Always Loyal*, which captures the scarred and amputated bodies of soldiers, almost all of whom appear in the nude with their genitals covered only by the trappings of battle. Henline was photographed too late to make it into the book, but Stokes has laid him bare in near-nude photos from outlets like CNN to Tumblr. In one photo, Henline faces the camera with only enhanced shoulder straps covering his upper body and operational camo pants below his waist. His face is stoic, and the tattooed sleeve on his right arm stands out in stark contrast to his withered left arm with its amputated hand. Also in full view is the calligraphic tattoo that arcs across Henline's upper chest, and reads: "Truly Blessed."

Staged photos of Henline tend to reinforce so many touchstones of the comic gesture, like ambiguity, juxtaposition, exaggeration, and even caricature. It helps (or hurts) that Henline identifies as a heterosexual white male who is at ease with his gender identity even with (or except for) his disabled body. The right parts still work, one can assume. He is broken but still all man. His comic performance is "charged."[78] It challenges audiences to incorporate differently abled citizens as beings of a common culture. But this does not make it less conventional in its gendered politics. Henline's abject comedy demonstrates the tension between the comic charge and the rhetorical force of convention in displaying how war can be edged with the ridiculous; photos like these portray the abject itself as "edged with the sublime."[79] To subject disfigured soldier bodies to the public gaze via photography, then, is to show forth the abject as a mode of recovery, rebuilding, and even remaking of civic selfhood. It is to channel the still life of a Bakhtinian carnival and all its exaggerations of the human body, from utter grotesqueries to sexual appeals (and thus from degenerations to renewals). In Henline's own words, such (comic) subjection is to "show the beauty without the arm, the leg." Furthermore, while "some people are weird about [them]," the photos show who the soldiers are in juxtaposition to who they were.[80]

The social knowledge embedded in wounded bodies is even more evident in the images of Henline that are circulated widely online. Stokes is fond of sharing his work on Instagram. Henline, too, was active on Twitter, regularly posting or retweeting images and information that reinforce the advocacy he later moved to Instagram and TikTok. In December 2015, for instance, Henline tweeted a photo from Stokes's Instagram feed, which reveals Henline completely nude except for dog tags hanging from his neck and an assault rifle that he holds in his right hand, covering his penis. His text: "My mom just called to tell me I could have used a smaller gun lol." Amidst the many comments in response to Henline's tweet is his own expression of "a big Thank You to everyone for your support and to Michael Stokes for helping us Vets with your talent and vision." Henline also tweets inspirational quotes, selfies he takes at the gym, links to news reports about his comedy and activism, references to time he ("BurntPa") spends with his granddaughter, and more. From the stage to online networks, Henline nurtures his comic intellectualism to foster visibility, mobilize the cause of returning soldiers, and even create "mini-public spheres" within the broader US war culture.[81] His publicity makes wounded bodies less abject, and war itself less a dirty word.[82]

CONCLUSION: " . . . THE WAR NEVER ENDS."

Following the journalist Mike Sager, if we truly learn the lessons of returning soldiers, then it is okay if they entertain, guide, and enrich us—so long as they haunt us, too.

There is much that is enriching, guiding, and entertaining in Henline's civic education about coming back from war. What haunts me, though, is the not so tacit acceptance of US military engagements abroad that emerges out of his comic intellectualism, not to mention his veteran advocacy. Do not mistake: those individuals who have been damaged and disfigured while serving at arms in our name deserve our appreciation, assistance, and attention. Henline's body constitutes his combat *bona fides*, and his comedy routine shows forth an exercise in civic engagement. Nevertheless, if his veteran advocacy devolves into simplistic celebrations of the civil liberties and pursuits of happiness that war—or at least a strong national security state—can protect, his comedy reminds us that sometimes laughter "is not only *not* therapeutic but also pathological."[83] One way of understanding this has to do with acknowledging that comedy, even if subversive (i.e., with Henline's insights into the utterly social relations that can actually provoke combat trauma), also preserves the status quo. Henline accepts the fact that advances in health care and enhancements in medical equipment mean fewer troops will die on the battlefield.[84] His comic intellectualism implies that the ties binding citizens together are often more loosely knit than those that sustain a combat unit. This is partly why he works so hard to include citizens in the deployment cycle via their engagement with returning soldiers. It is also why one can see in his routines the potential for a slippery slope from so-called "war-is-hell" theory to a view of war as home.

There remains some conventional wisdom that "disabled vets are constructed as problems within American culture—problems to be solved, problems to be exposed, and problems to be ignored."[85] Henline upends this truism by laughing at himself and the ways in which others allow their ignorance of warfare to undermine more social forms of support on the home front. Confronted with puns and punchlines that work like disjointed shot/reverse shot sequences, audiences of Henline's comedy routines "are forced to turn and look, look again, look back, modulate, mediate, hesitate, and finally see."[86] In interviews, films, and photo shoots, Henline makes his corporeality less and less transgressive, and even eventually beautiful in spite of the ugliness of war. In doing so, he exposes the real civic monstrosities in the activities of those at home who lack compassion for the war-torn. And he carries this type of exposure into the public sphere, when he wears t-shirts that are all black except for white text that reads "got burns?" But after the smoke clears, we are left with the peculiar imbrication of pleasure and pain that comes from recognizing that war is increasingly the norm, that peace (like the freedom from strife that Henline seeks) is the deviation, and that identification with wounded veterans can be cast as disidentification with the foundational principles of war culture writ large.

I began this chapter with an image of a scorched earth—explicitly to encourage attention to the idea that war comedy can, at times, blacken the rhetorical resources that could be used to critique, if not resist, war culture even while we as a citizenry find ways to help returning soldiers heal. My concern remains: if we are caught between the norm of armed conflict and its production of wounded warriors on one side, and the prospect of peace as the safekeeping of soldiers for a civic self-defense on the other, then we are very likely burning the "good" reasons for war culture from both ends.

Notes

1. Howard Chua-Eoan, "Cocktails & Carnage: Dinner With Staff Sergeant Henline," *Roads & Kingdoms*, http://roadsandkingdoms.com/2013/cocktails-carnage-dinner-with-staff-sergeant-henline/.

2. Henline almost exaggerates his embroilment with the institutional and everyday practices that enable some bodies to matter while disabling others, and so amplifies the roles of public speech and performativity in the exchanges of cultural knowledge. Moreover, he both performs and portrays his body as a "rhetorical body," embellishing his gross corporeality with persuasive—or at least coded—speech. Such exaggerations and embellishments open up the possibility for a transgressive body to reinscribe and even rewrite itself in spite of a tinge of the normative. See Judith Butler, *Bodies that Matter: On the Discursive Limits of "Sex"* (New York: Routledge, 1993); Bruno Latour, "How to Talk about the Body? The Normative Dimension of Science Studies," *Body & Society* 10 (2004): 205–29; *Rhetorical Bodies*, ed. Jack Selzer and Sharon Crowley (Madison: University of Wisconsin Press, 1999); and more.

3. David Gillota, "Stand-Up Nation: Humor and American Identity," *The Journal of American Culture* 38 (2015): 102–12.

4. Debra Hawhee, *Moving Bodies: Kenneth Burke at the Edges of Language* (Columbia: University of South Carolina Press, 2012).

5. Rebecca Krefting, *All Joking Aside: American Humor and Its Discontents* (Baltimore, MD: Johns Hopkins University Press, 2014), 150.

6. John Limon, *Stand-Up Comedy in Theory, or, Abjection in America* (Durham, NC: Duke University Press, 2000), 4.

7. José Esteban Muñoz, *Disidentifications: Queers of Color and the Performance of Politics* (Minneapolis: University of Minnesota Press, 1999), 185. See also Lawrence E. Mintz, "Standup Comedy as Social and Cultural Mediation," *American Quarterly* 37 (1985): 74.

8. Ian Wilkie, *Performing in Comedy: A Student's Guide* (New York: Routledge, 2016), 110.

9. Wilkie, *Performing*, 110.

10. Posted on YouTube by Henline himself, sponsored by organizations like Red Boots Talent and Promotion, and recorded at venues like the Laughing Skull Lounge.

11. Gail Finney, "Introduction: Unity in Difference?" in *Look Who's Laughing: Gender and Comedy*, ed. Gail Finney (Langhorne, UK: Gordon and Breach, 1994), 7.

12. John Taylor, *Body Horror: Photojournalism, Catastrophe and War* (New York: Manchester University Press, 1998); and Joshua Gunn, *Modern Occult Rhetoric: Mass Media and the Dream of Secrecy in the Twentieth Century* (Tuscaloosa: University of Alabama Press, 2005), xxi. See also Elisabeth Bronfen, "Gothic Wars—Media's Lust," in *Monstrous Media/Spectral Subjects: Imagining Gothic from the Nineteenth Century to the Present*, ed. Fred Botting and Catherine Spooner (New York: Manchester University Press, 2015), 21.

13. Bob Woodward and Carl Bernstein, *The Final Days* (New York: Simon & Schuster, 1976), 194.

14. Kathie Costos, "Military Intelligence Lacking when Troops Are Blamed for PTSD," *Wounded Times*, February 4, 2014, http://www.combatptsdwoundedtimes.org/2014/02/military-intelligence-lacking-when.html.

15. Ashley Fantz, "'The Evil Hours': Authors' Deep, Personal Take on Post-traumatic Stress," *CNN*, February 2, 2015, http://www.cnn.com/2015/02/01/us/ptsd-evil-hours/.

16. Thomas B. Farrell, "Knowledge, Consensus, and Rhetorical Theory," *Quarterly Journal of Speech* 62 (1976): 12.

17. Cara A. Finnegan, *Making Photography Matter: A Viewer's History from the Civil War to the Great Depression* (Urbana: University of Illinois Press, 2015), 180.

18. Christopher J. Gilbert and John Louis Lucaites, "Bringing War Down to Earth: The Dialectic of Pity and Compassion in *Doonesbury*'s View of Combat Trauma," *Quarterly Journal of Speech* 101 (2015): 379–404.

19. Christopher J. Gilbert, "Standing Up to Combat Trauma," *Text and Performance Quarterly* 34 (2014): 146, 153. See also Gilbert, "Bawdy Blows: VET Tv and the Comedy of Combat Masculinity," *Women's Studies in Communication* 42 (2019): 181–201.

20. Paul Achter, "Rhetoric and the Permanent War," *Quarterly Journal of Speech* 102 (2016): 79.

21. See Col. Lloyd J. Matthews, "The Uniformed Intellectual and His Place in American Arms," *Army*, August 2002; and Joe Byerly, "Anti-Intellectualism and the Army," *The Bridge*, https://medium.com/the-bridge/anti-intellectualism-and-the-army-3b502b90c40a#.rb8kn4wdq.

22. John M. Kinder, *Paying with Their Bodies: American War and the Problem of the Disabled Veteran* (Chicago: University of Chicago Press, 2015), 3. See also Paul Achter, "Unruly Bodies: The Rhetorical Domestication of Twenty-First-Century Veterans of War," *Quarterly Journal of Speech* 96 (2010): 46–68.

23. Joanne R. Gilbert, *Performing Marginality: Humor, Gender, and Cultural Critique* (Detroit, MI: Wayne State University Press, 2004), 35.

24. Gilbert, *Performing Marginality*, 24.

25. David Livingstone Smith, *Less than Human: Why We Demean, Enslave, and Exterminate Others* (New York: St. Martin's Press, 2011), 12.

26. Richard Hofstadter, *Anti-Intellectualism in American Life* (New York: Vintage Books, 1962), 292.

27. Megan Garber, "How Comedians Became Public Intellectuals," *The Atlantic*, May 28, 2015.

28. Michael André Bernstein, *Bitter Carnival: Ressentiment and the Abject Hero* (Princeton, NJ: Princeton University Press, 1992), 33.

29. Pankaj Mishra, "Is It Still Possible to Be a Public Intellectual?" *The New York Times*, November 24, 2015, http://www.nytimes.com/2015/11/29/books/review/is-it-still-possible-to-be-a-public-intellectual.html.

30. J. Jeffery Auer, "Discussion Programs and Techniques in the Armed Forces," *Quarterly Journal of Speech* 32 (1946): 303.

31. James Fallows, "The Tragedy of the American Military," *The Atlantic*, January/February 2015, http://www.theatlantic.com/magazine/archive/2015/01/the-tragedy-of-the-american

-military/383516/. See also Andrew J. Bacevich, *The New American Militarism: How Americans Are Seduced by War* (New York: Oxford University Press, 2005), 28.

32. Andrew J. Bacevich, "Rationalizing Lunacy: The Intellectual as Servant of the State," *The Huffington Post*, May 8, 2015, http://www.huffingtonpost.com/andrew-bacevich/rationalizing-lunacy_b_6828460.html. It is worth noting here that during the 2016 presidential campaign, Henline publicly pegged himself as a "defense intellectual" in order to express his willingness to advise the next president.

33. Jonathan Paul Rossing, "Dick Gregory and Activist Style: Identifying Attributes of Humor Necessary for Activist Advocacy," *Argumentation and Advocacy* 50 (2013): 59–71. Note that Henline has even organized some of this advocacy into the Crosshairs Comedy Troupe, supporting other soldier-comedians as they bring the comedy of war to veterans and civilians alike.

34. Rosemarie Garland Thomson, *Extraordinary Bodies: Figuring Physical Disability in American Culture and Literature* (New York: Columbia University Press, 1997), 136.

35. Jane Gallop, *Thinking through the Body* (New York: Columbia University Press, 1988).

36. Jay Timothy Dolmage, *Disability Rhetoric* (Syracuse, NY: Syracuse University Press, 2014), 90.

37. D. Diane Davis, *Breaking Up (at) Totality: A Rhetoric of Laughter* (Carbondale: Southern Illinois University Press, 2000), 180.

38. Jonardon Ganeri and Clare Carlisle, "Introduction," in *Philosophy as Therapeia* (New York: Cambridge University Press, 2010), 2.

39. Claire Sisco King, *Washed in Blood: Male Sacrifice, Trauma, and the Cinema* (New Brunswick, NJ: Rutgers University Press, 2012), 116. Also, for a discussion of the unmasking capacities of tragedy and comedy, see Nathan Crick and John Poulakos, "Go Tell Alcibiades: Tragedy, Comedy, and Rhetoric in Plato's 'Symposium,'" *Quarterly Journal of Speech* 94 (2008): 1–22; and Adrienne E. Christiansen and Jeremy J. Hanson, "Comedy as Cure for Tragedy: Act Up and the Rhetoric of Aids," *Quarterly Journal of Speech* 82 (1996): 157–70.

40. Gilbert, *Performing Marginality*, 141.

41. See Deborah Caslav Covino, *Amending the Abject Body: Aesthetic Makeovers in Medicine and Culture* (Albany: State University of New York Press, 2004), 6, 36.

42. Krefting, *All Joking Aside*, 120.

43. Muñoz, *Disidentifications*, 31.

44. Arthur W. Frank, "What's Pharmakos? From Pseudotheology to Presence," *Body & Society* 5 (1999): 59.

45. Gary L. Albrecht, "Disability Humor: What's in a Joke?" *Body & Society* 5 (1999): 72.

46. Covino, *Amending*, 109. See also Nathan Crick, "Rhetoric, Philosophy, and the Public Intellectual," *Philosophy and Rhetoric* 39 (2006): 127–39.

47. Susan Keating, "Inspiring Wounded Veteran Hopes to Open Restaurant to 'Empower' and Employ Other Veterans: 'God Kept Me Alive for a Reason,'" *People*, March 8, 2016, https://people.com/human-interest/wounded-veteran-to-open-restaurant-to-employ-other-veterans/.

48. Sharon Ko, "Wounded Warrior Aspires to Open Restaurant, Empower Veterans," KENS 5, February 26, 2016, https://www.kens5.com/article/news/local/wounded-warrior-aspires-to-open-restaurant-empower-veterans/273-301333490.

49. David Wood, "Beyond the Battlefield: Saved from the Brink of Death, Veteran Keeps Chasing His Dreams," *The Huffington Post*, December 21, 2011, http://www.huffingtonpost.com/2011/10/21/beyond-the-battlefield-10-henline_n_1017579.html.

50. Limon, *Stand-up Comedy*, 6.

51. See Josh Gross, "Laugh Is a Battlefield: Injured Veterans Use Standup Comedy to Heal in 'Comedy Warriors,'" *Boulder Weekly*, November 6, 2014, http://www.boulderweekly.com/entertainment/screen/laugh-is-a-battlefield/.

52. John Durham Peters, *Courting the Abyss: Free Speech and the Liberal Tradition* (Chicago: University of Chicago Press, 2005), 160, emphasis added.

53. Andrea Greenbaum, "Stand-Up Comedy as Rhetorical Argument: An Investigation of Comic Culture," *Humor* 12 (1999): 33–46; Deborah Wrigley, "Wounded Veterans Bring Healing through Comedy," *ABC 13 Eyewitness News*, July 3, 2014, http://abc13.com/entertainment/veterans-bring-healing-through-comedy/154564/.

54. Gilbert, *Performing Marginality*, 163.

55. Krefting, *All Joking Aside*, 5.

56. Susan Seizer, "On the Uses of Obscenity in Live Stand-Up Comedy," *Anthropological Quarterly* 84 (2011): 230.

57. John Durham Peters, "Preludes to a Theory of Obscenity," in *Obscenity and the Limits of Liberalism*, ed. Loren Glass and Charles Francis Williams (Columbus: Ohio State University, 2011), 154.

58. Sebastian Junger, "How PTSD Became a Problem Far Beyond the Battlefield," *Vanity Fair*, June 2015, http://www.vanityfair.com/news/2015/05/ptsd-war-home-sebastian-junger.

59. Amy Davidson, "The 'Soldier's Disease,'" *The New Yorker*, November 11, 2010, http://www.newyorker.com/news/amy-davidson/the-soldiers-disease.

60. William M. Welch, "Trauma of Iraq War Haunting Thousands Returning Home," *USA Today*, February 28, 2005, http://usatoday30.usatoday.com/news/world/iraq/2005-02-28-cover-iraq-injuries_x.htm.

61. This comes directly from the synopsis available online at http://www.hbo.com/documentaries/wartorn-1861-2010/synopsis.html.

62. See also David Finkel, "The Return," *The New Yorker*, September 9, 2013, http://www.newyorker.com/magazine/2013/09/09/the-return-9.

63. Peter van Agtmael, "From the Battlefield to the Comedy Stage: Healing Bobby Henline," *TIME*, November 10, 2013, http://time.com/3803958/from-the-battlefield-to-the-comedy-stage-healing-bobby-henline/.

64. van Agtmael, "From the Battlefield."

65. Rajiv Chandrasekaran, "A Legacy of Pain and Pride," *The Washington Post*, March 29, 2014, http://www.washingtonpost.com/sf/national/2014/03/29/a-legacy-of-pride-and-pain/.

66. The film has since shown almost exclusively at film festivals, and has been honored at the Television Academy's 2014 Emmy Awards show.

67. Karen Rubin, "From Gold Coast Film Fest: 'Comedy Warriors' Showcases Healing Power of Humor," *Examiner*, December 4, 2013, http://www.examiner.com/article/from-gold-coast-film-fest-comedy-warriors-showcases-healing-power-of-humor.

68. Elaine Scarry, *The Body in Pain: The Making and Unmaking of the World* (New York: Oxford University Press, 1985), 169, 308.

69. Jeffrey C. Alexander, *Trauma: A Social Theory* (Malden, UK: Polity Press, 2012), 68.

70. Wood, "Beyond the Battlefield."

71. Ian Wenger, "Lessons I Learned from a Wounded Warrior," *Today*, May 30, 2011, http://www.today.com/news/lessons-i-learned-wounded-warrior-1C9016263.

72. Pablo Villa, "Former NCO Burned in IED Blast Wants to Open Restaurant, Empower Veterans," *NCO Journal*, March 28, 2016, http://ncojournal.dodlive.mil/tag/bobby-henline/.

73. Pauline Boss, *Loss, Trauma, and Resilience: Therapeutic Work with Ambiguous Loss* (New York: W. W. Norton & Company, 2006), 190.

74. In February 2015, performed with Steve-O at Tommy T's, a comedy club in Pleasanton, California.

75. Abby Ellin, "Photographing Veterans Back from War," *The New York Times*, November 24, 2015, http://well.blogs.nytimes.com/2015/11/24/photographing-soldiers-back-from-war/.

76. See David Jay's series at http://www.unknownsoldier.org/. See also Elizabeth Blair, "It's Not Rude: These Portraits of Wounded Vets Are Meant to Be Stared At," *NPR*, May 25, 2015, http://www.npr.org/2015/05/25/408505821/its-not-rude-these-portraits-of-wounded-vets-are-meant-to-be-stared-at.

77. See Pearsall's portraits of Henline at http://stacypearsall.photoshelter.com/index.

78. Krefting, *All Joking Aside*, 79–82.

79. Julia Kristeva, *Powers of Horror: An Essay on Abjection* (New York: Columbia University Press, 1982), 11.

80. Ellin, "Photographing Veterans."

81. Peter Dahlgren, "From Public to Civic Intellectuals via Online Cultures," *Participations* 10 (2013): 402.

82. I borrow inspiration for this turn of phrase from Bernard Alan Miller, "Rhetorics of War: Dirty Words and Julia Kristeva's Statement of the Abject," *CEA Critic* 77, no.3 (2015): 320–28.

83. David B. Morris, *The Culture of Pain* (Berkeley: University of California Press, 1991), 103.

84. See also an interview with David Wood on *Fresh Air*, available at "Rebuilding Soldiers Transformed by War Injuries," *National Public Radio*, October 13, 2011, http://www.npr.org/2011/10/13/141266015/rebuilding-wounded-soldiers-when-they-return.

85. Kinder, *Paying*, 8.

86. Judith Halberstam, *In a Queer Time and Place: Transgender Bodies, Subcultural Lives* (New York: New York University Press, 2005), 107.

MARIA BAMFORD
A/Way with Words

Rebecca Krefting

> I really do think that comedians are the modern-day philosophers.... And I think that gives us a very important role, because who else is doing that? Who else has that commentary that quickly, and also, is able to make light of painful things and give it some perspective.
>
> —Hari Kondabolu[1]

INTRODUCING MARIA BAMFORD

From comedic web series, to voice-overs for animated television shows, to experimental documentary, to comedy concert films, to star of the Netflix series *Lady Dynamite* (2016–2017), Maria Bamford's résumé as an entertainer is (like those of most comedians who cross over to television and film) as eclectic as it is impressive. According to her official website, her comedy career began at the age of eleven when "she starred in the Chester Park Elementary production of *How the West Was REALLY Won!*" She has been chasing after laughs ever since. You never know what Maria Bamford will say next, or with which voice. Her alternative comedy stylings, most notably a cavalcade of voices and characters that draw inspiration from family members, friends, and even enemies, inspired Zack Ruskin of *SF Weekly* to call her "one of the most innovative stand-up comics working today."[2] During her guest appearance on *The Late Show* (2015–), Stephen Colbert said to Bamford in all earnestness: "You are my favorite comedian on planet earth."[3] Judd Apatow echoes this, almost verbatim: "Maria Bamford is my favorite comedian ever. Nobody makes me laugh harder. To all my friends who are comedians, I apologize for saying this. I hope it didn't hurt you. But it's just a fact. And deep down, you know I'm right."4 They are not alone in their assessment. Over time, Bamford has created a cult-like following from fans drawn to the wacky cast of characters that inhabit her body and her deft treatment of an array of social issues—as in this joke:

> Certain English phrases you really don't learn until you've been here at least a couple hundred years. Things like [*assumes a dyspeptic nasally voice*]: "Why vote? Who cares? It doesn't even fucking matter [*laughter*]." And like [*assuming an indignant tone*]: "Yeah, I'm not racist but they're lazy [*laughter*]." [*Assumes normal voice*] Sounds racist when you say it [*laughter*]. My favorite English phrase that I have been hearing a lot frequently is [*assumes a spoiled tone*]: "Yeah, I need money but I'm not going to work as a fucking . . . [*assumes normal voice*] fill in the blank [*laughter and clapping*]." Very difficult to enunciate that. [*Speaks as if her mouth is full and gestures to her cheeks*] Got to keep the silver spoon between my cheek and gum.5

This recitation of statements weighted with privilege, entitlement, apathy, and judgment boldly skewers the attitudes and the systems that sustain such problematic beliefs. For Bamford, the payoff for performing stand-up comedy is twofold: validation of her experiences and sense of humor, and the possibility that her comedy might unmask social issues and coax new ways of thinking about them. To that effect, she says: "[T]here's something wonderful about hearing people laugh, especially if it's something that's important to me like mental illness. Those laughs can feel really affirming."6 Without being heavy-handed, Bamford's humor tasks us with confronting social stratifications, global inequality, issues of gender parity, and negative attitudes towards mental illness. Over time, she has become a spokesperson especially in matters of mental illness. Given her profession, her sex, and her conscientious efforts to destigmatize mental illness, Bamford—an anxious blonde white woman of slight frame and a childlike voice—seems a surprising choice as a public intellectual.

Bamford was born in Port Hueneme, California on September 3, 1970, but her family moved shortly thereafter to Duluth, Minnesota, where they stayed. When speaking of her childhood, Maria Bamford refers to herself as a "dark kid" who "would occasionally stage my own death for fun. . . . I never really thought of myself as depressed though as much as *paralyzed by hope*."7 She channeled her energies and anxieties into building an arsenal of wacky characters, performing both stand-up and improv while attending college. Believing she could turn those voices into a profitable profession, Bamford moved to LA at the age of twenty-two and quickly infiltrated the thriving West Coast alternative comedy scene of the 1990s. It was not long before she secured well-paying jobs for voice-over work for shows like Nickelodeon's *CatDog* (1998–2005), *Hey Arnold!* (1996–2004), and *Back at the Barnyard* (2007–2011).[8] She earned her chops as a comedy writer by signing on as a staff writer for *Second City Headlines & News* (1996–) in 1997, and later snagged a sweet gig writing for *The Martin Short Show* (1999–2000) in 1999.[9] Stand-up comedy was a constant passion and continuous focus while she was working other jobs as a comedy writer and voice-over actor.

The early aughts brought greater success and notoriety, as Bamford exercised innovative branding through new technologies and platforms circumventing traditional pathways to fame. She pumped out an impressive four comedy albums in the span of eight years (2003–2010)[10] and became a celebrated must-see comic after participating in the Comedians of Comedy Tour with Patton Oswalt, Brian Posehn, Zach Galifianakis, and (later, when he joined the tour) Eugene Mirman.[11] Notably, Bamford adapts her comedy to multiple media; as an early adopter of the platform, she used YouTube to launch the popular web series *The Maria Bamford Show* (2006) and *Ask My Mom!* (2013). The first of these shows offers a prophetic answer to the hypothetical question: "What will happen if I have a mental breakdown?"[12] She shocked and delighted fans with her low-tech, low-cost version of a stand-up special, which she playfully titled *Maria Bamford: The Special Special Special!* (2012), essentially a self-produced full-length stand-up routine.[13] A skeleton crew filmed the show in her living room with only her parents in attendance, and Bamford made it available through Chill.com for a mere $5. In 2013, she caught the attention of *Arrested Development* (2003–2019) creator Mitchell Hurwitz, who cast her in the rebooted season of the show; she went on to become one of the creators and writers of *Lady Dynamite*, a semi-autobiographical digitally streamed Netflix series based on Bamford's life released in May of 2016. After a few more years of experimentation with form and audience, Comedy Dynamics produced her first traditional stand-up special. *Weakness Is the Brand* (Cohen, 2020) landed her on a number of top ten lists for what would be one of the strangest years in comedy history. Not surprisingly, Bamford was at the vanguard of visionary performance during the COVID-19 pandemic. You would be hard pressed to find a working comedian unaware of Bamford's comedic brilliance. She has established herself as an innovator in the field of stand-up comedy—a critical voice with a loyal and growing fan base of public intellectual proportions.

What follows is an exploration of the qualities necessary to inhabit the role of public intellectual, and how charged humor commands this designation.

By charged humor, I mean the humor that intentionally seeks to reveal social inequalities while also doing its own work to celebrate difference, cultivate cultural citizenship, and present suggestions for change.[14] The questions about which I am most curious are: What are the criteria necessary to be cast as public intellectual? Do the criteria have inherent biases, and how does that play out? For example, androcentrism informs the collective choices that continually reify men as more able to serve in such distinguished positions, illuminating the difficulty women have achieving status as a public intellectual. This, along with the fact that Maria Bamford's comedy takes on many issues of inequality, not just stigmas about mental illness, makes her position as cultural mouthpiece all the more impressive. Using her corpus of comedy work, including concert films, audio recordings, web series, YouTube clips, and television work, I aim to frame, contextualize, and analyze the myriad ways that Bamford uses her profession to generate charged humor or urge social consciousness and political change, most particularly around long-held negative attitudes toward and stereotypes about mental illness. Widespread respect for Maria Bamford—her life and her creative work—has catapulted her into the role of public intellectual, which is not that surprising since comedians are frequently included in *Time Magazine*'s lists of 100 most influential people. When *Foreign Policy* gave readers the chance to offer suggestions for whom to include in a list of the world's top twenty public intellectuals, Stephen Colbert received the most votes.[15] Popular opinion demonstrates that someone like Jon Stewart or Whoopi Goldberg can be stacked up against the likes of Maya Angelou, Ayaan Hirsi Ali, Al Gore, or Umberto Eco. Though laughter may be a primary objective for stand-up comics, their words are freighted and fertile with possibility. Indeed, this is what makes comics suitable as public intellectuals in the first place.

THIS PUBLIC INTELLECTUAL *IS* CHARGED

Comedians have been called a lot of things—not all of them nice, either. Humor studies scholars confer upon stand-up comedians many roles, among them: "comic auteurs,"[16] cultural and community spokespersons,[17] and "*cynical insider[s]*."[18] Stephanie Koziski positions stand-up comics as cultural anthropologists, a designation that entails closely observing a community or group, commenting on community norms and cultural contradictions, offering new interpretations and ways of envisioning the past and present, and connecting language and forms of expression to social roles (e.g., the way certain dialects and mannerisms evoke regional, class, or racial/ethnic distinctions).[19] Beyond securing the yuks, comics also function to hold up a mirror to our shared assumptions, values, and cultural practices, bringing new kinds of awareness to who we are and what we deem important. Because they "see" our culture from many angles, comedians can use humor to make the normal seem strange, so that we might reexamine our behaviors. In other words, comics scrutinize aspects of life so we have to rethink our norms. They do not have to be purveyors of charged humor, nor must they be actively seeking to raise social consciousness, but they can and do these things, and the most accomplished of them at filling these roles become our public intellectuals.

Scholarship framing modern conceptions of public intellectuals may not use the precise term yet may refer to the same kinds of social savvy, authority, visibility, and cultural critique. Antonio Gramsci characterizes organic intellectuals as holding positions of leadership (this could be in any profession), having specialized skills, and raising awareness around economic, social, and political issues.[20] For Maria Bamford, lecherous bosses, quirky coworkers, and all manner of humiliations common to temporary work became fodder and fuel for stand-up comedy.

> I used to have this really creepy, creepy boss. He would always come up to me and say stuff like: [*heavy breathing into the microphone*] "I really like it when you wear your hair like that. Hehehe. [*breathes heavily into the microphone while audience laughs*] Why don't you come in the meeting, take shorthand, cheer up the guys with your pretty face? Come on smile for me. You look so much more beautiful when you smile. Hehehe" [*breathes heavily into the microphone while crowd laughs*]. Like I go in his office and say stuff like [*assumes a sexy voice*]: "Hi, I really love the way your gray curly neck hair comes up over the edge of your peach polyweave sweat-stained sport shirt [*laughter*]. Why don't you come in my cubicle and tell me more about my partial dental benefits after ninety days [*she winks seductively and crowd laughs and claps*]? Come on, smile for me. The fact that I net $6.49 an hour to provide you with the sexual stimulation you're not man enough to get in your personal life [*smattering of cheers and laughter*] is so much more apparent [*she drops the voice and looks directly at her audience*] when you smile" [*clapping and cheering*].[21]

Bamford offers an agentic response to the ubiquity of being devalued as object or decoration for male pleasure, and by drawing attention to these matters she knocks a small but mighty chink in the armor of patriarchy.

On stage, in a position of authority (read leadership), she nimbly moves from character to character, each with their own voice, body language, and idiosyncrasies (read specialized skills) to reveal the gendered dimensions of inequality.

Gramsci's organic intellectual presents a facsimile for public intellectuals, though one not quite as nuanced as Edward Said's discussion of the same. Using different terminology but banging on the same set of drums, Said positions the "role of the intellectual as outsider, 'amateur,' and disturber of the status quo."[22] He goes on: "Insiders promote special interests, but intellectuals should be the ones to question patriotic nationalism, corporate thinking, and a sense of class, racial or gender privilege."[23] For Said, it is not enough to report what you see; rather, the public tasks intellectuals with maintaining critical distance from our political and social institutions. For this reason, Elizabeth Bruenig, a writer for *New Republic*, does *not* believe that comedians should be deemed public intellectuals. She suggests that televised comedy—whether stand-up or late-night talk shows—panders to the broadest possible audience. This generally dilutes excoriating critiques of society or our political system. Bruenig writes: "Mistaking gentle jokes about Republicans for subversiveness is dangerous because it convinces those in the center that they're on the vanguard, which severely delimits their view of the range of political possibilities."[24] Her point is well taken and is echoed in Edward Said's scholarship about public intellectuals (i.e., the degree to which one can occupy that role while being subject to corporate interests).[25] Comedians *are* subject to media censure and do make career decisions to maximize profit, which can work to minimize the extent of the critiques they offer. The degree to which anyone can locate themselves outside the system is debatable; however, most important here for Said and Gramsci is the imperative of a critique leveled at systemic inequality. Comedians such as Hannah Gadsby, Steve Martin, Dave Chappelle, Marc Maron, and Wanda Sykes remain beneficiaries of the system while pointing to its flaws.

To be clear, being a comedian does not a public intellectual make. Generalizing statements identifying all comedians as public intellectuals ignore the reality of the banal comedy so readily available to consumers. Not all comics portend to play such a part, and most people would reserve that designation for stand-up comedians who comment on social and political issues, critique the status quo, and deliver profound maxims all steeped in humor. Carrot Top and Adam Carolla are, for instance, in no danger of being misidentified as public intellectuals. As Stephanie Koziski puts it, "The unreflective artist may merely betray and depict covert traits of culture without analysis. The more sensitive and critical artist will discover, analyze and account for the discrepancies found in their observations of how things *should* operate in culture but *don't*" (italics hers).[26] Koziski's "critical artist" is just another way of alluding to charged humor or the comedy that pays particular attention to unmasking social inequalities, troubles the notion that there is anything "natural" about disenfranchisement, and stokes cultural citizenship. Just as with Edward Said's description of an intellectual, this kind of charged humorist positions themselves as an outsider, divested of the interests of the ruling classes and invested in pointing out where the trouble lies in our production and reproduction of social and political institutions. Nearly everyone agrees on what constitutes a public intellectual and that comedians can serve in such a capacity, but this does nothing to diminish the reality that women are less likely to rise to such a status in the first place.

Dimensions of inequality inform whom we choose to view as public intellectuals. Whether we are talking about captivating orators, celebrated specialists, or public intellectuals, these positions of authority tend to be held by those occupying dominant categories of identity: e.g., able-bodied, white, male, heterosexual, Christian, affluent, etcetera. Some time ago, in a conversation with colleagues, someone compared Hillary Clinton to Barack Obama as an orator, citing Obama's abilities for public oration as superior to Hillary Clinton's. Both are compelling leaders, savvy political strategists, and intellectual giants. But put up one against the other when it comes to delivering speeches that inform, counsel, and motivate, and most people will agree that Obama executes better than Clinton. Indeed, an article in the *Huffington Post* lauded Obama as the third greatest orator in the modern era.[27] Hillary Clinton was not even a contender, perhaps because she lacks what Eliana Johnson, a writer for *National Review*, describes as willingness to offer "exposure, access, the illusion of intimacy."[28] In an ironic twist, based on those descriptors, it appears that Clinton does not do a good enough job of exuding feminine traits. Or it could mean that people interpret differently the careful balancing act of exhibiting authority versus vulnerability when the subject is female versus male. The point is not whether Obama is a better orator; rather, it is that women will be judged differently while performing in exactly the same ways as men. Clinton's public speaking abilities are not deficient; they just ring oddly to ears accustomed to hearing men speak. We are socialized to accept men as political leaders; that power looks good, if not exactly right, when nestled in the arms of men.[29] Historically we designate mainly white male comics as cultural critics. It's true that some African American men have attained such status, such as Dick Gregory and Richard Pryor, but in the United States people more readily accept white men in the role of public intellectual. Comics—Black, white, and brown; men and women; straight and queer; Christian, Muslim, Jewish, and atheist have all performed in the role of public intellectual at some time or other. This is not to say that women have not served in such capacities; rather, the point is that women will struggle more than their male counterparts to demonstrate aptitude as public intellectuals, because we are socialized to believe that men are more efficacious orators, critics, observers, and leaders.

In the mid–twentieth century, comedians like Mort Sahl, Dick Gregory, Richard Pryor, George Carlin, and Lenny Bruce took up roles as public intellectuals, using humor to speak with cultural authority. Their commonality: *wide-spread visibility and charged content destabilizing cultural norms and critiquing political and social institutions*. In using charged humor to challenge what was assumed to be natural or normal, and then to imagine otherwise, they captivated the public's ear; consequently they continue to exist in our history and cultural imagination as comic icons and public intellectuals. There have always been smart comics who pack a moral wallop in their jokes; the question is whether we buy what they are selling and enable them to break into the mainstream. The same charged humor that catapulted Gregory, Carlin, and Pryor in the 1970s fell out of favor in the 1980s alongside the rise of neoliberalism, making room for a sharp rise in comedy that was apolitical, gag-heavy, and television appropriate.

The rise of the conservative Right in the 1980s shaped public attitudes, and changing technologies delivered more content to more people, forever altering modes of distribution and consumption of comedy.[30] In his history of anti-intellectualism in the early to mid–twentieth century, Richard Hofstadter charts the ebb and flow of public ambivalence bordering on hostility toward intellectuals, demonstrating that a confluence of political events and cultural beliefs can produce or quash the people's faith in and need for public intellectuals. Sometimes we want our public intellectuals to remind us of ways we can improve; sometimes we don't. Neoliberalism propelled shifts in public opinion around our social contract, and formerly celebrated words like "welfare state" and "government aid" took on increasingly negative connotations. Individuals, not the government, were to blame for poverty, homelessness, medical illness, and disability. Those same beliefs that gave rise to neoliberalism in the 1980s diminished the gravitas granted to intellectualism—not altogether, but enough to diminish the public's desire for vocal spokespersons critiquing a system that had been soundly declared democratic and equal for all citizens.[31] Visible inequalities like poverty became not a reason to doubt the American Dream, but a sign of bad choices and individual failure. The centralization of media used to distribute comedy to the masses in the 1980s was another crucial factor in the heft that comedians—or anyone, for that matter—could bring to topics when subject to censorship and advertisers' restrictions. The big bucks were in television, especially in sitcoms, and producers had no intention of jeopardizing ratings by signing on a comedian with polarizing political views. The later twentieth century was an era in which cultural critics need not apply. When it comes down to who we turn to for guidance—excepting religious or political authorities—public allowances for social critique matter as much as the communication systems we have in place to share and connect with one another.

In a world with gender parity (not this one), it takes only two important components to achieve status as comic-*cum*-public intellectual: *critical comedic commentary* and *visibility*. Charged comics already have the content; it is the visibility that proves more difficult to procure, particularly when the most effective and widespread forms of media exposure have vested interests in trafficking ideas palatable to middle America. The fact is that one cannot be a public intellectual if no one is listening, but when a comic has a captive audience they may wield a great deal of power to unpack and transform the American Mind. Having worked diligently for decades as a charged stand-up comic, Bamford is more than up to the task. She takes on mental health struggles and a number of other social issues related to gender, race, sexuality, and class. For this, she attracts fans from many communities and groups who can identify with her critiques of sexism, racism, classism, and stigmas about mental illness. I discovered Bamford in the early aughts and was initially impressed with the way she critiqued gender inequalities, offering incisive perspectives on the female condition while never losing the funny.

> I wanna do a makeup commercial. I'd do one. [*Pretends to narrate for a commercial, assuming an upbeat voice*] My old lip color can barely keep up with my busy schedule. Ha ha! In the time it takes to notice the wide discrepancy between my salary and that of my male peers, I'd have to reapply, ha ha [*laughter*]! In the seconds it takes to count the number of women in high political offices, seated on corporate executive boards, and featured in film and television over the age of forty, my lip color would be as invisible as this glass ceiling only inches above my head [*laughter*]. L'Oreal, because I am worth it and because holding myself to an impossible standard of beauty keeps me from starting a riot [*laughter, clapping, and several "yeahs" from the audience*]![32]

This charged humor identifies ways gender disparities play out in politics, business, and entertainment. Moreover, the way preoccupations with beauty serve to distract us from important issues that perpetuate the subordination of women—like essentialist beliefs about women's biological inferiority that interfere with women's professional success, a gendered income gap, and the lack of complex female protagonists over the age of forty in film and television. Bamford's sweet voice, her delivery, her femininity, and of course her whiteness help to make this kind of excoriating critique palatable. She serves as a Trojan horse, using multiple media to champion society's underdogs. Her comedy grapples with a variety of social ills and inequalities, but it is her discerning critique of social treatment of mental illness that has commanded the most public interest and praise.

DESTIGMATIZING MENTAL ILLNESS

Mental illness is tough, and especially so when it remains undiagnosed or controlled. Falling prey to bulimia during her teenage years was just one of many coping mechanisms, including performing stand-up comedy, that Bamford used to stave off depression and anxieties—what she now knows was undiagnosed bipolar II disorder. When she was sixteen, she attended an eighteen-week workshop for a Dale Carnegie sales training and management course that gave her another set of strategies for coping with negative thoughts and suicidal ideations.[33] At the age of twenty-one, not long after spreading her wings as a fledgling comic, she sought professional treatment for her eating disorder.[34] This was the first of a series of hospitalizations for mental health issues. It also became the wellspring from which she draws her comedy. Maria Bamford's bipolar II disorder remained undiagnosed until 2010, when her depression and suicidal thoughts were too overwhelming to control. She canceled shows in Chicago and checked herself into the hospital for what would be the first of three hospitalizations over the next year and a half. Psychiatrists suggested and prescribed mood stabilizers, which she was reluctant to take—she felt that doing so would be an admission that she was dealing with something bigger than depression. Bamford explains this resistance in her stand-up comedy and interviews: "I was fine with saying I was depressed, but I was not fine with saying that I was bipolar. For whatever reason—it's very odd because there's tons of mental illness in my family—I had some deep prejudice against it."[35] After accepting the bipolar diagnosis, acceding to her daily dose of Depacon, and realizing that she could still perform comedy, she came to acceptance: "'I like how I feel now,' she says. 'This is how people should feel.'"[36] And the things that make her happy are not always congruent with societal expectations like competition, success, and wealth. Early on Bamford's history of mental illness forced her into a position as outsider, and it is from here that she has been able to use charged humor to recast our norms and challenge prevailing assumptions and ideologies in ways both funny and subversive.

Just as Hannah Gadsby has become a spokesperson for gender nonconformity and neurodiversity, Bamford has become a respected voice around matters of mental illness. David Gillota, a humor studies scholar, writes, "most stand-ups also represent the point-of-view of a particular demographic defined by race, gender, class, or sexual orientation."[37] Niche marketing capitalizes on the same categories of identity, helping to promote comedians as spokespersons for various communities; in Bamford's case, she speaks on behalf of the disenfranchised across many communities, and most clearly for those dealing personally with mental illness. She goes off script on stage and in interviews, saying all manner of things countering pervasive narratives circulating about mental illness. Cultural forces, religious practices, and political and social institutions overtly and tacitly condemn suicide—those who do it and those who contemplate it. Although it is no longer criminalized in the United States, there were state laws making suicide a felony well into the 1990s. In *Ask Me about My New God!* Bamford uses her comedy to get these views across, joking: "Over seven thousand US veterans die of suicide every year which is funny [*she starts chuckling*] because you would think they would die over there but they come home, right [*pause and audience laughter*]. [*Fake goofy laughter from Maria*] I thought it must be funny because nobody was taking it that seriously [*clapping and cheering*]."[38] By telling her audience about her own thoughts about suicide and demonstrating that suicide is endemic to US veterans—a respected segment of the population—she exposes the social and cultural forces that discourage admission of depression and silence discussion on the topic of suicide, simultaneously revealing how problematic and dangerous that can be. When asked about her objectives whilst performing comedy targeting mental illness, she says: "For myself, it's all very selfish. I would like to make it okay to ask for help in a major way like in an embarrassing way. . . . [P]eople need to know that maybe there is hope."[39]

As early as 2007, Maria Bamford's stand-up comedy referenced battles with OCD, depression, and suicidal ideation; and after being hospitalized in 2010 and 2011, she went public with having bipolar II disorder. She reports that at the outset she was terrified of talking about her personal experiences, but that the more she did, the easier it became. Being frank about what happened, according to Bamford, "has been a real gift to me too, that the art form allows, that you can talk about anything. . . . Like it doesn't become this private horrible, horrible thing."[40] Mental health was not a focus early on in Bamford's comedy—or at least it does not show up on her comedy albums until her second album *Maria Bamford: How to WIN!* (2007)—when it does, it is referenced sparingly. For instance, when she sings her famous "Anxiety Song" and for the first time reveals that she is seeing a therapist.

> [*Sings in a faltering voice while repeatedly clenching one fist then the other*] If I keep my ice cube trays filled it'll be okay. As long as I clench my fists at odd intervals then the darkness that's within you won't force me to do things I don't want to do that are inappropriately violent [*laughter*]. As long as I keep singing this song I won't turn gay and God can't kill me. It can't get you if you're singing a song, yeah [*laughter and clapping*]![41]

The antidote to a barrage of repetitive negative thoughts becomes an incongruous assemblage of preventive measures like singing this song. It doesn't require having OCD to identify with Bamford and find this bit humorous. We all exhibit idiosyncratic behaviors that are only sensical given our personal and social histories, experiences, and dispositions. Most other jokes on this album are about her family, living in LA, and bad credit, but she also targets other global issues like child labor.

> I wish I could get mad about something that actually mattered [*laughter*]. Go in Target, be like: "You know what, if you can't help me then I need to speak to someone who can because this is a $3 pair of flip-flops made by a five-year-old Guatemalan girl and I'm not leaving until she gets benefits and an education under the NAFTA Fair Trade Agreement [*clapping and laughter*]. You better go get a manager [*laughter*]." [*Speaking to the audience*] This could take a while [*laughter*].[42]

It is easy to admire Maria Bamford. Never preachy, the humor often comes at her own expense, as she fails time and again to live up to society's standards or to take appropriate action against inequality. Her messages are clear: social standards need to be revised to account for diverse identities and experiences, and we are all complicit in national/global wealth disparities.

Anyone who has dealt with mental health issues will tell you that in order to be functional, healthy, and happy you have to find new ways of approaching life and new methods for drowning out the din of social demands. It's the same mental short-circuiting required for challenging representations of any "Other," a never-ending process of unlearning. This means eschewing maxims and ideologies engrained in the very fabric of American identity—beliefs that what we produce or how much we earn is a measure of our worth, that independence is more valuable than interdependence, and that different physical and mental abilities equate to deficiency. Bamford explains this further:

> Either people put it into terms of like you can get yourself out of it. It's not a genuine illness, a moral failing. And/or the moral failing as in spirituality like [*assumes a sanctimonious tone*]: You're blocking your chi. You're not being honest with yourself about something [*assumes regular voice*]—and that the brain isn't an organ like any other part of the body that can malfunction.[43]

Bamford alludes to these beliefs in her comedy and chides Americans for perpetuating a myth of triumphalism—that the strong will triumph over anything, which makes it hard for anyone with mental illness to feel adequate.[44]

> I get mad and stuff 'cause there's still stigma, you know, talking about any kind of mental illness. They don't talk about mental illness the way they do other illnesses. [*Assumes woman's voice*] "Yeah apparently, Steve has cancer. It's like fuck off, we all have cancer, right [*laughter and clapping*]?! Right?! [*Sustained laughter*] I have cancer pretty bad right now but I get it taken care of. I go to chemotherapy. I get back to work" [*laughing and clapping*]. [*Assumes man's voice*] "Yeah I was dating this chick and apparently, you know, she needs contact lenses, you know, all this time. She wears glasses and yeah, I was just like I don't believe in all that Western medicine shit, you know [*laughter*]. If you wanna see, like, other people, it's all about attitude [*laughter*]. You gotta want it! [*laughter*] You gotta want it" [*laughter*]. [*Switches voice to a sad women*] "You would think you'd be able to stop vomiting for me and the kids" [*laughter*]."[45]

Bamford makes visible the range of stigmas leveled at folks with mental illness: that you should take care of it (quietly), that using willpower you can overcome all manner of physical and mental ailments, and that caring for others means ignoring your own needs. Her charged comedy compels listeners to examine their own beliefs, biases, and assumptions about mental illness. This is the power wielded by Stephanie Koziski's "cynical insider" who writes: "The comedian can use [their] power as a symbol-maker, interpreter and articulator of information to transform past and present experiences into a new cultural focus."[46] In this case, the new cultural focus pinpoints attitudes and behaviors surrounding mental illness and health, drawing admiration from a broad swath of people who have been affected themselves or know someone who has.

In a *New York Times* article, "The Weird, Scary and Ingenious Brain of Maria Bamford," Sara Corbett writes, "After the show, a crowd lingered late in front of the theater, waiting to speak with Bamford. She is frequently approached by people who view themselves as part of her tribe, who want to talk about their own diagnoses and tell their own tales of being misunderstood."[47] Mental illness cuts across all categories of difference—race/ethnicity, class, sex, gender presentation, sexuality, etcetera—making Bamford's fans a diverse tribe. She describes the way comedy becomes an invitation to connect with her fans—whom she describes as "super-sweet"[48]—based on shared experiences, saying: "So all of a sudden I have a ginormous community of strangers who say: 'Oh that happened to me or my friend.' You know, where it makes it less of a freak show thing."[49] Bamford reports that she struggled with internalized stigmas and intolerance toward mental illness, and that it wasn't until after going through what she did that she was able to confront her lack of acceptance. What the audience gets from her is a humanized view of working through society's dicta and cultural conditioning around these topics. Her comedy exposes her identity-in-the-making as she processes her own mental illness while simultaneously becoming a beacon for people in various stages of acceptance and understanding. Edward Said argues that public intellectuals are representative of something: a cause, a set of beliefs, a set of political strategies. Moreover, "in so doing [intellectuals] represent themselves to themselves . . . you do what you do according to an idea or representation you have of yourself as doing that thing."[50] Bamford's role as cultural spokesperson is repeatedly reflected back to her in the many exchanges between her and her fans both on stage and off. Her comedy oscillates between her own experiences and broader critiques of the institutions and beliefs fueling misperceptions about people with mental illness.

> If you ever start thinking [*assumes a depressed voice*]: "Oh, but I'm a waste of space and I'm a burden." [*Resumes normal voice*] Remember that also describes the Grand Canyon [*laughter*]. [*Assumes a dejected voice*] "Oh oh, but I owe people a lot of money and everybody hates me." [*Resumes normal voice*] Hello Europe [*laughter*]! [*Assumes a guilty voice*] "Oh oh, but I've done some other horrible, unspeakable, unforgivable thing." [*Resumes normal voice*] GOOGLE IT!

> Somebody has done exactly what you have done or worse, has gotten past it and is currently on a book tour. You're never alone [*applause and cheering*]![51]

She turns self-doubt into a natural wonder—something to be admired because it simultaneously inspires awe and evokes fear—and humorously reminds listeners that no situation is experienced in isolation. Comedy albums she recorded during the 2010s reflect Bamford's awareness that she has become a trusted ally and critical voice waged against the silence, the stigma, the condescension, the judgments, and the pity. In her own words, "I went through a nightmare, but it means a lot to me that other people with mental illness tell me the show [*Lady Dynamite*] has helped and made them laugh."[52] She has stepped up to and settled into a role as public intellectual, a position she didn't ask for but was given anyway.

Though delighted by the popular reception of her comic performances and proud to play the role of public intellectual, Bamford isn't angling for more fame. In an interview for *Esquire*, she explains: "Well I like to work, but I feel a bit afraid of fame and stuff. It seems a little frightening. But I also know that people who are very successful work really hard, and I have to admit I'm not the hardest worker. And I think that's okay."[53] She chooses to reject Western notions of success if those efforts compromise her mental well-being. As she sees it, she has already achieved what she wants and is happy with her current level of fame.

> Oh my god, I feel like I made it five years ago. Or ten. I've got a joke about how people in LA are always asking [*dons a peppy voice*], "So what are you working on? What's going on with you? What's the next page? What's coming up for you? What's going on? What's on the horizon?" and I say [*resumes normal voice*], "Oh. I'm done. Yeah, I finished early. I'm actually living in a gravy boat filled with gravy." And I do feel like that. I just want to have more potluck dinner parties and walk around with my dogs. Those are my main goals now.[54]

Maria Bamford's stage persona and life serve as a model for approaching issues of mental health in new ways that value individual differences and needs regardless of whether they fly in the face of American beliefs about independence that denigrate anyone who needs help. Others, like Josh Blue, Maysoon Zayid, Danielle Perez, Nicki Payne, and Brett Leake, use their positions as comic performers and motivational speakers to advocate on behalf of those who are differently abled—physically, mentally, or otherwise—but none have as broad an audience as Maria Bamford does. When COVID-19 gutted the stand-up comedy industry, she exercised ingenuity by creating virtual performances. She spoke openly about her mother's battle with cancer alongside offering free therapy to fans and fellow comics—not necessarily *good* therapy, but she tried. These intimate exchanges illustrated the depth of respect and gratitude the public has for her work. A fellow comic, Erin Foley, describes Bamford as "all parts smart, honest, poignant, imaginative, brilliant and silly. I think she might be from the future."[55] If her comedy portends the future, then we have much to look forward to.[56]

Notes

1. Max Levine, "Hari Kondabolu Talks Bobby Jindal, Stand-up during Political Unrest, and Why Comedians Are Like Philosophers," *City Paper*, August 18, 2015, accessed September 3, 2015. http://www.citypaper.com/arts/stage/bcp-081915-stage-hari-kondabolu-20150818-story.html.

2. Zack Ruskin, "Dispatches from SF Sketchfest: Sally Field, Maya Rudolph, Maria Bamford and More," *SFWeekly*, January 25, 2015, accessed February 22, 2016, http://www.sfweekly.com/exhibitionist/2016/01/25/dispatches-from-sf-sketchfest-sally-field-maya-rudolph-maria-bamford-and-more.

3. *The Late Show with Stephen Colbert*, "Maria Bamford Performs Stand-Up," filmed January 16, 2016, YouTube video, 4:17, posted January 16, 2016, https://www.youtube.com/watch?v=Oe17RymMqWI.

4. Judd Apatow, *Sick in the Head: Conversations about Life and Comedy* (New York: Random House, 2015), 493.

5. *Maria Bamford: Ask Me About My New God!* CD, Comedy Central Records, 2013.

6. Matthew Kitchen, "Q & A: Maria Bamford on Her Hilarious New Show," *Esquire*, June 18, 2013, accessed March 10, 2016, http://www.esquire.com/entertainment/tv/interviews/a23127/maria-bamford-interview-ask-my-mom/.

7. *Maria Bamford: How to WIN!* CD, Stand Up! Records, 2007.

8. For a complete list of Maria Bamford's voiceover work, you can consult IMDB: http://www.imdb.com/name/nm0051469/.

9. Marah Eakin, "Maria Bamford on Our 11 Questions and *My Cat From Hell*," *The AV Club*, October 29, 2014, accessed February 22, 2016, http://www.avclub.com/article/maria-bamford-our-11-questions-and-my-cat-hell-211049.

10. Bamford's comedy albums include: *The Burning Bridges Tour* (2003); *How to WIN!* (2007); *Unwanted Thoughts Syndrome* (2009); *Plan B* (2010); *The Special Special Special* (2012); *Ask Me about My New God!* (2013); *20%* (2016); *Old Baby* (2017); and *Weakness Is the Brand* (2020). Many of these are available free of charge on Spotify.

11. Portions of the tour were filmed in 2004 and premiered as a documentary of the same name at the South by Southwest film festival in 2005. The film features some of their stand-up comedy interspersed with lively behind-the-scenes footage. *The Comedians of Comedy: Live at the El Rey*, DVD, directed by Michael Blieden, Red Envelope Entertainment, Netflix Co.

2006. 12. "Maria Bamford: A Seriously Funny Comedian," *Fresh Air with Terry Gross*, Podcast, audio, July 18, 2013, http://www.npr.org/2013/07/18/202374622/maria-bamford-a-seriously-funny-comedian.; Sean L. McCarthy, "Interview Maria Bamford," *The Comic's Comic*, accessed February 6, 2015, http://thecomicscomic.com/2008/10/14/interview-maria/.

13. *Maria Bamford: Special, Special, Special*, online download, Chill.com, 2012.

14. The first chapter of my monograph-length treatment on the subject of charged humor offers a more complete description and discussion of charged humor and its connections to cultural citizenship. See Rebecca Krefting, *All Joking Aside: American Humor and Its Discontents* (Baltimore, MD: Johns Hopkins University Press, 2014).

15. Brad Amburn, "The World's Top 20 Public Intellectuals," *Foreign Policy*, October 7, 2009, accessed July 12, 2016, http://foreignpolicy.com/2009/10/07/the-worlds-top-20-public-intellectuals/.

16. Linda Mizejewski, *Pretty/Funny: Women Comedians and Body Politics* (Austin: University of Texas Press, 2014), 5.

17. David Gillota, "Stand-Up Nation: Humor and American Identity," *Journal of American Culture* 38, no. 2 (2015): 102–12; Lawrence E. Mintz, "Standup Comedy as Social and Cultural Mediation," *American Quarterly* 37, no. 1 (Spring 1985): 71–80.

18. Stephanie Koziski, "The Standup Comedian as Anthropologist: Intentional Cultural Critic," *Journal of Popular Culture* 18, no. 2 (Fall 1984): 57–76.

19. Koziski, "Standup Comedian," 64–67.

20. Antonio Gramsci, *Selections from the Prison Notebooks of Antonio Gramsci* (1971), ed. and trans. Quintin Hoare and Geoffrey Nowell-Smith (New York: International Publishers, 2005).

21. Rich Writer, "Just For Laughs—Maria Bamford—Patrice O'Neal," YouTube video, 8:19, posted June 9, 2012, https://www.youtube.com/watch?v=mVzbsqgUm4I.

22. Edward Said, *Representations of the Intellectual* (New York: Pantheon, 1994), x.

23. Said, *Representations*, xiii.

24. Elizabeth Breunig, "Comedians Are Funny, Not Public Intellectuals," *New Republic*, June 3, 2015, accessed September 22, 2015, https://newrepublic.com/article/121956/stewart-and-colbert-are-no-substitute-intellectuals.

25. Said, *Representations*.

26. Said, *Representations*, 65.

27. Richard Greene, "Obama Is America's Third Greatest Presidential Orator in Modern Era," *Huffington Post*, January 25, 2011, accessed June 10, 2016, http://www.huffingtonpost.com/richard-greene/obama-is-americas-3rd-gre_b_813868.html.

28. Eliana Johnson, "Hillary Clinton Can't Give a Decent Speech. Does it Matter?" *National Review*, June 16, 2015, accessed June 10, 2016, http://www.nationalreview.com/article/419818/hillary-clinton-cant-give-decent-speech-does-it-matter-eliana-johnson.

29. Sandra Harding, "Rethinking Standpoint Epistemology: What Is 'Strong Objectivity'?" in *Feminist Epistemologies*, ed. Linda Alcoff and Elizabeth Potter (New York & London: Routledge, 1993), 49–82.

30. Krefting, *All Joking Aside*.

31. Richard Hofstadter, *Anti-Intellectualism in American Life* (New York: Alfred A. Knopf, 1963).

32. *Maria Bamford: How to WIN!*

33. *Maria Bamford: How to WIN!*; "Bamford: Seriously Funny," *Fresh Air with Terry Gross*.

34. Patrick Gomez, "Comedian Maria Bamford: My Battle with Mental Illness," *People*, July 25, 2016, 74–75.

35. q on cbc, "Maria Bamford Brings Her Dark Comedy to Studio Q," filmed November 11, 2014, YouTube video, 24:47, posted November 11, 2014, https://www.youtube.com/watch?v=kIorvIdMexY.

36. Gomez, "Comedian Maria Bamford."

37. Gillota, "Stand-Up Nation," 103.

38. *Maria Bamford: Ask Me About My New God!*

39. q on cbc, "Maria Bamford Brings Her Dark Comedy."

40. *Misery Loves Comedy*, DVD, directed by Kevin Pollak, Tribeca Film, 2015.

41. *Maria Bamford: How to WIN!*

42. *Maria Bamford: How to WIN!*

43. KCET SoCalConnected, "In 'Special Special Special,' Maria Bamford Finds the Funny in Her Mental Illness," filmed April 5, 2013, YouTube video, 7:08, posted April 5, 2013. https://www.youtube.com/watch?v=S0lxkDv0D5E.

44. q on cbc, "Maria Bamford Brings Her Dark Comedy."

45. *Maria Bamford: Ask Me About My New God!*

46. Koziski, "Standup Comedian" 66.

47. Sara Corbett, "On the Road with Maria Bamford," *The New York Times*, July 17, 2014, accessed February 22, 2016, http://6thfloor.blogs.nytimes.com/2014/07/17/on-the-road-with-maria-bamford/.

48. Emma Zemler, "The Greatest Joke (According to Maria Bamford)," *Esquire*, May 28, 2015, accessed February 22, 2016, http://www.esquire.com/entertainment/a35297/maria-bamford-greatest-joke/.

49. PBS, "Maria Bamford—Crazy Meds/Modern Comedian—Episode 29," filmed August 22, 2014, YouTube video, 12:10, posted August 22, 2014, https://www.youtube.com/watch?v=f6fKarmaphY.

50. Said, *Representations*, xv.

51. Comedy Central, "The Meltdown with Jonah and Kumail—Maria Bamford—You're Never," filmed September 9, 2014, YouTube video, 1:55, posted Sept. 9, 2014, https://www.youtube.com/watch?v=InNjt2GO5w4.

52. Gomez, "Comedian Maria Bamford."

53. Kitchen, "Q & A: Maria Bamford."

54. Kitchen, "Q & A: Maria Bamford."

55. Art Levine, "Maria Bamford Tells (Almost) All About Her Comedy, Mental Illness and Sloppy Psych Care before the American Comedy Awards," *Huffington Post*, May 7, 2014, accessed February 22, 2016, http://www.huffingtonpost.com/art-levine/maria-bamford-tells-almos_b_5251231.html.

56. The following publications offer additional analyses on Maria Bamford's comedy: David Gillota, "Beyond Liveness: Experimentation in the Stand-Up Special," *Studies in American Humor* 6, no. 1 (2020): 44–61; Kathryn Mears, Eric Shouse, and Patrice Oppliger, "An Incongruous Blend of Tragedy and Comedy: How Maria Bamford Lightens the Dark Side of Mental Illness," in *The Dark Side of Stand-Up Comedy*, ed. Patrice Oppliger and Eric Shouse (Cham, Switzerland: Palgrave Macmillan, 2020), 173–93.

4

AWKWARD EMBRACE
Tig Notaro and the Humor of Social Discomfort

Kathryn Kein

Tig Notaro's comedy isn't "edgy." On stage, she doesn't curse, do political material, or talk about race, sex, or sexuality. In a 2015 interview at *New York Magazine*'s "Vulture Fest," Notaro labeled her own stand-up as "not . . . hard to take."[1] Given her avoidance of controversial material, then, you wouldn't expect to watch or listen to one of Notaro's shows and feel uncomfortable. But despite her lack of so-called edge, Notaro's comedy is *all* about discomfort. Her material relies on stories of social awkwardness and embarrassment—mistaken gender, a bombed show, a repeated scoff from a beloved pop star in response to her compliments—in which she doesn't escape the discomfort, but basks in it. The jokes themselves are not one-liners, big punch lines, or surprise incongruous endings. Rather, they move slowly, forcing the audience to linger in the discomfort, often waiting for a punch line the words of which they already know are coming. Notaro's joke setups draw out the comic tension, rendering the tension itself a main feature of the act.

In this way, Notaro's comedy encourages audiences to examine their social boundaries and notions of awkwardness and social propriety. Notaro does similar work in multiple venues away from the stand-up stage—in interviews, talk show appearances, her popular podcast, and her book—cementing her place as a public intellectual widely known for awkward encounters and challenges to social expectations. As a comedian she challenges notions of the performance space—at times performing in fans' basements, backyards, and crowded kitchens—and in so doing she calls into question the socially scripted roles of performer and audience. On and off stage she hones in on situations and affects from which we would generally run, but instead asks us to stay put, to fully and collectively experience the discomfort rather than retreating. In doing so, Notaro calls into question the types of interactions that have value, and upends social hierarchies that privilege certain bodies, behaviors, or experiences over others.

Many have noted the significant place comedians have held in the public discourse in recent years as not just entertainers, but public intellectuals. Writing for *The Atlantic* in 2015, Megan Garber argued that in the current political moment—and enabled by the internet to reach greater audiences—comedians are increasingly performing comedy with a message, telling "jokes that tend to treat humor not just as an end in itself, but as a vehicle for making a point."[2] As public intellectuals, comedians explore important ideas and prompt discussions among an audience that is looking to them to do so.

This chapter examines the stand-up comedy and public presence of Tig Notaro within this era of comedians as public intellectuals, highlighting the role of awkwardness and discomfort in both the form and the content of her work. It will do this with two main areas of focus, the first of which is Notaro's signature, slow comedic delivery and joke style. Next, it turns to the content of her material, focusing particularly on Notaro's material on gender and the body. I argue that Tig Notaro's stand-up comedy highlights boundary transgression and discomfort, challenging and deconstructing societal assumptions of the value and function of awkwardness and boundaries of belonging. Notaro's over-performance of awkwardness works to redeem this usually negative affect, assigning it value that pushes against its association with social rejection and shame. By valuing abject interactions and bodies this way, Notaro publicly urges a reframing of social boundaries that contribute to social hierarchy and marginalization. In so doing, she renegotiates relationships between bodies in a universal framing that rejects identity politics. Despite the seemingly democratizing effect of such a view, I ultimately argue that Notaro's use of awkwardness as a framing for her social encounters depoliticizes sexual and gender identity, rendering invisible the power hierarchies that render nonnormative bodies abject in the first place.

JUST A PERSON

Tig Notaro began doing stand-up in Los Angeles in the 1990s. For years she enjoyed moderate success, touring the country and developing a cult following. She was known among fans for her androgynous style, flat affect, relishing of awkward moments, and self-proclaimed love of "silliness." In one bit on her album *Good One* (2011), she describes in detail a mental image that makes her laugh: the thought of an infant taking a shower. In another she recounts her repeated real-life run-ins with 1980s pop star Taylor Dayne, who coldly rebuffed her compliments at each meeting.

All of that changed in 2012 when Notaro went from enjoying relative success as a touring comedian to being a household name. The turning point was an unexpected and emotional show at the Largo Theater in Los Angeles just days after Notaro was diagnosed with stage II bilateral breast cancer. Rather than doing her usual material, Notaro took the stage with the now famous opening line, "Good evening . . . Hello . . . I have cancer."[3] She went on to fill the half-hour set with details of what she'd endured over the past few months: pneumonia, hospitalization with the deadly intestinal bacteria *clostridium difficile*, the tragic death of her mother from a freak accident, a break-up, and the cancer diagnosis. Comedian Louis C.K., who witnessed the set backstage, later tweeted that it was one of the greatest sets he'd seen in 27 years. Shortly after, C.K. released the audio of Notaro's set on his website. The album, titled *Live*—pronounced like the verb—was later nominated for a Grammy in the category of Best Comedy Album.[4]

The success of *Live* propelled Notaro from comedy club regular to mainstream star. Since the 2012 set and her successful double mastectomy, Notaro has taped dozens of episodes of her hit podcast *Professor Blastoff* (2011–2015),[5] created and starred in two seasons of a semi-autobiographical Amazon series *One Mississippi* (2015–2017), and been the subject of two documentaries, one of which, *Tig*, premiered at the Sundance Film Festival. She went back on tour, visiting dozens of cities with an hour of new material, culminating in her first HBO special, *Boyish Girl Interrupted*. Notaro released her first book, *I'm Just a Person*, in 2016, in which she reflects on the events of her famous year of tragedies as well as some memories of her childhood and career.

THIS IS AWKWARD

Notaro makes no secret of her appreciation for awkwardness. In an August 2015 *Vogue* article on Notaro, Julia Felsenthal notes that in her comedy, "the humor is always in the awkwardness."[6] Fellow comedian Marc Maron once introduced Notaro as a guest on his podcast by saying "I've always felt a little uncomfortable with her, but she kinda likes to do that."[7] In an interview with the *Madison Cap Times* in February 2015, Notaro declared simply, "I love awkwardness and I imagine I will continue to explore that."[8]

Many have noted a recent drastic increase in use of the term "awkward" to describe uncomfortable situations or individuals. In 2013, *The New Yorker* staff writer and essayist Adam Gopnik told a story for *The Moth* in which he frames "awkward" as a symbol of generational difference between his son and himself. In the story, an unexpected encounter at a local gym—Gopnik brings his son into the steam room only to find two men having sex—leaves Gopnik upset, agonizingly negotiating between his perception of the event's inappropriateness and self-described liberal guilt in deciding his requisite response. His son, in contrast, is able to shrug off the event—"awkward!" To Gopnik, the label of awkwardness represents an equal opportunity discomfort, one unburdened by identity politics or social hierarchy.[9]

Elif Batuman and Ben Yagoda both go so far as to label our current cultural moment "The Awkward Age," the former in a 2014 *New Yorker* piece, the latter in the deconstruction of trends in spoken English, *You Need to Read This*.[10] Batuman suggests, "As the Eskimos were said to have seven words for snow, today's Americans have a near-infinite vocabulary for gradations of awkwardness."[11]

In *Awkwardness: An Essay*, Adam Kotsko argues that themes of social awkwardness are so prevalent in American humor today that "it's becoming increasingly difficult to remember laughing at anything other than cringe-inducing scenes of social discomfort."[12] Kotsko's description of cringe-inducing social discomfort works as a succinct, all-purpose definition of awkwardness, which he goes on to separate into two distinct categories. The first of these is "everyday awkwardness," or awkwardness originating in individuals. "Severely awkward individuals," he explains, "are those who have particular difficulty relating to their social context."[13] He further clarifies that while certain individuals may have a penchant for awkwardness, awkwardness requires and is rooted in a social situation and is measured in relation to social norms. The second kind, "radical awkwardness," causes the greatest discomfort, as it occurs when no norm exists to dictate a social situation, leaving no basis for navigating it. "Most often, this happens because of an encounter between two sets of norms," Kotsko explains.[14]

Understood in this way, awkwardness has the potential to depoliticize social interaction, divorcing bodies from cultural hierarchies and placing them instead in a context wherein we can all be awkward—privilege (white, heterosexual, etc.) saves no one. As Batuman notes, "nobody is exempt" from awkwardness, because "awkwardness comes from the realization that, when you look around the world, it's difficult to identify anyone who isn't either the victim or the beneficiary of injustice . . . and reminds us that we are never isolated individuals."[15]

Awkwardness, like humor, is dependent on shared social norms—or, in the former case, the lack thereof. Bergson's theory of laughter insists upon laughter's social function. In *Laughter: An Essay on the Meaning of the Comic*,

Bergson argues, "Laughter must answer to certain requirements of life in common. It must have a SOCIAL signification."[16] While the incongruity theory of humor, originating with Kant, states that we laugh when our assumptions are disturbed, Simon Critchley emphasizes that "social incongruity" is required for comic incongruity, emphasizing that our assumptions are socially dependent.[17] This means, first, that awkwardness and humor are perhaps inherently compatible.[18] More than that, though, it means that the line between humor and awkwardness is a fine one. Notaro's comedy often moves back and forth over that line; her relation to that line, in fact, may often be in the eye of the beholder.

EMBRACING THE TENSION

In her 2015 HBO comedy special, *Boyish Girl Interrupted*, Notaro recounts a story of taking her then girlfriend to visit the grave of her recently deceased mother. Setting the scene, Notaro explains that after her mother's funeral, she learned that her stepfather had purchased five additional burial plots along with her mother's: one for himself, one each for Notaro and her brother, and "two extras" for their future partners. Notaro lingers on that wording—"two extras!"—emphasizing the unlikely juxtaposition of the somber occasion of choosing a resting place for a deceased loved one with the trivial tone of "extras," remarking, "That is *serious* bargain shopping!"[19]

Having informed the audience of her stepfather's purchase, Notaro fast-forwards to the day in the graveyard with her girlfriend. "So, my girlfriend and I pull up to the graveyard," she begins, to boisterous laughter from the audience. Notaro is far from reaching the anticipated payoff of the story, where she will be forced to explain to her girlfriend that one of the plots before them—the two of them not married or even engaged—was already reserved for her, yet the anticipation of that ending brings laughter at every step. Notaro tells the story slowly, with plenty of long pauses to emphasize her discomfort, so that the audience experiences that discomfort as well. In drawing out the story and delaying the punch line, which is all but a foregone conclusion, Notaro draws out the tension of the joke, or the period between set-up and punch line.

In her stand-up style, Notaro often draws on tension in this way, making tension and discomfort main features of her acts. The jokes themselves[20] do not feature big punch lines (although the graveyard story contains a twist in its conclusion, where Notaro informs her girlfriend, "That's where you'll be 'gay-buried'"[21]). Rather, they move slowly, with details added one by one between long pauses wherein the audience is encouraged to fill in the blanks. She might recount a conversation whose content can be inferred by the first line, yet she commits to detailing it line by line, forcing the audience to wait.

Simon Critchley emphasizes the tension in the space between joke set-up and punch line. When a joke begins, Critchley explains, a listener must first assent, or recognize the set-up and agree to go along with the joke. Assent creates tension, a kind of discomfort broken only when the punch line comes. He argues, "In thus assenting and going along with the joke, a certain tension is created in the listener and I follow along willingly with the story that is being recounted. When the punch line kicks in, and the little bubble of tension pops, I experience an affect that can be described as pleasure, and I laugh or just smile."[22] In delaying the payoff of a joke or story, Notaro extends that tension. As a result, the discomfort of tension becomes a predominant affect of her performances, taking up more space than does the pleasure of laughter. In this way, Notaro redeems discomfort, valuing the affect of discomfort alongside, or even above, pleasure. The effect of this is to challenge the expectation that discomfort be avoided at all costs—an expectation that drives social conformity.

Even when the discomfort on stage is not intentional, Notaro steers her act into, not away from, awkward moments. A prime example of this came on an appearance on Conan O'Brien's *After-Hours Stand-Up Series* in 2012. Notaro told her story about run-ins with the pop star Taylor Dayne, arguably her most famous material at that point. The story is long—so long that it contains a self-conscious joke questioning the wisdom of telling "a *fourteen-minute story* about a pop singer that nobody's heard of."[23] Notaro had told the story many times before, including on her 2011 album *Good One*, but this time around, in the middle of the story, she forgets what comes next. After a drawn-out silence, not unlike the others in the story so far, Notaro laughs to herself before confessing, "Oh my gosh . . . I'm completely blanking on what happens next."[24] Rather than ad lib to cover her mistake, Notaro continues to draw attention to her failure, at times repeating the last line she'd delivered correctly in hopes of jogging her memory, or laughing at herself and pointing out the rising discomfort in the room. At one point she clarifies that her memory lapse is not part of the bit, confirming both that social awkwardness is part of her normal act to such an extent that her current state could be interpreted as planned performance, and that the horror she is experiencing as a performer frozen on stage is real. "This is me taping something and realizing I'm forgetting my story," she insists. "Then you guys are like, 'Oh my gosh, this is horrifying.' Then the people from *Conan* (2010–2021) are watching this on monitors going, 'This *is* really horrifying.

We've paid you . . . we had a limo take you here to forget your story.'" After one long pause she says matter-of-factly, "Yeah, this is awkward, I know! I don't know what to do."[25]

All told, Notaro's on-stage memory lapse lasts nearly two minutes. The *Conan* staff offered to edit out the mistake in the taped version, but Notaro declined, choosing instead to let online viewers see her awkward fumble as it happened.[26] In an interview with segment host Pete Holmes after the show, Notaro reflects, "I did different layers of comedy accidentally tonight."[27] To Notaro, her moment of amnesia, which to many performers would be a worst nightmare, ended up being a valued element of the performance. This is not to say that Notaro reframed the situation optimistically, though. When Holmes comments that she "took a crisis and turned it into an opportunity," she corrects him: "No, I took a crisis and turned it into *another* crisis."[28] In this way, Notaro is assigning a value to awkwardness for its own sake. Awkwardness isn't useful if it can be turned into something else—perhaps it is useful just as it is.

In many ways, then, Notaro's set defied many of the assumptions we have about stand-up comedians and what makes them successful. Many who study comedy—scholars and comedians alike—stress that the figure of the stand-up comedian is an aggressive one who wields power over their audience.[29] But in this case, Notaro is not in a powerful, aggressive position: she is vulnerable. She stands on stage in front of a crowd of people at a microphone and admits that she doesn't know what to say. At one point she opens her mouth as if to speak, but says nothing and then looks around helplessly. What's most surprising, though, is that Notaro's hiccup doesn't ruin the set. The audience laughs throughout, including during and after the portion in question. The comedian Tina Fey suggested in her bestselling book *Bossypants* that "comedy is about confidence, and the moment an audience senses a slip in confidence, they're nervous for you and can't laugh."[30] Notaro's memory loss is nothing if not a slip in confidence, though, and yet Fey's assertion does not pan out.

The slip-up on *Conan* shows the way Notaro's embrace of awkwardness challenges social boundaries and expectations. Rather than retreating, Notaro brings the audience into the vulnerable moment with her, and in doing so generates a shared affective experience that highlights mutual vulnerability. Kotsko notes, "The participants in an awkward situation might flee the scene, but in the moment of awkwardness, they are strangely exposed, forced to share to varying degrees in the experience of awkwardness. . . . The experience of awkwardness, then, is an intrinsically social one. And this means that, paradoxically, certain violations of the norms we rely on to navigate our way through social encounters . . . actually create a weird kind of social bond."[31] If this is true, then Notaro's orchestration of awkwardness for the audience generates a bond among audience members wherein mutually existing in the discomfort emphasizes their shared human condition and social vulnerability.

This sentiment is perhaps best exemplified in Notaro's frequent refrain, "I'm just a person!" Also the title of her 2016 book—and, I would argue, the thesis statement of her comedy—this is a phrase Notaro deploys often in her acts and on social media. In her 2015 special *Boyish Girl Interrupted*, she repeats it as she descends the stairs into the audience during a bit. Her approach is met by cheers and applause, to which she responds in a mocking tone, "Guys, relax! Relax, I'm just a person!"[32] Notaro awkwardly mocks the false modesty of celebrities, exploiting her refrain half-heartedly. Clearly, she does not truly discourage her fans' adoration. Paradoxically, her performance of celebrity modesty also acts as a tongue-in-cheek *immodest* elevation of herself to celebrity status, boldly assuming that people need to be reminded that she is "just a person." At the end of that same special, Notaro receives a standing ovation from the crowd (she set this up earlier in the show, when she told the crowd that she had never *not* received one), and again implores the audience to "relax," as she is "just a person."[33] She vacillates between this false modesty and requests for more attention, peppering her insistence of "just a person" with checks of her watch for how much time is left in the standing ovation (she had asked for three minutes).[34] By using this phrase, Notaro plays with the boundaries between celebrity and fan, performer and audience. She simultaneously erases and redraws that boundary, traversing it in physical space while drawing it verbally, mocking the boundary while brazenly claiming it. In crossing this boundary in different directions simultaneously, she effectively renders it moot, eliminating boundaries between herself and her audience, and in a broader sense, boundaries that elevate certain people and bodies above others.

Notaro breaks down these boundaries between performer and audience on a grander scale in the 2015 Showtime documentary, *Knock Knock, It's Tig Notaro* (LaHaie and Wilcha, 2014). The project follows her and fellow comedian Jon Dore on a trip around the country to perform in people's homes and yards. Notaro had reached out to her "most loyal" fans weeks earlier to announce her upcoming tour, and had encouraged fans to send her suggested locations. "We're looking for venues for me to perform in," she explained. "So, if you'd like for me to be on your rooftop, your basement, backyard, living room, garage, in your barn . . . you tell me where I'm going!"[35] The tour sees the two comedians performing across rural America in a basement, a backyard, and an empty church space. Some venues include stages, while in others Notaro and Dore stand on the same level as their audience, who may be seated or standing, in some cases barely a foot away. In one performance in a host's kitchen, the comics perform in front of a kitchen table, around which some spectators are seated, while other members of the audience sit and stand around the room. The effect appears to an outside observer like a group of people mingling in a space as opposed to a single performer and a separate viewing audience.

Notaro's performances in people's homes and other unconventional venues blur the lines between performer and audience and between performance and other types of human interaction. The proximity to her audiences can be severely awkward, often leading Notaro to point out the discomfort of the nontraditional setup. This tour and documentary serve as an extension of Notaro's broader work of using awkwardness to question social boundaries; they represent perhaps the most literal iteration of her project, using space and staging—or lack thereof—to eliminate a hierarchy between participants in the interaction.

AWKWARD BODIES

Notaro's comedy does not just explore awkwardness through comic form—the drawing out of tension and breaking down of barriers—and setting; it also features awkwardness as a topic in its content. Notaro recounts countless stories of awkwardness she has experienced, particularly concerning gender and bodies. One of her signature bits before 2012 was a story about a man on the street mistaking her gender: "I was walking through my neighborhood, down the sidewalk, and uh, I was passing this guy. And, uh, right when we were passing each other he said to me—*right* when we were passing each other: [Notaro imitates a high-pitched, surprised voice] 'Ahhhhh! Dem are little titties! I thought you was a man!'"[36] Back in her own voice, Notaro maintains an unfazed tone, as if considering the stranger's input. "It's like—okay," she says, "Okay if you think that. And okay if you say that. [pause] *To yourself!*" Notaro goes on to emphasize the brashness of the stranger choosing to share this particular thought, pointing out that our thoughts go through "several layers of filter" before we speak them aloud. "Think of all the things he decided *not* to say," she suggests, like "good afternoon" or "Uh . . . I was going to say something but I decided not to."[37] Notaro highlights the rudeness, the ridiculousness, of shouting such a thing to a stranger on the street. In her telling, the anonymous man is the social outcast, not the woman mistaken as a man at first glance. Notaro reframes this encounter away from one of conflicting ideas of normative gender to one of conflicting norms of general politeness.

The encounter on the Los Angeles sidewalk is far from the only time Notaro reports her gender publicly coming into question. The title of her 2015 HBO special, *Boyish Girl Interrupted*, positions her "boyish" appearance as her identifying quality. During that special, Notaro jokes about sitting in the exit row of a commercial flight and being asked to help in the event of an emergency. Wondering whether flight attendants would "really hold [her] to that," Notaro takes on the role of a flight attendant attempting to track her down. "Where's that woman from 12E?" she yells. When she asks a second time, she makes a correction: "Where's that guy from 12E? . . . He said he'd help us out!"[38] In the famed Largo set shortly following her cancer diagnosis, Notaro recounts an encounter with a stranger on her walk home from the doctor. The stranger was walking beside her and looking closely at her face before attempting to grab her attention with exclamations of "'Sir! Sir! Sir!' And usually I have a sense of humor about that," she explains, suggesting these encounters happen all the time. This time, though, Notaro snaps back, telling the stranger, "I just got diagnosed with breast cancer! In both breasts! That's how much I'm not a man."[39]

Notaro offers another story in *Boyish Girl Interrupted*, where she recounts an experience going through airport security after her double mastectomy. When Notaro required additional security screening, the TSA agent called out a request for "female assist," as passengers get physically searched by agents of their same gender.[40] Notaro mimes the role of the agent, her arms outstretched in front of her as if to pat someone down. Her hands are flat, palms out, as she moves as if to feel around the chest. Here, Notaro interrupts to clarify that she did not have reconstructive surgery following her double mastectomy, leaving her with scars on her chest and no breasts. She begins to mime more frantically, moving her outstretched hands more quickly with a puzzled look on her face.

At this point in Notaro's story, the woman returns to the original agent for clarification. "And she walked only maybe *this* far away [Notaro walks a couple of steps away on stage], and she whispered something to the other officer, and I just heard him say, 'Yes, I'm positive!'"[41] Now, the woman returns to Notaro to continue the search. "But this time she stopped before she touched me," Notaro said, "She looked up [pause] at my face. She *really* took it in. But apparently, that was not helpful. At all! And she said 'hold on a second.'"[42] Even with an up-close examination of Notaro's face, the agent still sought clarification of her gender, leaving Notaro to stand and wait again. Notaro describes the woman whispering to the original agent yet again, to which he responds *"YES!"*[43]

Notaro goes on to reflect on her role in the situation:

> And the thing is, I knew exactly what was happening. And I knew that all I needed to do was speak, and then she would know that I was female. But, I just [pause] *did not* [pause] want to help her out. At all. I was enjoying the awkwardness *so much*! I just loved standing there like: [Notaro stands with a blank look on her face, glancing around innocently and occasionally shrugging and looking down at her own chest].[44]

As if to have given up, the female agent in Notaro's story returns to where she is standing and informs her that she may leave.

The pace of Notaro's story and her physicality on stage draw extra attention to the awkwardness of the scenario as it played out. She takes long pauses, stretching out the moments of social awkwardness and discomfort. In telling the story she moves between acting out her part and the TSA agent's, emphasizing their close physical proximity as the woman questions the other agent about her body—whispering as if secretly, yet right in front of her. Her movement between the two characters in the scene draws attention to Notaro's position as a subject of public scrutiny and what for many would be public humiliation. She stands under the scrutiny of physical inspection, in plain sight of onlookers in the airport, unable to leave until the agent can properly categorize her body.

Both of these stories—Notaro's encounter with the man on the sidewalk and her experience with airport security—explore anxiety over properly gendered bodies and policing when bodies fall outside normative bounds. Yet, in both of these stories she reframes the awkwardness, shifting the burden of discomfort from herself to the man on the sidewalk or the TSA agent. In the first, the onus of the awkwardness is applied not to the deviant body that defies gender labeling, but to the observer who sees her body as such and calls it out. When Notaro emphasizes, "Okay if you say that ... *to yourself*," she highlights the breach of social boundaries of the man's outburst instead.[45] By listing things he chose not to say, she points to a standard level of accepted social interaction, rendering even more blatant the man's violation of social decency that ostensibly called out Notaro's nonnormativity. If awkwardness threatens us all equally, the cisgender man is not privileged in this encounter over the queer, gender nonconforming woman.

In the airport story, Notaro points to the expectation placed on her shoulders to make the TSA agent more comfortable. She rejects this expectation, instead forcing the agent to navigate her job in light of a body that she cannot properly categorize. Notaro shifts the placement of embarrassment in the situation away from herself and onto the woman unable to operate in a situation where she is not perfectly comfortable. In doing this, Notaro questions notions of normative and nonnormative bodies, placing ridicule of outsider status on the TSA agent whose understanding of bodies is rigidly bound by traditional expectations of gender.

In this way, the individualizing language of awkwardness removes the situation from the context of identity politics, divorcing actors from subjugated identity categories. In other words, Notaro frames the encounters as misunderstandings between individuals, rather than as experiences of homophobia and gender policing directed at a queer, gender nonconforming woman by straight, cisgender men and women, one of whom is acting on behalf of a government agency.

While this universalizing effect may ostensibly liberate individuals from hierarchies of identity politics, ultimately it renders invisible the power structures still operating behind these hierarchies. Much like the post-racial ideology of colorblindness, Notaro's framing of awkwardness amounts to a denial of power dynamics within the encounters, though perhaps not actual subversion of them.

This reading is consistent with many of Notaro's off-stage interviews. Despite being open about her relationships with women and her acknowledgment of gender nonconformity, Notaro has often distanced herself from, if not blatantly denied, queer, feminist, and transgender politics. The most famous of these instances happened in a public feud with fellow comedian Amy Schumer, in which Notaro took offense to Schumer's claim that Notaro faced extra challenges as a queer female comedian. Speaking about Notaro in a *Vanity Fair* piece, Schumer claimed, "Looking masculine and being gay, the challenges of the road are twenty times harder for Tig than other female comedians. People fear what they don't understand."[46] Notaro railed against Schumer's remarks in an interview with *The Guardian*, calling them "offensive nonsense." She added, "If you knew me well, you would never say that."[47] Notaro's objection not only distances her from any claims of discrimination in comedy—or in the broader world of "the road"—but positions her rejection of such claims as central to who she is. Knowing her well entails knowing she sees claims of queer discrimination in comedy as "nonsense."

Notaro has pushed back against claims of injustices against women and gays at other times as well. Despite the common refrain that comedy as a profession is unkind to women—high-profile comedians who have claimed as much include Tina Fey, Amy Poehler, Kathy Griffin, Samantha Bee, Amy Schumer, Leslie Jones, and many, many others—Notaro resists these assertions in lieu of an understanding of comic success or failure based solely on individual merit. "I really don't have a complaint in the world about being a woman or how I've been treated," Notaro explains in a *Time* magazine Interview. "If people didn't like me I never blamed it on any particular thing. I just figured they didn't like me."[48] In other words, Notaro is not a woman in a profession notoriously known as a boys' club, but "just a person" who could succeed or fail like anyone else.

In a 2012 interview Notaro not only denied identification or allyship with the transgender community, but denied even basic knowledge of it. She revealed in a *HuffPost Live* interview that following her mastectomy, she had received congratulations from a few fans on her "free top surgery."[49] Notaro, who does not identify as transgender and who underwent a traumatic diagnosis and surgery, was understandably upset by these comments. She responded in the interview, "I guess when you make a decision that's not medical to remove your breasts, it's called top surgery. I wasn't familiar with it, and I never wanted that."[50] Notaro's response goes far beyond expressing her offense at the comments' insensitivity or clarifying that she did not *want* the surgery, to deliberately distancing herself from the transgender community. The comment treats awareness of transgender issues as a cause for embarrassment that ought to be denied, despite her reference to top surgery in an earlier stand-up set. In the Largo set just days after her diagnosis, Notaro refers to her upcoming double mastectomy as "[her] forced transition."[51] This joke certainly supports the assumption that Notaro is at least minimally familiar with transgender therapies or surgeries. Further, it suggests that she is not being truthful in her claim that she was not familiar with the concept of top surgery, but rather that she fabricates this out of a desire to distance herself from any association with transgender identity or politics. These examples and others like them suggest that denial of identity politics is part of Notaro's overall agenda as a public intellectual and performer. The universalizing effect of awkwardness serves as a vehicle to achieve these ends.

CONCLUSION

Adam Kotsko argues, "The tension of awkwardness indicates that no social order is self-evident and no social order accounts for every possibility. Awkwardness shows us that humans are fundamentally social, but that they have no built-in norms."[52] Tig Notaro uses awkwardness in her comedy and other work to draw attention to this very fact: that social boundaries are not inherent, and we can determine where they are drawn and which norms are valued. She does this with the very form of her stand-up, using slow delivery and long pauses to make awkwardness the prevailing affect of her shows. She challenges the boundaries between performer and audience—often with awkward results—to eliminate the power differential between parties. Her performances give value to awkwardness itself, calling into question the social impulse to retreat from social discomfort and the very social hierarchies that contribute to that impulse. Moreover, Notaro questions normativity pertaining to gender and bodies, using stories of her flat chest both pre- and post–double mastectomy to raise questions of belonging and social appropriateness.

Ultimately, this democratizing effect of awkwardness operates as a rejection of identity politics, divorcing actors in an encounter from their context in social hierarchies. Notaro's ostensibly "safe" material, along with her personal interviews, writing, and performance style, mocks and challenges social boundaries and hierarchies, reminding us in the end that everyone is "just a person."

Notes

1. Tig Notaro, interviewed by E. Alex Jung, "Tig Notaro at Vulture Festival 2015," *New York Magazine*, June 10, 2015, accessed June 18, 2016, https://www.youtube.com/watch?v=-V3AbusILpI.

2. Megan Garber, "How Comedians Became Public Intellectuals," *The Atlantic*, May 28, 2015, accessed October 11, 2019, https://www.theatlantic.com/entertainment/archive/2015/05/how-comedians-became-public-intellectuals/394277/.

3. Tig Notaro, *Live*, produced by Secretly Canadian, 2012, iTunes MP3.

4. Kathy Griffin's "Calm Down Gurrl" won.

5. The podcast, which Notaro cohosted with fellow comedians and friends Kyle Dunnigan and David Huntsberger, ended in July 2015.

6. Julia Felsenthal, "Comedian and Cancer Survivor Tig Notaro on Going Topless in Her New HBO Special," *Vogue*, August 20, 2015, accessed July 9, 2016, http://www.vogue.com/13296744/tig-notaro-topless-hbo-boyish-girl-interrupted/.

7. Marc Maron, host, "Episode 81 (Tig Notaro)," *WTF with Marc Maron*, MP3 Podcast, iTunes.

8. Laurel White, "Cancer, Topless Comedy and Being Awkward on Purpose: 11 Questions for Tig Notaro," *The Capital Times* (Madison), February 23, 2015, accessed July 9, 2016, http://host.madison.com/ct/news/local/writers/laurel-white/cancer-topless-comedy-and-being-awkward-on-purpose-questions-for/article_37f63898-9323-56ba-a473-075ece85b157.html.

9. Adam Gopnik, "The Pieties of Perspiration," *The Moth: True Stories Told Live*, online podcast, accessed August 14, 2016, https://themoth.org/stories/the-pieties-of-perspiration.

10. See Elif Batuman, "The Awkward Age," *New Yorker*, September 9, 2014, accessed August 4, 2016, http://www.newyorker.com/culture/cultural-comment/awkward-age; Ben Yagoda, *You Need to Read This: The Death of the Imperative Mode, The Rise of the American Glottal Stop, The Bizarre Popularity of 'Amongst,' and Other Cuckoo Things that Have Happened to the English Language* (New York: Riverhead Books, 2014).

11. Batuman, "Awkward Age."

12. Adam Kotsko, *Awkwardness: An Essay* (Blue Ridge Summit, PA: John Hunt Publishing, 2010).

13. Kotsko, *Awkwardness*, 6.

14. Kotsko, *Awkwardness*, 7.

15. Kotsko, *Awkwardness*,

16. Henri Bergson, *Laughter: An Essay on the Meaning of the Comic* (Whitefish, MT: Kessinger, 2010), 5.

17. Simon Critchley, *On Humor* (New York: Routledge, 2002), 3.

18. While Bergson's social theory of laughter argues that laughter as a behavior works as a corrective, I argue that Notaro's use of awkwardness reframes it such that the "correction" is aimed at the social structure that creates it rather than the breach of that norm.

19. *Boyish Girl Interrupted*, produced by Funny or Die, originally aired August 22, 2015, HBO.

20. I use the term "joke" loosely here to include her on-stage comedic material, which is often in the form of longer stories rather than traditional jokes.

21. *Boyish Girl Interrupted*.

22. Critchley, *On* Humor, 5.

23. Tig Notaro, "Taylor Dayne," *Good One*, produced by Secretly Canadian, 2011.

24. Tig Notaro, "Tig Notaro Tells a Deeply Personal Story about Taylor Dayne," *The After-Hours Stand-Up* Series, July 10, 2012, accessed July 10, 2016, https://www.youtube.com/watch?v=V97lvUKYisA.

25. Notaro, "Deeply Personal Story."

26. Boris Kachka, "Tig Notaro on Public Humiliation and the Trifecta of Heartbreak that Made Her Career," *Vulture*, May 16, 2016, accessed July 9, 2016, http://www.vulture.com/2016/05/tig-notaro-on-public-humiliation-and-heartbreak.html.

27. Tig Notaro, interviewed by Pete Holmes, "*After-Hours Stand-Up Series*: Pete Holmes Interviews Tig Notaro," July 5, 2012, accessed July 10, 2016, http://teamcoco.com/video/tig-notaro-interview.

28. Notaro, "*After-Hours Stand-Up* Interview."

29. See Linda Mizejewski, *Pretty/Funny: Women Comedians and Body Politics* (Austin: University of Texas Press, 2014), 15, 191; Cynthia Willett, Julie Willett, and Yael D. Sherman, "The Seriously Erotic Politics of Feminist Laughter," *Social Research: An International Quarterly* 79, no. 1 (2012): 217–46.

30. Tina Fey, *Bossypants* (New York: Little, Brown, and Co., 2011), 127.

31. Kotsko, *Awkwardness*, 8.

32. Notaro, *Boyish Girl Interrupted*.

33. Notaro, *Boyish Girl Interrupted*.
34. Notaro, *Boyish Girl Interrupted*.
35. "Knock Knock, It's Tig Notaro," YouTube Video, 0:59, posted by "Showtime," July 2, 2013, https://www.youtube.com/watch?v=mYZvvKYci5c.
36. Tig Notaro, "Little Titties," *Good One*.
37. Notaro, "Little Titties."
38. Notaro, *Boyish Girl Interrupted*.
39. Tig Notaro, *Live*.
40. Notaro, *Boyish Girl Interrupted*.
41. Notaro, *Boyish Girl Interrupted*.
42. Notaro, *Boyish Girl Interrupted*.
43. Notaro, *Boyish Girl Interrupted*.
44. Notaro, *Boyish Girl Interrupted*.
45. Notaro, "Little Titties."
46. Vanessa Grigoriadis, "Survival of the Funniest," *Vanity Fair*, December 18, 2012, https://www.vanityfair.com/culture/2013/01/tig-notaro-breast-cancer-dont-connect-with-jokes.
47. Hadley Freeman, "Tig Notaro: 'People Were Wanting to Take Care of Me, Just to Look Good,'" *The Guardian*, June 11, 2016, https://www.theguardian.com/stage/2016/jun/11/tig-notaro-people-wanting-take-care-look-good.
48. Lily Rothman, "Comedian Tig Notaro Looks Back—and Forward," *Time*, July 11, 2013, http://entertainment.time.com/2013/07/11/comedian-tig-notaro-looks-back-and-forward/.
49. Emily Tess Katz, "Tig Notaro: People Saw My Double Mastectomy as 'Free Top Surgery,'" *HuffPost*, August 13, 2015, https://www.huffingtonpost.com/entry/tig-notaro-people-saw-my-double-mastectomy-as-free-top-surgery_us_55cbb89de4b0898c488670a4.
50. Katz, "Tig Notaro."
51. Tig Notaro, *Live*.
52. Kotsko, *Awkwardness*, 16.

5

COMEDY FROM THE INTERSECTIONS
Chris Rock on Class and Race

Philip Scepanski

As part of his 2016 Academy Awards hosting duties, Chris Rock confirmed but also poked fun at criticism that the Oscars had ignored African American talent. In one bit, he asked Black movie patrons their opinions on the best picture nominees. Black theatergoers, it seemed, had neither interest in nor knowledge of the nominated films. Though played for good-natured laughs, the segment reinforced the idea that there was a gulf between the Academy and African Americans. The next day, *The New York Post* ran an editorial titled "Oscar's Problem Isn't Really Race—It's Class," arguing, "So much of what Hollywood makes—and even more of what it singles out for honors—just doesn't connect to the lives of most Americans, black or white." Though a thinly veiled excuse to criticize Hollywood's left-leaning elitism, it was nevertheless odd to accuse Chris Rock of class-blindness, considering that his career is in many ways built on an awareness of the ways race and class intersect and interact in America. This is most acutely clear in his most famous routine: "N---as Versus Black People" from 1994's *Bring the Pain*, which articulates different class identities within African American culture. In fact, Rock frequently explored the same idea proposed by the *Post*: that many of the characteristics attributed to race are actually determined by class.

Rock occupies a number of positions in that bit, as host of the Oscars, and as a public figure more generally. His star persona is that of a Black man who escaped lower-class poverty by enacting middle-class respectability and work ethic while maintaining working-class authenticity. Through this combination of working-class realness and middle-class responsibility, he has attained means as a member of the upper class. So, while his persona, values, and lifestyle represent a complex mélange of class positions, each mark of class mobility is always connected to and defined in relation to his Blackness.

Rock's perspectives thus reflect both the influence of and his awareness of his intersectionality—that numerous social identities (race, class, etc.) interact in his personal experience and in larger social discourses.

David Gillota argues that this ability to occupy and shift between different identity positions not only allows Rock to joke from whatever position best suits the humor of any given routine, but also places him in the liminal state of simultaneously occupying both insider and outsider positions.[1] In the case of the Oscars, he is an insider to both the Hollywood glitterati and the regular Black folks he interviews. At the same time, his insider position in each group makes him an outsider to the other. This multivalence gives him unique perspectives and abilities to speak to different aspects of his persona as well as to those with whom he shares certain but not all identity positions, such as middle-class whites. He offers insight to the outsiders and outsight to the insiders.

These points are readily apparent in Rock's most (in)famous routine, which critically though troublingly examines race and class. The bit, "N--- as Versus Black People," attacks aspects of working-class Black culture, and it proved highly controversial, placing Rock at the center of larger cultural debates on race and class.[2] This chapter examines Chris Rock's early recorded stand-up comedy, from his first album and his first two HBO specials, to track the development of themes that would culminate in his breakout moment.[3] Rock developed this style and outlook over a number of years, culminating in the special that would secure his position as a public intellectual. Over the course of his early career and beyond, Rock engaged, questioned, attacked, and sometimes reinforced common notions of Black intersectionality with regularly revisited if not consistent theme of disarticulating assumptions that understand Blackness as inextricably linked to lower-class economic struggle and cultural expression.

WHITE TOXIC WASTE

Chris Rock's first comedy album, *Born Suspect* (1991), tackles many of the themes that would become regular features of his ensuing work. In addition to topics like male–female relations and fashion, he demonstrates that even at this early point he is thinking about the relationship between race and class.[4] Although he shows hints of his eventual ethical perspective on this topic, his approach is not fully developed and at times contradicts his later insights.

In one track from this album, titled "Poor Whites," Rock explains how he was bused to a poor white neighborhood for school. Instead of interrogating the logic that would send a poor Black child to a poorer white neighborhood, as he would in a later routine, Rock launches into an essentialist attack on lower-class whites.

> I got bused to school to a poor white neighborhood. That shit was scary. Everybody's scared of n---as, everybody's scared of Puerto Ricans. Ain't nothing more horrifying than a bunch of poor white people, boy. That's the scariest shit in the world, boy, because they're capable of anything, boy. They blame n---as over everything. You get some poor trailer-trash motherfuckers, boy, they will blame n---as on everything. Space Shuttle blew up. "Those damn n---ers, that's who it was!" Shit. Shit is crazy man. Motherfuckers got no education. They just blame shit on n---as and shit.
>
> White people don't need to be poor. All white people should have money, because they don't know how to handle that shit when they don't got no money. N---as is like, "I'm broke, fuck it, lemme go hang out." [unintelligible] some broke white people? Them motherfuckers is damn near ready to cry in the middle of the street. "[unintelligible] I have no money. I have no money. How did this happen? I'm white!"
>
> This shit is crazy. With all this homelessness. You got white bums now and shit. Shit is crazy. My mother would never give money to a white bum. Never. Just look at them and say, "No reason for that." See I don't know everything but I figure being white's like always having five bucks. Being Black's like always being fifty cents short.

There are some defensible positions in this routine that hint at Rock's later work. Most basically, it reminds the audience that poor white people exist, upsetting simplistic understandings of race that paint whites as always economically advantaged compared to African Americans. He also attacks a certain form of racism born of ignorance and poor education, although that element of this routine is underdeveloped and devolves into simplistic attacks. Toward the end, however, Rock also argues that the relatively low socioeconomic status of African Americans is the result of larger cultural structures rather than inherent racial characteristics. But Rock rejects the opportunity for class-based identification across race because he believes that if white people are poor, it is likely their fault. In contrast, the whole of Black America suffers under the metaphorical disadvantage of being fifty cents short and are therefore deserving of sympathy.

In relying on economic and racial essentialism, this segment runs counter to much of Rock's later material on race and class. While his belief that

African Americans typically work at a disadvantage is defensible, his apparent belief that there is no excuse for white poverty belies the typically more thoughtful and complex comedy that he developed later. The ethics of these jokes contrast with other attacks on poor whites in later routines. In this case, he mocks people as a general category without pushing back against racism in any particularly intellectual capacity. Additionally, by ignoring the larger sociocultural factors that can lead to poverty for anyone, Rock uses an essentializing logic that privileges race over class—a logic his work would eventually dismantle.[5]

Despite its shortcomings, the title track of *Born Suspect* gestures toward complicating essentialist notions of race and class by suggesting that culture is responsible for associating Blackness with being disadvantaged. "Sometimes I hate life. Know why? Because I was born a suspect. All Black people: born a suspect. Came out of my momma's stomach; anything that happened within a three-block radius, I was a suspect." The comic develops this idea with a number of examples of how he is continually treated as a potential threat: "I walk down the street and women are grabbing hold of their mace, everybody's tucking in their chains, people hitting their car doors, people getting into karate stances." Based on feelings of superiority, this directing of ridicule at those who overreact to Rock's presence implies a critique of their flawed logic in assuming all Black men to be violent criminals. To the extent that criminality is a product of poverty, then, laughter at least in part attacks Rock's straw men for not disarticulating race from class and class-related behaviors.

Although his audience laughs at the imagined people that fear Rock for little reason, there is a sense that they also laugh at Rock's misfortune at always being a suspect. Lawrence E. Mintz believes that the two primary roles of stand-up comedians are to present themselves as butts of jokes and to express frustrations with society. In other words, comics are most important when criticizing themselves or others, but "the separation of the two roles is rarely absolute or even entirely clear."[6] In Rock's case, his position as a member of the underclass allows the audience to laugh at his misfortune while acknowledging the racial injustices he must suffer. Although this articulation of Blackness to underclass and victim positions would never entirely disappear from his act, Rock's evolving persona, adoption of middle-class ideological positions, and success would complicate his approach to these issues later in his career.

While Rock jokes from the position of victim in this routine, he also notes that performances of race that confirm suspicions of threat may be advantageous in certain situations. In a bit where he talks about being arrested for driving too slowly, he advises that the best course of action if you are in jail for that offense is to invent something more threatening. And in the "Born Suspect" track, he opines, "one good thing about being Black [is that] you can bluff having a gun any time. White people always think you always have a gun." As with the rest of this routine, the humor revolves around depicting white people as overly anxious and gullible based on their prejudices and thus disabusing audiences of those prejudices. What distinguishes this section of the routine from those in which white people simply overreacted at his presence is that in the scenario of bluffing a gun, Rock seems to turn their prejudice to his advantage—or at least use it for survival. Such jokes tap into larger discussions of why people in positions of poverty sometimes perform assumptions about their class out of expediency or necessity.[7] In his most infamous routine, "N---as Versus Black People," Rock turned against performances of working-class Blackness and even more so against activities that articulate Blackness with criminality as part of his larger work to distinguish class and race. In response, his critics would attack Rock's routine using these arguments about how survival necessitates these performances.

By the time of his first HBO special, *Big Ass Jokes* (Truesdell, 1994), Chris Rock's perspectives on these issues had evolved into a more complex rhetorical argument. Again drawing from his childhood experiences, and even repeating aspects of his earlier routine word for word, Rock nevertheless finds new angles from which to approach these topics.

> I do a lot of racial humor. Do a lot of racial humor. You know why? I was bused to school when I was a kid. Very hard being bused, man. . . . You're supposed to get bused to a better neighborhood to get a better education and all that shit. I got bused to school into a poor white neighborhood. A neighborhood worse than the one I lived in. And everybody's scared of Black people; everybody's scared of Puerto Ricans. Yo! There ain't nothing scarier than poor white people. Even white people are scared of poor white people. "Hey, keep them white people away from us." Yo, these mothers—they lived *under* the trailer home, alright? They weren't white trash; they were like white toxic waste. A bunch of Shaggy-from-*Scooby-Doo*–looking people. That's who I went to school with. And they hated my guts. They hated me. They couldn't—because my family had more money than them. We didn't even have money, but we had more money than them. And right then I learned my lesson, boy. Nothing a white guy with a penny hates more than a n---a with a nickel.[8]

In this routine, Rock again shows off his talent for comic insults and exaggerated metaphor to work through a childhood trauma resulting from integrationist school busing programs. Although some of the attacks remain crude, he begins to interrogate issues including cross-racial, intra-class conflict and flawed social programs. One significant problem, according to Rock, is that the busing program of which he was a part narrowly focused on race while ignoring class, busing Black children into white neighborhoods without considering whether the white school was actually well equipped to aid its new students. Rock's routine focuses explicitly on expressions of class among his white peers while also denouncing their racist class resentment to explain the failure of busing programs.

At a deeper level, this routine attacks what Rock sees as a flawed social policy of desegregation busing. Indeed, Black intellectual leaders and communities across the United States opposed busing programs for myriad reasons.[9] Rock's routine argues that busing programs negatively affected students of color. "I had to get up every morning at six in the morning to compete with white kids who didn't have to get up until eight," he explains. "I got a teacher saying 'Chris can't read.' I'm like, 'No, Chris is fucking tired.'" Though he is certainly simplifying the interaction of these different factors and ignoring other factors, Rock is arguing that his poor scholastic performance was a product of neither race nor class, but of a flaw in the busing strategy.

Based on his personal experiences, Rock's jokes offer a corrective to the logics and assumptions of busing programs. In describing his own troubles, he challenges the audience to consider the goals and consequences of such programs in ways that allow for more nuanced understandings of class and race. Noting the difficulties facing school desegregation by the end of the 1970s, busing champion Willis D. Hawley described the optimistic hopes for desegregation as the hope that "children of all colors learning side by side would bring about the end of prejudice and would substantially undermine social inequalities."[10] Rock articulates a more pragmatic, and arguably more popular, notion of busing as a way to remedy economic inequality by bringing students from poorer, lower-performing schools to those with more resources. He exposes the flaws in both ways of thinking by drawing out these contradictions through comic exaggeration. The hope of dismantling future racism proves overly optimistic, since his classmates' racism was too firmly entrenched. And Rock troubles the popular belief that busing brought poor minority students into wealthier white neighborhood schools by citing his experience with "white toxic waste." This routine about busing, while personal and humorous, also placed him in the public sphere as he turned the stage into a soapbox. By entering into longer, larger, and continuing discussions and debates over civil rights and desegregation policy, Rock signaled even at this relatively early point that his routines could be personally, politically, and intellectually provocative.

Like his earlier attacks on poor whites, aspects of this strand of his humor arose from *schadenfreude*: even those of low status get to laugh down at the toxic waste. There is also a subtler jab at the hypocrisy of attacking other poor kids when coalition-building and class uplift would be more useful. Rock suffered prejudice as a child that mixed subtle class infighting with overt racism. Karl Marx made similar arguments about race and class, explicitly connecting his observations regarding Irish–English relations to the way poor white Americans treated African Americans:

> Every industrial and commercial centre [sic] in England now possesses a working class divided into two *hostile* camps, English proletarians and Irish proletarians. The ordinary English worker hates the Irish worker as a competitor who lowers his standard of life. In relation to the Irish worker he regards himself as a member of the *ruling* nation.... His attitude towards him is much the same as that of the "poor whites" to the Negroes in the former slave states of the U.S.A. (emphasis in original)[11]

Marx believed that racism is a wedge that keeps workers from recognizing their common interests. Although Rock did not take his observations to that fully Marxist conclusion, his joke points out a perceived hypocrisy that socioeconomically similar people hate each other based on superficial differences while disparaging his targets and intensifying the humor. Though Rock attacks the hypocrisy of class infighting, he nevertheless performs contradictions similar to those Marx criticized. From this perspective, his is a problematic attack that reflects and encourages discord among working-class members of different races. So, although it most significantly troubles assumptions that race and socioeconomic class are inseparable and speaks to the complexities and unpredictable consequences of well-meaning social policy, it cannot fully escape the ideologies it criticizes. Nevertheless, the hierarchy constructed by Rock exposes a larger theme that was common in his work going back to 1991: assumptions that race and class can be neatly articulated as whites being economically better off and nonwhites being worse off are too simplistic. In this routine, the comic notes that integration does not automatically mean bringing Black students into neighborhoods of higher economic status (nor, logic demands, does it mean lowering the economic status of white neighborhoods). However, Rock does not express much sympathy for or solidarity with his worse-off white classmates; instead he largely recreates the antagonism from which he suffered by skillfully mocking them.

These early routines demonstrate a preoccupation with race and class that Rock explicitly links to his experiences as a poor Black child who moved across racial, but not economic, geography. In so doing, he focused his comedic ire on his white peers, on their racism, and on well-meaning but flawed social programs that only considered race and not class. As he worked through these issues, Rock developed a more complex view of the situation. With the release of his breakout special, *Bring the Pain* (Truesdell, 1996), Rock would add considerable nuance to his discussion of these issues. And although Rock would not ignore troubling aspects of white culture, he would, in his best-known routine, make distinctions between African Americans of different classes that would launch him to heights of success and controversy.

"N---AS VERSUS BLACK PEOPLE" (VERSUS RICH PEOPLE)

In 1991's *Born Suspect* and 1994's *Big Ass Jokes*, the most discernible theme is that any neat hierarchy assuming whites to be of a higher class than African Americans is overly simple. Chris Rock primarily makes this point by noting that there are white people of a lower class than himself, but he also explains the role of larger sociological structures that can cause race and class to appear inextricably linked when in fact they are not. Moreover, he mounts an ethical argument that assumptions like this can counteract well-meaning attempts to uplift working-class Black populations and fight racism. In his second HBO special, *Bring the Pain*, Rock continued to joke about and thus dismantle monolithic constructions that understand race and class as one and the same.[12] But this special differs from his earlier work. Rather than focusing on the existence of working-class whites, Rock turns his attention to different economic classes of African Americans. Specifically, his jokes attack those of the lower and, to a lesser extent, upper classes, implying that middle-class bourgeois values are those most worth emulating.

Rock's treatment of celebrity reflects his valuation of middle-class over upper-class values. When discussing Black notables like Colin Powell and O. J. Simpson, his jokes frequently rely on distinctions between classes within African American culture. The most explicit example of this in any of his specials may in fact be in his discussion of the O. J. Simpson trial. "Black people way too happy, like [skipping across the stage] 'Yay! We won! We won!

Yay! We won!' What the fuck did we win?! Every day I look in my mailbox for my O. J. prize. Nothing! Nothing!" Rock echoes widespread beliefs that Simpson was neither representative of nor loyal to African American communities.[13] But in light of Rock's continual discussions of race and class, this joke also deconstructs the notion of a singular Black "we" by which working- and middle-class African Americans should identify with Simpson or take his acquittal as a symbolic victory. "That shit wasn't about race," he intones, "that shit was about fame. Because if O. J. wasn't famous, he'd be in jail right now. If O. J. drove a bus, he wouldn't even be O. J., he'd be Orenthal the bus-driving murderer." Though this kind of self-positioning is common in Rock's work more generally, this routine is an especially pointed example of David Gillota's reading of the comic as one who alternately adopts the position of insider or outsider depending on the issue at hand. In this case, Rock rejects racial loyalties in order to perform populist anger against wealth and privilege. In particular, the comic taps into larger anger and concern over how class structures intersect with race in the justice system as well as the ways in which people of racial and economic privilege garner special treatment.

Rock's use of "fame" as the explicit reason for the acquittal seems to imply rather than explicitly state wealth and social advantage, but as Jeffrey Sconce notes, celebrity has come to stand for such privileges in its cultural articulation. This is especially true, he argues, when it comes to class resentment against celebrities. "In a culture that chooses to repress the politics of class division," argues Sconce, *schadenfreude* towards celebrities "may well be the last simmering refuge of populist hatred for the spoiled rich."[14] Sconce notes the connections, both symbolic and economic, between contemporary celebrity culture and larger class structures. In keeping with Sconce's diagnosis, Rock expresses populist anger towards celebrity and class privilege through his discussion of celebrity. Simpson's experience is hardly that of a working-class African American. O. J. the star of football and cinema walked free; Orenthal the bus driver, on the other hand, would have been convicted of murder. Rock and the populist audience with which he seeks solidarity see Orenthal as their surrogate, not O. J.

Rock's strategy in articulating the importance of class in relation to race varies depending on the celebrity in question. He is less concerned in this routine with Simpson's actions than with his power to represent race and class within mass media discourse and the justice system; his larger point is that while the fate of a poor Black man in the justice system would be overdetermined, class privilege may in some cases be powerful enough to supersede the disadvantages of being Black in America. Colin Powell serves a different function in Rock's routine, in that Powell normalizes middle-class respectability.

> You know how I can tell Colin Powell can't be president? Whenever Colin Powell's on the news, white people always give him the same compliments. Always the same compliments. "How do you feel about Colin Powell?" "He speaks so well." "He's so well-spoken." "He speaks so well." "I mean he really speaks well." "He speaks so well." Like that's a compliment. "Speaks so well" is not a compliment, okay? "Speaks so well" is some shit you say about retarded people that can talk. What do you mean he speaks so well? What'd he have a stroke the other day? He's a fucking educated man, how the fuck do you expect him to sound you dirty motherfucker, what are you talking about!? He speaks so well. What are you talking about? He speaks so well. What voice were you looking to come out of his mouth? [effects a minstrel-like smile and accent] "Imma drop me a bomb today. I be prez-o-den."

Compared to his feelings on Simpson, Rock is more positive towards Colin Powell. In fact, Powell is one of few celebrities in Rock's routines to emerge relatively unscathed by his jokes. Powell embodies middle-class respectability, a point made explicit by Rock's counterexample that imagines Powell as a minstrel-like figure. Nevertheless, the surprise Rock's straw men express at the politician's eloquence betrays unfair assumptions that because he is Black, Powell cannot be middle-class. With regards to white prejudice against Powell, Rock highlights his own Blackness, which gives him an outsider's viewpoint on dominant white culture. This is in contrast to his more insider/ everyman perspective on O. J.'s class advantages. In other sections of this special, Rock would formulate and adopt still more complex identity positions.

In what has since become his most famous and controversial bit, Rock argues that there are different classes within the Black community.

> Who's more racist, Black people or white people? It's Black people. You know why? Because we hate Black people too. Everything white people don't like about Black people, Black people *really* don't like about Black people. And there's two sides: there's Black people and there's n---as. The n---as have got to go. You can't have shit when you around n---as, you can't have shit. You can't have no big screen TV. You can have it, but you better move it in at 3 in the morning. Paint it white, hope n---as think it's a bassinet. Can't have shit in your house! Why?! Because n---as will break into your house. N---as that live next

door to you break into your house, come over the next day and go, "I heard you got robbed." N---a, you know who robbed me. You didn't *see* shit 'cause you was *doing* shit! You can't go see a movie, you know why? 'Cause n---as is shooting at the screen, "This movie's so good I gotta bust a cap in here!" You know the worst thing about n---as? N---as always want credit for some shit they supposed to do. A n---a will brag about some shit a normal man just *does*. A n---a will say some shit like, "I take care of my kids." You're *supposed* to, you dumb motherfucker! What kind of ignorant shit is that? "I ain't never been to jail!" What do you want, a cookie?! You're not *supposed* to go to jail, you low-expectation-having motherfucker!

When Rock attacked lower-class whites in earlier routines, he complicated neat hierarchies presuming whites to be of a higher class than African Americans. This section of *Bring the Pain* is similar in both its disdain for lower-class cultures and its attempt to differentiate race and class, but it is more concerned with noting the differences that exist within larger Black culture. In the process, as Bambi Haggins notes, he "pressur[es the audience] (black and white) to recognize issues of difference (in terms of class and social practices) *within* the black community" (emphasis in original).[15]

Christine Acham notes this particular routine as a prime example of a Black comic airing dirty laundry.[16] She borrows this critique from Malcolm X's speech "A Message to the Grassroots," in which the leader argued that such information could be used as a "means to divide and conquer."[17] Such criticism bears a strong resemblance to the Marxist ideal that members of the working class transcend race in order to create a stronger and more unified proletariat, except that it privileges racial over class solidarity. But Rock appears no more interested here in constructing racial solidarity across class lines than he appeared in earlier routines to create class solidarity across racial lines. Rock's humor is not about smoothing over distinctions within groups; he's more interested in highlighting them. And because of his intersectional ability to highlight different aspects of his identity, there are multiple ways in which the comic can go about drawing out these distinctions. In practice and as Haggins notes, this troubles the notion that there is but one Black people as much as his earlier routines troubled a notion of poverty as racially homogenous.

Rock's routine obviously chastises those he believes to be acting inappropriately, but with each criticism he implies that the inverse is the proper way to act. While the majority of the routine focuses on lower-class behavior, the routine's introduction characterizes "Black people" (like Rock) as a relatively silent majority of responsible performers of bourgeois values. That is, to be "Black" as opposed to "famous" or a "n---a" is to be middle-class. This erasure of class labels for only the middle normalizes the bourgeois behavior and renders it invisible. To be Black is to be middle-class and to be middle-class is both normal and correct.

Christopher Alan Bracey notes this routine in his study of the history of Black conservatism: "Rock's routine was driven by serious and sincere conservative values of hard work, family, self-sufficiency, and law and order—the same values that provide the grist of cultural critiques by leading black neoconservative intellectuals and public figures."[18] Writing at *Salon*, Mychal Denzel Smith traces Rock's intellectual legacy in similar terms, arguing that this routine "hewed to the same line of respectability politics that had been a part of black political life since the days of Reconstruction. Even W. E. B. Du Bois, perhaps the most important sociologist in all of American history, posited a theory for black liberation that rested on the idea that 90 percent of black people ain't shit and could only be saved by the 'talented tenth.'"[19] *Respectability politics* refers to the strategy by disadvantaged groups to win the favor of those in power by adopting and performing the dominant group's values. With this routine, Rock throws his lot in with the respectability politics crowd.

Although Malcolm X's warning against criticizing Black people and culture within earshot of whites explicitly framed it as a way in which whites could attack African Americans, there are clearly other hazards associated with discourses like "N---s Versus Black People." Most notably, there is a danger in the ways white audiences could make sense of this routine. Humor like this may be enjoyed because it confirms rather than complicates racist assumptions about Black people. Moreover, the fact that such criticism comes from the mouth of a Black man makes it more comfortable for whites to enjoy racist humor and confirm their prejudices. More generally, Rock's argument that Black people are more racist than whites disguises deeply ingrained cultures and structures of American racism by focusing on the superficial prejudices of individuals rather than the deeper issues. So while Rock might shift identity positions to highlight his class in relation to other members of his race, complex reading strategies allow whites to identify with Rock's argument while maintaining white identity and downplaying the complexity of class, ultimately reinforcing senses of white supremacy.

Toward the end of this routine, and in an echo of his criticism from *Big Ass Jokes*, Rock discusses poor whites. Most of America, he argues, "is filled up with broke-ass white people. Broke-ass, living in their trailer home, eating mayonnaise sandwiches, fucking their sisters, listening to John Cougar

Mellencamp records." He reprises this theme not only to remind his audience once again that Black America does not have a monopoly on poverty, but also to move to a larger point about his attacks on poor African Americans. "It ain't all Black people on welfare. Shit, white people on welfare too. But we can't give a fuck about them. We just gotta do our own thing. You can't go 'oh they fucked up, we can be fucked up.' That's ignorant."[20] Rock builds on a tradition of thought that can be traced back through the rhetoric of Malcolm X and Marcus Garvey arguing that African Americans should work toward self-reliance more than integration. This hearkens back to Rock's earlier discussion of busing in the sense that integration's narrow focus on race ignores the effects of class, but also suggests that *intra*racial uplift strategies like discouraging the excesses of working-class culture are the most effective ways to help African Americans succeed.

The Mychal Denzel Smith article cited above ultimately settles on criticizing the hypocrisy of attacking working-class Black behavior from the perspective of middle-class mores, because these actions were often necessary to survive. Furthermore, these tactics were often necessary to make class mobility possible. Smith quotes Damon Young in making this point:

> Because if you actually go to a hood, you'll find that if there is a young person with actual academic or athletic potential—basically, someone who seems to have a ticket out of the hood—there will usually be waaaaaaaaaaaaaaaaaaaay more people rooting for and even protecting them than actively wanting them to fail. Maybe their methods of protection and support might be unorthodox and even occasionally counterproductive, but the supporters, the ones genuinely happy to see someone from their block who's "made it," tend to outnumber the haters.[21]

The point made by both Smith and Young echoes aspects of *Born Suspect*, where Rock also notes the sometimes necessary expediency of performing as the "bad Black" for short-term survival.

"N---as Versus Black People" relies on the same kind of insulting comedy Rock demonstrated in his discussion of "white toxic waste." A number of significant differences likely played into this routine's notability over and above his earlier performances. Rock's style had grown more consummate and his jokes cleverer. That is, comparatively bland insults had given way to a more intricately developed theme-and-variation mode of building ideas from the basis of his setup to a feverish comic pitch. There is also a culturally conservative element within this bit's wider appreciation that revels in its stereotype confirmation, sense of moral and cultural superiority, and having come from a Black man. Nevertheless, it fits into Rock's larger discussions of race and class by reminding the audience that African Americans are not a monolithic group—a fairly uncontroversial opinion. And although this is the routine that people often think of when Rock's name comes up, it was neither his first nor his final word on the topic.

CONCLUSION

Rock's stand-up continues to elaborate with variation on these themes after *Bring the Pain*. In *Bigger and Blacker* (Truesdell, 1999) he discusses racism and class explicitly, albeit reverting to the racial essentialism characteristic of his earlier work.

> Shit, there ain't a white man in this room that would change places with me. None of you would change places with me. And I'm rich! [. . .] There's a white, one-legged busboy in here right now that won't change places with my Black ass. He's going, "No, man, I don't wanna switch. I wanna ride this white thing out. See where it takes me."

His 2004 special *Never Scared* (Gallen, 2004) attacked the hypocrisy that allows white people to become wealthy from harmful products while African Americans are punished for similar actions. "White man makes guns; nobody gives a fuck. White man makes guns; kids shoot up each other in school; nobody gives a fuck. White man makes guns; no problem. Black rapper says 'gun'; congressional hearing." But whether this is the result of an artist seeking greater variety or of Rock being further removed from his working-class past, class seems to be less of a concern even if race remains central in his routines.

Following his breakout moment in the mid-1990s, Rock branched into a wider variety of creative outlets, creating and starring in *The Chris Rock Show* (1997–2000) on HBO, expanding his cinematic presence to include voicing animated children's films, regularly appearing in *Saturday Night Live* (1975–) friend Adam Sandler's films, and hosting the Academy Awards twice. Clearly, these expanded offerings present different degrees of possibility for exploring these issues, as it would be difficult to imagine overt discussions of uplift ideology or racial performance coming out of the mouth of an animated zebra, despite the black-and-white animal's rich symbolic potential.

Perhaps the most logical place to seek Rock's commentary on race and class outside of stand-up is in his semi-autobiographical television show *Everybody Hates Chris*, which ran from 2005 to 2009.[22] After all, the series is based on Rock's experiences growing up, including his family life and busing to a mostly white school. As in his early routines, he faces difficulties in these situations. However, much more than in his more fully autobiographical stand-up, this show focused on Rock's home life and drew much of its humor from the problems of economic struggle among working-class African Americans. Moreover, racism in the series was less ubiquitous and virulent than what Rock describes in his early routines and in interviews. Instead of attending an overwhelmingly hostile school with whites who are worse off than his family, he attends a moderately better-off school where the racism and torment are muted and mostly limited to a single bully character. So while race and class are certainly significant issues within its narrative universe, the show lacks some of the critical edge and rhetorical punch of Rock's stand-up. However, besides ignoring the particular demands of genre and medium, such criticism also elides that Rock was never a perfect, nor perfectly consistent, intersectional analyst. Rather, his continued expansion into different media and appeals to different audiences highlights his popular appeal, which is critical to his status as a *public* intellectual.

Nevertheless, Rock's intellectual engagement with issues of race and class remains most obvious in his stand-up comedy. But exposure has allowed him to take his observations and arguments on these topics into different venues. And even though his appearances in films like *Grown Ups* (Dugan, 2010) and *Madagascar* (Darnell and McGrath, 2005) may disqualify Rock for the kind of public intellectualism that defines his most notable stand-up routines, films like *Head of State* (Rock, 2003), *Good Hair* (Stilson, 2009), and *Top Five* (Rock, 2015) function in many ways as venues for his more challenging ideas. So while certain of his projects may appear less intellectual, Rock has grown more public and popular. And publicity means that he can take pointed stances in genres and venues that support such discourses: interviews, stand-up, and more public venues like the Oscars.

Notes

1. David Gillota, "Stand-Up Nation: Humor and American Identity," *The Journal of American Culture* 38, no. 2 (June 2015): 102–12.

2. Notable examples include citation of this routine in a speech by then presidential candidate Barack Obama and in a *Harvard Law Review* article. Paul Butler, "(Color) Blind Faith: The Tragedy of Race, Crime, and the Law," *Harvard Law Review* 111, no. 5 (March 1998):

1270–88; Nick Baumann, "Obama Channels Chris Rock," *Mother Jones*, June 16, 2008, http://www.motherjones.com/mojo/2008/06/obama-channels-chris-rock.

3. Although Rock had already established himself by this period due to his presence on *Saturday Night Live* and film roles in *I'm Gonna Git You Sucka* (Wayans, 1988) and *New Jack City* (Van Peebles, 1991), these stand-up routines show Rock developing his comic style and outlook into the special and routine that would launch him to high prominence.

4. Chris Rock, *Born Suspect*, Atlantic Records, Atlantic 82159-2, 1991, compact disc.

5. Although distinct from the specific attacks on poor whites, this routine also contains an even more racially essentialist joke about race and boxing ability. In it, he states, "white guys cannot box. Black guys fight better. Puerto Ricans fight even better. Guess the lower you go on the social ladder, the better you fight. When you think about it, for every good Puerto Rican fighter, there's an American Indian that's waiting to kick his ass."

6. Lawrence E. Mintz, "Standup Comedy as Social and Cultural Mediation," *American Quarterly* 37, no. 1 (Spring 1985): 71–80. 75.

7. The scope and length of this chapter prevent me from evaluating these claims and the larger, complex discourses of which they are a part.

8. *Big Ass Jokes*, first aired June 16, 1994, HBO.

9. Richard A. Pride and J. David Woodard, *The Burden of Busing: The Politics of Desegregation in Nashville, Tennessee* (Knoxville: University of Tennessee Press, 1985), 169–224; Christine H. Rosell, *The Carrot or the Stick for School Desegregation Policy: Magnet Schools or Forced Busing* (Philadelphia: Temple University Press, 1990) 120.

10. Willis D. Hawley, "The New Mythology of School Desegregation," *Law and Contemporary Problems* 42, no. 4 (1978): 214–33.

11. Karl Marx, "Marx to Sigfrid Meyer and August Vogt in New York," in *Marx, Engels: Selected Correspondence*, 3rd edition (Moscow, Russia: Progress Publishers, 1975), 220–24. 222.

12. *Bring the Pain*, first aired June 1, 1996, HBO.

13. Maxwell Strachan, "O. J. Simpson Didn't Want to Be Associated with Black America. Then He Came to Symbolize It," *The Huffington Post*, June 14, 2016, http://new.www.huffingtonpost.com/entry/oj-simpson-race-black_us_575ee2d9e4b0e4fe51431080.

14. Jeffrey Sconce, "See You in Hell, Johnny Bravo!" in *Reality TV: Remaking Television Culture*, ed. Susan Murray and Laurie Ouellette (New York and London: New York University Press 2004), 251–67. 255.

15. Bambi Haggins, *Laughing Mad: The Black Comic Persona in Post-Soul America* (New Brunswick, NJ and London: Rutgers University Press, 2007), 83.

16. Christine Acham, *Revolution Televised: Prime Time and the Struggle for Black Power* (Minneapolis: University of Minnesota Press, 2004). The fact that I, as a white man, have access to and can thus comment on this material, of course, proves the point.

17. Malcolm X, "A Message to the Grassroots," in *Malcolm X Speaks*, ed. George Breitman (New York: First Grove Press, 1966), 3–17. Cited in Acham, *Revolution Televised*, 179.

18. Christopher Alan Bracey, *Saviors or Sellouts: The Promise and Peril of Black Conservatism, from Booker T. Washington to Condoleezza Rice* (Boston: Beacon Press, 2008). 182.

19. Mychal Denzel Smith, "Chris Rock's Poisonous Legacy: How to Get Rich and Exalted Chastising 'Bad Blacks,'" *Salon.com*, November 12, 2014, http://www.salon.com/2014/11/12/chris_rocks_poisonous_legacy_how_to_get_rich_and_exalted_chastising_bad_blacks/.

20. Of course, Rock cannot control his audience's ability to digest this section of the routine in the way he intends, which would blunt its tendency to reinforce white racism.

21. Damon Young, "Dear Black People: Please Stop Spreading the Lie that 'Bad' Blacks Are Holding 'Good' Blacks Back," *Very Smart Brothas*, October 27, 2014, http://verysmartbrothas.com/dear-black-people-please-stop-spreading-the-lie-that-bad-blacks-are-holding-good-blacks-back/comment-page-7/. Cited in Smith, "Chris Rock's Poisonous Legacy."

22. *Everybody Hates Chris*, first aired 2005–2009 by UPN and the CW.

6

WHITE COMEDIANS, STRATEGIC RACIST HUMOR, AND THE (RE)NORMALIZATION OF RACISM
Lisa Lampanelli as a Case Study

Raúl Pérez

> I have always used in my act every racial slur there is for Asians, blacks, gays, and Hispanics. To me, it's acceptable if the joke is funny and if it is said in a context of no hate. It's about taking the hate out of the word.
> —Lisa Lampanelli[1]

INTRODUCTION

There is a tendency to regard comedians not only as joke tellers, but as well-intended "truth-tellers."[2] Increasingly, comedians are viewed as "cultural mediators" and "public intellectuals" who serve as moral guides to steer us "through the cultural debates of the moment" by enlightening the public with their comic cultural criticism.[3] This current rendering of comedians as public intellectuals and cultural mediators largely reproduces a celebratory narrative that has become the dominant framework for understanding contemporary comedy,[4] where comics are often regarded as "heroes" who speak "truth to power."[5]

At the same time, over the last decade there has been growing criticism and protest against comic speech that continues to rely on racist, sexist, and homophobic discourse.[6] The use of racist jokes and slurs in particular appears to be at the center of many of these humor controversies. From the Michael Richards incident at the Laugh Factory in 2006, where Richards verbally abused a Black audience member with racial insults and slurs,[7] to the #CancelColbert campaign that took Stephen Colbert to task for his Asian minstrel character "Ching Chong Ding Dong,"[8] these and other recent incidents have created much debate over the legitimacy of audience criticism and whether such contestation harms or benefits comedy in particular, and free speech in general.[9]

Many prominent comedians and "free speech advocates" have increasingly condemned such criticism and audience reaction as "political correctness" and as an attack on freedom of expression.[10] Yet it is worth noting that such a move by comedians is in many ways a resurfacing of a conservative "anti-intellectual" position that frames criticism of abusive language by the more privileged as a form of "liberal totalitarianism." From Jerry Seinfeld to Chris Rock, numerous prominent comedians have denounced "political correctness" as a great threat to comedy and society. From this perspective, any criticism of comedy and comedians is unwarranted, as critics are regarded as humorless killjoys.[11]

One potential solution to this problem, according to Krefting, is for audiences and critics to try to decipher the "comic intentionality" of performers before jumping to conclusions. Krefting contends that while "shock comics" make use of racist/sexist/homophobic jokes, these may not necessarily be "world views they believe or to which they adhere."[12] Mintz regarded such comics as *negative exemplars* who perform defective social identities to amuse and instruct the audience.[13] In turn, Krefting suggests that audiences and critics should pay close attention to what comics say and do off stage, which may "belie what might otherwise appear as virulent bigotry."[14]

Weaver contends that deciphering the authorial intentions of comedians has become more difficult in late neoliberalism or "liquid modernity," as comic discourse has become more ambiguous, audiences more fragmented, and interpretations of their discourse more varied.[15] Moreover, Weaver contends that "unserious" comic racism often has the rhetorical potential to reactivate and support "serious racism." That is, while humor is "polysemic," having multiple levels of interpretation, racial humor and comedy can be used to support racist ideologies, as there is a prior reliance on racist discourse to support racism more generally. Take for instance the appropriation and circulation of "ironic" and often violent racist jokes by the alt-Right and far-Right white supremacists.[16] In other words, when humor, jokes, comic discourse, and intentionality are viewed primarily as "good," and comedians are celebrated and protected as "well-intentioned," they are shielded from critical analysis.

Over the last two decades, Lisa Lampanelli has bolstered her reputation as an "insult comic" and an "equal opportunity offender" who has managed to capitalize on her unabashed use of racist jokes, slurs, and stereotypes, all while largely evading serious social criticism. In this essay, I examine Lampanelli's use of racist jokes, narratives, and racial slurs in order to illustrate how Lampanelli has worked to *maximize* racist talk while *minimizing* and denying a racist interpretation of her comedy. Drawing on Feagin's notion of a *white racial frame*,[17] I analyze public interviews where Lampanelli describes and defends her style of comedy in order to examine how Lampanelli "manages" her public persona and "frames" her use of racist humor as "not racist." That is, by publicly articulating and denying a racist reading in her work, I contend that Lampanelli articulates a *neoliberal white racial comedy*—a commercial racial comedy where the history, significance, and persistence of racism and racial inequality is minimized, trivialized, and ignored. This denial and trivialization of racism works to grant white comics discursive license to use and profit from racist jokes, narratives, and slurs unapologetically, under the guise of humor and comic free speech. A *neoliberal white racial comedy* is upheld and reinforced through a deliberate set of comic performance practices and strategies that work to veil the use of comic racist talk as "not racist." This allows for the racist jokes of white comedians like Lampanelli to be consumed as publicly palatable, and to remain economically viable, in an ostensibly colorblind society where racist talk has been disavowed more broadly.[18]

Lampanelli has played a leading role in this regard. Moreover, by publicly challenging and delegitimize audience criticism as "political correctness," and by framing such criticism as a form of "censorship," Lampanelli has, I argue, produced a comic "anti-intellectualism" that has worked to steer critical public discourse and debate away from analyzing such comedy as potentially harmful, racist, political, and ideological, and to position it instead as primarily a form of amusement, fun, and pleasure. Furthermore, by taking aim at college-educated audiences and universities for allegedly fueling the cultural rising tides of the "politically correct" who "can't take a joke," such a critique by Lampanelli and other comics falls in line with the ongoing efforts by conservative and right-wing anti-intellectuals, organizations, and politicians working to dismantle the cultural changes that have emerged in the aftermath the of the civil rights movement.[19] One of the central changes of the post–civil rights era was in limiting the acceptability of racist speech in public, which conservatives swiftly branded as "political correctness." But while twenty-five years ago it was right-wing public anti-intellectuals, writers, and journalists leading the charge against so-called political correctness (e.g., Dinesh D'Souza), today it is seemingly comedians like Lampanelli.[20]

THE LEGACY OF WHITE RACIST COMEDY

To better understand the cultural impact of Lampanelli's racial comedy, it is important to situate her use of racist humor historically and theoretically within the legacy and evolution of racial discourse, comedy, and ridicule in the US.

In the history of US comedy, the pre–civil rights era can be characterized as the era of overt racial ridicule. Blackface minstrelsy, for instance, which originated in the early nineteenth century, was one of the most prominent forms of comedy and entertainment from the pre–Civil War period until the civil rights era.[21] This genre of humor began with white humorists painting their faces black while offering "authentic" depictions of blacks as stupid, childlike, inarticulate, buffoonish, and unassimilable.[22] While the development of this comic genre would later include Blacks as blackface minstrels, Black performers needed to engage in self-ridicule and reproduce white portrayals of Blackness as buffoonish and inferior in order to survive in this cultural industry.[23]

It is also important to understand that this form of racist entertainment and comedy was not something that occurred by mere historical accident; rather, it evolved as a cultural practice that operated centrally through what the sociologist Joe Feagin calls a "white racial frame."[24] According Feagin, this white racial frame originated from the historical, social, political, and economic development of the US as a white-dominated society. A white racial frame became the dominant "meaning making" system in the US for understanding racial matters and social life, as whites were believed to be innately superior to nonwhites. Through this racial frame racist images, stereotypes, beliefs, and cultural practices were created, accepted, and circulated as cultural knowledge in virtually every social sphere in US society, which in turn worked to normalize, reproduce, and reinforce notions of white superiority and supremacy as the natural order of things.

These everyday beliefs regarding the natural inferiority of nonwhites would soon emerge in the cultural arena. From the early nineteenth until the mid-twentieth century, white entertainers in blackface became the comic "truth-tellers" who were articulating an ideology of white supremacy via racial ridicule on stage, radio, and film for the collective pleasure and consumption of white audiences.[25]

And it was precisely this version of racial "truth" that nonwhites began to challenge publicly during the civil rights movement, as protests against racial ridicule signaled a turning point in the history of racist humor in the US.[26] People of color began to challenge their status of inferiority in a "racial dictatorship" by combating a white racial framing of society with calls for racial democracy and equality[27]—in this case with regard to ending the practice of comic racial ridicule.

As a result of organized public protests against the use of racial ridicule by whites during and after the civil rights movement, scholars argued that white comedians and humorists now had greater difficulty ridiculing racial and ethnic minorities in public.[28] For instance, during the civil rights era groups like the NAACP protested comedy shows that continued the legacy of blackface minstrelsy, such as *Amos 'n' Andy* while organizations such as the Mexican American Anti-Defamation Committee (MAADC) and the Involvement of Mexican Americans in Gainful Endeavors (IMAGE) challenged racist comic portrayals of Latinos as inarticulate buffoons, such as comedian Bill Dana's Latino minstrel character "José Jiménez."[29] Such comedy shows were protested as forms of racist media and entertainment and were soon taken off the air.

This decline in the acceptability of public racial ridicule by white comedians and humorists reflected the overall unacceptability of explicit and offensive racist talk in public by whites more generally.[30] In turn, this cultural shift in public race talk in the post–civil rights era contributed to the notion that a new cultural moment had arrived, a shift that conservatives increasingly described as "political correctness." For the first time in US society, white entertainers could no longer make use of racist discourse, slurs, and ridicule freely and without social consequence.[31]

FROM RACIAL RIDICULE TO EQUAL OPPORTUNITY OFFENDER

The civil rights movement made it challenging for whites to make use of racial ridicule and racial slurs in the arena of comedy. While nonwhite comics could continue to engage in self-racial ridicule and make liberal use of racial slurs (e.g., Redd Foxx, Richard Pryor),[32] in the post–civil rights era public audiences were less willing to accept overt racial ridicule from whites. Moreover, white comedians increasingly began to police their own racial discourse. For instance, in the early 1970s the comedian George Carlin expressed his refusal to perform race- and ethnicity-based jokes in his comedy: "There isn't a lot that outrages me . . . except racial jokes, ethnic jokes. I find nothing funny about that—just tasteless."[33] Over the last several decades, Carlin has been broadly celebrated as a comic "truth-teller," a champion of "free speech," and has been widely regarded as an influential and unfiltered critic of American culture and society.[34] Yet, the motivation to self-censor the use of racial ridicule on the part of Carlin and other white comics during and after the civil movement stems in part from the moral stigma of racism that emerged after the civil rights era.

The historical context in which comedians like Carlin came of age is also important to consider. The free speech movement, the civil rights movement, the feminist movement, and the antiwar movement were all backdrops for the "rebel comedians" of the 1950s and 1960s.[35] During this time, comedians increasingly voiced their opinions with regard to racism, political corruption, and the war in Vietnam. That is, the sociopolitical context of this era shaped the political orientation of many of these comics broadly toward the "Left" wing of the political spectrum. In turn, many influential comedians of this era increasingly used their comic criticism as a weapon that "kicked up" the social and political hierarchy (e.g., mocking the power elite and the racist power structure), rather than "kicking down" in the way that blackface and other forms of racist ridicule had during the pre–civil rights era.[36]

However, conservative figures increasingly challenged the policing of racist discourse as an attack on "free speech" and began to demonize such efforts with the term "political correctness." During the 1980s and 1990s, leading conservative "public intellectuals" branded political correctness as a "catch-all" phrase that was intended to marginalize progressive ideas like racial equality, gender equality, environmentalism, and anti-imperialism.[37] These ideas gained popularity during the civil rights, women's rights, and antiwar movements of the 1960s and 1970s. But as Wilson observes, the framing of "political correctness" as a form of "liberal totalitarianism" became a way for leading conservative anti-intellectuals to publicly challenge "multiculturalism, affirmative action, sexual harassment codes, and the so-called politicization of higher education."[38] In turn, leading conservative voices worked to frame "political correctness" as "the greatest threat to the First Amendment in our history."[39] This included the inability of white conservatives to tell racist jokes in public. As the conservative radio talk show host Rush Limbaugh noted in the early 1990s: "How come you can't have a little fun about blacks? . . . What protects them? Why are they immune from legitimate forms of humor?"[40]

This social tension around public racial discourse created a social context in which some comedians attempted to indulge in the "forbidden fruit" of racism in their comedy.[41] For instance, during a period in which "equal opportunity" was offered as the remedy for the historical and continued social harm of racial oppression, comedians like Don Rickles took to the stage and produced a more ambiguous form of racial ridicule.[42] That is, rather focusing comic racial ridicule on one particular racialized group (e.g., blackface), Rickles and others began to *diversify* their targets of racial ridicule, increasingly coming to be regarded as "equal opportunity offenders." In turn, humorists made use of this new rhetorical strategy as a way to circumvent accusations of racism during the post–civil rights era.[43]

In other words, this new polarizing social, political, and cultural context created a discursive, artistic, and commercial opening that emboldened some white humorists to challenge "political correctness" by becoming "politically incorrect." Soon, joke books like the *Truly Tasteless Jokes* series became national best sellers by trading in racist, sexist, and homophobic jokes,[44] while comedians like Jackie Mason were receiving national attention for their brand of "politically incorrect" humor that was unafraid to insult "everyone."[45] By framing themselves as "equal opportunity offenders," white humorists were able to offer a successful and commercial counterattack to so-called "political correctness."

Over the last two decades, Lisa Lampanelli became one of the most commercially successful comedians to carry the mantle of "equal opportunity offender" and attack "political correctness." This brand of commercial racial comedy has allowed Lampanelli to articulate a defense of her use of racist jokes and slurs in her comedy, during a period in US society ostensibly dominated by "colorblindness."[46] For instance, take the following jokes from Lampanelli's comedy special *Dirty Girl: No Protection* (Higby, 2007): "What do you call a black woman who's had seven abortions? A crime fighter! [audience laughter] How many 'hispangics' [*sic*] does it take to clean a bathroom? None! That's a n----r's job! [audience laughter]."[47] How did a white comedian like Lisa Lampanelli get on stage and tell such jokes in front of a racially diverse audience and receive laughter, applause, and commercial success, with seemingly no opposition? Lampanelli has worked to legitimize her use of racist jokes and slurs in public by *minimizing* a racist interpretation of her work, while *maximizing* her use of racist speech in a strategic way. That is, I contend that Lampanelli learned to strategically navigate the cultural terrain of public racial discourse, both in her comedy and in public interviews, by articulating and performing a *neoliberal white racial comedy*.

ARTICULATING A NEOLIBERAL WHITE RACIAL COMEDY

Because of the nature of her racial comedy, over the last two decades Lampanelli has worked to publicly deny and distance herself from racism and racist intent in her work. Numerous interviewers have sought to understand how it is that Lampanelli, a white woman, can "get away" with using extreme and explicit racial slurs and racist jokes in a historical context where such discourse was largely disavowed in public. Other white comedians have faced public backlash and have had their reputations and careers ruined for making careless use of racist jokes and racial slurs on stage. For instance, in the aftermath of the Michael Richards incident in 2006, where Richards verbally abused a Black audience member with racist slurs and violent racist imagery, interviewers asked Lampanelli if she had reassessed her own work given the public outcry against Richards's performance: "Nope, because I know what's in my heart and I have nothing but love for people."[48] And: "I have this likeability where I can say whatever I want. I'm not going to edit because some prick who's an actual racist says the N-word."[49] Moreover, when asked whether she believed that the audience goes along with her comedy because "everyone's a little bit racist," Lampanelli responds: "You're absolutely right. And you know what's weird, I like to think of myself as not at all."[50] In other words, over the last two decades, Lampanelli worked to craft her comic brand as a "non-racist" who "plays with racism." Moreover, by marketing herself as a "politically incorrect" "non-racist" who "loves everyone," Lampanelli justifies her use of extreme racist language and slurs by seemingly refusing to "edit" herself in order to uphold the principles of "free speech."[51] It is worth taking a closer look to reveal *how* exactly Lampanelli articulates, denies, and profits from racism in her work.

Below, I examine 15 interviews with Lisa Lampanelli (from 2006 to 2019) where she discusses the use of racist jokes and racial slurs in her comedy. These interviews were published in venues ranging from national and local newspapers and magazines to blogs, magazines, and websites dedicated to analyzing comedy. In analyzing these media interviews, I make use of Richardson's method for newspaper analysis, which relies on critical discourse analysis (CDA) to (1) *interpret* the meanings of the texts, (2) situate "*what* is written or said in the *context* in which it occurs," and (3) argue that textual meanings "are *constructed* through an interaction between producer, text and consumer."[52]

Throughout these interviews, I find that a pattern emerges in the ways Lampanelli and her interviewers justify her command of racist jokes and racial slurs. Using CDA to analyze these interviews, I examine how Lampanelli and interviewers work to explain her use of racist humor by crafting narratives that suggest: 1) she does not use racist jokes and slurs out of "hate," because she "loves everyone"; 2) she uses racist discourse strategically and responsibly; and 3) she makes use of racist discourse to "subvert" racism. In turn, I argue that this construction of her use of racist jokes and racial slurs allows Lampanelli to frame criticism of her work not only as hurting comedy, but as harmful to freedom of speech, artistic expression, and the business of comedy more generally.

RACISM WITHOUT HATE?

One of the key ways Lampanelli has crafted her public image regarding the use of racist humor in interviews has been by emphasizing her "love for everyone," her "likability," and her "warmth"—in other words, her "good intentions." In turn, by publicly stating that she has no racial animus or hatred, Lampanelli believes she is absolved from being viewed as "racist." Take the following examples:

> With my style of comedy, you can't do comedy like that unless you really like people—I mean like every race. . . . I have love in my heart for everybody, even though I do edgy stuff.[53]
>
> You have to be a warm person who cares about other people. And have good karma and people love you. It's warmth and likeability and then you can say whatever you want.[54]
>
> The fact is, if I say the "n" word or the "cunt" word or the "spic" or the "chink" or whatever, and there is good intention in my heart, people can sense it.[55]

Repeatedly, Lampanelli suggests that it is her "good intentions" that allow her to circumvent criticism from the audience regarding her use of explicit racist discourse on stage. She suggests that the audience can readily decode that her use of racial insults and slurs is not a result of "hatred," but of her "love" for people. And based on her argument that her use of racist language is "without hatred," Lampanelli believes it is acceptable.

Lampanelli further articulates this point by rhetorically distancing her brand of racist humor from more obvious forms of racial hatred. Asked in an interview about how and when she started doing racist humor, Lampanelli jokingly responds: "I used to put on a hood and just go to the rallies on the weekend. When you find out you can get paid to be in the Klan, it's really good. I think there's too many unemployed Klan members out there. No, I did show comedy, and it just developed."[56] Here, Lampanelli attempts to comically and rhetorically distance her brand of racist humor from obvious and extreme racism by suggesting that her use of racist discourse is intended as "play."⁵⁷ Lampanelli later suggests that her decision to make use of racist language in her work was not the result of racial animus; rather, she says it came from realizing that she enjoyed engaging and insulting the audience while on stage: "I really liked f*cking with them and not having anybody get mad at me."⁵⁸ Lampanelli has also noted that the "comic inspiration" for her work stemmed in part from her mother, whom she described as a "genteel and often clueless bigot."⁵⁹ But while she has branded herself as a raw and unedited insult comic and "free speech warrior,"⁶⁰ Lampanelli notes that making use of racist discourse on stage is not an easy task: "I don't think any comic is good enough in the first seven years to say the 'N' word ... you have to be lovable and good, and have sort of a handle on your craft to be able to take those chances."⁶¹ Lampanelli recalled an early experience where her use of racist insults failed: "I didn't meet a Jewish person until I went to college ... I think I called somebody a kike. I was just joking around. The fucking guy had a fit. So I think early on I learned that, uh-oh, you've got to really know how to do this right. You can't be doing it just indiscriminately."⁶² Such incidents were early learning experiences for Lampanelli, who understood that if she was going to "get to say the 'n' word on stage and get paid money,"⁶³ she would have to learn to edit her delivery by performing her racist discourse strategically. As she notes: "If you're good enough ... you can make it all humorous, but you *have* to do it right."⁶⁴ By articulating her experiences with racist comedy in this way, Lampanelli was able to use such interviews to frame her use of racism as "responsible," which worked to minimize accusations and interpretations of racism in her work.

STRATEGIC RACIST COMEDY

Many of Lampanelli's interviews over the last decade focus on a seeming contradiction: her reliance on explicit racist discourse and the diversity of her audience. Lampanelli attributes her ability to make use of racist humor in front of a diverse audience to her "good intentions" and "love for everybody," but her success largely stems from a careful crafting of her incongruous stage persona and the strategic delivery of her racist jokes. For instance, some interviewers observed how the incongruity of her stage character contributes to the acceptability of her brand of humor: "While Ms. Lampanelli talks like a truck driver, she dresses pure girly-girl. In performance she resembles a '50s housewife in her pearls, shirtwaist dresses and button-down sweaters. 'The more conservative you dress, the more you can get away with,' she said, twirling a long blond curl."⁶⁵ Lampanelli notes that this aesthetic incongruity is strategic and that it has helped her perform her style of insult comedy: "The more I look like a June Cleaver type, the more shock value it has, and the more it takes you by surprise. If a joke's good and you have warmth and likability, (an audience) will let you get away with it."[66] While female comedians have gained more visibility in the world of stand-up comedy in recent years, comedy largely remains a male-dominated profession.[67] But over the last two decades, Lampanelli was able to stand out precisely because of her brand of racist comedy. She created a stage persona that allowed her to capitalize on glaring incongruity of that character—a 1950s white suburban housewife with a "trucker mouth"—and the social/cultural climate regarding the declining acceptance of racist speech in public. As Allyson Jaffe, the manager and part-owner of the DC Improv comedy club, suggests: "It's much more shocking to hear a woman saying what she does than a man.... It's just really surprising. That's why she's playing 800-seat theaters instead of smaller clubs. You just don't expect women to say those things."[68] This context and incongruity was not lost on Lampanelli, as she speculated on why she was able to stand out while other female comedians were largely unsuccessful in the comedy industry:

> I kind of almost have a male approach to comedy.... If you took any of [my material], a guy could do those jokes. The reason women comics suck is, they do chick jokes, they do chick humor. And, really, does a guy want to pay to hear some cunt moaning and groaning about the things women talk about onstage? No. If he really wants to hear that he can stay home and his wife won't charge him.[69]

In a male-privileged and male-dominated culture industry, the perceived incongruity of her character, a soccer mom with a foul mouth, a woman who "talks like a man," and the audience's distaste for "chick jokes" all work together to account for Lampanelli's comic appeal.

Lampanelli's strategic delivery of racist language also facilitated her ability to capitalize on racist comedy. Lampanelli relies on two performance strategies in particular: (1) *self-deprecation*, such as mocking her gender, weight, appearance, and sexual transgressions, all of which facilitates her ability to be (2) an *equal opportunity offender* that insults "everyone," nonwhites in particular. As Farmer notes, Lampanelli is "often the butt of her own jokes, she ridicules herself for her weight and for being an easy catch."[70] This strategy in turn facilitates Lampanelli's use of racist jokes and slurs. Take the following joke:

> My problem is, I can't get a good-looking white guy, I just don't have the looks to get that. I get hot blacks but also, blacks are now starting to get uppity and go for the skinny white ones and the Asians, which is very offensive to me that they don't stick with their roots—the chubby white girl. What I have to do now is get super famous and rich so I could get a big black boy toy to follow me around on the road and give me a fluff. . . . I want a guy who's so dumb, he has a plate in his head. I banged a bouncer two days ago in West Palm Beach, he must've had 'plate in the head' action going on because he could not spell his name and I thought, this is the type of n----r for me. Here's the thing though and also, I was a little scared, I hardly got any sleep because my purse was in the same room and when they're black, you have to hide your money because they steal. And Hispanics and even dirty Arabs steal, they're so dirty, really, I can't trust any of those f*ckers.⁷¹

A recurring theme in Lampanelli's comedy during the mid- to late 2000s was her sexual appetite for Black men, which she mined for comic gold. Lampanelli's self-deprecating jokes about being unattractive, which were a setup for her jokes about sleeping with Black men, became a strategic routine in her racial comedy. Lampanelli often used her "black boyfriends" as an entry point into "diversifying" the racial targets of her racist jokes and slurs onstage. Lampanelli recalls how she hit on this strategy:

> I did a show once in Dayton, Ohio, and I was all upset, going, "Oh my God," because that's right near where the Klan started. And I had a black boyfriend at the time. I said, what if they're laughing for the wrong reasons? And he goes, "well, just as long as you stick with your jokes about having a black boyfriend so they know you really aren't racist, then you're OK and you're not to be held responsible for anybody else's ignorance." So I just do it, I put it out there, and the right people get it, the wrong people don't. And it's like I know what's in my heart, so that's really all that counts.⁷²

The rhetorical impact and conceit of such stories for readers is that they are intended to frame Lampanelli as "not racist," even while much of her comedy relies on using blatantly racist discourse. Moreover, as she notes above, while some audience members may laugh at her racist jokes and slurs for the "wrong reasons," ultimately Lampanelli denies responsibility for "their ignorance," thus *minimizing* the possibility that she may be reinforcing and legitimizing their racist beliefs with her public use of racist jokes and slurs.

SUBVERTING OR EXPLOITING RACISM?

Over the course of her career in comedy, Lampanelli has come to believe that her use of racial slurs and insults might actually have a positive social function by making the audience see themselves as "equals." This was not her original intention; Lampanelli notes that she was initially more interested in "cursing at people and calling them names." Over time, though, Lampanelli suggests that her comedy started "taking on a different tone," where she believes the appeal and power of her comedy was in "bringing different groups of people together." "I think what happens is they all feel like they're all on the same page and everybody's equal when they come out of the show."[73] When pressed about whether she might be exploiting racist discourse and racial slurs in her comedy, Lampanelli now insists that her use of racist discourse is intended to subvert racism:

> The whole point is to make fun of stereotypes. You're making fun on two levels. Your audience could get it on two levels. The first level would be like, "Oh, she said the N-word." Well, that's not really the people you want to appeal to. And the second is the level of, "Wow, she's really making fun of the people who say the N word and who really believe that all Hispanics steal or all blacks kill people." Because the stereotypes are so stupid, that to hear them put out there in such a blatant way sort of pokes fun at the people who believe them. So it's better to do that.... I mean, it's so blatantly untrue, that it's funny.[74]

While her comedy makes frequent use of racial expletives and insults, Lampanelli maintains that it ultimately works to combat racist views among her target audience. When asked how she decides what racial slurs to use on stage, she notes:

> Well, I just do which ones flow off the tongue easiest for me because the audience seems to accept every word I say. So if I use the "N-word," that does flow off the tongue quite nicely in some jokes. And I like "spick" a lot better than "wetback" because the "c" sound at the end of "spick" is a lot funnier and crisper than "wetback." "Wetback" is kind of boring. The two syllables water it down.[75]

Lampanelli prefers to read her work as an act of "subversion" of racism, and suggests that her core audience readily deciphers the "subversive" and "ironic" intent of her work. Yet she acknowledges that part of the audience may enjoy her comedy for the explicit use of racial slurs and stereotypes. While she notes that this not the audience she intends to appeal to, others view this as a frequent pitfall in her work. As her 2008 interview with the *New York Times* suggests: "She uses the most blatant, politically incorrect quips so that people will laugh at the absurdity of them ... although she routinely encounters audience members who commend her afterward for sticking it to some group."[76] Lampanelli contends that she "feels sorry for those people" and maintains that her comedy helps level social differences and inequalities among the audience by fostering a sense of "solidarity." But Lampanelli does so by *minimizing* a racist reading in her work and by discounting the part of her audience she believes is misinterpreting her work. When faced with those who are critical of her work, Lampanelli has developed coping strategies to deal with their criticism: "Once I did a thing where this guy from the NAACP got mad. I felt so bad, because I know what I really feel. So I was like, 'Oh, let me donate something and see what I could do.' What else can I do? ... I'll donate some money to the NAACP just to make myself feel better."[77] Lampanelli prefers to believe that her audience is largely composed of individuals who see the "subversive irony" in her work, and she suggests that it is only a few who may have their racist views reinforced. She also downplays audience criticism by emphasizing her racial charity, which is intended to actively shield her from negative criticism not only of her comedy but also of herself as a person. Asked about the "worst reactions" to her work, Lampanelli jokingly notes: "Well, here's the problem, or maybe actually it's good really, I have my assistant delete any negative emails I get from fans so I can delude myself into thinking everyone loves me. So basically, I'm not really sure if anybody out there doesn't like me, but from what I hear I'm fantastic."[78] While she jokingly suggests she intentionally filters her fan mail, she also notes her intolerance of criticism from fellow performers in the comedy industry: "Guess who the fuck is buying the Gucci purses, motherfucker. Not you. Spend more time writing a joke too."[79] By minimizing the racist impact of her work, and actively shielding herself from the criticism of others who believe her use of racist discourse is harmful or exploitative, Lampanelli further strengthens her brand of *neoliberal white racial comedy*—emphasizing the seemingly well-intentioned, subversive, and commercial success of her comedy. In this way, Lampanelli denies the possibility that she has been exploiting and profiting from her use of racist discourse in her work.

CONCLUSION

In a society where public racist discourse was disavowed following the civil rights movement, comedians like Lampanelli have worked to publicly challenge constraints on public racist discourse by embracing and monetizing "political incorrectness." From this perspective, racist jokes are attacking not the racial and ethnic minorities they spotlight, or calls for racial equality and justice, but the "politically correct" policing of speech and censorship. According to these enterprising humorists, this use of racist humor is but an exercise in "freedom of expression." As Lampanelli contends: "By being politically correct, you're closing your mind to a different point of view. Which sounds a lot like prejudice. Which is definitely not politically correct."[80] While three decades ago it was conservative pundits leading the charge against political correctness, today it seems to be comedians like Lampanelli, who are raising the battle-cry by using their reputations as fearless "free speech crusaders" unafraid of using racial slurs and racist jokes in public to combat racism.

By framing the use of racist jokes as an act of "subversion" and limiting the definition of racism to "hate,"[81] Lampanelli and others reinforce an individualized neoliberal notion of racism that centers racism and racial ideology as merely expressions of individual prejudice.[82] But their perspective obscures the role that racist discourse, jokes, and comedy have long played in reinforcing and legitimizing racial inequality and racial violence. As Patton and Leonard contend:

> racial jokes allow white America to claim that race no longer matters, even as there's talk whizzing in every direction about how blacks and Latinos are outbreeding whites, are criminals and welfare queens, are "stealing jobs" and victimizing whites through affirmative action policies and denying them the right to use the n-word. Comedy allows these comforting ideas to be shared with a built-in defense mechanism that protects white innocence.[83]

As illustrated above, a *neoliberal white racial comedy* is also about protecting the white innocence of comedians profiting from the use of racist slurs and racist jokes while denying the possibility that such comedy may be socially harmful. But in an era where police and white supremacist racism and violence has become difficult to ignore, some white comedians have started changing their tune. Like Lampanelli, Sarah Silverman developed her reputation as a "shock comic" who made liberal use of racial stereotypes and slurs in her comedy during the 2000s.[84] Yet, in 2015, at the height of the Black Lives Matter protests, Silverman reflected on the nation's racial climate and questioned the use of racial jokes by comedians: "Racial jokes that were just kind of being absurd have less charm in a world where we're all very aware that white cops are killing black teenagers on a daily basis."[85] While police brutality and violence against people of color have long been the norm in US society, this history of police racial violence only emerged into significant public attention following a series of high-profile police shootings. In particular, Ferguson, Missouri became a focal point, after the mass demonstrations and civil rebellion that erupted following the shooting of Black teenager Michael Brown by white police officer Darren Wilson. The police department in Ferguson underwent a federal investigation by the US Justice Department, in order to determine whether racial bias was present within a mostly white police department in a predominantly Black city.

Some of the key evidence used by the DOJ in determining the presence of racial bias among officers was the circulation of racist jokes within the department. Take the following joke: "An African American woman in New Orleans was admitted into the hospital for a pregnancy termination. Two weeks later she received a check for $5,000. She phoned the hospital to ask who it was from. The hospital said, 'Crimestoppers.'"[86] This joke is eerily reminiscent of Lampanelli's joke referring to Black mortality as a form of crime-fighting. When Lampanelli shared that joke, she was heralded as a "fearless" comic who does not cater to audience sensibilities and political correctness. When white police officers shared essentially the same joke, it was used as evidence of "derogatory, dehumanizing and . . . impermissible bias" among Ferguson police.[87]

While it is important to keep "context" in mind when evaluating such humor, we should also keep in mind that a *neoliberal white racial comedy* has encouraged the societal acceptability, profitability, and continued circulation of racist jokes, slurs, and ridicule in a purportedly free speech and colorblind society as harmless fun. This same free speech society frames criticism and opposition to such comedy as "political correctness" and a danger to free speech. And it is this same society in which a racist political demagogue built a political campaign largely by attacking so-called "political correctness," while simultaneously ridiculing and insulting people of color all the way into the White House.[88]

In late 2018, two years after the election of Trump, Lampanelli, a former contestant on Trump's reality TV show *The Apprentice* (2004–2017), announced her departure from comedy, noting that perhaps the "message of including people through insults is getting lost."[89] But that message, it seems, was never lost on Trump, who understood the power of racist jokes and insults to uphold racist ideologies and structures, even when shared with "good intentions." By the time the "Queen of Mean" had her fill of racist jokes, began to have some doubts, and has since cashed out, it appears that a *neoliberal white racial comedy* fulfilled its true purpose.

Notes

1. Kristen West Savali, "Lisa Lampanelli and Her 'N***a': How a Comedian Became a Cliché," *Huffington Post*, February 22, 2013.

2. See, for example, Inkoo Kang, "How Amy Schumer Became this Generation's Latest Truth-teller," *The Village Voice*, May 20, 2015; Scott Raab, "Comedians as Prophets," *Esquire*, September 18, 2013.

3. See, for example, Megan Garber, "How Comedians Became Public Intellectuals," *The Atlantic*, May 28, 2015; Lawrence E. Mintz, "Standup Comedy as Social and Cultural Mediation," *American Quarterly* 37, no. 1 (1985): 71–80.

4. See, for example, Simon Weaver, *The Rhetoric of Racist Humour: US, UK and Global Race Joking* (Farnham, UK: Ashgate Publishing, 2011); Michael Billig, *Laughter and Ridicule: Towards a Social Critique of Humour* (Thousand Oaks, CA: Sage, 2005).

5. See, for example, Rebecca Krefting, *All Joking Aside: American Humor and Its Discontents* (Baltimore, MD: Johns Hopkins University Press, 2014); Jonathan P. Rossing, "Emancipatory Racial Humor as Critical Public Pedagogy: Subverting Hegemonic Racism," *Communication, Culture & Critique* 9, no. 4 (2015): 614–32; Jonathan P. Rossing, "Critical Race Humor in a Postracial Moment: Richard Pryor's Contemporary Parrhesia," *Howard Journal of Communications* 25, no. 1 (2014): 16–33.

6. In addition to Patton and Leonard, see Amanda Holpuch, "Daniel Tosh Apologises for Rape Joke as Fellow Comedians Defend Topic," *The Guardian*, July 11, 2012; John Hudson, "Tracy Morgan Under Fire for Homophobic Jokes," *The Atlantic*, June 10, 2011.

7. Paul Farhi, "'Seinfeld' Comic Richards Apologizes for Racial Rant," *The Washington Post*, November 21, 2006.

8. Jay C. Kang, "The Campaign to 'Cancel' Colbert," *The New Yorker*, March 30, 2014.

9. See for example Nicholas Barber, "Comedy in the Age of Outrage: When Jokes Go Too Far," *BBC Culture*, August 4, 2015; Jason Zinoman, "Political Correctness Isn't Ruining Comedy. It's Helping," *The New York Times*, October 20, 2015.

10. Lisa Lampanelli, "How Political Correctness is Killing Comedy," *The Hollywood Reporter*, May 2, 2013; Greg Lukianoff, "The Story Behind the New Documentary 'Can We Take a Joke?'" *The Huffington Post*, August 11, 2016.

11. Anna Silman, "10 Famous Comedians on How Political Correctness Is Killing Comedy: 'We Are Addicted to the Rush of Being Offended,'" *Salon.com*, June 10, 2015.

12. Krefting, *All Joking Aside*, 29.

13. Mintz, "Standup Comedy as Social and Cultural Mediation," 75.

14. Krefting, *All Joking Aside*, 29.

15. Weaver, *The Rhetoric of Racist Humour*.

16. See, for example, Michael Billig, "Humour and Hatred: The Racist Jokes of the Ku Klux Klan," *Discourse & Society* 12, no. 3 (2001): 267–89; Jason Wilson, "Hiding in Plain Sight: How the 'Alt-Right' is Weaponizing Irony to Spread Fascism," *The Guardian*, May 23, 2017.

17. Joe R. Feagin, *The White Racial Frame: Centuries of Racial Framing and Counter-framing* (Abingdon, UK: Routledge, 2013).

18. Raúl Pérez, "Learning to Make Racism Funny in the 'Color-blind' Era: Stand-up Comedy Students, Performance Strategies, and the (Re)Production of Racist Jokes in Public," *Discourse & Society* 24, no. 4 (2013): 478–503.

19. See, for example, John K. Wilson, *The Myth of Political Correctness: The Conservative Attack on Higher Education* (Durham, NC: Duke University Press, 1995); Moir Weigel, "Political Correctness: How the Right Invented a Phantom Enemy," *The Guardian*, November 30, 2016.

20. Anna Silman, "10 Famous Comedians on How Political Correctness is Killing Comedy," *Salon.com*, June 11, 2015.

21. Joseph Boskin, *Sambo: The Rise & Demise of an American Jester* (Oxford, UK: Oxford University Press, 1986).

22. See, for example, Alexander Saxton, "Blackface Minstrelsy and Jacksonian Ideology," *American Quarterly* 27, no. 1 (1975): 3–28; Eric Lott, *Love & Theft: Blackface Minstrelsy and the American Working Class* (Oxford, UK: Oxford University Press, 2013).

23. Joseph Boskin and Joseph Dorinson, "Ethnic Humor: Subversion and Survival," *American Quarterly* 37, no. 1 (1985): 81–97.

24. Feagin, *The White Racial Frame*.

25. In addition to Lott, see Saidiya V. Hartman, *Scenes of Subjection: Terror, Slavery, and Self-making in Nineteenth-Century America* (Oxford, UK: Oxford University Press, 1997).

26. See, for example, M. Alison Kibler, *Censoring Racial Ridicule: Irish, Jewish, and African American Struggles over Race and Representation, 1890–1930* (Chapel Hill, NC: University of North Carolina Press, 2015); Raúl Pérez, "Brownface Minstrelsy: José Jiménez, the Civil Rights Movement, and the Legacy of Racist Comedy," *Ethnicities* 16, no. 1 (2016): 40–67.

27. Michael Omi and Howard Winant, *Racial Formation in the United States* (Abingdon, UK: Routledge, 2014).

28. In addition to Boskin, see Mahadev L. Apte, "Ethnic Humor Versus 'Sense of Humor': An American Sociocultural Dilemma," *The American Behavioral Scientist* 30, no. 3 (1987): 27.

29. Pérez, "Brownface Minstrelsy."

30. See, for example, Lawrence Bobo, James R. Kluegel, and Ryan A. Smith, "Laissez-faire Racism: The Crystallization of a Kinder, Gentler, Antiblack Ideology," in *Racial Attitudes in the 1990s: Continuity and Change* (Westport, CT: Praeger, 1997), 23–25; Eduardo Bonilla-Silva, *Racism without Racists: Color-Blind Racism and the Persistence of Racial Inequality in America* (Lanham, MD: Rowman & Littlefield Publishers, 2013).

31. Jane Littlewood and Michael Pickering, "Gender, Ethnicity and Political Correctness in Comedy," in *Because I Tell a Joke or Two: Comedy, Politics, and Social Difference* (Abingdon, UK: Routledge 1998), 289–307.

32. Bambi Haggins, *Laughing Mad: The Black Comic Persona in Post-Soul America* (New Brunswick, NJ: Rutgers University Press, 2007).

33. Stephen Ford, "Comedian Carlin's Point Is to Make Point," *Daily News*, November 24, 1974.

34. Richard Zoglin, *Comedy at the Edge: How Stand-up in the 1970s Changed America* (London: Bloomsbury Publishing, 2009).

35. Gerald Nachman, *Seriously Funny: The Rebel Comedians of the 1950s and 1960s* (New York: Watson-Guptill Publications, 2004).

36. Littlewood and Pickering, "Gender, Ethnicity and Political Correctness in Comedy."

37. Weigel, "Political Correctness."

38. Wilson, *The Myth of Political Correctness*, 12.

39. Wilson, *The Myth of Political Correctness*, 7.

40. Peter Baker, "Now No Laughing Matter," *Washington Post*, March 21, 1993.

41. Peter L. Berger, *Redeeming Laughter: The Comic Dimension of Human Experience* (Berlin: Walter de Gruyter, 2014).

42. Raúl Pérez, "Rhetoric of Racial Ridicule in an Era of Racial Protest: Don Rickles, the 'Equal Opportunity Offender' Strategy, and the Civil Rights Movement," in *Standing Up, Speaking Out: Stand-Up Comedy and the Rhetoric of Social Change* (Abingdon, UK: Routledge, 2017): 71-91.

43. Raúl Pérez, "Racist Humor: Then and Now," *Sociology Compass* 10, no. 10 (2016): 928–38.

44. Edwin McDowell, "Ethnic Jokebooks Flourish Despite Criticism," *New York Times*, July 30, 1983.

45. Ben Brantley, "Jackie Mason; Politically Incorrect," *The New York Times*, April 6, 1994.

46. Bonilla-Silva, *Racism without Racists*.

47. Lisa Lampanelli, *Dirty Girl: No Protection*, (Seattle, WA: Jack Records, 2007).

48. Terry Armour, "Lampanelli Relishes the Leap from Deadlines to Punchlines," *Chicago Tribune*, December 1, 2006.

49. Todd Jackson, "Interview: Lisa Lampanelli, Stand-Up Comedian," *Dead-Frog.com*, February 19, 2007.

50. Jackson, "Lisa Lampanelli, Stand-Up Comedian."

51. It is worth noting here that Michael Richards's own defense, regarding his use of racist slurs, was that he believed he was "not a racist." See Judy Faber, "Kramer Apologizes. Says He's Not Racist," CBS News, November 20, 2006.

52. John E. Richardson, *Analysing Newspapers: An Approach from Critical Discourse Analysis* (Basingstoke, UK: Palgrave Macmillan, 2006), 15.

53. Armour, "Lampanelli Relishes the Leap from Deadlines to Punch Lines."

54. Jackson, "Lisa Lampanelli, Stand-Up Comedian"

55. Jeanine Budd, "Lisa Lampanelli Insults Her Way through NU," *The Huntington News*, February 27, 2008.

56. Askmen.com, "Lisa Lampanelli . . . Wants You to Take It Like a Man," *Askmen.com*, July 20, 2007.

57. Pérez, "Learning to Make Racism Funny."

58. Askmen.com, "Lisa Lampanelli . . . Wants You to Take It Like a Man."

59. Paul Farhi, "'Insult Comic' Lisa Lampanelli Is on a Roll and at the Warner Theatre," *The Washington Post*, January 24, 2009.

60. Lampanelli, "How Political Correctness is Killing Comedy."

61. Askmen.com, "Lisa Lampanelli . . . Wants You to Take It Like a Man."

62. Dylan Gadino, "Lisa Lampanelli: Highly Insulting!" *Laughspin.com*, February 5, 2006.

63. Budd, "Lisa Lampanelli Insults Her Way through NU."
64. Nicole Powers, "Lisa Lampanelli: Queen of Mean," *Suicidegirls.com,* January 30, 2009.
65. Ann Farmer, "Fearlessly Foul, and on the Verge of Respectability," *The New York Times,* February 10, 2008.
66. John Wenzel, "Don't Let the Dress Fool You: Lampanelli's no June Cleaver," *The Denver Post,* June 25, 2008.
67. Raúl Pérez, "Race, Gender, and Comedy Awards: From Civil Rights to Color-blindness," *Comedy Studies* 8, no. 1 (2017): 68–80.
68. Farhi, "Insult Comic" Lisa Lampanelli Is on a Roll and at the Warner Theatre."
69. Farhi, "Insult Comic" Lisa Lampanelli Is on a Roll and at the Warner Theatre."
70. Farmer, "Fearlessly Foul, and on the Verge of Respectability."
71. Askmen.com. "Lisa Lampanelli . . . Wants You to Take It Like a Man."
72. Gadino, "Lisa Lampanelli: Highly Insulting!"
73. Powers, "Lisa Lampanelli: Queen of Mean."
74. Gadino, "Lisa Lampanelli: Highly Insulting!"
75. Powers, "Lisa Lampanelli: Queen of Mean."
76. Farmer, "Fearlessly Foul, and on the Verge of Respectability."
77. Gadino, "Lisa Lampanelli: Highly Insulting!"
78. Powers, "Lisa Lampanelli: Queen of Mean."
79. Jackson, "Lisa Lampanelli, Stand-Up Comedian."
80. Lampanelli, "How Political Correctness is Killing Comedy."
81. Raúl Pérez, "Racism without Hatred? Racist Humor and the Myth of 'Colorblindness,'" *Sociological Perspectives* 60, no. 5 (2017): 956–74.
82. Bonilla-Silva, *Racism without Racists.*
83. Stacey Patton and David J. Leonard, "Don't Believe Her Defenders. Amy Schumer's Jokes are Racist." *Washington Post,* July 6, 2015, https://www.washingtonpost.com/posteverything/wp/2015/07/06/dont-believe-her-defenders-amy-schumers-jokes-are-racist/.
84. Fiona Sturges, "Sarah Silverman: Funny Woman or Foul-Mouthed Racist?" *The Independent,* October 18, 2008.
85. Benjamin Lee, "Sarah Silverman: Ferguson Changed My Attitude to Race Jokes," *The Guardian,* September 16, 2015.
86. United States Department of Justice, "Investigation of the Ferguson Police Department," *Civil Rights Division,* March 4, 2015, 72.
87. Pérez, "Racism without Hatred?"
88. Jessica Gantt Shafer, "'Donald Trump's 'Political Incorrectness': Neoliberalism as Frontstage Racism on Social Media," *Social Media + Society* 3, no. 3 (2017).
89. *The Howard Stern Show,* "Lisa Lampanelli Announces Her Retirement from Stand-Up Comedy," filmed October 2018, YouTube video, 1:28, posted October 2018, https://www.youtube.com/watch?v=i7tQKSeBLyA.

7

LEGUIZAMO'S COMIC FRAME
Identity and the Art of Impersonation

Miriam M. Chirico

> The comic frame should enable people to be *observers of themselves, while acting*. Its ultimate would not be *passiveness*, but *maximum consciousness*. . . . It considers human life as a project in "composition," where the poet works with the material of social relationships.
> —Kenneth Burke[1]

INTRODUCTION: IDENTITY AS NEGOTIATION

In describing the creative process behind her performance piece *Fires in the Mirror*, Anna Deavere Smith notes, "In America, identity is always being negotiated."[2] Smith, a monologist working in the genre of mimetic realism, relies on techniques of impersonation to enact the dynamic and contested process of identity formation. John Leguizamo also incorporates impersonation into his monologues to explore identity, but unlike Smith, he involves *comedic* impersonation. Over a twenty-five-year career in the theater, from his early one-man shows *Mambo Mouth* (1991) and *Spic-O-Rama* (1991), to his later autobiographical pieces, *Freak* (1998), *Sexaholix . . . A Love Story* (2002), and *Ghetto Klown* (2010), to his most recent work *Latin History for Morons* (2016), he uses his on-stage persona to explore Latino identity and to contribute to a public discourse about identity politics.[3] He enacts the construction of Latino identity either by creating imaginary characters or by sharing personal anecdotes; his experiences as a Colombian immigrant growing up in Jackson Heights, Queens, or as an actor moving into the majority white TV and film industry are all material for his one-man shows.

Moreover, his use of comedy as his generic motif, interacting with the audience as a stand-up comedian might do, allows him to observe himself—in Kenneth Burke's terms—in this process of identity negotiation, and to do so publicly. Leguizamo uses comedic impersonation to stand outside himself; he becomes the dominant other and views himself from the other's oppositional gaze. In other words, his humorous impersonations are more than entertainment; they endeavor to intellectualize the process of identity formation, contingent as it is upon the dominant-majority gaze. His intellectual contribution to identity politics is to dramatize the marginalized status of the "scrappy outsider,"[4] as he phrases it, within a multicultural society. Furthermore, his performances reveal the insubstantiality of his own identity.

"Identity is negotiated," Smith explains, expressing that humans do not have one fixed, essential identity, but shuffle between various selves based on context, physical location, and interpersonal relationships. The depiction of any identity, as social psychologists are quick to point out, is not simply a projection of personality, but a dynamic involvement with another. Identity is not a solid core consisting of a bundle of traits, but actually a series of malleable roles that evolve through interactive relationships and that shift depending on social circumstances. In an oft-cited phrase from *The Principles of Psychology*, William James attributed personal identity not to the individual himself or herself, but to the perception others hold of that individual; he contended, "A man has as many social selves as there are individuals who recognize him."[5] Within a homogeneous society, this malleable self does not pose a problem; an individual might easily mitigate his or her identity moving between similar social environments, such as work, places of worship, and community organizations. Regardless of where he goes, the view that others hold of him is more or less uniform and does not require radical adjustments nor create moments of self-doubt. However, within a heterogeneous society, the individual receives less reassurance or affirming feedback. Growing up in a multiethnic neighborhood, Leguizamo experienced inconsistent attitudes and internalized the racist labels applied to him by others: "When you are by yourself [i.e., the only Latino family in a neighborhood], and somebody calls you names, you believe it. I thought 'we are the parasites of the universe.'"[6] Leguizamo's monologues frequently speak to this process of absorbing the negative perception of others and making adjustments to his identity in order to assimilate to mainstream culture.

IDENTITY AND THE AWARENESS OF STEREOTYPES

The individual member of an ethnic or racial minority attempts to construct an identity in contradistinction to larger social forces, to modify his or her behavior to that of the dominant social norms. Whether it is assimilation (i.e., trying to *appear* like everyone else) or opposition (i.e., rebelling against cultural norms), the identity is still constructed in a dialectical relation to a dominant US majority. The sociological model of the "looking-glass self," a concept introduced by the sociologist Charles Cooley, helpfully describes the process of identity formation as an individual seeing him- or herself reflected in the reactions of other people. That is, as we read the subjective responses of others to our speech and behavior, we correct our identities to align with or even to challenge those views. However, from the perspective of racial or ethnic minorities, the model of the "looking-glass self" presents a precarious position, as the individual is never certain whether he or she is acting true-to-self or fulfilling an expected stereotype. The reflection he or she receives back from others will be distorted based on biased expectations, and thus the interchange of the looking-glass self will be limited by these circumscribed perceptions. Some Latino/a writers have described this model of identity-making positively, as a collaboration. For example, William Luis metaphorically describes the interdependent association of Anglo-Americans and Latinos: "Once the two partners engage in the dance, both will change; neither one will remain the same."[7] Leguizamo sees this partnered relationship as slightly more one-sided, where one partner must temper his moves according to the dominant partner's cues and feedback. "That's what culture is," Leguizamo wrote in an early opinion piece for the *New York Times*: "you are permitted particular codes of behavior."[8] In this way, one's cultural or ethnic identity is not so much a revelation of personal traits as a specific slate of attributes that the dominant culture inscribes onto the minority group.

Latinos growing up in majority white America often feel like second-class citizens, as Leguizamo readily attests,[9] because of the dominant white majority's perception of Latinos' inferiority. Leguizamo has a history of challenging such negative representation, through public advocacy but mostly through his performances. He began creating and performing his dramatic pieces at a time when the public saw very few positive representations of Latino actors.[10] In fact, Leguizamo and Paul Rodriguez were considered the only prominent Latino comic actors of the 1980s and 1990s, and Leguizamo's shows released on HBO were arguably the "first significant exposure of Latino culturally intimate humor to a substantial non-Latino audience."[11]

Latinos represented 13 percent of the American population in the 1980s, while programs televised at that time contained only 3 percent Latino characters, typically on crime drama TV series such as *CHiPs* (1977–1983), *Miami Vice* (1984–1989),[12] or *L.A. Law* (1986–1992).[13] Other shows that featured Latinos typically depicted them as gang members or criminals, manipulating the public's impressions of Latinos. In his play *Freak* Leguizamo humorously spoofs on the disproportionate number of televised Latino lawbreakers, although the joke is double-edged. He refers to one of his cousins, Speedy, as "that shirtless Latin guy that you see on *Cops* [1989–2020] each week,"[14] toying with the stereotypical depiction of Latinos as criminals. He describes how his cousins would engage him in play-acting these televised weekly run-ins with police officers, in a game called "police brutality." Tossing a gun into the young John's unsuspecting hands, they would apprehend him violently and beat him up. The story cheekily satirizes the media's programmatic reliance upon such adverse portrayals as a consumer good. This perpetuation of stereotypes for entertainment purposes is not without repercussions; as Leguizamo noted in an op-ed piece for the *New York Times*, the lack of positive Latino representation in history books and televised media paved the way for Donald Trump's racist campaign rhetoric.[15]

The public dissemination of such biased representation is not the entertainment industry's only collateral damage; the limited acting roles available to Latinos and the subsequent necessity of accepting stereotypical parts damages an ethnic minority's understanding of him- or herself as a professional and as an individual. Leguizamo has pointed to the irresponsibility of the entertainment industry in choosing to cast non-Latino actors in Latino parts in movies such as *The House of the Spirits* (August, 1993), *Death and the Maiden* (Polanski, 1994), and *The Perez Family* (Nair, 1995),[16] a practice that further limits acting opportunities for Latinos. During the successful run of *Mambo Mouth*, he wrote an editorial for the *New York Times* exposing the danger Latino actors face of being cast in acting roles where they are required to play a stereotype of themselves; not only does the limited nature of these roles reify the public's perception of the minority group, but it corrupts the actor's own sense of identity. He described his meager options as being asked to play only the "drug pusher/terrorist/immigrant/gigolo" within the "Spicorama of television and film": "In *Miami Vice* I am the cocaine mafia prince from a big Colombian drug-dealing family; in the movie *Revenge* [Scott, 1990], I'm a silent Mexican—a gun-toting lackey; in *Die Hard 2* [Harlin, 1990], I'm a terrorist; in *Regarding Henry* [Nichols, 1991], I'm the mugger. I turned four film parts down in February: two were gang members and two were drug dealers."[17] It is worth drawing attention to Leguizamo's use of the verb "to be" in this passage (i.e., "I *am* the cocaine mafia prince"), as if these acting roles were somehow intrinsic to his own self-identity. This construction is a telling rhetorical maneuver indicating the psychological harm that such restricted roles inflicted upon him and his fellow Latino actors. Furthermore, he and his colleagues acknowledged that they perpetuated such negative ethnic representations out of financial necessity. They understood that the economic reality of the movie industry required that they compromise their identities. They would "act ghetto" during their auditions for these roles portraying negative stereotypes, well aware that "we were denigrating our race, but we were making paper at the same time."[18]

Many of Leguizamo's monologues testify to the internalized racism inculcated by viewing oneself through the assumed superiority of the European aesthetic. His character impersonations reveal, as he describes it, the "toxic shame that is ingrained into you,"[19] even as they critically interrogate the power the "white gaze" has over identity formation. The opening vignette of *Mambo Mouth* illustrates the destructive self-awareness of the white gaze as mediated by the TV and film industry. The self-idolizing talk-show host, Agamemnon, shares with his audience a love scene he performed with an older white woman in a feature film, identifying himself as the lascivious Latin lover, RRRRRRRamón, the Cuban cabana boy. "I'm dark, devilish, desperate, *Catolico*, and illegal, oh yes, very illegal," he says, humorously acknowledging how he played the stereotype expected of Latino men: i.e., dark hair and olive complexion, with assertive masculinity, an obsessive sexual drive, and an illegal status. Agamemnon is thus aware of himself objectively, playing the "type" the viewing audience expects. Furthermore, the two characters project their stereotypical fantasies onto each other, as absurd as they are, fulfilling William James's notion that a person has "as many social selves as there are persons who recognize him"[20]: "She calls me Chocolate Eyes," Agamemnon says, reenacting the dialogue with the older, white tourist; "I call her Albino Beauty. She calls me her greasy, treacherous raven. I call her (*licks fingers and yanks her imaginary hair*) Grandmother!"[21] He enacts the camera angles as they occur, referring to "close-up" and "dolly shot," framing his face with his hands, or crossing the stage in a semi-crouch to mimic a camera following him at a low angle.[22] By enacting both the camera's movement and that of the character of Ramón, the mediated public gaze and the objectified actor, Leguizamo satirizes media distortion, emphasizing that two actors are no more realistic than the anticipated demands of the moviegoing audience make them out to be. Caught in the lens of the camera, their identities are dictated by what the filmmaker wishes to portray and are constructed by what the audience wishes to consume. The representational layering of Leguizamo playing Agamemnon playing Ramón is a brilliant metatheatrical device used to explode our reliance upon stereotypes. It also speaks to Leguizamo's use of creative acting techniques "that produce authentic breakdowns in the dominant images of the American mass media."[23]

Another character, Rafael Gigante, from *Spic-O-Rama*, is based on Leguizamo's experiences of being excluded from acting roles because of his accented speech patterns. He demonstrates a ludicrously exaggerated awareness of the white gaze when he tries to pass himself off as the purported love child of Sir Laurence Olivier, with the help of Clorox and British Received Pronunciation. Disguising his ethnic markers of identity before he leaves for an audition, Rafael literally assembles his self onstage. He increases his height with platform shoes and puts on a striped shirt to give him "that lengthy look" that Euro-American male actors possess (he also stuffs his shorts for a similar "lengthy look"). Casting glances in the mirror to appraise his newly constructed identity, he fabricates a looking-glass encounter with an imaginary interlocutor: "Excuse me, squire, aren't you that famous actor?"[24] he inquires of himself. The entire skit is an identity con job; Raphael is delighted to be subverting the institutional dictates that require a white physiognomy. The only moment he experiences self-doubt is when he notes the unusual color of his skin, a mid-tone between black and white: "I'm urine-colored" he declares, horrified.[25] Leguizamo's portrayal of Rafael demonstrates a Latino who examines his mirrored image not in the spirit of self-reflection, but as he supposes others see him, driving home the point that in trying to pass as white, he embraces a level of self-denial that results in a loss of self-worth.

Leguizamo frequently highlights how ethnicity and race are tropes. In addition to this comic skit about racial passing, he emphasizes identity's fungible nature in performance by playfully manipulating ethnic, gender, and class markers. For example, in both *Mambo Mouth* and *Spic-O-Rama* he changed his clothing and wigs in full view of the audience—with the help of his assistant: the two hid behind a scrim, and backlighting projected their shadows as they donned and removed accessories. In his later plays, Leguizamo interchangeably impersonates dozens of characters, putting on accents, gestures, behaviors, and postures. The rapidity with which he transforms from one person into another drives home the point that racial or ethnic identities can be performed. Ben Brantley specifically underscores the remarkable fluidity of transformations in his review of *Freak*: "Mr. Leguizamo carries on four- and five-person dialogues without any noticeable clicks of transition. One moment he is clearly and unconditionally one person; one moment he's another. It's as simple and unfathomable as that. . . . Like the great Richard Pryor, [Leguizamo] understands that race is less a matter of skin color than a way of talking, walking, dancing and just standing."[26] By thus showcasing the accessories or the actions that constitute each character, Leguizamo demonstrates that the traits we assume to be inherent in our identity—mannerisms, attire, hair style—are choices, both chosen as well as imposed.

It is this imposition of ethnic markers that concerns minority actors in television and film: they worry about fulfilling the majority culture's stereotypical beliefs when they play to type. The minority individual is burdened by such imaginary projections from other members of society, never being sure if he or she is acting naturally or fulfilling stereotypical expectations. Wanda Sykes, in fact, created a comic routine around the white gaze prompting a heightened awareness of her racial identity in her TV special, *I'ma Be Me* (McCarthy, 2009). She recounts a scene from her childhood where her mother chastises her and her sister because their desire to dance fulfilled a racial stereotype: "you ain't dancing in my car. White people are looking at you."[27] The self-consciousness Sykes describes as a Black woman under the gaze of a white majority society undermines her personal expression of joy, and she consequently works to discover her true self—i.e., "I'ma be me"—regardless of white culture's expectations. Likewise, Leguizamo draws attention to this loss of an authentic sense of self in his autobiographical plays. In *Freak*, he enacts a scene from early in his career when a director insisted that he act "More Latino [on the stage]. I wanna feel the agony and patheticness of your people . . . more junkie, think Latino!"[28] Later, in *Ghetto Klown*, he shares how the film crew from *Casualties of War* (De Palma, 1989) wanted him "to talk like Cheech and Chong"[29] to correlate with their fantasy image of a Latino. For the racial minority who is fabricating an identity or the immigrant who is struggling to conform to the expectations of the community, Cooley's concept of a reflected self becomes a downright existential burden.

QUANDARY: THE SEARCH FOR AUTHENTIC IDENTITY

Leguizamo's autobiographical pieces contend with this particular existential quandary of identity formation, but he goes one step further. Through his skills of impersonation he embodies both himself and the looking-glass spectator, literally transforming himself into the other "looking" characters and adopting their race, age, ethnicity, gender, or class. In so doing, he both narrates and dramatizes a dialectical development of identity. In one scene from his show *Freak*, he plays both his father and himself. The name "freak" is given to him as a young boy when his intoxicated father invites his son to give him a kiss but then berates him for kissing him on the mouth instead of the cheek: "Not on the lips, you little freak!"[30] In accepting this given identity as a "freak," Leguizamo acknowledges his sense of familial and societal dislocation. His youth is filled with tales of difference, reinforcing his identity as culturally deviant: first he recounts his encounter with the Fresh-Air Fund family of WASPs who mark John as "primitive" because he is uncircumcised (one brother describes his penis as "a mouse in a garden hose")[31]; then he imitates the boys in the Irish neighborhood who threaten to "wipe up the street with ya, you little wetback"[32]; next he portrays the Italians who yelled at him "Youse douchebags ruined this neighborhood" after Leguizamo's family arrived.[33] He spoofs the German woman at Kentucky Fried Chicken with whom his father arranged for John to lose his virginity saying, "Your swarthy looks are so dark and I feel sorry for you, so I will fuck you. I'll think of it as war reparations,"[34] and he transforms himself into his African American girlfriend who laughingly tells him, "Oh, my God, you are the whitest motherfucker I ever saw. You glow in the dark."[35] Like Wanda Sykes, who was sensitive to the white gaze, Leguizamo explores the various interpretations of his identity through the eyes of others; he is either primitive, or inferior, or subjugated, or too light-skinned, or too dark. Even his friendship with Latino college students results in a perception of himself as politically naïve because of his accidental use of the word "Hispanic": "Shut up, stupid! Stop talking shit! It's Latino, you colonized eunuch," they upbraid him.[36] These childhood scenarios, based on dialectical interactions with diverse people, imbue him with contradictory views of himself. But Leguizamo goes one step beyond the looking-glass model through his use of impersonation. Not only does he see himself from the viewpoint of the WASPy father, or his Black girlfriend, or his classmates—he *impersonates* these individuals and thus dramatizes for the audience the process by which he sees himself subjugated to the other person's gaze.

In *Ghetto Klown*, Leguizamo shares anecdotes through which he constructs his identity oppositionally, this time within the white-coded world of Hollywood—or "Holly-wouldn't," as Leguizamo quips about the industry's inaccessibility to minorities.[37] He reenacts various conflicts he experienced with established white male actors. Steven Seagal punched him in the solar plexus and threw him against a wall, for example, and he got into fisticuffs with Patrick Swayze on the set of *To Wong Foo* (Kidron, 1995). He offers a sketch about working with Sean Penn while filming the movie *Casualties of War* where Penn was required to strike the side of Leguizamo's face. Penn's choice as a method actor to put real force behind his blow resulted in Leguizamo's face becoming significantly swollen and bruised as they filmed the scene multiple times. Unfortunately, the scene was later edited out of the film. Leguizamo interprets this interaction from a racial perspective, wherein a prominent white man physically abuses a Latino under the approval of an authority figure, the director, only to have the evidence destroyed. He compares his experience of licensed battery to the history of whites conquering Latinos, reflecting back to the time "when my great, great Incan grandmother was being raped by conquistadores . . . when the CIA turned our countries into Banana Republics . . . when Madonna stole Latin Freestyle from Lisa Lisa and the Cult Jam!"[38] Even with the comedic twist at the end, the narration makes the metaphor of racial domination explicit. By impersonating Sean Penn and Brian De Palma in this act of condoned aggression, Leguizamo adopts the perspective of the white actor and director who insist upon his acquiescence within an employment sector defined by white rules.

Another conflict occurred while filming the movie *Carlito's Way* (De Palma, 1993). Leguizamo started ad-libbing dialogue as an acting technique in order to find his center during a critical scene, but his experimental playfulness angered Al Pacino. In his rebuke, Pacino's language was emasculating: "Who said you could act with men? I don't know *who you know* or *whose cock you're sucking* to keep this job, but I swear, I will to go the *head of the studio*."[39] He then calls Leguizamo a clown: "Just be yourself, you clown. Take off your clown makeup and be yourself, John. Because you're a clown. You're a clown."[40] As much as this conflict shows once again an established white actor denigrating a Latino, it also reveals how Leguizamo sees himself from Pacino's perspective as a "Klown," because in his monologue he is playing both roles: Pacino and himself. He perceives himself as foolish and immature, but he simultaneously positions himself as the object of the dominant white gaze, as a minority struggling against the paternalistic authority of directors and fellow actors. Reappropriating the term "Klown," Leguizamo casts himself as an anarchist funny-man rebelling against the inherent hubris of the movie industry. In other words, he both absorbs Pacino's abusive comment and subverts it, aligning himself with the comedic court jesters of yesteryear whose special status allowed them to mock the king. Through his mocking impersonations of Sean Penn and Al Pacino, Leguizamo is able get the last laugh by reducing these men to ciphers of pomposity, and he gains the audience's approval and agreement.[41]

TRYING IT ON: IDENTITY AND IMPERSONATION

Leguizamo developed his impersonation skills in his youth, using spot-on imitations to avoid confrontations by eliciting laughter from police officers in his neighborhood or from the bullies who threatened to beat him up. He honed his skills working for The First Amendment Comedy Troupe, an improv group, as well as the Off Center Theater, a diverse children's theater troop that revised fairy tales to showcase Black and Latino characters.[42] Leguizamo's ability to impersonate different people comes from his improvisational receptiveness to adopting multiple identities. In other words, his work in improvisation enabled him to liberate the self to become the other.[43] Moreover, Leguizamo's impersonation of multiple characters is what stands out in performance, and critics emphasize his protean talent in theater reviews. John Lahr uses the term "one man universe" to describe the sensation of watching Leguizamo,[44] and Brantley, referring to the play *Freak*, describes the "whole city of people inside this young man's slender frame."[45] Anna Deavere Smith, whose dramatic work evolved from reflecting deeply about the acting process, emphasizes how she uses impersonation as a mode of empathy, a bridge towards understanding the other person's world view or experiences, a method of "travel from the self to other."[46] Smith develops her documentary-style theater from interviews with real-life individuals, and uses her talents of mimicry as an acting technique whereby she can experience another person's perspective by inhabiting his or her speech and gestural pattern. According to her reasoning, if identity consists of the words a person speaks and the actions he or she does, then adopting those speech and gestural patterns can give some insight into the other's perspective. Leguizamo follows a similar formula in his two early plays, *Mambo Mouth* and *Spic-O-Rama*, incarnating multiple characters in order to showcase a collective Latino identity. In *Mambo Mouth*, for example, he portrayed a talk-show host, a thirteen-year-old hyperkinetic boy, a transvestite, a man arrested for domestic battery, an illegal alien, and finally an image consultant worried about "passing" in the corporate world.

In his autobiographical pieces, however, the functionality behind his impersonation shifts. No longer is he an actor universalizing the Latino identity through various characters. Instead, he enacts himself in relationship with the dominant other. In *Freak, Sexaholix,* and *Ghetto Klown*, he impersonates the diverse people with whom he interacts on a social or professional level, switching quickly between roles of self and other to enact himself as the subjugated other. As he dramatizes these dialectical interactions, he is able to act out the power differential that subjugates his identity to another's expectations. From the WASPy father or Irish neighborhood thugs in *Freak* to Sean Penn and Al Pacino in *Ghetto Klown*, Leguizamo adopts the identity of the dominant other and *acts out* or *impersonates* in front of an audience these separate selves that in turn determine his own identity. Through embodying the "Other," he shows how he witnesses himself through their eyes; in other words, he dramatically enacts Cooley's "looking-glass" model of self-formation on stage. He fabricates his own identity in contradistinction to the imposed racial and ethnic norms, playfully dramatizing a process of "oppositional improvisation"[47] in response to these dominant expectations.

Leguizamo shares many personal details about his life through his monologues, such as his need for the approval of others and his frequent bouts of depression and near professional collapse (*Ghetto Klown*, 2014). It is no surprise that his work of transforming himself based on the expectations of others could create self-doubt: "You don't even know yourself," his father rebukes him in *Freak*. Ben Brantley comments on Leguizamo's lack of a defined core personality in performance and attributes it to the comedian's multitudinous impersonations. He even alludes to the amorphous character in the Kurt Vonnegut story "Who Am I This Time?" a figure who so thoroughly lacks a core identity that he depends upon the roles he plays in the local community theater to define his life.[48] However, it is important to see Leguizamo's strength in sharing with the audience his quest for self. His choice to admit to an inchoate self that he shapes and reshapes upon a stage before the audience is to make himself vulnerable. Laurie Stone praises Leguizamo for his courage in sharing this vulnerability, particularly in light of the typical "strut and chest-thump" associated with Latino machismo.[49] Leguizamo's one-man shows are marked by the same vulnerability in front of an audience that stand-up comedy possesses, with its presumed expression of the comedian's "naked self"[50] or its "illusion of intimacy."[51] As Stephen Holden notes in his review of *Mambo Mouth*, "In an increasingly conformist social climate, where appearances of propriety account for so much, [monologists] strip naked psychically, revealing fantasies that may be universal but that are still socially unmentionable."[52] Leguizamo makes visible the mask that he wears by allowing the audience not only to see the mask, but to view the struggle for selfhood that lies behind the mask.

On an aesthetic level, another principle is at work in Leguizamo's monologues: the comic frame. Comedy, according to Kenneth Burke, is a frame of acceptance. In his work *Attitudes Toward History*, Burke describes various modes of artistic representation, such as comedy, tragedy, satire, or the grotesque, as frames of acceptance or rejection, based on how these literary forms enabled people to cope with a given set of historical circumstances.

"Like tragedy," he writes, "comedy warns against the dangers of pride, but its emphasis shifts from crime to stupidity.... The progress of human enlightenment can go no further than in picturing people not as vicious, but as mistaken."[53] Contemplating the idea of comedy as a strategy of living does much to explain the benefit Leguizamo derives from writing his plays—particularly his latest one, *Latin History for Morons*, where he admits that his inability to instill self-pride in his son is due to a lack of historical grounding in his own heritage.[54] This quest for self-education originates as a family drama; Leguizamo states his intention to learn about Latino history in an effort to fortify his twelve-year old son against ethnic harassment by his classmates. During his educational journey, Leguizamo discovered the significant number of Latino accomplishments absent from the historical record. Reflecting upon these absences, Leguizamo experiences a mixture of emotions: "First of all, you're angered, then you're heartbroken, and then you feel empowered. It's incredible. It's like the stages of empowerment, you know? Anger, sadness or loss, and then hilarity. I definitely did feel that."[55] Although one of the reviewers criticized the play for its "easy" laughter and for its failure to castigate European colonizers for their wrongs-doings,[56] Leguizamo's monologue purposefully points to his own agency; he considers himself one of the "morons" of the play's title because of his ignorance. He understands that educating himself and sharing his history is imbricated into the shifting perception of Latino identity within the United States. In an interview, he acknowledges that his early work in the theater was his attempt to "test the waters of what [he] could and couldn't be" and to see how far he could "push the boundaries. But I soon saw the boundaries were mostly in my own head. What I saw on TV and in movies and books did not apply to the real world. I found that the real world, once I gave it a chance, was pretty open and tolerant and curious."[57] The boundaries of ethnic identity are both real and fictional, according to Leguizamo—that is, both socially contingent and open to interpretation. As Burke notes, "The comic frame, in making a man the student of himself, makes it possible for him to 'transcend' occasions when he has been tricked or cheated."[58] Leguizamo's comedic impersonations allow him to explore how his ethnic self-identification depends upon such boundaries of difference, and inculcates in him a desire to transcend such fatuous perspectives.

In the conclusion to his book, *Ethnic Humor in Multiethnic America*, David Gillota asks an interesting question about whether or not multiethnic humor could serve the function that comedy typically purports to serve, which is to unify: "what might an American ethnic humor, based on solidarity rather than ethnic boundaries, look like?" He appreciates the difficulty behind his question in its totalizing nature, but nevertheless believes that "it is possible for humorists to be deeply entrenched in their ethnic affiliation and simultaneously embrace a distinctly American identity."[59] Leguizamo's work may justifiably be considered an example of such unifying ethnic comedy. His intellectual contribution to the discourse on race resides in performing the ethnic body on stage and using it to lampoon the biased representation of Latinos in the United States. His monologues dramatize the fragmented sense of identity known to so many immigrants. In his autobiographical pieces, his use of impersonation demonstrates how identity is a social and cultural construction; i.e., by impersonating the self as well as the other, he demonstrates how so much of his own sense of self is contingent upon the acknowledgment of a majority white gaze, real or imagined. Most importantly, over a prolific thirty-year career, Leguizamo has shared his authentic search for identity, as he presses against the limitations that minorities experience and expresses his right to take part in the pluralistic realm that is America.

Notes

1. Kenneth Burke, *Attitudes Toward History*, 3rd edition (Berkeley: University of California Press, 1984), 171–73.

2. Anna Deavere Smith, "Introduction," in *Fires in the Mirror: Crown Heights, Brooklyn and Other Identities* (New York: Anchor Books, 1993), xxxiii.

3. Leguizamo is easily one of the most accomplished Latino actors on the stage and screen. David Román explores the success of Leguizamo's play *Freak* in *Performance in America: Contemporary Culture and the Performing Arts* (Durham, NC: Duke University Press, 2005), 100–136. *Mambo Mouth* won a 1991 Obie and Outer Critics Circle Award, followed by *Spic-O-Rama* (1993). Equally popular, the autobiographical *Freak* earned him Tony Award nominations for Best Actor and Best Play. *Latin History for Morons*, which premiered at Berkeley Repertory Theater in 2016, had an entirely sold-out run after transferring to Public Theater in New York in 2017. It moved to Studio 54 on Broadway and was nominated for a Tony in 2018.

4. Charles Isherwood, "Theater Review: Ghetto Klown. A Queens Guy Toughs It Out in Hollywood," *New York Times*, March 22, 2011.

5. William James, *The Principles of Psychology*, 2 vols. (New York: Henry Holt and Company, 1918), 294.

6. Somini Sengupta, "The Stuff of Memories and Manic Wit: A Comic Revisits Queens, the Source Of Material for His Broadway Show," *New York Times*, May 4, 1998.

7. William Luis, *Dance between Two Cultures: Latino Caribbean Literature Written in the United States* (Nashville, TN: Vanderbilt University Press, 1997), xv.

8. John Leguizamo, "New Voices from Latinolandia Whisper in America's Ear," *The New York Times*, July 14, 1991.

9. Recently, Leguizamo met an older Latina woman backstage after his show *Latin History for Morons*, and she shared how his performance helped lessen her feelings of low

self-worth. Michael Schulman, "John Leguizamo's Latino-History Lecture," *The New Yorker*, November 15, 2017.

10. The history of comedic Latino performers in American mass media is not only paltry but guilty of fostering stereotypes: Desi Arnaz played the heavily accented Ricky Ricardo on *I Love Lucy* (1951–1957), Freddie Prinze took a role many saw as simplistic and clownish on the sit-com *Chico and the Man* (1974–1978), and Cheech Marin embraced a lazy, unintelligent persona in the *Cheech and Chong* films.

11. Evan Cooper, "Looking at the Latin 'Freak': Audience Reception of John Leguizamo's Culturally Intimate Humor," *Latino Studies* 6 (2008): 437.

12. Leguizamo starred in a two-episode sequence on *Miami Vice* at the age of nineteen, playing the part of a Colombian cocaine dealer who comes to Miami to avenge his father's death. As much as he deplored the part, it earned him an agent and membership in the Screen Actors Guild (SAG).

13. Ed Morales, "We Ought to Be in Pictures," in *Mass Media Issues*, 7th ed., ed. Denis Mercier (Dubuque, IA: Kendall/ Hunt, 2002); quoted in John Markert, "*The George Lopez Show*: The Same Old Hispano?" *Bilingual Review/La Revista Bilingüe* 28, no. 2 (May–August 2004–2007): 149.

14. John Leguizamo, *Freak*, in *The Works of John Leguizamo: Freak, Spic-O-Rama, Mambo Mouth and Sexaholix* (New York: HarperCollins, 2008), 9–10.

15. John Leguizamo, "Too Bad You're Latin," *New York Times*, October 21, 2016.

16. Valerie Menard, "In Living Color," *Hispanic* 8, no. 4 (May 1995): 16.

17. Leguizamo, "New Voices from Latinolandia."

18. John Leguizamo, *Pimps, Hos, Playa Hatas, and All the Rest of My Hollywood Friends: My Life* (New York: HarperCollins, 2006), 51.

19. Leguizamo, *Pimps, Hos*, 113.

20. James, *Principles*, 218.

21. John Leguizamo, *Mambo Mouth*, in *Works*, 197.

22. Leguizamo, *Works*, 197–98.

23. Gastón Adolfo Alzate, "When the Subaltern is Politically Incorrect: A Cultural Analysis of the Performance Art of John Leguizamo," in *The State of Latino Theater in the United States: Hybridity, Transculturation, and Identity*, ed. Luis A. Ramos-García (New York: Routledge, 2002), 133.

24. John Leguizamo, *Spic-O-Rama*, in *Works*, 129.

25. Leguizamo, *Mambo Mouth*, 127–29.

26. Ben Brantley, "A One-Man Melting Pot Bubbling Over with Demons," *New York Times*, February 13, 1998.

27. Wanda Sykes, *I'ma Be Me*, TV movie, 2008.

28. Leguizamo, *Freak*, 56.

29. John Leguizamo, *Ghetto Klown: A Graphic Novel*, illustrated by Christa Cassano and Shamus Beyale (New York: Abrams Comicarts, 2015), 37.

30. Leguizamo, *Freak*, 18.

31. Leguizamo, *Freak*, 25.

32. Leguizamo, *Freak*, 35.

33. Leguizamo, *Freak*, 36.

34. Leguizamo, *Freak*, 40.
35. Leguizamo, *Freak*, 39.
36. Leguizamo, *Freak*, 49.
37. Dan Rather, *The Big Interview with Dan Rather*, AXS Television, July 14, 2015.
38. Leguizamo, *Ghetto Klown*, 42.
39. Leguizamo, *Ghetto Klown*, 91.
40. Leguizamo, *Ghetto Klown*, 92.
41. As Joanne R. Gilbert has noted: "By performing their marginality, social outcasts call attention to their subordinate status; by commodifying this performance, they ensure that the dominant culture literally pays a price for this disparity." See Gilbert, *Performing Marginality: Humor, Gender, and Cultural Critique* (Detroit, MI: Wayne State University Press, 2004), xi.
42. John Leguizamo, "The First Time I Faced a Hostile Audience: Kids," *New York Times*, March 21, 2017.
43. Improvisational work—that is, the spontaneous and collaborative creation of imaginary roles and scenarios—requires not only experimental playfulness, but the ability to read signals from the other group members. Violin Spolin, in her work on improvisation, emphasized the elimination of the "ego-self" in order to be responsive to the suggestions of others and to see the world from their perspective.
44. John Lahr, "One-Man Universe," review of *Spic-O-Rama*, *The New Yorker*, November 9, 1992.
45. Brantley, "One-Man Melting Pot."
46. Smith, "Introduction," xxvi.
47. Annie Eysturoy notes that this oppositional self-development is seen in a variety of Latinx narratives, where the Latino patriarchal norms and values are so strong that women create an identity "out of a conscious opposition to patriarchal norms and values" (*Daughters of Self-Creation: The Contemporary Chicana Novel* [Albuquerque: University of New Mexico Press, 1996], 131). I am indebted to José R. Rosario for coining the term "oppositional improvisation" in his article "On the Ethics and Poetics of How We Make Our Lives: Esmeralda Santiago and the Improvisation of Identity," *Centro Journal* 22, no. 2 (Fall 2010): 106–27.
48. Brantley, "One-Man Melting Pot."
49. Laurie Stone, "Escape Artist," *The Nation*, April 6, 1998.
50. David Marc describes stand-up as a genre focused on the performance of an exposed individual in *Comic Visions: Television Comedy and American Culture* (Boston: Unwin Hyman, 1989).
51. Ian Brodie refers to the illusion of intimacy upon which stand-up is predicated as the sharing of one's autobiographical details in performance, the seemingly true nature of these details, and the "visual intimacy between performer and audience and the audience's investment in [the comedian's] life story" whose details often spill out into the public sphere. Brodie, "Stand-Up Comedy as a Genre of Intimacy," *Ethnologies* 30, no. 2 (2008): 175.
52. Stephen Holden, "All Alone, Peering into the Abyss," *New York Times*, December 14, 1990. Lawrence E. Mintz also describes the comedian's positionality of being both a negative exemplar of the community (i.e., an outsider) and a spokesperson for the community. See Mintz, "Standup Comedy as Social and Cultural Mediation," *American Quarterly* 37, no. 1 (Spring 1985): 74.

53. Burke, *Attitudes Toward History*, 41.

54. Leguizamo considers his play *Latin History for Morons* as a corrective history to the pervasive Eurocentric narrative. Intended to empower other Latinos, the play rectifies a sense of omission in a history spanning from the Incas to Sonia Sotomayor; Leguizamo includes such figures as Loreta Janeta Velázquez, a Cuban-born woman who dressed like a man to join the Confederate Army and fought in the battles of Shiloh and Bull Run.

55. Adam Hetrick, "How John Leguizamo Turned Heartbreak into Broadway History," *Playbill*, October 19, 2017.

56. Jesse Green, "Review: John Leguizamo Goes for Easy Laughs in 'Latin History,'" *New York Times*, November 15, 2017. Green was disturbed by the "falseness of [Leguizamo's] effort to wring sarcastic pride from disasters retooled as comedy," particularly when the purported objective of the piece was to target racial bias and omission from the historical record.

57. Leguizamo, "The First Time I Faced a Hostile Audience: Kids."

58. Burke, *Attitudes Toward History*, 171.

59. David Gillota, *Ethnic Humor in Multiethnic America* (New Brunswick, NJ: Rutgers University Press, 2013), 156.

8

"OF COURSE, BUT MAYBE"
Louis C.K. and the Contradictory Politics of Privilege

David Gillota

On November 9, 2017, *The New York Times* released a story about Louis C.K. masturbating in front of various women in the entertainment industry.[1] The story gave credence to rumors that had been circulating around C.K. for years. The next day, C.K. himself released a statement in which he admitted that "these stories are true."[2] The next several days saw various think pieces about C.K.'s actions, his statement, and what the revelations would mean both for his legacy and for the comedy world in general. Other major figures within the comedy industry—notably Marc Maron, Sarah Silverman, and Jon Stewart—weighed in and largely denounced C.K.'s behavior. Within a week, the television networks FX and HBO—with whom C.K. had worked for years—cut all ties with the comedian; he was fired from his role in the sequel to the children's film *The Secret Life of Pets* (Renaud, 2016); he was cut from the roster of the autism benefit *Night of Too Many Stars*; and the release of his upcoming movie *I Love You, Daddy* (C.K., 2017) was cancelled. C.K. had fallen from most respected living comedian to industry pariah.

The news about C.K., of course, came at a cultural moment in which powerful men throughout the entertainment industry—Harvey Weinstein, Kevin Spacey, and many others—were being outed for sexual misconduct, abuse, and assault. However, for many people (myself included), the news about C.K. was particularly saddening and disappointing. C.K. wasn't just a popular comedian; he was one of the few straight, white, male celebrities who seemed aware of the unequal ways in which power operates in our world, and he even appeared at times to be committed to combatting such inequality. His work addressing gender and race had received praise from activists and progressives. C.K.'s behavior, then—as well as his refusal over the years to address the rumors about his sexual misconduct—felt like something of a betrayal. While C.K. may *be* committed to combatting inequality, the revelations about his abuse of power show that he also benefited from it.

About six weeks before the November 9 *New York Times* article, I submitted what I then thought was the final draft of this essay about Louis C.K. and privilege. After the news, the editors of this collection graciously asked if I wished to revise. I did. The essay you're reading, however, is not a major overhaul of my argument about C.K.'s humor and its complicated attitude toward privilege. Rather, it is the same argument with an attempt to recontextualize it in light of what we now know about C.K.'s behavior and his position in the industry. Of course, by the time this essay collection is in print, readers will surely know more about the impact of these events on both C.K.'s reputation and his future career prospects than I do now. Regardless of his legacy and/or future in the comedy world, or in the culture at large, I do hope that critics and scholars continue to think about C.K.'s work. As I hope to suggest, stand-up comedy is a cultural form that is particularly suitable for exposing the rifts and contradictions of our culture. The analysis of a comedian like C.K., who has both abused his power and used his humor to critique abuse, can be incredibly fruitful in a number of ways. For example, the fallout of the revelations about C.K.'s behavior will hopefully spearhead further, much-needed discussions about sexism in the comedy world. The case of C.K. can also help us to explore more abstract topics, such as the ability of critics to separate the art from the artist or the comedian from the comic persona.[3] And, as I hope this essay demonstrates, C.K.'s humor can help us to better understand the complicated workings of privilege and inequality in our culture.

The central argument here is that C.K.—or at least his stage and screen persona—often uses the stand-up stage as a forum through which to explore his own privilege as an affluent, heterosexual, white male and as an American citizen who reaps the benefits of a global economy that is built upon the labor force of poorer countries. I argue further that C.K.'s approach to privilege is often inconsistent, contradictory, and problematic. It is important, however, because it elucidates a concept in the public sphere that is often only discussed in academic settings, and because it is ultimately revelatory of the contradictory ways in which inequality is understood and continues to operate in the contemporary United States. In light of the recent revelations about C.K., this argument still stands, but his "problematic" approach to privilege is likely more obvious now. Originally, I was concerned that this essay would come across as being too hard on C.K., whom I had always admired. I am not concerned about that anymore.

The concept of privilege, as it is used in this essay, is attributed to an oft cited and frequently anthologized 1988 essay by Peggy McIntosh. McIntosh asserts that males and white people receive certain benefits simply for being male and/or white. She famously uses the metaphor of an "invisible knapsack" to describe the unearned benefits that white people often take for granted.[4] Since McIntosh's original essay, numerous scholars and activists have taken up the topic—Michael Kimmel, Tim Wise, and Abby L. Ferber, to name a few—and it has been explored in relation to numerous identity positions. Today, for example, scholars discuss privilege regarding not only race and gender but also sexual orientation, class, religion, ability, and age. Scholars have also begun to take into account issues of intersectionality,[5] teasing out the ways in which individuals may benefit from some aspects of their identity while simultaneously suffering oppression due to others.[6] Most scholars who study privilege agree that it is a necessary component for understanding the ways in which race, gender, class, sexual orientation, and other factors impact our day-to-day lives. Furthermore, privilege is a major hurdle in the attempt to ultimately dismantle oppression and inequality.

The largest issue in privilege studies is not much changed today from how it was in McIntosh's 1988 essay, in which she asserted that white privilege was "invisible." Nearly every scholar or activist who addresses privilege asserts the importance of raising awareness of the existence of privilege. Tim Wise argues that white privilege is "off the radar screens of most people,"[7] and Michael Kimmel, in an anthology of essays on privilege designed for students, argues simply that "privilege needs to be made visible."[8] Peggy McIntosh herself, in a 2012 essay focusing on the future of privilege studies, maintains that "United States ideology, media, and institutions as a whole still deny that systems of privilege exist and powerfully shape individual identities and societal institutions."[9] She goes on to assert the need for discussions of privilege that extend beyond academia: "colleges and universities are the main institutions that are raising awareness of the relationship between privilege and oppression, but ... this awareness is needed throughout all public and private sectors of the United States."[10] In those rare cases when the concept of privilege *is* explicitly explored in the public sphere, the mainstream backlash is often considerable.[11] In this cultural climate, then, C.K.'s humor related to privilege is undeniably important. While his take on privilege is less nuanced—and certainly less consistent—than the scholars cited above, he nonetheless uses the stand-up stage as a forum through which to expose millions of viewers to the topic. At the same time, the fact that he managed to rise to stardom despite the open secret of his sexual misconduct underscores the manner in which he benefited from entrenched sexism within the comedy industry. In other words, both his onstage performance and his offstage behavior can serve to raise awareness of privilege.

C.K., it should be noted, has always been an innovative comedian, and there are numerous other themes and topics that one *could* explore in discussing him as a "public intellectual." Much of his humor, for example, continues the tradition of piercing, R-rated social critique exemplified by pioneers like Lenny Bruce or George Carlin; his tendency towards absurdity, however, marks him as a comic descendant of meta-comedians like Steve Martin and Albert Brooks. At the same time, C.K.'s frank routines about fatherhood, for which he has already received critical attention,[12] mark him as a comic successor of Bill Cosby, and his self-deprecating humor and notoriously bleak vision of himself, his body, and the world are most reminiscent of Woody Allen or Richard Pryor. His work related to privilege and inequality, however, may be his most unique and important contribution to contemporary American humor. Of course, numerous nonwhite, queer, or female comedians have used their humor to critique structural inequalities. Before C.K., however, most white male comedians tended to avoid the issue of race (unless they could find some way to distance themselves from whiteness, like any number of Jewish comedians) and to restrict their discussion of gender to fairly stereotypical differences between men and women. In fact, in the work of the majority of white male comedians, their race and gender serve as markers of universality, thus distancing the performer from any particular group identification and allowing them to speak, in theory, for "everyone."[13]

This type of "universal" impulse is not absent in C.K.'s humor, but unlike most other mainstream comics, he frequently calls attention to his wealth and his white masculinity and the various advantages that come from them. It speaks to the sad state of American culture that C.K.'s critique of inequality—coming from a wealthy white man—has gained more attention than other critiques that have been offered by any number of nonwhite or nonmale comedians. Precisely because it comes from the center (rather than the margins), C.K.'s take on privilege proves very fruitful for close analysis. C.K.'s idiosyncratic take on the topic ultimately reveals the contradictory ways in which the beneficiaries of unequal systems of power might understand and rationalize their privilege. It is important to point out that C.K. is explicitly *not* seeking to dismantle current hierarchies. Rather, his onstage attitude toward privilege is a tangled web of guilt, pride, confusion, anger, and happiness.

C.K.'S HUMOR AND A THEORY OF STAND-UP

We see a clear example of this tangled web in one of C.K.'s most famous routines about whiteness, which he performed in his stand-up special *Chewed Up* (C.K. and Hartman, 2008). Here, C.K. offers a lengthy discussion about the benefits of being white:

> Oh God, I love being white. I really do. Seriously, if you're not white, you're missing out 'cause this shit is thoroughly good. Let me be clear by the way; I'm not saying that white people are better. I'm saying that being white is clearly better. Who could even argue? . . . Here's how great it is to be white. I could get in a time machine and go to any time, and it would be fucking awesome when I get there. That is exclusively a white privilege. Black people can't fuck with time machines. . . . I could go to any time—in the past. I don't want to go to the future and find out what happens to white people because we're gonna pay hard for this shit. You gotta know that. We're not just gonna fall from number one to two. They're gonna hold us down and fuck us in the ass forever, and we totally deserve it. But for now, wheeeeee!

Toward the end of the same routine, C.K. brings gender into the equation. With a note of amazement in his voice, he says, "I'm a *white man*. How many advantages can one person have? You can't even hurt my feelings." This sort of frank admission of systemic advantages is rare, not only in stand-up but anywhere in popular culture.

With routines like this, it was often tempting to view C.K. as something of a political spokesperson for a progressive and liberal ideology, and before his downfall many commentators had done just that.[14] But there is something more complex going on in the humor itself. Indeed, C.K. is well aware of how various structural and cultural institutions operate, and he often uses the stand-up stage to explore inequities. However, C.K.'s onstage persona should not be perceived as that of a progressive activist. In the segment quoted above about whiteness, C.K. is clearly trying to get white viewers to admit to and examine their own privilege. At the same time, though, his stated goal in pointing out white privilege is to assert how "awesome" it is. He expresses fear about his privilege coming to an end, and his final childlike "wheeeee!"—no matter how tongue-in-cheek—is a far cry from an activist's call to action. In this sense, the routine is as much a celebration of inequity as it is a criticism of it. C.K.'s approach to privilege could therefore be characterized as a "complicit critique"[15] in which he acknowledges and criticizes racial and gender inequalities even as he benefits from them and, arguably, perpetuates them himself.

My formulation of the inconsistent attitudes toward inequality that can be found in C.K.'s performances is developed, in part, from my ongoing exploration into how stand-up comedy works as an art form, and the particular role stand-up comedy may play in contemporary American culture. A dominant approach offered by much contemporary criticism is to view stand-up comedy as a forum for marginalized voices or as a platform for a particular ideological worldview. Plenty of excellent scholarship has emerged from this approach, but often the result is that critics focus only on stand-up comedians who can serve as joke-telling pundits or funny activists.[16] In particular, Rebecca Krefting offers a fascinating study of what she calls "charged humor." Practitioners of "charged humor," for Krefting, "intentionally produce humor challenging social inequality and cultural exclusion."[17] And she goes on to assert that "charged humor relies on identification with struggles and issues associated with being a second-class citizen."[18] Not surprisingly, C.K.— even before his recent scandal—does not conform to Krefting's definition of a charged humorist. Krefting argues that C.K. "has achieved enormous success by most industry standards; however, his use of charged humor, while laudable, is not consistent throughout his shows."[19] I completely agree with this assessment. I suggest, however, that the inconsistencies Krefting points out can actually teach us about the workings of privilege and about our culture's contradictory attitudes toward inequality.

As I have argued elsewhere, stand-up comedy is an important art form primarily *because* of its formal ability to reveal contradictions and inconsistencies that are a part of the culture itself.[20] John Limon points out that a stand-up performance "does not require plot, closure, nor point."[21] This openness of the medium allows the stand-up comedian to move among a variety of ideological viewpoints and to align and realign herself in relation to any number of group affiliations or allegiances, no matter how contradictory they may be. A politically minded viewer may find, in a single stand-up act, a series of both regressive and progressive viewpoints. The impulse of some audience members may be to chide the comedian for failing to live up to his or her activist potential. The frequent charge that Chris Rock "airs the dirty laundry" of the Black community, or the widely held perception of Ellen DeGeneres's often shaky relationship with LGBTQ scholars and activists, may help to illustrate this point.[22] Rather than viewing the contradictory aspects of a stand-up performance as a failure on the part of the comedian, however, I contend that we ought to view them instead as opportunities to evaluate and better understand the rocky terrain of ideology itself.

"I HAVE A LOT OF BELIEFS, AND I LIVE BY NONE OF THEM"

My claim about C.K.'s incongruous approach to privilege is built upon the idea that contradiction and inconsistency are key features of the stand-up genre. It thus follows that nearly all stand-up comedians exhibit this sort of fluidity to some degree. C.K., however, may be the quintessential example. A survey of his major stand-up specials reveals that C.K. has been explicitly interested in using stand-up to explore contradictory ideas for much of his career. Very early in his special *Live at the Beacon Theater* (C.K., 2011), for example, C.K. explains his belief system (or lack thereof): "I have a lot of beliefs, and I live by none of them. That's just the way I am. They're just my beliefs. I just like believing them. . . . They're my little *believies*. They make me feel good about who I am, but if they get in the way of a thing I want, or if I want to jack off or something, I fucking do that." The routine, while foreshadowing C.K.'s sexual misconduct scandal, also echoes the pragmatist philosopher Charles Sanders Peirce and goes to the heart of what we really mean when we speak of "beliefs." C.K. suggests that rather than being a meaningful set of convictions that guide our lives, the things we call beliefs are actually hollow, and that more often than not our actions will contradict our so-called value system. In the world of Louis C.K., beliefs are never stable, and political positions are rarely fixed. Instead, C.K.'s performance highlights the ways in which value systems may be constantly negotiated or revised.

C.K. thus reveals a gap between beliefs and actions. The implications of this gap for his approach to structural inequalities are immediately clear. C.K. reflects an American culture that *believes* in classic American values like freedom and equality. At the same time, he also reflects the attitudes of a privileged group of Americans who, due to some combination of their race, gender, or class, have grown accustomed to the advantages they have reaped from an unequal power structure. These Americans are unwilling to give those advantages up. Three years after his sketch about his belief system, C.K. explicitly makes this very point in what has since become one of his signature routines. In the concluding segment of his stand-up special *Oh My God* (C.K., 2013), C.K. returns to the idea of beliefs and once again uses the stand-up stage as a forum in which to explore contradictory visions of the world. C.K. explains that "everybody has a competition in their brain of good thoughts and bad thoughts, and hopefully the good thoughts win. For me, I always have both. I have like the thing I believe, the good thing . . . and then there's *this* thing, and I don't believe it, but it *is* there." He goes on to explain that "it's become a category in my brain that I call 'of course, but maybe.'"[23]

From here, C.K. provides a series of examples of how this "category in his brain" works. He asserts that "of course" children with nut allergies need to be protected no matter how inconvenient it is to segregate their food. A moment later, however, he says, "but *maybe*, if touching a nut kills you, you're supposed to die." While performing this bit, C.K. literally tiptoes around the stage, visually reinforcing the sensitive nature of his topic and driving home the idea that he is stating thoughts that may exist in people's minds but that they rarely admit. C.K. saves his most controversial example—and the one most clearly related to inequality—for last: "*Of course* slavery is the worst thing that ever happened, of course . . . but *maybe* every incredible human achievement was done with slaves." C.K. goes on to explore the concept in more detail:

> "How did they build these pyramids?" They just threw human death and suffering at them until they were finished. "How did we traverse the nation with the railroads so quickly?" We just threw Chinese people in caves and blew them up and didn't give a shit what happened to them. There's no end to what you can do when you don't give a fuck about particular people. You can do anything! That's where human greatness comes from, is that we're shitty people.

The contradictions that C.K. suggests are palpable. Human progress comes from human oppression, and human greatness comes from human "shittiness." So far, though, C.K. keeps his examples safely in the past, affording both himself and audience members the ability to judge historical atrocities without fully admitting their own complicity. As he concludes, however, C.K. pulls his cell phone out of his pocket, holds it up, and says, "even today." He goes on to ask:

> "How do we have such amazing micro technology?" Because in the factory where they're making these they jump off the fucking roof 'cause it's a nightmare in there. You really have a choice: you can have candles and horses and be a little kinder to each other, or let someone suffer immeasurably far away, just so you can leave a mean comment on YouTube while you're taking a shit.

Mike Hale calls the bit a "problematic and risky segment."[24] This might be true, but by the end of the routine, the risk feels fairly low, for C.K. structures the sequence in such a way that viewers are left not with a defense of the institution of slavery, but with a condemnation of those—including himself—who are complicit with it. In this light, the segment emerges as a satire of privilege and of humans' ability to put out of their minds the ways in which their own comforts are born out of suffering. This complicity is a direct result of C.K.'s "two minds" toward slavery. When he asserts that we have a choice between being "a little kinder to each other" and letting "someone suffer immeasurably far away," there is no suggestion that C.K., or any of us, will choose the former and willingly give up the privileges and benefits those inequalities produce.

"MEN ARE WORSE THAN WOMEN"

In the examples above, C.K. makes his ideological contradictions both clear and overt. He signals to audience members that his explicit goal is to highlight the tension between beliefs and actions, and he unambiguously explains that he often has two or more competing feelings about the same issue. In this sense, C.K.'s humor works well as a satire of American hypocrisy. There are other places in his humor, though, where C.K.'s statements are just as contradictory but where his acknowledgment of those contradictions is not made explicit. In these cases, C.K. is no longer a satirist, but rather an example of the ways in which political positions can be slippery and the ways in which those who benefit from structural inequality—even those who are aware of it—can inadvertently reproduce or become complicit with the very same power structures they are attempting to highlight. In other words, there are moments in C.K.'s oeuvre where he himself slips back and forth between progressive and regressive viewpoints. This slippage demonstrates the ways stand-up comedy may serve as a window into the workings of privilege and inequality itself.

There are many cases in C.K.'s body of work where we can locate an ideological slipperiness, but nowhere is this more pronounced than in his discussion of gender. First, it is important to point out that there are numerous moments in C.K.'s humor which—before the sexual misconduct story—could have established him as a sort of feminist comedian. His feminism, however, was never built upon a call for equal rights and representation; instead it was based on a critique of the behaviors of men. In his 2014 *Saturday Night Live* monologue, for example, C.K. says, "I don't think women are better than men, but I do think men are worse than women." Logically, the statement makes no sense, but the suggestion seems to be that while neither men nor women are particularly great, the behavior of men *is* particularly bad. C.K. performs an extended version of this same *Saturday Night Live* monologue on the season 4 episode of *Louie* (2010–2015) titled "Pamela: Part 1." Here, C.K.'s fictionalized version of himself—which is yet another step removed from his already constructed stand-up persona—discusses in more detail the ways in which "men are worse than women." C.K. takes a broad historical perspective, saying, "I think that we made God a man because we wanted men to be in charge." A few moments later, he goes on to assert that

> Women are really kept down, even today. A lot of people like to argue that things are equal, but they're really not, and American history hasn't been kind to women. Women couldn't vote until 1920. How crazy is that, that women couldn't vote in America until 1920? . . . They couldn't vote until 1920, which means that America wasn't really a democracy until 1920. You can't call it a democracy if the whole sex of women can't vote. . . . That means American democracy is really 93 years old.

The routine here requires little analysis. In fact, there is very little overt humor in it, as C.K. in this instance simply asserts the existence of gender inequality in unambiguous terms. In the context of the episode in which this routine occurs, there is plenty to talk about, but as a stand-up set—which is my focus here—the routine emerges as a fairly clear critique of patriarchy.[25]

C.K.'s approach to gender doesn't always work this way, though. In *Chewed Up*, for example, C.K. lays out what he sees as the difference between boys and girls, which then leads him into a fuller discussion of essential differences between men and women:

> Boys fuck things up. Girls are fucked up. . . . Boys just do damage to your house that you can measure in dollars, like a hurricane. Girls like leave scars in your psyche that you find later, like a genocide or an atrocity. . . . That's the difference between boys and girls, and it becomes the difference between men and women really. Because a man will like steal your car or burn your house down, or beat the shit out of you, but a woman will ruin your fucking life. Do you see the difference? Like a man will cut your arm off and throw it in a river, but he'll leave you as a human being intact. . . . Women are nonviolent, but they will shit inside of your heart.

While the hyperbolic nature of C.K.'s descriptions successfully generates humor for many viewers, his assessment is similar to any number of reductive and essentialist comparisons between men and women that can be found in the work of many run-of-the-mill comedians. Perhaps even more importantly, the gender ideology that C.K. is buying into here—that women "mess" with men's heads and ruin their lives—is born out of the very same system of gender inequality that C.K. critiques in other instances.

The juxtaposition of C.K.'s feminist humor with his essentialized gender humor is similar to the "two minds" that C.K. has explicitly elucidated in the routines discussed above. C.K. can acknowledge and even work against sexism, but this doesn't mean that his visions of gender have not also been shaped by the patriarchal culture of which he is undeniably a part. We see this more explicitly in a very recent bit from *Oh My God*, in which C.K. slips from one vision of gender politics to another within the very same routine. The ostensible topic of the sequence is dating rituals, and C.K. uses the idea of men and women dating as an avenue for discussing broader issues related to gender:

> A woman saying "yes" to a date with a man is literally insane and ill-advised, and the whole species' existence counts on them doing it. ... How do women still go out with guys when you consider the fact that there is no greater threat to women than men? We're the number one threat to women. Globally and historically, we're the number one cause of injury and mayhem to women. We're the worst thing that ever happens to them. That's true! You know what our number one threat is? Heart disease. That's the whole thing. That's it.

So far, the routine is a scathing attack on patriarchal violence. Yes, C.K. imagines a very traditional courting ritual in which men ask women out on dates, and yes, a routine like this takes on another level of meaning after C.K.'s own confession of sexual misconduct. However, what we know about sexual abuse and domestic violence—not to mention the less immediately tangible effects of a patriarchal culture—certainly supports C.K.'s claim that men are the worst thing to happen to women. And his method of contrasting violence against women to heart disease for men suggests that one aspect of male privilege is that men do not have to worry about sexual and domestic violence to the same extent as women.

As he moves deeper into his routine about dating, however, C.K. suddenly shifts gears and begins describing an actual date that men and women are on together:

> You can tell it's a first date by the way they're walking together, and she's looking up at his face trying to figure him out, and he's just a

mess. A guy on a first date . . . has no actual personality. He's just a mishmash of different kinds of dudes for a couple of seconds each . . . no cohesive, just like a ransom note cut out of a lot of magazines.
. . . There's something that happens on a date that I never get to witness because women do this. They get to do it inside, they get to just decide quietly, "I'm gonna let him fuck me." They just get to decide. Something he says, and she's like "that was good. He's gonna fuck me later." And he has no idea . . . he's already in there.

The change in tone and content from the first half of the routine is astounding. Earlier, C.K. spent a good deal of time asserting the dangers that women encounter when they interact with men on a date. In the second half, however, the man on a date, rather than being prone to inflicting patriarchal violence, is changed into a clueless yet affable doofus who simply has no idea how to talk to women.

More important, however, is the contradictory ways in which C.K. imagines women. When his goal is to highlight and critique patriarchy, C.K. speaks of women as vulnerable victims of masculine violence. By the end of the same bit, however, he has transformed them into the gatekeepers of sex who decide whether or not to "let men fuck them." In this scenario, women have *all* of the power on a date, and men are simply subject to their whim. In addition to having this inconsistent vision of gender, C.K. seems unaware of the ways in which his stereotypical description of women as mysterious figures who may on a whim decide to grant or withhold sex is perhaps part of the root cause of the masculine violence he critiques in the first half of the routine. One does not have to look far in this culture to find a man who uses such stereotypes of women as a way of rationalizing the physical violence that is inflicted upon them. C.K. thus perpetuates the very systems of privilege and inequality that he elsewhere attacks.

I assert that we can use this inconsistency as an entry point to a discussion of much larger cultural contradictions. In the above routine, C.K. describes a man on a date as a "mishmash of different kinds of dudes for a couple of seconds each . . . like a ransom note cut out of a lot of magazines." This description may just as easily refer to the stand-up comedian him or herself, who uses the stage as an avenue through which to explore and dramatize a variety of cultural positions and attitudes. And in a broader sense, the description can refer to the inconsistent and slippery views of any number of privileged Americans who at some times are able to acknowledge their privilege, but at other times may be completely unaware of it, or unwilling to sacrifice it. C.K.—like many Americans who believe in equality but are hesitant to sacrifice the benefits they reap from the lack of it—stands upon these cultural fault lines and occupies a series of contradictory and inconsistent positions. The gap between his onstage persona and his offstage behavior only further demonstrates this point.

C.K.—as a comedian, as a fallen celebrity, and as a public intellectual—serves as a mirror for our culture's own confused attitudes toward privilege. From a progressive viewpoint, what we of course hope to see are men who emerge as feminist allies and white people who fight for racial equality. We want to see people who recognize the privileges that go along with whiteness and masculinity and who actively reject the most problematic aspects of American culture. What we actually *get*—in both popular culture and everyday life—is more of a disjointed hodgepodge of progressive efforts marked by traditional or regressive impulses, or vice versa. Enter stand-up comedy. The contradictory and fluid nature of the stand-up performance can reveal to us how certain people are articulating and understanding privilege. It can also offer resistant audiences a nonacademic, non–"politically correct" entry point into conceptualizing the ways in which privilege is constructed and how some of our culture's most harmful aspects can begin to be challenged.

Notes

1. Melena Ryzik, Cara Buckley, and Jodi Kantor, "Louis C.K. Is Accused by 5 Women of Sexual Misconduct," *New York Times*, November 9, 2017, https://www.nytimes.com/2017/11/09/arts/television/louis-ck-sexual-misconduct.html.

2. Dave Itzkoff, "Louis C.K. Admits to Sexual Misconduct as Media Companies Cut Ties," *New York Times*, November 10, 2017, https://www.nytimes.com/2017/11/10/movies/louis-ck-i-love-you-daddy-release-is-canceled.html

3. For a detailed exploration of stand-up personae and their construction, see Bambi Haggins, *Laughing Mad: The Black Comic Persona in Post-Soul America* (New Brunswick, NJ: Rutgers University Press, 2007). In this essay, I will be examining C.K.'s persona—which can be seen as a fictional construct—when discussing his stand-up performances. When discussing his offstage behavior, I am obviously discussing the real person.

4. Peggy McIntosh, "White Privilege and Male Privilege," in *Privilege: A Reader*, 3rd ed., ed. Michael S. Kimmel and Abby L. Ferber (Boulder, CO: Westview Press, 2014), 15–27.

5. The concept of intersectionality originated in the Black feminist work of Kimberlé Crenshaw, who argues against "dominant conceptions of discrimination" which "condition us to think about subordination as disadvantage occurring along a single categorial axis." Kimberlé Crenshaw, "Demarginalizing the Intersection of Race and Sex: A Black Feminist Critique of Antidiscrimination Doctrine, Feminist Theory and Antiracist Politics," *University of Chicago Legal Forum* (1989): 140. Since Crenshaw's original Black feminist analysis, other scholars have utilized the concept to explore ways in which privilege and discrimination may intersect. For an overview of the term's varied usage, see Devon W. Carbado and Cheryl I.

Harris, "Intersectionality at 30: Mapping the Margins of Anti-Essentialism, Intersectionality, and Dominance Theory," *Harvard Law Review* 132, no. 8 (2019): 2193–2239.

6. See, for example, Bethany M. Coston and Michael Kimmel, "Seeing Privilege Where It Isn't: Marginalized Masculinities and the Intersectionality of Privilege," *Journal of Social Issues* 68, no. 1 (2012): 97–111.

7. Tim Wise, *White Like Me: Reflections on Race from a Privileged Son* (Berkeley, CA: Soft Skull Press, 2011), ix.

8. Michael S. Kimmel, "Toward a Sociology of the Superordinate," in *Privilege: A Reader*, 3rd ed., ed. Michael S. Kimmel and Abby L. Ferber (Boulder, CO: Westview Press, 2014), 3.

9. Peggy McIntosh, "Reflections and Future Directions for Privilege Studies," *Journal of Social Issues* 68, no. 1 (2012): 194.

10. McIntosh, "Reflections and Future Directions," 195.

11. See, for example, Cory Weinberg, "The White Privilege Moment," *InsideHigherEd*, May 28, 2014, https://www.insidehighered.com/news/2014/05/28/academics-who-study-white-privilege-experience-attention-and-criticism. The essay discusses the hate mail many scholars who work in privilege studies report getting, and it also discusses a cultural backlash against the existence of privilege after Fox News pundit Bill O'Reilly discussed the topic.

12. See Peter C. Kunze, "Fatherhood, Feminism, and Failure in Louis C.K.'s Comedy," in *Pops in Pop Culture: Fatherhood, Masculinity, and the New Man*, ed. Elizabeth Podnieks (New York: Palgrave McMillan, 2016), 51–66.

13. There are numerous scholarly discussions of the ways whiteness is typically seen as an unmarked norm in contemporary culture. See, in particular, Richard Dyer, who asserts that whiteness "needs to be made strange"—*White: Essays on Race and Culture* (New York: Routledge, 1997), 10.

14. See, for example, Francie Latour, "Louis C.K.'s Stand-up Offers Powerful Insights on Race," *Boston Globe*, December 8, 2013, https://www.bostonglobe.com/business/2013/12/08/wiseguy/w291yxuEYqk8xAZcueHP4L/story.html.

15. The term "complicit critique" is borrowed from Linda Hutcheon's *The Politics of Postmodernism* (New York: Routledge, 1999), in which Hutcheon asserts that postmodern literature reproduces the structures and themes of classical and modernist literature even as it critiques them.

16. Key examples of this approach can be found in Joanne R. Gilbert's *Performing Marginality: Humor, Gender, and Cultural Critique* (Detroit, MI: Wayne State University Press, 2004); in many of the essays in the recent collection *Standing-Up, Speaking Out: Stand-Up Comedy and the Rhetoric of Social Change*, ed. Matthew R. Meier and Casey R. Schmitt (New York: Routledge, 2017); and in Rebecca Krefting's *All Joking Aside: American Humor and Its Discontents* (Baltimore, MD: Johns Hopkins University Press, 2014), discussed in more detail below.

17. Krefting, *All Joking Aside*, 2.

18. Krefting, *All Joking Aside*, 5

19. Krefting, *All Joking Aside*, 3

20. See David Gillota, "Stand-up Nation: Humor and American Identity," *Journal of American Culture* 38, no. 2 (2015): 102–12; David Gillota, "Reckless Talk: Exploration and

Contradiction in Dave Chappelle's Recent Stand-up Comedy," *Studies in Popular Culture* 42, no. 1 (2019), 1–22.

21. John Limon, *Stand-up Comedy in Theory, or, Abjection in America* (Durham, NC: Duke University Press, 2000), 13.

22. Both Rock and DeGeneres are often viewed as public intellectuals in their own right, but both have had fraught relationships with the particular communities they are thought to represent. I have argued elsewhere that both DeGeneres and Rock exemplify the complicated terrain of American identity politics, in which individual interests are often at odds with larger group affiliations. See Gillota, "Stand-up Nation."

23. Sonia Saraiya provides an excellent rereading of this routine after the revelations of C.K.'s sexual misconduct. Saraiya explains that she "always thought C.K. ended up on the side of the 'of course.' It turns out he was more than happy to end up on the side of the 'but maybe.'" Sonia Saraiya, "I Admired Louis C.K. What a Mistake," *Variety*, November 11, 2017, http://variety.com/2017/tv/news/louis-ck-scandal-sexual-harassment-mistake-louie-1202612558/#article-comments.

24. Mike Hale, "Lessons on Bacon, Sex and Nixon, Not Available in a Sitcom," *New York Times*, April 12, 2013. http://www.nytimes.com/2013/04/13/arts/television/louis-ck-oh-my-god-a-stand-up-special-on-hbo.html?_r=0

25. In the episode of *Louie* in which this set is performed, the fictionalized Louie—who is a less successful and in many ways less intelligent version of C.K.'s stage persona—attempts (and fails) to force himself upon Pamela, his long-term love interest on the show. There was much discussion about whether or not Louie's actions here could be called "attempted rape"; suffice to say, the fictional Louie's actions completely undermine the progressive ideology of the stand-up performance.

JERRY SEINFELD VERSUS PC SOCIAL MEDIA

Professional Dissonance and the Public Intellectual as Gatekeeper

Timothy J. Viator

On June 10, 2015, Jerry Seinfeld appeared on *Late Night with Seth Meyers* (2014–) along with David Remnick, the editor of *The New Yorker*. The two discussed changes they perceived in the audience's reception of comedy and humor from audiences, and Seinfeld added,

> They keep moving the lines in for no reason. I do this joke about the way people need to justify their cell phone: "I need to have it with me because people are so important." I said, "Well, they don't seem very important, the way you scroll through them like a gay French king."
>
> I did this line recently in front of an audience—comedy is where you can kind of feel, like, an opinion—and they thought, "What do you mean, *gay*? What are you talking about *gay*? What are you saying *gay*? What are you doing? What do you mean?" And I thought, "Are you kidding me?"
>
> I can imagine a time—and this is a serious thing—I could imagine a time now where people would say that's offensive to suggest that a gay person moves their hands in a flourishing motion, and you now need to apologize.
>
> There's a creepy PC thing out there that really bothers me.[1]

Seinfeld also addressed this issue when he appeared on Colin Cowherd's ESPN radio program earlier that same month: "I have no interest in gender or race or anything like that. But everyone else is kind of, with their calculating—is this the exact right mix? I think that's—to me it's anti-comedy. It's more about PC-nonsense."[2]

By using the phrases "creepy PC thing" and "PC nonsense," Seinfeld ostensibly enters a larger political debate about comedy and its audience, and given his fame, he attracts considerable attention. As Meier and Schmitt write in their introduction to *Standing Up, Speaking Out*, "The stand-up comic performing live before an audience is literally 'speaking out' to the crowd, and inherent to this practice is a social engagement, with the potential to encourage social reflection and social change. Certainly not all stand-up comedy is performed with social commentary in mind, but the mere act of standing up and speaking out always holds this potential."[3] While Seinfeld's observational humor may not be intentionally political, subversive, or critical of power, he appears to reject that any stand-up is speaking out. Yet, in turning his talk show appearances and newspaper interviews promoting his series, *Comedians in Cars Getting Coffee* (*CCC*), toward a "PC culture" he perceives as a threat to the comedy club, Seinfeld comments on a problem that he rarely defines. Again and again in various venues, he asserts that the only measure of a comedy set is its funniness. Seinfeld appears to suggest that PC culture politicizes comedy, yet his speaking out against such criticisms, social media, and changing sensibilities somehow remains apolitical. Writing about George Carlin's and Daniel Tosh's jokes about rape, Christopher A. Medjesky argues that "Simply being a comedian [does not grant] immunity from criticism when joking about subjects" that audience members find troublesome.[4] By extension, speaking out against criticism of comedians and jokes is social commentary, a political argument that Seinfeld wants to deny simultaneously to critics and to audience members.

In "What Does It Mean to Be a Public Intellectual?" John Issitt and Duncan Jackson put forth six conventional types of the public intellectual: the dissenter, the revealer of truth, the thinker, the expert, the media superstar, and the knowledge gatekeeper.[5] Those who are quick to quote Seinfeld offer him up as the expert, the "voice" of a practitioner who speaks for "the generality of folk [that] are not in a position to know specific things."[6] On one hand, Seinfeld's views align with those who see the issue as one of "free speech," including conservative commentators on Fox News and comics such as Chris Rock, Bill Burr, and the noted left-libertarian Bill Maher—critics of PC culture who portray it as a dangerous force that suppresses or censors individual speech. On the other, his reaction goes against those who prefer fair treatment for all. His comments have prompted responses from several commentators: Sarah Silverman, who says comedians have to change; a college student, who in an open letter asks Seinfeld and other comedians to write material that does not offend audiences; and a blogger, who considers Seinfeld a hack.[7]

Seinfeld seemingly wants to project a public persona of a hard-working, apolitical comedian who strives only to make audiences laugh—yet more and more he contradicts this persona by speaking out publicly. In so doing, he positions himself as the gatekeeper, who Issitt and Jackson explain offers "short packaged and served up pieces of information [that can] never do justice to the information or idea itself" and that lack "in-depth, nuanced, and critical understanding . . . convenient in inevitably simplistic accounts."[8] Seinfeld's insistence that in comedy "funny" is all that matters is the type of "served-up" explanation that they associate with gatekeepers. In an episode of *CCC* featuring Steve Harvey, for example, Seinfeld insists that "The audience is all the police we [comedians] need; if something's not funny, it will get removed."[9] Throughout *CCC*, he argues in a quasi-religious tone about the sanctity of the comedy club, the long-standing tradition that for comics and their audiences funny is all that matters.[10] For him, that "creepy PC thing" fails to take into account that fundamental truth.

Implicit in many of Seinfeld's comments about stand-up is that it is not and should not be political; yet by arguing what comedy is or must be, Seinfeld contradicts his own views about his role. Columnists and bloggers quote Seinfeld as an authority supporting their views about how PC culture curtails free speech, while his critics argue he is "reading from the playbook of bloviating pundits like Rush Limbaugh and Bill O'Reilly."[11] Seinfeld himself never asserts his freedom to say whatever he wants; instead he seems genuinely perplexed by the situation. Comedians often note that a comic knows when a joke or bit does not hit, and Seinfeld shares that observation when he tells Meyers and Remnick that "comedy is where you can kind of feel, like, an opinion." Assured that he knows what his audience was thinking, he initially fixates on the word *gay* as the reason for its reaction, yet he quickly turns to the hand gesture he used to represent the smug indifference he sees when people swipe the touch screens of smartphones. Trying to say that we insist on having smartphones to maintain constant contact with our friends and family, Seinfeld wants to make a joke about the seemingly absurd way we use our phones. Accustomed to hearing his audiences laughing, Seinfeld is incredulous, imagining a time "where people would say that's offensive to suggest that a gay person moves their hands in a flourishing motion, and you now need to apologize."

What he fails to realize is that humor based on stereotypes has offended many audience members for a long time. His hand gesture and the haughty facial expression that accompany his line about a gay French king invoke for some audiences the cliché that gay men are effeminate and theatrical. For example, writing for *TalkingPointsMemo*, Amanda Marcotte concludes her essay about Seinfeld's joke in this way: "It's a good thing for comedy if hackish comedians are finding it harder and harder to rely on half-baked and unfunny jokes that rest on the premise that straight guys are better and cooler than everyone else."[12] Marcotte implies that Seinfeld's bit depends upon familiar jokes, clichés, and stereotypes about gay men. The reactions from some Twitter users mirror those of Marcotte. One user tweeted, "Political correctness cannot ruin Jerry Seinfeld's 'gay French king' joke. Because it wasn't funny in the first place,"[13] while another asserted, "Seinfeld told a 'gay French king' joke about swiping that isn't actually very funny but 'PC GONE MAD IS WHY THEY DIDN'T LAUGH.'"[14]

In his effort to understand how stand-up comedy and its audiences are changing, Seinfeld offers PC culture as a cause, and in so doing he speaks out in the shouting match that Erica Hellerstein and Judd Legum label a "phony debate" in which "angry responses often come from people who hold more institutional power than [those] they critique."[15] During the Cowherd interview, Seinfeld said, "I don't play colleges, but I hear a lot of people tell me, 'Don't go near colleges. They're so PC.'"[16] Commentators on both sides of the issue were quick to quote him as an authority. Writing in the *Chicago Tribune*, Chris Jones titles his editorial "Why Seinfeld Took a Stand Against Political Correctness."[17] For his piece in *Salon*, Mick Hume starts with "It's worse than Jerry Seinfeld says: PC is undermining free speech, expression, liberties."[18] Unsurprisingly, comebacks came as quick and sharp as the title of the alternet.org essay by Adam Johnson suggests: "Jerry Seinfeld—White Hetero Male Worth $820 Million—Thinks World Is Too 'PC.'"[19]

Seinfeld plays the reluctant gadfly, but this incident provides an illuminating case study into the contentious, problematic, and fragile relationships between comedians and audiences. I try here to understand Seinfeld's status and influence as one of America's most well-known observational comedians, the commentary about stand-up and humor from his web series *Comedians in Cars Getting Coffee,* and the use of social media by audiences as a platform for criticism. At the same time, I once again call up theories about humor, its function, and its targets as victims that critics and commentators alike have debated for centuries.

To further this discussion, I want to adapt a theory from studies of social workers, because I sense that Seinfeld's comments come more from perplexity than from politics. In "Professional Dissonance: A Promising Concept for Clinical Social Work," Melissa Floyd Taylor articulates the concept of "professional dissonance," defined as "a feeling of discomfort arising from the conflict between professional values and expected or required job task."[20] I propose that the clash that Floyd Taylor and her colleagues see in social workers is evident in all professions. Professionals with an idealized view of their work as noble, pure, and important feel discomfort when they confront the reality of said work. As a result, the incongruity, disharmony, and discord confuse, frustrate, and stress a professional required to perform a "task" that conflicts with that idealized view. This aggravation, in turn, causes dissonance. Social workers, teachers, lawyers, and comedians can all experience professional dissonance in their attempts to negotiate their perception of and the response to their work.

Professionals who have yet to recognize professional dissonance may be feeling malaise, an undetermined anxiety that somehow things are off and things are beyond one's control. One way to approach Seinfeld's comments on PC culture is to keep in mind this notion of work-related malaise. Furthermore, social media allows for a revised relationship between the comedian and the audience in ways that potentially frustrate gatekeepers such as Seinfeld. The audience for stand-up has expanded to include those not in the live audience, and comedians face the consequences that ensue.

Despite this changing comedic landscape, Jerry Seinfeld remains one of the most prominent and influential American comedians. First, he is generally acknowledged to be one of American's best and best-known "observational comics." Nearly twenty years since its last episode, *Seinfeld* (1989–1998) continues in syndication—with Hulu buying the streaming rights and a 2014 *New York* magazine article reporting that the "*Seinfeld* economy" has generated over $3 billion in earnings.[21] Unlike other stand-up comedians who starred in their own television series, Seinfeld returned to the comedy clubs instead of retiring or trying another film role after the mixed results of the critically disappointing box office hit *Bee Movie* (Hickner and Smith, 2007). In Ricky Gervais's *Talking Funny* (Moffitt, 2011) on HBO, Seinfeld explained that more than success, he just always wants to be one of those guys—that is, a working, professional stand-up comedian.[22] Fellow comedians continually praise his desire to face the audience.

More recently, Seinfeld has returned to television through the web series *Comedians in Cars Getting Coffee*, where he purposefully subverts the conventions of the talk show. He and his mobile, limited production staff film roughly three and a half hours of driving, coffee drinking, and conversation that are edited down to episodes of about sixteen minutes, on average. Seinfeld has mentioned in interviews that he wanted a talk show without an audience and without promotion. Seinfeld explains that getting into cars and driving to coffee shops gives the show "movement" that a studio talk show lacks.[23] As his 2015 appearance on Seth Meyers makes clear, Seinfeld dislikes the inauthenticity of the typical talk show chatter, in which a "host" reads a list of questions and topics that come up during the preshow interview with the guest looking to plug a project, something Seinfeld now refuses to do. Playing off the notion that *Seinfeld* was a show about nothing, reviewers presumably want to see *CCC* as a talk show about nothing, yet the series has now, after more than fifty episodes, established its own conventions: a discussion of the automobile Seinfeld has chosen, the telephone call to the guest, the drive to and from the coffeeshops. *CCC* plays off the tensions that Judith Yaross Lee notes in the sitcom *Seinfeld*, "between authenticity and illusion, seriousness and joking, reality and play."[24]

Seinfeld's fame and fortune afford him what few comedians have—license. Because of his wealth and enduring popularity, he is free to play only on select weekends and only in select venues. The sponsors of *CCC* allow him control over content. Although convention holds that web series episodes should not exceed five minutes, Seinfeld's typically run from twelve to twenty minutes. *CCC* seems intimate, conversational, unscripted, and unplanned, offering a seemingly authentic interaction between acquaintances getting coffee and walking (or driving) around town. Being "in the car" or "at the table" with Seinfeld and his guest, the viewers are not audience members in the same way they might be with a studio talk show. Unlike Bill Maher's *Real Time*, which is deliberately political, *CCC* is more social and less formal, an unabashed celebration of comedians and the art of comedy.

In several episodes of *CCC*, Seinfeld describes the comedy club in what might seem to some listeners deferential tones. In the comedy club, the comedian and the audience have only one measure: is it funny? As he said on *CBS This Morning* (1992–) in February 2014, "Funny is the world that I live in. You're funny; I'm interested. You're not funny; I'm not interested."[25] Seinfeld seems to want to position his humor away from the type of explicitly "political" humor of programs like *Real Time with Bill Maher* (2003–), *The Daily Show* (1996–), and *The Colbert Report* (2005–2014). Being able to perform in large venues to large audiences while charging top dollar and working where, when, and how often he wants to, Seinfeld enjoys a position of privilege that few comedians ever attain. As a result, the media and comedy fans alike afford his opinions greater weight than those of many of his peers.

Many of his comments about PC culture arise from that view of the comedy club, its comedians, and the audience as sacrosanct. Several times, Seinfeld has noted how emergent sensibilities about social justice issues such as gender and race—what critics are quick to dismiss as the "PC culture" commonly associated with college campuses—has had an impact on stand-up audiences. Seinfeld dismisses these concerns as "PC nonsense," which he views as "anti-comedy."[26] Some views center more on audiences than on material. As "anti-comedy," PC culture forces audiences to stifle laughter if the subject is deemed inappropriate. If it is potentially controversial, it cannot be funny. To Seinfeld, an audience should be free to laugh and enjoy all comedy, no matter the premise. If the joke is not funny, the audience will not laugh, and the comedian must rework the material.

What he and others label "PC culture" questions and challenges the process by which comedians rework and revise material. Even though he cannot play college campuses, Seinfeld wants to explain that colleges are so politicized that audiences become humorless. Jokes are no longer either funny or not; now they can also be offensive. Since audiences may be insulted, slighted, or upset, Seinfeld contends that PC culture demands that comedians work to assure that all jokes do not offend, and in so doing it undermines the joke-writing process. Seinfeld's frustration belies an anxious dismay that his profession is changing.

In a discussion of comedy, Seinfeld and fellow comedian Steve Martin discussed the question of whether or not comedy evolves. Martin explains his decision to stop doing stand-up comedy because his persona as an absurdist—a silly, playful "wild and crazy guy"—was "linked to the era we were coming out of, which was Vietnam."[27] Seinfeld, somewhat defensively, argues that "comedy doesn't change that much, I think. It's kinda like being a boxer." For Seinfeld, the rules, game, and basic truth of comedy remain unchanged. He does not mean to imply that comedians and their audiences are battling; rather, his point is that the elemental work of comedians is trying to make strangers laugh. As he told Howard Stern, who admits several times during their time together to his own ongoing anxiety and self-doubt, "You should worry if [your listeners are] enjoying the show or not."[28] Comedy rises above its historical moment: it either works—or it doesn't.

Seinfeld's comments about PC culture as anti-comedy may not be as overtly political as Bill Maher's *Real Time*, for example, but his fascination with the power dynamics between comedian and audience reveals a political interest nevertheless. As an observational comedian, Seinfeld has never been one to confront his audiences. He wants to find humor in the incongruity and absurdity of everyday situations that are common, recognizable, and perhaps even universal. The monologues are not self-directed, but relational, asking the audience to recognize the bizarre, the incompatible, the inconsistent, the strange, and the silly in everyday things. The observational comic wants an audience to laugh along. And Seinfeld's approach to his stand-up has remained the same for his entire career, demonstrating his belief in the timelessness of good jokes.

Comedians often have a noticeable disdain for hecklers, but heckling is particularly disruptive for observational comedians whose humor depends upon pacing. In the *Seinfeld* episode "The Fire," Jerry struggles through an important stand-up routine as Toby—Elaine's coworker and Kramer's girlfriend—reacts to one of Jerry's jokes about the differences between men and women and starts to heckle him, thereby throwing off his timing and ruining his set. Jerry soon decides to enact a comedian's revenge by going to Toby's office at Pendant Publishing to heckle her at her job. The temptation of heckling the heckler points to the often complicated, problematic relationships comedians have with those members of their audience who speak out. Comedians routinely complain about their hecklers, whom they often consider unsettling, adversarial, and confrontational. At the same time, many admit that the anxiety they feel relates to losing control of the room. The pressure comedians experience is to be prepared with a comeback that redirects the audience's attention away from the heckler and back to themselves.

Jerry Seinfeld takes a different approach to heckling. In a Reddit chat with fans, Seinfeld responded to a question about how he handles heckling:

> Very early on in my career, I hit upon this idea of being the Heckle Therapist. So that when people would say something nasty, I would immediately become very sympathetic to them and try to help them with their problem and try to work out what was upsetting them, and try to be very understanding with their anger. It opened up this whole fun avenue for me as a comedian, and no one had ever seen that before. Some of my comedian friends used to call me—what did they say?—that I would counsel the heckler instead of fighting them. Instead of fighting them, I would say "You seem so upset, and I know that's not what you wanted to have happen tonight. Let's talk about your problem," and the audience would find it funny and it would really discombobulate the heckler too, because I wouldn't go against them, I would take their side.[29]

While his goal is the same—that is, to "discombobulate the heckler"—his strategy and tone differ. Saying that he "wouldn't go against them" exemplifies and corresponds to the philosophy of humor he embraces as an "observational comedian." Seinfeld rarely tells one-liners or a string of jokes, and generally doesn't use the zingers most comics use to "shut up hecklers" with confrontational putdowns. Instead he expresses his displeasure through his tone: he feigns concern for the heckler that the rest of the audience appreciates as indirect and insincere.

Social media provides a new space for audience members (or commentators) to "talk back" publicly to comedians, and this development inspires an ire in veteran comedians that we may view as professional dissonance. One prevalent topic that Seinfeld and many of his guests have discussed through *CCC* is how an audience can turn on a comic. "Turning" does not denote a single heckler; rather, it is about losing the entire audience completely. Clearly it is an anxiety that famous, established comedians still remember from the earliest parts of their careers. From Steve Martin, who feared that his audiences would tire of his stand-up persona, to Chris Rock, who wonders how Superman might turn to acts of physical strength to win back an audience, to Steve Harvey, who worries about losing a career over a joke, this anxiety arises from comedians' views of the fragility of each joke, each bit, and their entire careers.

One of the most emotional, authentic segments in the entire *CCC* series is the exchange between Seinfeld and his former co-star, Michael Richards, about the November 17, 2006 set at the Laugh Factory, where Richards's apparent efforts to counter heckling amounted to screaming racist epithets at the audience. Because of the growing popularity of cell phones with video-recording capability and internet platforms to share such recordings, the altercation became one the first and most consequential viral videos of a celebrity. Richards hit the talk shows to apologize, from *Late Show with David Letterman* ([1993–2015], accompanied by Seinfeld, where Richards tried to explain that he was initially trying to be outrageous) to the radio program of the Reverend Al Sharpton. The incident was widely parodied, from *South Park* (1997–) to *Family Guy* (1999–). Even Dave Chappelle, in a December 2010 appearance at the Laugh Factory, joked, "Every time I see this backdrop, I think about Kramer fucking up. I don't want to see any camera phones on my ass tonight."[30] In *CCC*, Richards admits to Seinfeld, "I busted up after that event," and "it broke me down."[31] In actuality, he "busted up" during the event. And as Chappelle's bit about camera phones demonstrates, comedians are anxious about how busting up can prompt intense media attention.

In several instances in *CCC*, Seinfeld worries about how the ways audiences can react to comedians have changed. Smartphones allow audiences to record and then share a routine immediately, while social media, especially Twitter, provides a forum to share reactions, challenge certain jokes, and criticize humor they find offensive or inappropriate. With these technological developments, even those who were not in attendance can watch a set and comment.

Unsurprisingly, Seinfeld discounts social media, agreeing with Bill Burr that audiences "think" they have power, but "it's not changing anything."[32] He and Steve Harvey mock the idea that something can be "all over the internet." Concurring with Margaret Cho's comparison of social media to the "Catholic Church" trying "to make sure everyone is living decently," Seinfeld believes that people post comments to social media to counter their insecurity that "no one is listening to me. Do you know that I exist?" He concludes, "No, I don't know that you exist, and I don't care that you exist."[33] That snarky conclusion signifies a professional dissonance and antagonism that comedians may feel when audience do not laugh. The power dynamic has clearly shifted.

The clash between comedians and their audiences brings to mind theories by Stuart Hall about how audiences understand texts. In "Theories of Consumption in Media Studies," David Morley precisely summarizes Hall's theory of intention and reception—what the latter calls "encoding" and "decoding":

1) The same event can be encoded in more than one way.
2) The message always contains more than one potential "reading." Messages propose and prefer certain readings over others, but they can never become wholly closed around one's reading: they remain polysemic.
3) Understanding the message is also a problematical practice, however transparent and "natural" it may seem. Messages encoded one way can always be read in a different way.[34]

The well-established notion of polysemy focuses on how "audiences" might "decode" or interpret any message in various ways. Whatever a "producer" of media like a comedian might intend, a "receiver" or audience member is never passive. Hall's theories may not address the full extent of how audience react and read, however. Audiences make assumptions and then judgments not just about the "decoding," but about the "encoding" as well. And all that has changed is that an outlet has become available through which the audience can comment in a widely visible way. Seinfeld tries to convince everyone that what is true for him is true for everyone: comedians tell jokes, and audiences either laugh or do not laugh. Yet because of social media, the way each and every individual audience member may feel about a joke is potentially shared and thus public. In other words, comedians tell jokes, and audiences may react to the joke itself, its subject matter, or its delivery by commenting online about their reactions to any aspect of a joke. The most important takeaway here is that audiences are not passive. Despite comedians' intentions to make them laugh, audiences exercise their free speech in how they respond. A joke, of course, can be funny or not, yet it also can be offensive and cliché. The audience decides, as Seinfeld notes, but the comedian cannot control that.

Viewing the target of the joke as a victim is a long-standing theory of humor, superiority. This concept is much older than the ideas of PC culture, victimhood, and call-out culture, and scholars trace it back to Plato and Aristotle, Hobbes, and Descartes. In this view, humor arises when one celebrates their superiority over someone else's perceived inferiority. As many have suggested, we laugh at—not with—someone. For this very reason, Plato wanted to banish laughter from the republic, and Hobbes argued that laughter as a celebration of one's perceived superiority is cowardly.[35]

Thus, humor seemingly fixates on difference between the joker and the target. The theory of superiority holds laughing at someone or something as mocking, insulting, and labeling. It presumes a dominant position and judgment. It is part of a larger power structure that names what is appropriate, normal, and good—and what is not. Those that view laughter as insult or a statement of dominance, power, and judgment quickly reject any joke that seems to aim at a member of a marginalized or disenfranchised group. Consequently, jokes that are sexist, homophobic, racist, or ableist can potentially marginalize, victimize, harm, and reject those targeted groups.

Seinfeld and his follow comedians are not much different from the critics that they feel threaten comedy. More and more commentators and bloggers are warning about the dangers of "PC culture." The phrase is used to criticize the political Left, college students, and so-called "social justice warriors." In defending comedy as a tool for dialogue and education that pushes the line instead of crossing it, Seinfeld and his colleagues argue for its special role in culture. As such, they imply that it merits special consideration, acceptance, and celebration. Trying to defend comedy and comedians is not much different from questioning it and them. Seinfeld's considerable wealth allows him to speak out with little concern for the effect on his career; and his professional status and enduring popularity mean that he can appear on talk shows on his own terms. His privilege ensures that he does not have to acknowledge the inherent politics of his stances, which critical audience members are attempting to draw attention to in their remarks. He may not turn to social media, but he can and does express his outrage on traditional talk shows and via his web series *Comedians in Cars Getting Coffee*. If the view that America is now in a period plagued by charges of victimhood is valid, then expressions of outrage coming from either side of the debate should not surprise anyone. And outrage often emerges from those who are ready to defend and protect even when they are not directly affected.

As previously noted, Seinfeld and his peers appear concerned that PC culture is a threat to comedy. In *CCC*, Seinfeld frequently argues that comedy and humor are necessary and effective—something to allow and celebrate and not to shut down or limit. He tells Judd Apatow that comedians "decode it all."[36] Talking with Trevor Noah, he is interested in the idea of apartheid South Africa outlawing comedy, even though he earlier introduced Noah as having "an interesting, complex ethnic background," "none of [which] matters" because Noah is funny.[37] And in what might be his most telling take on humor and stand-up comedy, Seinfeld says to Jim Carrey that humor has "a childlike fun to it. [A comedian] can be angry [here, in the sense of political] and smarter than us but make it funny for us."[38] In short, Seinfeld wants a freedom of expression that he will not readily extend to his audience.

Instead Seinfeld repeatedly maintains that "funny is funny." While he stresses that the burden of that falls upon the comedian, he nonetheless seems quick to question any other reaction from the audience than laughing or not laughing. What is now true, though, is that like any other profession, comedians need to recognize and accept how social media permits the audience to express themselves outside the comedy club and after the comedy set. In an internet age defined by user-generated content, comedians and their humor are open to the same feedback, reaction, and criticism as any other profession. Every professional must acknowledge that the most significant change since the emergence of social media and the smartphone is professional accountability. Not being able to understand that brings about the malaise Floyd Taylor deems professional dissonance.

That anxiety might explain Seinfeld's complaint to Meyers and Remnick that "they keep moving the lines in for no reason."[39] The line is and has always been moving—pushed out by comedians who are edgy and pushed back by the audience members who are critical. If Seinfeld truly believes what he says to Margaret Cho, that "comedy is always on the way; we're on the way somewhere else,"[40] then he and his fellow comedians need to accept that accountability. Instead of feeling like cornered animals, comedians should understand that not every joke is funny to everyone—that's always been true. If more audiences are sensitive about subject matter, tone, and gestures, then comedians should either rework their material to make the audience laugh or put up with criticism about their sets.

Notes

1. Jerry Seinfeld, "Jerry Seinfeld Is Tired of Political Correctness," *Late Night with Seth Meyers*, filmed June 2015, YouTube video, 4:11, posted June 2015, https://youtu.be/KXDHjwaUtPI.

2. Jerry Seinfeld, Interview with Colin Cowherd, *The Herd with Colin Cowherd*, ESPN, June 4, 2015, ESPN Audio http://www.espn.com/espnradio/play/_/id/13010973.

3. Matthew R. Meier and Casey R. Schmitt, "Introduction," in *Standing Up, Speaking Out*, ed. Matthew R. Meier and Casey R. Schmitt (New York: Routledge, 2017), xxvi.

4. Christopher A. Medjesky, "How Can Rape Be Funny? Comic Persona, Irony, and the Limits of Rape Jokes," in *Standing Up, Speaking Out*, ed. Matthew R. Meier and Casey R. Schmitt (New York: Routledge, 2017), 195–212.

5. John Issitt and Duncan Jackson, "What Does It Mean to Be a Public Intellectual?" March 2013. https://www.heacademy.ac.uk/system/files/resources/12_march_presentation.pdf.

6. Issitt and Jackson, "What Does It Mean to Be a Public Intellectual?" 6.

7. See Sarah Silverman, interview with Parker Molloy, September 15, 2015, http://www.upworthy.com/sarah-silvermans-answer-to-this-question-about-political-correctness-was-totally-unexpected; Anthony Berteaux, "An Open Letter to Jerry Seinfeld from a 'Politically Correct' College Student," *Huffington Post*, June 9, 2016, http://www.huffingtonpost.com/anthony-berteaux/jerry-seinfeld-politcally-correct-college-student_b_7540878.html; and Amanda Marcotte, "Hey, Seinfeld: Don't Blame PC Culture For Your Lackluster Jokes," *TalkingPointsMemo*, June 11, 2015, http://talkingpointsmemo.com/cafe/seinfeld-pc-culture-seth-meyers.

8. Issitt and Jackson, "What Does It Mean to Be a Public Intellectual?"

9. *Comedians in Cars Getting Coffee*, "Steve Harvey: 'Always Do the Banana Joke First,'" Season 6, Episode 2.

10. See for example CCC episodes with David Letterman ("if you're funny, you survive; if you're not, you don't"), Seth Meyers ("your whole career is an act of charity. That you devote yourself to this somewhat painful existence, to make the world a little brighter"), Trevor Noah ("He has an interesting, complicated ethnic background. To me, none of that matters; to me, he's just a funny guy").

11. Mick Hume, "It's Worse than Jerry Seinfeld Says: PC Is Undermining Free Speech, Expression, Liberties," *Salon*, July 19, 2015, http://www.salon.com/2015/07/19/its_worse_than_jerry_seinfeld_says_pc_is_undermining_free_speech_expression_liberties/.

12. Marcotte, "Hey, Seinfeld: Don't Blame PC Culture For Your Lackluster Jokes."

13. @wallflower_91, Twitter, June 10, 2015, 7:57 a.m.

14. @arthur_affect, Twitter, September 9, 2015, 8:47 a.m.

15. Erica Hellerstein and Judd Legum, "The Phony Debate about Political Correctness," *Think Progress*, January 14, 2016, https://thinkprogress.org/the-phony-debate-about-political-correctness-f81da03b3bdb#.xyfpoire6.

16. Seinfeld, *The Herd with Colin Cowherd*.

17. Chris Jones, "Why Seinfeld Took a Stand against Political Correctness," *Chicago Tribune*, June 12, 2015, http://www.chicagotribune.com/entertainment/theater/comedy/ct-seinfeld-political-correctness-column.html.

18. Hume, "It's Worse than Jerry Seinfeld Says."

19. Adam Johnson, "Jerry Seinfeld—White Hetero Male Worth $820 Million—Thinks World Too 'PC,'" *Alternet*, June 12, 2015, http://www.alternet.org/culture/jerry-seinfeld-white-hetero-male-worth-820-million-thinks-world-too-pc.

20. Melissa Floyd Taylor, "Professional Dissonance: An Important Concept for Clinical Social Work," *Smith College Studies in Social Work* 77, no. 1 (2007): 89–100.

21. Matt Giles, "Breaking Down the Multi-Billion-Dollar *Seinfeld* Economy," *Vulture*, June 29, 2014, https://www.vulture.com/2014/06/breaking-down-the-seinfeld-economy.html#_ga=2.215750359.1375570055.1569994557-707847364.1569994557.

22. *Talking Funny*, HBO, http://www.hbo.com/comedy/talking-funny.

23. Katla McGlynn, "Seinfeld Schools Letterman On 'Comedians In Cars,' A.K.A. The 'Anti-Show About A Nonevent," *Huffington Post*, June 12, 2014, http://www.huffingtonpost.com/2014/06/10/jerry-seinfeld-david-letterman-comedians-in-cars-paley_n_5480298.html.

24. Judith Yaross Lee, *Twain's Brand: Humor in Contemporary American Culture* (Jackson: University Press of Mississippi, 2012), 67.

25. Jerry Seinfeld, "Jerry Seinfeld Talks Comedy, 'Seinfeld' reunion and Newman," interview with Peter Laura, "Buzzfeed Brews with *CBS This Morning*," filmed February 4, 2014, http://www.cbsnews.com/videos/jerry-seinfeld-talks-comedy-seinfeld-reunion-and-newman/.

26. Seinfeld, "Seinfeld Talks Comedy."

27. *Comedians in Cars Getting Coffee*, "Steve Martin: 'If You See This on a Toilet Seat, Don't Sit Down,'" Season 7, Episode 2.

28. *Comedians in Cars Getting Coffee*, "Howard Stern: 'The Last Days of Howard Stern,'" Season 3, Episode 7.

29. Reddit (2014). "Jerry Seinfeld Here. I Will Give You an Answer." Accessed September 16, 2016, https://www.reddit.com/r/IAmA/comments/1ujvrg/jerry_seinfeld_here_i_will_give_you_an_answer/.

30. Dave Chappelle, "Kramer," December 20, 2010, Laugh Factory YouTube video, 2:46, posted December 2010, https://www.youtube.com/watch?v=Kth0UOU5a_M.

31. *Comedians in Cars Getting Coffee*, "Michael Richards: 'It's Bubbly Time, Jerry,'" Season 1, Episode 10.

32. *Comedians in Cars Getting Coffee*, "Bill Burr: 'Smoking Past the Band,'" Season 3, Episode 7.

33. *Comedians in Cars Getting Coffee*, "Margaret Cho: You Can Go Cho Again," Season 8, Episode 2.

34. David Morley, "Theories of Consumption in Media Studies," in *Cultural Studies: An Anthology*, ed. Michael Ryan (Malden, MA: Blackwell, 2008), 1096–1111, 1098–99.

35. See John Morreall, "The Superiority Theory," in *Taking Laughter Seriously*, by John Morreall (Albany: State University of New York Press, 1983), 4–14.

36. *Comedians in Cars Getting Coffee*, "Judd Apatow: 'Escape From Syosset,'" Season 8, Episode 3.

37. *Comedians in Cars Getting Coffee*, "Trevor Noah: 'That's the Whole Point of Apartheid, Jerry,'" Season 6, Episode 5.

38. *Comedians in Cars Getting Coffee*, "Jim Carrey: 'We Love Breathing What You're Burning, Baby,'" Season 6, Episode 3.

39. Seinfeld, "Jerry Seinfeld Is Tired of Political Correctness."

40. *Comedians in Cars Getting Coffee*, "Cho."

STANDING FLAT-FOOTED AND TALKING
W. Kamau Bell Talks Race in an Age of "Post-Race"

Monique Taylor

> Blacks could sing and dance in the white night clubs but weren't allowed to stand flat-footed and talk to white folks, which is what a comic does.
> –Dick Gregory

WHAT'S THAT BUZZ?

In the spring of 2015, radio ears tuned to *This American Life* (1995–) were treated to a lesson in bias and microaggression by W. Kamau Bell. His tale, about the fallout and follow-up of an incident that took place in very liberal Berkeley, California, was the race chapter in the week's episode, "Birds and Bees." (That's birds and bees as in difficult things to discuss with children.) In the segment, "If You See Racism, Say Racism," Bell recounted a weekend afternoon when he found himself on the wrong side of a café worker's assumptions about race. On the day in question, Bell had stopped at the Elmwood Café to meet his wife and some of her friends who were seated in the outside dining area. A series of sharp raps on the glass window from inside the café were followed by hand gestures from one of the staff indicating that Kamau should scram/get lost/move on or something to that effect. Bell, his wife, and her friends were stunned.

SPOILER ALERT: In his comedy routines and writing, Bell often draws attention to the physical—at six feet four inches he calls himself a "big black male" (BBM). Another oft-mentioned biographical detail is the fact that he is married to a white woman. Theirs are mixed-race kids. Whatever was in the mind of the Elmwood staff person that day, she told Bell's wife that it wasn't "a race thing."[1] Bell and his wife disagreed. Bell blogged about the incident and, with his wife, penned a "dear Elmwood Café" letter to the owner inviting a public conversation (#SoYouCanComeToo). The post went viral and was vigorously debated online. A town hall reckoning on racial bias in Berkeley followed. During the town hall, community angst turned on uncomfortable facts about the intersection of racism and spatial politics. From the center of a racial storm, Bell had transformed the personal to the political in the blink of a social media eye.

It is not surprising how easily Bell could harness the power of the hashtag. He is a solid presence across today's media/social media landscape, and much cyber ink has been spilled about him. Google "Kamau Bell" and he appears to have been everywhere. Today Bell is the host of *United Shades of America*, a documentary series on CNN that has captured an Emmy for "Outstanding Unstructured Reality Series." Ranging across a broad comedy universe, Bell tackles the contradiction of racism in a (so-called) post-racial age head-on. His is a distinct antiracist perspective in blogs, podcasts, magazine essays, a televised series, and CDs of his stand-up work.

In an age where old media meets new, W. Kamau Bell embodies a current generation of comedians who square in every way with the criteria that critic Megan Garber identified as the connection between public intellectuals and comedy. Comedians, she writes, "are fashioning themselves not just as joke-tellers, but as truth-tellers—as intellectual and moral guides through the cultural debates of the moment."[2] While it is useful to ask whether Garber overreaches in her claim, academic definitions of public intellectuals have been subject to endless but unresolved debate: public intellectuals are claimed to be generalists, specialists, well-traveled and broadly educated, or cultural icons.[3] Never mind the high-minded characterization of public intellectuals as "a small and select group who kept themselves apart from the masses."[4] Garber's universe is populated by a "crop of culturally influential comedians in league with pretty much any human who has ever, in the face of an awkward silence, decided to make a fart joke."[5]

A closer look at scholarship on humor suggests that Garber's claim is neither bold nor entirely new. Lawrence E. Mintz, for one, points to anthropologists Mary Douglas and Victor Turner, who situated comedians in a broader social context as subversive commentators who use jokes to "tear down, distort, misrepresent, and reorder usual patterns of expression and perception."[6] To Mintz, the comedian operates as "comic *spokesperson*, mediator, articulator of culture, and as contemporary *anthropologist*."[7] In this position, Mintz argues, "modern American standup comedians provide . . . some of our most valuable social commentary."[8] Stripped of academic credentials, this position is not much different from Garber's.

Similarly, the "charged humor" of Rebecca Krefting fixes another framework in which comedy is wedded to public intellectualism. "Charged humor," Krefting argues, is used where "terms such as satire, political humor, or biting humor do not quite capture ... proactive qualities."[9] Rather, charged humor is "a metaphor [used] to describe humor intending to incite social change, develop community, and lobby for civil rights and acknowledgment."[10] Read closely, strategies employed repeatedly in Kamau Bell's comedy exhibit proactive and provocative intentionality. Most significantly, Bell's work—on-stage and off—invites a form of cultural citizenship which, as Krefting describes, "is not simply resistant; it can unite, edify, and rally on behalf of minority communities."[11]

When he introduced himself to the Elmwood Café's owner, Bell claimed a higher calling for his comedy: "I'm known for something that *The New Yorker* called 'intersectional progressivism,'" wrote Bell. "That basically means I use jokes to fight for the people who don't get a fair shake in the world.... I have tried to learn as much as I can about oppression in all forms so that I can help make the world slightly more bearable with a few jokes." The Elmwood episode revealed that Bell's work could command a public platform. And Bell's careful attention to audience development among a latte-liberal crowd makes him a pioneer in integrating the space of progressive politics through comedy.

Born in 1973, W. Kamau Bell updates and redefines civil rights conversations with an eye to present realities that is always informed by the past. While his intersectional worldview represents a generational shift, Bell situates his laughs with a legacy, nodding often in his work to Martin Luther King and Malcolm X, Rosa Parks, the Black Panthers, and slave ancestors. Trey Ellis, the author of the 1989 essay "New Black Aesthetic," was an early arrival to designate the post–civil rights generation as inheritors of "what *Village Voice* critic Greg Tate calls a 'post-liberated aesthetic.'"[12] And while this generation of Afro-punks and soul babies (as they have been tagged) might be liberated, they would not be free from what the critic Nelson George identified as a major contradiction of the 1980s. While it signaled an "unprecedented acceptance of black people in the public life of America," this acceptance, George noted, existed alongside "persistent poverty, poor education and lingering deep-seated social discrimination."[13]

In his work, W. Kamau Bell routinely calls attention to these contradictions. The ways in which Bell stands flat-footed and talks race in an age of post-race will be reviewed more systematically in this chapter through what Bertram D. Ashe calls the post-soul matrix—an analytical framework for cataloging and sorting the artistic sensibilities of a new generation that relies on fluid rather than fixed markers or containers of "Blackness." For Ashe, "post-soul" artists were born or came of age in the post–civil rights movement era. They produce work that grapples with the *cultural mulatto archetype*, attempts *"blaxploration,"* and/or employs strategies to achieve a *"'troubling' of blackness."*[14] The comic work of W. Kamau Bell contains each of the defining traits of the post-soul matrix.

THE CULTURAL MULATTO

A self-identified "blerd," or Black nerd, Bell's public/private comic persona is a study in cultural eclecticism and contrasts. Comic books and superheroes figure prominently throughout Bell's work. "Much like a member of the X-Men," he wrote in the inaugural entry of *Ending Racism*, the blog that accompanied his one-man show of the same title, "I was born with a superpower. I have an eye for racism. And like many mutants, I tried to ignore my superpower for years, hoping it would go away. But unfortunately for me it did not. My mom, who also has the eye, tried to prepare me, 'Professor Xavier-style' to learn how to harness and use my power for good."[15]

There's also the fanboy crush he has carried for years on Living Colour guitarist Vernon Reid. "Living Colour seems to summon . . . the appropriate level of black rage mixed with intellect and scathing criticism that I need to pull off ending racism in about an hour," Bell wrote in another *Ending Racism* post.[16] Eventually, Bell would co-host a podcast with Reid, *The Field Negro's Guide to Art and Culture* (2010–2014). Under a surreal and slippery system of numbering, the podcast's 56(-ish) episodes satisfy a psychic need for the cultural mulatto, delivering intimate talk on wide-ranging subjects with a precise theme that is hard to pinpoint. Their vision reaches toward a space for grappling with race beyond containers.

The Field Negro strategy of "geeking out" is the thread that ties Bell and Reid to Greg Tate and Trey Ellis; it places them among those longing for an expressive practice of culture that unlooses a sensibility at odds with presumably fixed racial identities outside the influence of history or social context. The sly reference to Malcolm X's house and field Negro dichotomy positions a posture of resistance, in this case, resistance to a (Black) box. The obsessive attention to detail that fanboys bring to superheroes and comic book culture is wielded as an analytical knife in unraveling the politics and culture of race. Bell and Reid hold great admiration for genre-busters like Prince, Hendrix, and Gil Scott-Heron. They could be serious and silly at the same time. One day the geeks bring a surgeon's skills to dissecting Swedish vampire movies;

another day, rage and raw emotion process news of the shooting of Trayvon Martin. The aftermath unfolds in real time across several podcasts.

As a cultural mulatto, Bell attracts and challenges a diverse audience of progressives, geeks, and nerds willing to embrace critical race thinking through engagement with multiple perspectives. Bell once used a catchy hook for his stand-up shows—bring a friend of a different race and get in two for one—which he often worked into his routine. "Y'all here taking my money," Bell would jibe, chiding but sounding pleased at the same time. On multiple occasions he has joked that not even MLK offered that kind of break. He frequently comments on the necessity of audience diversity for tackling awkward conversations rather than avoiding them.

The two-for-one special allowed Bell to challenge his audience in advance. "In my experience," he notes, "white people don't think about their whiteness nearly enough. If you can't find a friend of a different race to bring to the show, then maybe you should think about why that is."[17] By pointing to the lack of integrated social networks as an obstacle to ending racism, Bell's understanding of his work aligns with a broader goal of charged humor in that it is "intentional" with "designs on an outcome . . . a change in attitudes or beliefs or action taken on behalf of social inequality."[18] Where many Americans tiptoe around topics of race, Bell doesn't shy away from images, vocabulary, or scenarios that call on his audience to enter directly into dialogue with moral dilemmas of racism.

Exhibiting another aspect of charged humor, which "charges audience members with complicity toward social inequities,"[19] Bell consciously tackles an Achilles' heel of today's progressive movement—accusations that it has downplayed race relations, police violence, and racial justice. Progressives are a favorite target of his jokes. Bell's early *San Francisco Chronicle* blogposts defending the Occupy Wall Street movement, as well as his support of marriage equality and his frequent discussion of issues in the LGBT community, fleshed out intersectional progressivism as more than a catchy turn of phrase. An indication of how broad Bell's big liberal tent is: he tours with Laughter Against the Machine, an issue-oriented comedy troupe started in 2008 which offers "humor in the service of creating cultural citizenship."[20] Across two seasons of *Totally Biased* (2012–2013), an FX comedy stand-up news program, Bell's guest lineup spanned a universe of popular progressive figures like Rachel Maddow, Melissa Harris-Perry, and Tom Morello (of Rage Against the Machine), who introduced a diversity of perspectives as they seamlessly hopscotched along hot topics from tech to social justice without ever avoiding race talk.

On intimate terms with issues of the progressive Left and delivering jokes that point out oversights among the liberals in his audience, Bell challenges unconscious and unacknowledged racism from an ally's perspective. Bell's comedic voice prods whites to think and talk about their whiteness. Overall, the cultural mulatto proves useful as a subversive insider/outsider persona that injects race relations into the current progressive movement. An emphasis on diversity also features importantly in the Blaxploration and Troubling Blackness work that Bell does on and off stage.

BLAXPLORATION

In season 2 of *Totally Biased,* Bell welcomes the comic Aisha Tyler. They agree that the worst enforcers of what they call "Black rules" are Black people who issue declarations like "Black people don't eat bagels." They share a laugh over distancing themselves from this mentality and judgments like not being "Black Black." Black Black is a good starting point for charting the blaxplorations of W. Kamau Bell. Black Black assumes that Black can be defined. As such, Black Black becomes a necessary site of resistance for soul babies, cult-nats, B-boys, and freaky dekes to PC-policing within the Black community.

When Bell welcomes the comedian and actress Issa Rae to *Totally Biased*, they discuss a shared sensibility informing their comedy. Rae, the creator of *Awkward Black Girl* (2011–2013), reveals her comedy inspirations: "I love *The Office* [2005–2013], *Parks and Rec*. I like that type of humor but I didn't see that humor in shows of color and it bothered me."[21] Discomfortt with the sources of a Black comedic sensibility is an oft-explored theme on *Totally Biased*. A video sketch titled Black Hipstery Month, a *Masterpiece Theatre* (1971–) spoof (including high-brow music, high-brow host in an armchair), celebrated the first Black woman to laugh out loud at the television show *Portlandia* (2011–2018; created by the comedians Fred Armisen and Carrie Brownstein as a satirical poke at Portland, Oregon's over-the-top hipness). Was the assumption that only white hipsters would find *Portlandia* funny, or that only whites are hipsters? Boundary crossers like Aisha Tyler, Issa Rae, and Kamau Bell deploy blaxploration as a necessary search for a fluid Blackness that reframes what is considered funny and who can author what jokes for which audiences.

For Bell, his white wife and biracial children up the ante on his blaxplorations. His family frequently features as the subject of his jokes, lessons, and stories. "Kamau," Bell says in an imitation of his wife's voice, "when we have kids you realize our kids will be half black and half white?"[22] The innocence of her question as voiced by Bell sets up a safe space for audience members to arrive at a celebration of mixed marriages and biracial kids. But when Bell lets loose the laugh of a comic book villain, telling the audience "I was like harharharhar," he sets up a rap on the knuckles. Bell's drawn out "Nooooooo," in response to his spouse's question is in fact the start of unraveling a flaw in the logic of racial definitions. "If the last election proves anything," Bell states matter-of-factly, "it's that black + white equals black. Barack is not our first half black, half white president. He's our first black president."[23] The joke is a lesson wrapped in Bell's rebuttal. It also critiques wedding Obama's election to a so-called post-racial transition. Loud peals of laughter signal that the audience is with him when he uses the joke's punchline to redirect responsibility back to them. "[Y]ou made that call white people,"[24] concludes Bell, calling attention to whiteness, but also leaving his audience to rethink the logic of Black + white.

Bell often calls attention to race when he is on stage, employing the blaxploration strategy to challenge whiteness. Bell will refer to himself as "that Negro," undoing through naming an erasure of Blackness and whiteness that is the unspoken logic of color blindness. When Bell identifies a character as a "white lady" or attributes certain traits to "white people," he assigns responsibility, not blame. Often he will clarify his use of whiteness. With a pumping of palms-down hands, he'll reassure audiences that he doesn't mean "you white people" before he pauses a beat and lands the joke: their friends and family deserve the blame. These strategies create a fluidity that manages the performer/audience dynamic. Bell conjures an intimacy that erodes racial lines he lays down, allowing him to bring an audience to his side or cast them across to another.

Bell's comedic discourse is about inclusion through education. His routines touch upon people and issues that bring audiences up to speed with a language of critical progressive discourse. "Keep up," he might joke, but he'll never leave you behind. "Too soon?"[25] he will ask the audience, adopting a somewhat protective tone. "Some of you know this" are words of praise Bell uses to reward an audience for its awareness. Even Bell is on a learning curve, like the time he admitted "I feel like I should Google"[26] during his interview with transgender trailblazer Laverne Cox of *Orange Is the New Black* (2013–2019).

Overall, in the hands of Bell, blaxploration (which also includes naming and examining whiteness) creates flexible definitions and safe places to (re)examine racial categories. This is a necessary approach given the difficulty of the social issues Bell takes on when troubling Blackness, which we will see in the following pages.

STANDING FLAT-FOOTED AND TROUBLING BLACKNESS

In a November 2014 VanityFair.com essay, "On Being a Black Male, Six Feet Four Inches Tall, in America," Kamau Bell unloads the anxiety of a big Black male (BBM, as he shorthands it). His tale of a bumbled transaction on the back end of a late-night trip in search of ice cream reads like a dark parody of Richard Wright's *Native Son*. As Bell's narrative descends into an imagined dreamlike state, he casts himself as kin to the murderous Bigger Thomas. His body, his bulk, his hands, his palms, even his nappy head could run imagination into fear as a dangerous weapon when scripted by others.

Bell's heightened awareness about microaggressions against Black bodies—which can be both psychologically destructive and potentially fatal—defines another aspect of the post-soul aesthetic undergirding his humor. Bell troubles Blackness through commentaries on racial profiling, unequal policing, and flawed criminal justice. Routines on these topics exhibit another aspect of Krefting's charged humor where "a performer ... foregrounds ... marginality in order to call into question and disrupt the terms of ... subordination."[27] In extended sketches on his *One Night Only* (2007) and *Face Full of Flour* (2010) CDs, Bell creates a nuanced understanding of terror and violence against Black bodies while breaking down the anatomy of white fear.

In the routine "Opportunity Knocks," Bell is friendly and chatty. He asks the audience for advice in a move that allows them to share his perspective: "I always find myself in these tenuous racial situations, man. Maybe I did the wrong thing."[28] His self-deprecating lines offer an opportunity to consider what happened and why. He invites the audience to help out, addressing them as "you guys" and sharing details about the seemingly innocent experience of walking alongside a fellow pedestrian on a city street. The space of the stage will become the street scene that Bell, an imaginary white woman, and the audience will share.

By designating the woman as white, Bell introduces race but doesn't pre-assign the audience to either role, the white woman or the Black man. Instead he constructs and dismantles identities at the same time. Bell's large frame paces the entire stage when he performs, lending his stories a slapstick silliness: "You walking down the street with somebody you don't know. Lock step like you practiced. And you can't seem to break it. You slow down. They slow down. You ever have that happen?"[29] Anyone could be in this two-person walking routine without race being an issue. But Bell's story is long on detail as he recreates the physical space and pinpoints the moment when, and how, it becomes defined by a (racially charged) mental state: "she's doing that walk. ... The tense, white lady walk. It's all knees and elbows ... trying to be 'I'm not afraid of anything. I've taken ten self-defense classes. And I've got my car keys between my fingers.'"[30] Alongside laughter Bell has introduced fear. This is white fear, to be more precise, but Bell has already cleverly given the audience permission to walk in his shoes.

Verbally punctuating the suspense, Bell makes the story funny, as we imagine the two characters continuing this joined-at-the-hip walk: "I'm like alright go white girl go and I let her take the lead. Suddenly she takes a right turn. I need to take that same right turn. Then she makes a left turn. I need to make that same left turn."[31] We are still on Bell's side, and we relate to his gentle chiding. Bell is not angry, the audience is not accused, the white girl is the focus. But then Bell interjects a (literal) darkness into the narrative space as the situation takes another turn. The two find themselves in a "dark, secluded, very quiet street" when the white woman suddenly turns around, Kamau narrates, "and went like. ..." Here, Bell makes a long, drawn-out gasping sound in imitation of a shrieking woman and confesses: "it so freaked me out I actually looked behind me."[32]

Bell continues with a shrill falsetto as his character voices a shared fear with this white lady: "Is somebody following *us*?" he asks, now placing everyone on the same side (Bell, the white lady, and the audience). And he has almost pulled off a transformation—the Black man who shrieks in the dark could not possibly be a brute. But then he gets it: "Oh wait," he says, "*I'm* following *us*. I thought we were about to get mugged. But apparently I'm the mugger." The audience is laughing. The pronouns are a mash-up. Bell's punchline is a disturbing QED of the twisted logic of racism: "She talked me into mugging her, ladies and gentlemen. I had never mugged anybody before. I didn't know what to do. Finally, I got confused, I handed her my wallet and ran away. I just got un-mugged. It happens, man."[33]

Bell's concluding address to his audience as ladies and gentleman calls to mind the calm tones of a lawyer resting a case before a jury. "It happens" is not angry, accusatory or a rage-filled denunciation but instead suggests passivity. Bell's reenactment of "white behaviors" such as linguistic tics, hand gestures, and posture casts him in the role Stephanie Koziski designates for the comedian as anthropologist. "The standup comedian and the cultural anthropologist," writes Koziski, "look deeper beneath the surface of human behavior at the thought forces at work in a society. They ask what is really at work in human consciousness.... This involves the capacity to stand outside themselves and to empathize with people who are different in order to more fully understand their actions and beliefs."[34] An autopsy of the mugging joke shows action, intention, and racism in the mind of the fast (white) walker encountering the BBM.

In another routine, "Am I Racist?" Bell sets up an absurd scenario to explore assumptions about criminal Black bodies. "Sometimes I'm in situations where something happens and I'm not sure if I'm racist or not and you'd think I would know because it's my head."[35] This joke is another in which Bell strikes a gentle tone, inviting the audience to explore the human consciousness. Here, he manages the audience through a spatial setup that places them in an imagined but familiar location. Racially driven logic will be placed under a microscope:

> Same coffee shop. I go there all the time and there's always lots of people in coffee shops with their laptops. We all know that, but you ever notice this phenomenon? At some point in coffee shops people will get up from their laptop and leave it for a long period of time like it's protected inside the Starbucks border . . . like we all signed a treaty on the way in or some shit. . . .[36]

Bell knows his audience well. This isn't just a coffee shop, but a Starbucks (imagined as a nation with borders and a treaty, no less). Through familiarity he brings them on board as insiders. "Recently I've had a compulsion to just want to take [a laptop]," Bell confides, adopting the musing mind of a criminal. "Give me that laptop. I've got that laptop. Leave that laptop. I'm taking your laptop,"[37] he blurts in a speeded-up series of demands in a Dr. Evil cartoon voice followed by a gravelly growl. What if one of us didn't share the same values? Bell imagines, undermining the assumed safety of the communal space. What if "a compulsion" drove someone to steal? Bell keeps it funny with his comic book villainy, but he's clearly testing boundaries and beliefs of security and belonging.

What follows is a challenge to the audience through a series of statements meant to unravel the source of fear and profiling:

> Like what's going on inside my head, man? I'm not a criminal. I've never been in trouble with the law. I have my own laptop in front of me that I've bought and paid for but wait, do I really want to steal this laptop or do I just think I do because I'm black? Oh shit. I am racially profiling myself. Somebody watch that Negro in the corner. . . . I don't trust him. I think I've seen him before . . . in the mirror.[38]

On the surface, the laugh is that Bell is the goof for profiling himself and even the absurd notion that *he* would steal, since he has a laptop, "bought and paid for." The absurdity steers the joke to a safe space for consideration. And since Bell is profiling Bell, there is no insinuation of white guilt. The scene allows Bell to dig deeper into views about the purported criminality of Black bodies:

> And this next thing is like that upper level of crazy . . . it's like just some crazy institutionalized racism . . . I don't even know where it comes from. Whenever I am in a store that has those, uh, security gates that you have to walk through before you get out . . . whenever I'm in a store with that beeper that go[es] off . . . before I walk out . . . I always check my pockets. Just to make sure I didn't accidentally steal something because I've got these untrustworthy black hands. I don't trust these black hands, they could have took something.[39]

In the physicality that defines Bell's storytelling, the power of charged humor "reveal[s] the immediate experience of second-class citizenship and . . . reveal[s] how a person belongs and conversely how and where they do not belong, showing us how they fit into the national body politic."[40] The surveillance he is exploring goes beyond Starbucks and into a more generic commercial space where, on stage and in real life, so too does the profiling.

This routine mines unexamined profiling. By suggesting that he himself might "accidentally" steal because of "untrustworthy" Black hands, Bell brings the audience to his side of an absurdist calculation. By drawing close attention to his own hands as he winds up the routine, Bell humanizes the abstract Black man:

> What's going in my head man . . . let me check myself man. I could have took something. I don't know these hands. They're black on this side . . . the black side, that's the grabbing side. That's the grabbing side. That's the "hi how you doing" side. The grabbing side is what steals stuff when I'm not paying attention . . . I get caught. "Oh damn," I knew my black hands weren't trustworthy. I don't even like Celine Dion. What am I doing? What are you doing black hands you got bad taste in music? Untrustworthy black hands.[41]

By questioning "what's going on in my head," Bell is inviting the audience members to examine their own thoughts. His conclusion, analyzing the relative merits of staying inside versus going outside, is funny, but it leads to an interesting point: "Inside is where it's at. You can control your environment inside. My black hands steal something; I can put it down."[42] But in spaces where Black hands have no control, the consequences can be deadly, as in the streets of Ferguson, Baltimore, Dallas, Charlotte, and (to be continued).

Racism is not just individual, as Bell teaches; it is also institutional. And Bell often takes on the larger issue of institutional racism in the criminal justice system. In part, this is personal. As far as his comedy goes, it is unquestionably political. By directly challenging the gap between individual awareness and institutional injustice, Bell exemplifies what Krefting sees as an indictment function in the use of charged humor. "The humorist . . . seeks to bring new worldviews that eschew inequality into public consciousness and discourse. . . . [Charged humor is] a call for viewers to refigure dominant beliefs and stereotypes about minorities and their respective communities."[43] Ripped from the headlines, news provides ample fodder for Bell's reality-based routines.

In a 2010 routine called "Henry Louis Gates," Bell recounted a well-known incident in which a nationally known Harvard University professor was arrested by Cambridge police officers for allegedly breaking into his own home. The arrest became a litmus test for how the newly elected first Black president would handle race. It ended in a "beer summit," where then-President Obama invited Professor Gates and the arresting officer to sit down and break bread by drinking beer.

In the routine, Bell illuminates the fact that class, status, and power offer no protection against stereotypes of Black males as criminals. Bell addresses the audience by collectively naming them America. The issue is framed as a violation of assumed rights and privileges of Americans: "Man, America, we will invent some new crime for Negroes, won't we?"[44] Having invited the audience to a conversation started with a question, Bell moves on to a tsk-tsk tone: "Never heard of that one before. Arrested for being in his own house." Then with reference to hip-hop artists Public Enemy (and their song "911 is a Joke"), Bell mocks the implicit bias that underpins the police officer's shift from blasé to red alert: "that's not really a crime," says Bell, imitating what he imagines the police officer initially telling the neighbor. This is followed by a quick and officious-sounding "we'll be right there" after the officer learns that a Black person is involved in the break-in. Bell plays both parts in the neighbor-and-police exchange and raises his voice to a shrill and shouted call and response to depict white fear.

Ever masterful at keeping the audience on his side even in an uncomfortable and challenging routine, Bell quickly shifts back to narrating with a tone of calm, just-the-facts professionalism: Gates was in his house. The cops showed up. Gates flipped out. But Bell's voice rises with this last detail about Professor Gates's emotional frame of mind. "You're supposed to flip out," he explains in a loud and incredulous voice. "That's your right and privilege as an American. Isn't that why we flip out? Isn't that why he flipped out?"[45] he asks, appealing to Americanness as a common identity. The audience murmurs. They are challenged. Bell moves to reassure, returning to a playful manner, like a teacher encouraging nervous students. "I don't mind the audience dividing up into teams," he says supportively, "That's when we're getting shit."[46]

When Bell narrates the next turn of events, he doesn't mask his disappointment about Obama's handling of the incident. "He backed off," Bell says, sounding downcast. "I wish he could at the most have sent out his press secretary to read a statement."[47] And so Bell offers a do-over with the lesson he would like America to learn. Playing the part of an Obama spokesperson, he voices a stiff bureaucrat reading stilted bureaucratese: "This is on the Henry Louis Gates situation. Fuck the police coming straight from the underground. . . . Fuck the, fuck, fuck, fuck the police."[48] By now, some audience members are howling and Bell pounces on a divide he must sense between those who know and those who are clueless to his satirical riff: "For the white people who aren't sure about what that was, that is from the rap group NWA. It's from a song entitled 'Fuck the Police,'"[49] he playfully explains. He concludes with a spontaneous thanks to the Greek chorus, rewarding those hip enough to be in on a discursive wavelength radioed from the world of hip-hop, where challenges to unfair policing in the Black community are commonplace. In his own retelling and reimagining of the Henry Louis Gates episode, Bell channels a level of anger not typical of Obama and explores rage as an appropriate emotional response on behalf of Gates. This exposes his audience to sides of the Black psyche that offer a glimpse into a guarded worldview that might surprise and unsettle those who have been becoming comfortable with the idea of an idealized post-Obama, post-racial America.

CONCLUSION

W. Kamau Bell's Gen X sensibilities place him in a comedy lineage that runs from current events sketch comedy like *SNL* back to sardonic observations of the everyday revolutionized by Letterman and Seinfeld and alongside the Stewart and Colbert takeover-through-talking-back-to the news. But it is comedy's racial integration that most thoroughly paved the way for Bell's explorations of race. Bell shrugs off the fact that his show, *Totally Biased*, has been called "The Black *Daily Show*," reasoning that it offers a way of helping people grasp the pop-culture fit with an "alt," Left-of-liberal sensibility. It appears that even by the early twenty-first century, Dick Gregory's observation about the challenges of crossing over still holds some truth: "I've got to go up there as an individual first, a Negro second. I've got to be known as a colored funny man not a funny colored man."[50]

Bell's roots also trace their lineage to comedians like Dick Gregory, Bill Cosby, Flip Wilson, and Richard Pryor who "came of age during the era of civil rights and black power . . . and set the stage for later black performers."[51] Each represents comic personae, according to Bambi Haggins, linked to "differing depictions of African American identity" which are "tied to changing notions of blackness during (and after) the civil rights era."[52] For next-generation Black comedians, Gregory's "Black activist," Cosby's "assimilationist observer," Wilson's "affable jokester," and Pryor's "crazy n----r cultural critic" are wise and witty elders who staked out performative possibilities at the intersection of humor and race.[53] A generational advantage that distinguishes Bell from these forefathers lies in an expanded consumerist universe where blogs, podcasts, and websites define a multicultural demographic connecting stand-up work to a widely circulated worldview.

Bell joins a current generation of Black comedians like Eddie Murphy, Chris Rock, and Dave Chappelle who all wrestle with delivering comedy for mixed audiences even as they move into the post–civil rights integrated spaces of comedy on shows like *SNL*, *The Tonight Show with Jay Leno* (1992–2009, 2010–2014), and *Late Show with David Letterman*. The "post-racial" sensibilities of W. Kamau Bell's comedy exhibit distinct features within a post-soul matrix that allow him to draw in and diversify audiences as a cultural mulatto, to explore fluid definitions of Blackness (and whiteness), and to use the space of comedy to challenge Americans to trouble Blackness. For Bell, this is a successful formula wedding comedy to a public intellectual stance of subversion through standing flat-footed and talking race in an age of (presumed) post-racialism.

Notes

1. W. Kamau Bell, "Happy Birthday Have Some Racism from Elmwood Café," *W. Kamau Bell* (blog), January 2015, http://www.wkamaubell.com/blog/2015/01/happy-birthday-have-some-racism-from-elmwood-cafe.

2. Megan Garber, "How Comedians Became Public Intellectuals," *The Atlantic*, May 28, 2015.

3. See Richard A. Posner, *Public Intellectuals: A Study of Decline* (Cambridge, MA: Harvard University Press, 2001); Daniel C. Brouwer and Catherine R. Squires, "Public Intellectuals, Public Life, and the University," *Argumentation and Advocacy* 39 (2003): 201–13; Kitty Calavita,

"Engaged Research, 'Goose Bumps,' and the Role of the Public Intellectual," *Law & Society Review* 36, no. 1 (2002): 5–20.

4. Amitai Etzioni, "Are Public Intellectuals an Endangered Species?" in *Public Intellectuals: An Endangered Species?* ed. Amitai Etzioni and Alyssa Bowditch (Lanham, MD: Rowman & Littlefield), 16.

5. Garber, "How Comedians."

6. Lawrence E. Mintz, "Standup Comedy as Social and Cultural Mediation," *American Quarterly* 37, no. 1 (Spring 1985): 73.

7. Mintz, "Standup Comedy," 75.

8. Mintz, "Standup Comedy," 75.

9. Rebecca Krefting, *All Joking Aside: American Humor and Its Discontents* (Baltimore, MD: Johns Hopkins University Press, 2014), 25.

10. Krefting, *All Joking Aside*, 26.

11. Krefting, *All Joking Aside*, 26.

12. Trey Ellis, "The New Black Aesthetic," *Callaloo* 38 (Winter, 1989): 233–43.

13. Nelson George, *Post-Soul Nation: The Explosive, Contradictory, Triumphant, and Tragic 1980s as Experienced by African Americans (Previously Known as Blacks and Before That Negroes)* (New York: Penguin, 2005), ix.

14. Bertram D. Ashe, "Theorizing the Post-Soul Aesthetic: An Introduction," *African American Review* 41, no. 4 (2007): 602–23; Bertram D. Ashe, Crystal Anderson, Mark Anthony Neal, Evie Shockley, and Alexander Weheliye, "These—Are—the 'Breaks': A Roundtable Discussion on Teaching the Post-Soul Aesthetic," *African American Review* 41, no. 4 (2007): 787–803.

15. W. Kamau Bell, "An Eye for Racism," *The W. Kamau Bell Curve* (blog), January 2008, http://thewkbellcurve.blogspot.com/2008/01/.

16. W. Kamau Bell, "Some Blogs Are Just for Me," *The W. Kamau Bell Curve* (blog). February 9, 2008, http://thewkbellcurve.blogspot.com/2008/02/.

17. Quoted in Nisha Chittal, "Love Is Love: Comedian W. Kamau Bell and Melissa Hudson Bell," *MSNBC*, February 13, 2015, www.msnbc.com/msnbc/love-love-comedian-w-kamau-bell-and-melissa-hudson-bell.

18. Krefting, *All Joking Aside*, 25.

19. Krefting, *All Joking Aside*, 25.

20. Krefting, *All Joking Aside*, 25.

21. *Totally Biased*, season 1, episode 5, directed by Joe Perota, aired September 11, 2013, on FX.

22. W. Kamau Bell, "The Rules Have Changed," on *Face Full of Flour*, Blonde Medicine Holdings LLC B00MXBKFRC, 2010, CD.

23. Bell, "The Rules Have Changed."

24. Bell, "The Rules Have Changed."

25. See Bell, *Totally Biased*, season 1 and season 2.

26. Bell, *Totally Biased*, season 2 episode 6, directed by Kevin Avery, aired September 6, 2012, on FX.

27. Krefting, *All Joking Aside*, 25.

28. W. Kamau Bell, "Opportunity Knocks," on *One Night Only*.

29. Bell, "Opportunity Knocks."

30. Bell, "Opportunity Knocks."
31. Bell, "Opportunity Knocks."
32. Bell, "Opportunity Knocks."
33. Bell, "Opportunity Knocks."
34. Stephanie Koziski, "The Standup Comedian as Anthropologist: Intentional Cultural Critic," *Journal of Popular Culture* 18, no. 2 (Fall 1984): 73.
35. W. Kamau Bell, "Am I Racist?" on *One Night Only*.
36. Bell, "Am I Racist?"
37. Bell, "Am I Racist?"
38. Bell, "Am I Racist?"
39. Bell, "Am I Racist?"
40. Krefting, *All Joking Aside*, 25–26.
41. Bell, "Am I Racist?"
42. Bell, "Am I Racist?"
43. Krefting, *All Joking Aside*, 26.
44. W. Kamau Bell, "Henry Louis Gates," on *Face Full of Flour*.
45. Bell, "Henry Louis Gates."
46. Bell, "Henry Louis Gates."
47. Bell, "Henry Louis Gates."
48. Bell, "Henry Louis Gates."
49. Bell, "Henry Louis Gates."
50. Dick Gregory and Robert Lipsyte, *Nigger: An Autobiography* (New York: Pocket Books, 1965), xx.
51. Bambi Haggins, *Laughing Mad: The Black Comic Persona in Post-Soul America* (New Brunswick, NJ: Rutgers University Press, 2007), 17.
52. Haggins, *Laughing Mad*, 17.
53. Haggins, *Laughing Mad*, 17.

SMARTPHONE SOCIOLOGY
Aziz Ansari on Intimacy in the Twenty-First Century

Ila Tyagi

In his book *Modern Romance*, cowritten with the sociologist Eric Klinenberg, Aziz Ansari mentions an emotionally draining text message exchange he once had with a woman with whom he thought he had a promising connection. Eager to see "Tanya" again, he sent her a message beginning with the word "Hey," inviting her to a concert. When she failed to respond, Ansari descended into a "tornado of panic and hurt and anger."[1] Should he have typed "Hey" with two y's instead of one? Had her phone fallen into "a river/trash compactor/volcano"?[2] Had *she* fallen into a river/trash compactor/volcano? Why did she not simply say she was not interested, thus allowing him to invite someone else? The hysteria he was tailspinning into while compulsively checking his cellphone, Ansari realized, would not have existed "twenty or even ten years ago."[3]

Much of Ansari's output—from *Modern Romance*, to his stand-up, to his Netflix show *Master of None*—asks how people's romantic relationships have recently changed. He offers three answers to that question. First, we now look for soulmates, rather than someone who is just good enough. Second, we have many more prospective partners. Third, phenomena like online dating, social media websites, and especially smartphones mediate our interactions with those prospective partners.

Other scholars have worked on the first two insights prior to Ansari. Stephanie Coontz, for example, shows how yearning for a perfect match has replaced companionate unions in *Marriage, A History: How Love Conquered Marriage*. The psychologist Barry Schwartz has demonstrated that having to choose from a seemingly infinite array of options engenders significant anxiety: how to find the best one? Ansari cites both Coontz and Schwartz in *Modern Romance*. However, he has an original intellectual contribution to make with his third insight, on technologically mediated human relationships. Irving Howe wrote of public intellectuals as seeking to embrace "the spirit of the age."[4] If one of their characteristics is that they are sharp interlocutors of the particular historical moment in which they live, Ansari's work shows him as one such interlocutor who cannily explores the dynamic influences of his time on its social spaces.[5]

In his stand-up and elsewhere, Ansari maps the topography of what he calls "phone world." Not a literal place, phone world is instead a figurative setting wherein "we are connected to anyone and everyone in our lives, from our parents to a casual acquaintance whom we friend on Facebook."[6] It is "the place you go when you want to find someone to see a movie with. It's where you go to decide what movie to go see. It's where you buy the tickets. It's where you let your friend know you have arrived at the theater. It's where your friend tells you, 'Shit, I'm at the wrong theater,' and where you say, 'What the fuck, man? You always do this. Fine. I'm off to see *G. I. Joe: Retaliation* [Chu, 2013] alone, AGAIN.'"[7]

Phone world, in short, is all-consuming. In this essay, I argue for the importance of better understanding its omnipresence, and also that Aziz Ansari helps us think through just what it means to live within it. I unfold this argument over three sections, in which I examine Ansari's attentiveness to writing text messages, a medium in which speed and brevity are key and tone is often difficult to glean as a result; his interest in how communicating via text message is affecting social etiquette; and finally, his investigation of the emotional toll that inhabiting a world whose social etiquette is in flux takes on us. Iain MacRury has said that stand-up "makes a defining contribution to contemporary culture, providing a valuable locus for the affective and reflective interplay of public culture and private intimacy."[8] The statement is especially applicable to Ansari's body of work: the torsion between public culture and private intimacy is an abiding preoccupation for him, traceable across his entire oeuvre.

At his stand-up performances, Ansari operates like a sociologist in the field, asking audience members to let him peruse their phones so he can collect data on how our public relationships with other people are filtered through our private relationship with a small glass and metal machine. This field research is supplemented by the numerous focus groups he and Klinenberg met with in a number of countries for *Modern Romance*, their method of talking to actual subjects complementing the theoretical approaches to interpersonal relations found in work such as Nancy K. Baym's *Personal Connections in the Digital Age*.[9] Ansari pushes past homilies like "all our new communications technologies are making it impossible for people to really connect with one another" or "our new media makes things better than ever."[10] The first viewpoint has been discussed at length by many scholars, including Sherry Turkle, who argues in *Alone Together* that we shield ourselves from intimacy by erecting technological barriers around us.[11] The latter point of view, technological triumphalism, appears in such works as David Rose's *Enchanted Objects* and Kevin Kelly's *The Inevitable*, which breathlessly foresee a world where computers, watches, and smartphones completely revolutionize how we learn, work, and spend.[12] Ansari provides a more nuanced take on these two diametrical positions, suggesting that even though the denizens of phone world frequently endure bruised hearts, smartphones also compensate for the brutalities of modern romance by opening up new opportunities for intimacy between friends, between colleagues, between parents and children, and between a stand-up comedian and his audience. "Relationships with robots," in Turkle's words, "are ramping up; relationships with people are ramping down."[13] Per Ansari, our relationships with gadgets are certainly ramping up, but gadgets foster ramped-up relationships with people in real life too.

WRITING TEXT MESSAGES

One way smartphones nurture real life relationships is through their text message function, which Rich Ling suggests operates as a kind of "gifting" economy: your message is a present to me, and I reciprocate by sending another back to you. "Failure to reciprocate," as Ling says, "and failure to do so in a timely manner with a message of similar value, can indicate a breach in the relationship."[14] A received message's value, in other words, is measured by how long it takes to arrive, by its length, by the degree to which the sender has tailored it for the recipient, and by how skillfully the sender has crafted its tone. Unfortunately, the literary effects we are used to seeing in longer pieces of writing, such as tone, are difficult to recreate within a text message's limited space.

Text messages' tone can be uncertain not just because they tend to be concise, thus giving the recipient little to go on, but also because they lack the social cues informing conversations in person, such as facial expressions, vocal inflections, gestures, and pauses. Emoticons and strategic punctuation use—perky exclamation points rather than dour periods—can only do so much.[15] Ansari mines text messages' tonal ambiguity for humor. In his *Live at Madison Square Garden* (Ansari, 2015) stand-up show, he looks through a phone belonging to a volunteer from the audience.[16] She has been exchanging messages with a man who wrote, "Hey Ashley . . . it's Chris. It was nice to hanging with you at BM." Ansari, mimicking Chris's voice, adopts a suave bass for the first sentence, but switches to comic nasality for the second sentence due to its typographical error ("Chris, no! Proofread!"). Text messaging being an unforgiving medium, the two sentences yield two completely different iterations of the same person—one debonair, the other gauche.

As Ian Brodie has shown in his work on stand-up comedy as a genre of intimacy, the format "allows for reaction, participation, and engagement" on the part of those with whom the stand-up comedian is speaking.[17] This moment in *Live at Madison Square Garden* is preceded by Ansari inviting audience members to come to the stage with their phones, opening up avenues for personal connection in what could be a depersonalized mass experience in the enormous arena. In her interviews with professional stand-up comedians, Sharon Lockyer found that large arenas are generally not conducive to asking for verbal responses from the audience, causing comedians to flatten their material to make it universal enough to elicit maximum laughs, as well as to make it clear and easily digestible rather than ambivalent or challenging.[18]

Not so with Ansari, who takes the bold step of building extended contingency into his routine: his conversations with volunteers about their dating communications are open-ended and unpredictable, even a little meandering, in contrast to the high polish of the rest of the material. By turning part of the show into an opportunity for him to home in on an audience member as intently as they focus on him throughout the performance, Ansari weaves his narrative in collaboration with her, just as ancient oral storytellers turned their texts into opportunities for negotiation as listeners expressed belief or disbelief, requested clarification, or offered corroboration.[19] With each such encounter, Ansari creates an intimate forum for the exchange of ideas, strengthening ties between himself and his audiences. A comedian, in Lawrence E. Mintz's words, must establish that his audience is "homogenous, a community, if the laughter is to come easily."[20]

Collaborating on composing a text message in the "Nashville" episode of *Master of None*'s first season similarly tightens the communal bond between Ansari's character, Dev, and his friends Arnold (Eric Wareheim) and Denise (Lena Waithe). Texting Rachel (Noël Wells) to ask her out on a date, Dev initially writes, "This may sound nuts, but would you want to go to Nashville for the weekend?"[21] "I think that text could use some seasoning, man. Maybe add a little of that classic Dev spice," Arnold says. Dev's second draft reads, "Are you down to clown in Nash-town?" "Fire it off, playboy," Denise replies, granting the revision her seal of approval. Working on the text message together is a testament to the camaraderie enjoyed by the group, just as

Dev soliciting the help of his coworker Benjamin (H. Jon Benjamin) to text his friend Brian (Kelvin Yu) back in an earlier episode serves to affirm and deepen his and Benjamin's intimacy.

In *Master of None*'s "Hot Ticket" episode, Dev, an actor, is in a makeup chair and cannot move his arms, so Benjamin types out replies to Brian. While doing so, he corrects Dev's tone. Brian has asked Dev if he wants to try a ramen restaurant, and Dev instructs Benjamin to write "No." "Just 'no'?" Benjamin says, scandalized. "That's incredibly rude." Research on emailing finds that senders overestimate their skill at transmitting their intended tone due to egocentrism, the "well-established social psychological phenomenon whereby people have a difficult time detaching themselves from their own perspectives and understanding how other people will interpret them."[22] Benjamin forces Dev to inhabit Brian's perspective and consider for a moment how he might feel receiving a monosyllabic rejection of his invitation. The time taken to contemplate a message's effect on a recipient is often elided in speedy text exchanges, but by deliberately typing out a longer response, Benjamin imbues the message with a more compassionate tone. His emendation is "Sorry, just ate, but I really admire you as a person." Brian is touched, vindicating Benjamin's composition.

In other words, verbosity is shown to be superior to brevity within the text message context. This violates a commonly accepted rule of good writing: that writers should not use more words than necessary. In his book *The Sociological Imagination*, C. Wright Mills lampoons fellow sociologist Talcott Parsons's long-windedness by quoting grandiloquent passages from the latter's *The Social System* and then supplying laughably brief summaries in plain English. Mills argues of circumlocutory academic writing that "'more fully' does not necessarily mean 'more adequately.'"[23] However, fleshing writing out more fully in phone world, Benjamin would counterargue, displays better social judgment, a more empathetic engagement with the message recipient's emotional life. Though they may seem a moldering relic of a predigital age, full sentences in a text message help raise the recipient closer to the level of information the sender has regarding her intentions and motivations, minimizing miscommunication. Living in phone world ideally sharpens our sensitivity to language, and heightens our capacity for empathy, by obliging us to imagine how others will construe our writing. Precisely because it is shorn of the cues that would normally signal our meaning, text messaging can refine our ability to express ourselves clearly in constrained space.

Ansari shares Mills's flair for condensed clarity. When comparing sociology to comedy in an interview, Ansari neatly boils two complex fields down to their essence as follows: sociology and comedy are both "about making observations that resonate with people and trying to work out why they do the things they do."[24] Parsons's much more unwieldy definition of sociology is that it has to do with "that aspect of the theory of social systems which is concerned with the phenomena of the institutionalization of patterns of value-orientation in the social system, with the conditions of that institutionalization; and of changes in the patterns, with conditions of conformity with and deviance from a set of such patterns, and with motivational processes in so far as they are involved in all of these."[25] Mills's translation of this almost impenetrable excerpt is simply, "Sociologists of my sort would like to study what people want and cherish. We would also like to find out why there is a variety of such values and why they change. When we do find a more or less unitary set of values, we would like to find out why some people do and others do not conform to them."[26] Ansari's professed interest in why people "do the things they do" is another way of saying that he wants to know what people value, why people value different things, and the manner in which people's values change. This interest in variable values emerges in the makeup-chair scene, where Dev's value system that deems a reply like "No" appropriate clashes with Benjamin's value system that considers such a terse response rude. Benjamin's values prevail; Dev's values change to conform to those of his colleague because he sees that taking time to type out a more thoughtful message generates considerable goodwill for the sender.

MORPHING SOCIAL ETIQUETTE

Ansari's sociological interest in variations in people's values, as well as in their evolution, also comes up in another "Hot Ticket" scene. Dev vents to Arnold, Brian, and Denise that a woman, Alice, whom he has invited to a concert has not bothered to text him back (a fictional scenario likely modeled on Ansari's real-life experience with Tanya). "They give you silence," Dev fumes. "Why?" Ansari's 2012 stand-up show "Dangerously Delicious" contains a similar bit, where he jokes that after he and a woman have been texting back and forth for a while, he will ask her if she wants to have pizza on Tuesday, "And then I don't hear anything! And I'm like, 'What just happened? I know you read that shit. You responded to twenty other things I just said. What, do you not like me anymore? You don't have two seconds to say, 'yes, I want to get pizza,' or 'no, I don't want to get pizza'? What, did you check your phone into a locker and go ride a roller coaster for a few hours?'"[27] Ansari expects a response; the woman in question does not believe one is required.

Ansari senses, in other words, that social codes are in flux, which means it is up to individuals to decide how to behave on a case-by-case basis. No one is sure anymore how to communicate with potential romantic partners. "With all these technological transitions, our feelings about when to use which medium have gotten pretty mixed up and confused," Ansari says in *Modern Romance*. "How do we figure out when to call, when to text, and when to just drop everything, stand outside someone's window, and serenade them with your favorite nineties R&B tune?"[28] While a majority of teenagers would be comfortable receiving an invitation to prom via text, for older generations "the idea of getting invited to something as special as prom by a text message may sound cold and impersonal."[29] Not only are there more options now for communicating with someone than before; a broader range of ways to interact with them is becoming increasingly socially acceptable—including abstaining from interacting with them altogether, which earlier would have seemed impermissibly rude.

In *Live at Madison Square Garden*, Ansari observes that we as phone world occupants have three main options when someone asks us out on a date and we want to decline: we can be honest and say we are not interested, we can pretend to be busy for as long as it takes for them to get the hint, or we can say nothing. His taxonomy helpfully extracts some order from the chaos unleashed by evolving social mores. Ansari's work also debates the pros and cons of each tactic. A recurring theme is that despite social etiquette's new laxity, not responding remains unacceptable. The growing absurdity of his imaginary conversation with the woman in "Dangerously Delicious"—"Well, guess who just got uninvited to the pizza party? You did, because I hate you now"—is funny, but his humor masks a real frustration with the callousness of failing to respond to an invitation to go on a date. In *Live at Madison Square Garden*, Ansari points out that being asked out is "a huge compliment, right? They're basically saying, 'Hey, out of the infinite number of things I could do with my time, what I'd like to do is spend some time with you.'" That compliment deserves to be acknowledged, at the very least.

In "Hot Ticket," though, Denise explains why some people might prefer simply not responding to the politer alternative of pretending to be busy. She draws from her ordeal with "Princess Love," who is leaving insistent, incessant voicemails on Denise's phone instead of registering that her "polite, busy excuses" mean no. "That's why you don't engage," Denise says firmly. Ansari is also leery of the option of being honest. "In our hearts we all want to give others honesty, but in practice it's just too damn hard," he says in *Modern Romance*. "Honesty is confrontational. Crafting the 'honest' message takes a lot of time and thought. And no matter how delicately you do it, it feels cold and mean to reject someone."[30] Ansari emphasizes this point in *Live at Madison Square Garden*, laying out a hypothetical "honest" text message exchange: "'Hey, you wanna get dinner sometime?' 'I'm not interested in getting dinner with you.' 'Goddamn! What are you, a demon?'"

So if honesty is too harsh and silence too rude, what does that leave? Pretending to be busy "until people get the picture," despite the risk that they will be as painfully oblivious as Princess Love.[31] None of the three options is ideal, but the busyness charade is least likely to hurt someone's feelings. Ansari pleads for using kindness as a behavioral guideline, as there seems to be no fixed, universally accepted protocol governing social relationships in phone world. "I'm a person," Dev says plaintively in "Hot Ticket." "I'm not just a bubble in a phone. Let's just be nice." "When you look at your phone and see a text from a potential partner," Ansari says in *Modern Romance*, "you don't always see another person—you often see a little bubble with text in it. And it's easy to forget that this bubble is actually a person. But it's so, so important to remember this."[32]

Ansari argues that we have two selves: a real-world self and a phone self. Since texting with someone keeps us at a slight remove from them, our phone selves can foreground "flakiness and rudeness and many other personality traits that would not be expressed in a phone call or an in-person interaction."[33] Bridging the split between real-world and phone selves, on the other hand, prevents us from hiding behind the bubbles. We may be dimly aware that there is another person just like us on the other end of the exchange, someone similarly stewing in anxiety as they anticipate our reply who therefore merits our empathy. However, as Stephanie Koziski says, comedians with anthropological or sociological leanings make us *consciously* reflect on "tacit operating knowledge."[34] When we witness Ansari deliberately scrutinizing our callous texting habits, behaviors that might otherwise have gone unacknowledged are brought to the fore. We are then more likely to visualize the people we text with as real human beings and to show them a shred of sympathy, instead of leaving them marinating in the anticipation, uncertainty, and anxiety that dominate phone world's emotional landscape.

HEFTY EMOTIONAL TOLL

Modern Romance offers an explanation as to why emotions in phone world are so fraught. Interviewing Natasha Schüll, an anthropologist studying gambling addiction, Ansari learns that "texting is a medium that conditions our minds in a distinctive way, and we expect our exchanges to work differently with messages than they did with phone calls."³⁵ In the landline era, people could wait up to a few days to call back before the person trusting to hear from them became concerned. Texting has habituated us to receiving faster responses. Schüll compares phone calls to cards, horse races, or the weekly lottery, all of which have waiting periods built in, whereas texting is akin to slot machines' instant gratification, obviating tolerance for delay. "Your whole system is primed to receive a message back," she says, "You want it—you *need* it—right away, and if it doesn't come, your whole system is like, 'Aaaaah!' You don't know what to do with the lack of response, the unresolved outcome."³⁶

Ian Bogost, one of the first media scholars to have written on the topic of smartphones, presents another explanation as to why our communications on these devices stoke anxiety. In *The Geek's Chihuahua*, he muses on how the pleasure afforded by slamming a telephone receiver down (thereby discharging acrimony) is vanishing. "It's not possible to hang up on someone via smartphone with deliberateness, because it's so much more likely that the network itself will disconnect of its own accord," he says, "The signal can be lost, the device's battery can deplete, the caller can accidentally bump the touch screen and end the call, the phone's operating system can crash. The mobile hangup never signals itself as such but remains shrouded in uncertainties."³⁷ Bogost adds that

> We've traded in our hangups for our hang-ups. The social disruption we now give or get via mobile devices is not the belligerence of hanging up or having been hung up on but the neurosis of not having received a response. In place of the threat of disengagement in fixed-line switched analog telephony, we find a subtly different fear in cellular telephony and its digital cousins: that of disregard. In the past the telephone was most threatening when it cut someone off; today its greatest menace is to reveal that you were never really connected in the first place.³⁸

The uneasiness of waiting for a text message response, in other words, is a noxious cocktail of dashed hopes for a prompt reply and suspicion that no reply is forthcoming after all because the sender unwittingly overestimated the closeness of her relationship with the recipient. While pining by a landline phone can be lonely enough, staring in anticipation at a smartphone screen is an exaggerated version of that loneliness, perhaps because smartphone screens usually produce such a rich cornucopia of new information every time they are stroked. The contrast between the powerful feeling of summoning fresh content at will and the powerlessness of being unable to conjure a longed-for message, no matter how much we caress our device, leaves us desolate. In *Master of None*'s "Parents" episode, Dev encounters the opposite problem. Unlike the dearth of text message responses marking his romantic life, an inundation of unwanted incoming texts defines his relationship with his parents, particularly his father. Dev grumbles to Brian about the barrage of text messages his father is sending him about his faulty iPad. "I don't think my dad knows how to text," Brian replies. Later in the episode, however, after Brian and Dev take their parents out to dinner, Brian's father has exchanged numbers with Dev's father, and the two of them are texting their sons avidly. Dev and Brian are initially reluctant to engage in a sustained relationship with their fathers and worm their way out of a second dinner invitation. Undeterred, Ramesh (played by the comedian's real-life father, Shoukath Ansari) continues texting his son regularly, per his habit. As Ramesh understands it, the new text message medium bolsters the parent–child bond even if children are remiss in keeping up their half of the exchange.

This is a quality specific to communications between people who are already close, or maybe unique to communications between parents and children: a tacit agreement that the message recipient, the child, is not required to respond. It is enough for the parent sender to have said, through their message, "I am here." Bogost argues that much digital communication, such as text messaging or online chatting, can be reduced to "variants of that one thing: *Here I am*. Are you here? Yes, yes, I'm here."[39] Bogost believes that today we often want to communicate, but "even more often we simply want to *meta-communicate*, to possess the knowledge that an individual or group will acknowledge us."[40] Ramesh communicates with his son selflessly, not desiring acknowledgement so much as wanting to remind his son that he is there for him. Their intimate relationship, built on many years of interactions in person, is available to his son whenever the latter wishes to resume it. Text messaging, in short, becomes another forum in which unconditional parental love can be expressed, providing succor for all the text message encounters Dev has with other people whom he does not know as well, encounters that bristle with disappointments.

By the end of the "Parents" episode, Dev's irritation at his father's relentless messages has transmogrified into gratitude that he is consistently laboring to keep a channel of communication open with his son. After Dev bombs an audition, his father's messages, painstakingly typed out in capital letters, become a source of comfort. Viewers see close-ups of two of them, "SORRY YOU CANT MAKE DINNER GIMME A CALL" and "YOU MUST BE BUSY CALL WHEN YOU CAN." His father is one of the few people with whom Dev actually uses his phone as a phone, befitting his father's age, but also denoting the specialness of their relationship. The text messages pave the way for an old-fashioned phone conversation in which Dev's father tells him that he is proud of him, despite the unsuccessful audition. The phone conversation, in turn, leads to Dev visiting his parents in person, bearing gifts: a framed photograph of the family for his mother, and a guitar for his father, whose own father had refused to buy him one as a child. On this visit, Dev fixes the trouble his father was having with the calendar on his iPad, scheduling a weekly call for them in the process. Through his work, Ansari makes the case that technology's advantages are manifold, but we should also remember to put our phones down from time to time and connect in person. Smartphones ought to facilitate or supplement face-to-face interactions, rather than displacing them entirely.

CODA

This lesson applies not just to relationships with parents, but also to romantic relationships and relationships with friends. In *Modern Romance*, Ansari proposes that online dating be thought of not as dating, but as an online introduction service—that is, it should be used as a springboard to meeting people in person, not as an end in itself, even though staying in and "clicking through profiles in your pajamas" may be tempting.[41] Likewise, smartphones in *Master of None* serve as the foundation for maintaining relationships between friends, but upon that foundation is built a wealth of interactions in person.

In the "Parents" episode, we see a close-up of Dev's phone as he types a text to Brian, followed by an establishing shot of Brian sitting on a couch, and a close-up of his phone receiving Dev's message. The close-up of Brian's phone is shot from the same angle as the close-up of Dev's phone, looking over both characters' right shoulders. The similarity between the shots has the effect of binding Dev and Brian together, even though they are in different places. The phone's annihilation of space and time has supported the development of formal techniques like parallel editing in moving images at least as far back as D. W. Griffith's *The Lonely Villa* (1909). Tom Gunning tracks films like *The Lonely Villa* even further back to one-act plays like *Au Téléphone* (1901), in which the protagonist helplessly hears his wife and child murdered by a robber over the phone. Rather than allowing him to overcome space and time, the device "torments him with distance and impotence. Electronic sound on the telephone can pass to and fro instantly, but the flesh and blood husband and father remains fixed."[42] Compressing space and time over the phone, though marvelous, is a pale shadow of the richness of flesh-and-blood presence. Thus, the message we see Dev sending and Brian receiving is "Headed over," an affirmation of the importance of physical interaction over the simulacrum of connection dispatching a text in one place and reading it immediately in another offers.

This is assuming we actually receive a response to the texts we beam out, of course. While awaiting a text back from Tanya that never came, it dawned on Ansari that "We each sit alone, staring at this black screen with a whole range of emotions. But in a strange way, we are all doing it together, and we should take solace in the fact."[43] Ansari went to a comedy club instead of the concert with Tanya. He told the audience there about "the awful frustration, self-doubt, and rage that this whole 'silence' nonsense had provoked in the depths of my being. I got laughs but also something bigger, like the audience and I were connecting on a deeper level."[44] Intimacy is a crucial component of comedy: as Noël Carroll has argued, humor "functions to build and to consolidate communities, however ephemeral," making it useful "to establish contact with strangers."[45] Our text messages are customarily intensely personal, but just as Ansari's audience grants him access to private corners of their lives by letting him probe their phones, Ansari likewise gives a great deal of himself to his audience. He harnesses the fact that the residents of phone world share more emotional ground than they might think in order to establish rapport, in person, with the attendees at his stand-up shows.

Ansari continues forging an intimate communion with his audience in his most recent stand-up show, *Right Now* (Jonze, 2019), as he takes stock of his life over the year and a half since a *Babe* exposé in January 2018 accused him of sexual misconduct.[46] Rather than striding confidently back and forth onstage, Ansari chooses to stay seated for most of this performance, his stool low and as close to the edge of the stage and to his audience members as possible. His posture is humble, his tone penitent. In a voice barely above a whisper, he confesses to having felt "terrible" after the article was published. According to the *Babe* account, Ansari was hell-bent on having his way with a 22-year-old woman he had met at an Emmy Awards after-party, hurrying her through dinner and back to his apartment on their first date. Once there, he repeatedly forced himself on her, despite her attempts to rebuff him. They stopped short of having what she called "actual sex," but "Grace" told *Babe* that she still felt "violated."[47] Ansari did not perpetrate a full-fledged criminal assault. Nevertheless, his boorishness came under fire. Referring to *Modern Romance* in her late-night talk show *Full Frontal with Samantha Bee* (2016–), host Bee pointed out that the author of a book about "how to sex good" ought to know better than to pressure women into sleeping with him.[48] Ansari had vocal defenders as well, such as the television news anchor Ashleigh Banfield, who accused "Grace" of cheapening the #MeToo movement by equating a "bad date" with rape.[49] Ansari released a statement in which he claimed to have understood his encounter with "Grace" to be consensual, and thereafter kept a low profile.[50]

He eventually returned to the public eye in the fall of 2018 with a new comedy tour, "Working Out New Material," upon which *Right Now* is based.[51] In *Right Now*, Ansari wins his audience over by straightaway acknowledging the *Babe* scandal, showing how he has used the shameful incident to become more considerate in his private life. Having established a baseline intimacy with his audience by openly discussing his humiliation, Ansari proceeds to build upon that intimacy, asking individual audience members questions as he moves through his set and soliciting spontaneous participation from them. Stand-up is live, unpredictable, and dynamically evolving, and as such it functions as something of an antidote to the difficulty we are supposedly increasingly having with real-time interactions as we become more used to communicating through asynchronously composed digital messages instead. Ansari had noticed that *Modern Romance* focus groups populated by older people differed from those populated by younger people: the former would be full of chatter, and the latter would be buried in their phones. This led him to wonder if "our ability and desire to interact with strangers is another muscle that risks atrophy in the smartphone world."[52] A comedian and his audience talking directly to each other, free from technological mediation, can counteract to some extent the smartphone age's diminished opportunities for sharing experiences with strangers. The attentiveness to phone world's details in Ansari's work sparks a feeling of recognition and kinship—at one time or another, we have all waited in agony for a text that took too long to arrive, or had a message we dashed off in haste misunderstood. What we experience as personal emotional toll is in fact collective. Ansari's comedy allows us to laugh over it together in the real world and, as a result, to feel less alone.

Notes

1. Aziz Ansari and Eric Klinenberg, *Modern Romance* (New York: Penguin, 2015), 5.
2. Ansari and Klinenberg, *Modern Romance*, 4.
3. Ansari and Klinenberg, *Modern Romance*, 5.
4. "From *A Margin of Hope* by Irving Howe," PBS.org, accessed August 30, 2017, https://www.pbs.org/arguing/nyintellectuals_howe_2.html.
5. Ta-Nehisi Coates, "What It Means to Be a Public Intellectual," *Atlantic.com*, last modified January 8, 2014, https://www.theatlantic.com/politics/archive/2014/01/what-it-means-to-be-a-public-intellectual/282907/.

6. Ansari and Klinenberg, *Modern Romance*, 31.

7. Ansari and Klinenberg, *Modern Romance*, 31.

8. Iain MacRury, "Humour as 'Social Dreaming': Stand-up Comedy as Therapeutic Performance," *Psychoanalysis, Culture & Society* 17, no. 2 (2012): 185.

9. Nancy K. Baym, *Personal Connections in the Digital Age* (Malden, MA: Polity Press, 2010).

10. Ansari and Klinenberg, *Modern Romance*, 251.

11. Sherry Turkle, *Alone Together: Why We Expect More from Technology and Less from Each Other* (New York: Basic Books, 2011), xii.

12. David Rose, *Enchanted Objects: Innovation, Design, and the Future of Technology* (New York: Scribner, 2014); Kevin Kelly, *The Inevitable: Understanding the 12 Technological Forces that Will Shape Our Future* (New York: Viking, 2016).

13. Turkle, *Alone Together*, 18.

14. Rich Ling, *The Mobile Connection: The Cell Phone's Impact on Society* (San Francisco: Morgan Kaufmann, 2004), 111, 153.

15. Eric Jaffe, "Why It's So Hard to Detect Emotion in Emails and Texts," *FastCoDesign.com*, last modified October 9, 2014, http://www.fastcodesign.com/3036748/evidence/why-its-so-hard-to-detect-emotion-in-emails-and-texts.

16. *Aziz Ansari Live at Madison Square Garden*, Netflix.com, accessed June 6, 2016, https://www.netflix.com/title/80038296.

17. Ian Brodie, "Stand-up Comedy as a Genre of Intimacy," *Ethnologies* 302 (2008): 153.

18. Sharon Lockyer, "Performance, Expectation, Interaction, and Intimacy: On the Opportunities and Limitations of Arena Stand-up Comedy for Comedians and Audiences," *The Journal of Popular Culture* 48, no. 3 (2015): 591–93.

19. Brodie, "Stand-up Comedy as a Genre of Intimacy," 155.

20. Lawrence E. Mintz, "Standup Comedy as Social and Cultural Mediation," *American Quarterly* 37, no. 1 (Spring 1985): 78.

21. *Master of None*, Netflix.com, accessed June 6, 2016, https://www.netflix.com/title/80049714.

22. Lea Winerman, "E-mails and Egos," APA.org, accessed June 7, 2016, http://www.apa.org/monitor/feb06/egos.aspx.

23. C. Wright Mills, *The Sociological Imagination* (New York: Oxford University Press, 1981–82 [1959]), 33.

24. Dan Rookwood, "Mr Aziz Ansari," MrPorter.com, accessed June 9, 2016, http://www.mrporter.com/journal/the-look/mr-aziz-ansari/587.

25. Mills, *The Sociological Imagination*, 35.

26. Mills, *The Sociological Imagination*, 35.

27. *Aziz Ansari: Dangerously Delicious*, Netflix.com, accessed June 9, 2016. No longer available via streaming.

28. Ansari and Klinenberg, *Modern Romance*, 38–39.

29. Ansari and Klinenberg, *Modern Romance*, 36.

30. Ansari and Klinenberg, *Modern Romance*, 66–67.

31. Ansari and Klinenberg, *Modern Romance*, 67.

32. Ansari and Klinenberg, *Modern Romance*, 240.

33. Ansari and Klinenberg, *Modern Romance*, 44.

34. Stephanie Koziski, "The Standup Comedian as Anthropologist: Intentional Culture Critic," *Journal of Popular Culture* 18, no. 2 (Fall 1984): 57.

35. Ansari and Klinenberg, *Modern Romance*, 60.

36. Ansari and Klinenberg, *Modern Romance*, 60.

37. Ian Bogost, *The Geek's Chihuahua: Living with Apple* (Minneapolis: University of Minnesota Press, 2015), 66.

38. Bogost, *The Geek's Chihuahua*, 68.

39. Bogost, *The Geek's Chihuahua*, 62.

40. Bogost, *The Geek's Chihuahua*, 61.

41. Ansari and Klinenberg, *Modern Romance*, 246.

42. Tom Gunning, "Heard Over the Phone: *The Lonely Villa* and the de Lorde Tradition of the Terrors of Technology," *Screen* 32, no. 2 (Summer 1991): 192.

43. Ansari and Klinenberg, *Modern Romance*, 6.

44. Ansari and Klinenberg, *Modern Romance*, 5.

45. Noël Carroll, *Humor: A Very Short Introduction* (Oxford: Oxford University Press, 2014), 84.

46. *Aziz Ansari: Right Now*, Netflix.com, accessed August 4, 2019, https://www.netflix.com/title/81098589.

47. Katie Way, "I Went on a Date with Aziz Ansari. It Turned Into the Worst Night of my Life," Babe.net, last modified January 14, 2018, https://babe.net/2018/01/13/aziz-ansari-28355.

48. *Full Frontal with Samantha Bee*, "#MeToo Backlash | January 17, 2018 Act 1 | Full Frontal on TBS," YouTube.com, last modified January 18, 2018, https://www.youtube.com/watch?v=II-OP6vdMs8.

49. Nick Romano, "HLN Host Ashleigh Banfield Blasts Aziz Ansari Accuser for 'Reckless' Claims," EW.com, last modified January 16, 2018, https://ew.com/tv/2018/01/16/hln-ashleigh-banfield-aziz-ansari-accuser/.

50. Megan Thomas, "Aziz Ansari Responds to Sexual Assault Allegation: 'I Was Surprised and Concerned,'" CNN.com, last modified January 16, 2018, https://edition.cnn.com/2018/01/15/entertainment/aziz-ansari-responds/index.html.

51. Eren Orbey, "Aziz Ansari's New Standup Tour Is a Cry Against Extreme Wokeness," NewYorker.com, last modified October 4, 2018, https://www.newyorker.com/culture/culture-desk/aziz-ansaris-new-standup-tour-is-a-cry-against-extreme-wokeness.

52. Ansari and Klinenberg, *Modern Romance*, 41.

12

STEWART HUFF, P.I.
Intellectual at Large

Susan Seizer and Aviva Orenstein

> This is eighty percent comedy, twenty percent is *I fuckin' have to tell somebody*.
> —Stewart Huff, 10/27/11

INTRODUCTION

In this essay we present and analyze the work of Stewart Huff, a stand-up comedian who, though less well known (and certainly less financially solvent) than the more famous entertainers discussed in this volume, presents a stellar example of truth-telling through humor. We focus on his show *God Hates Ann*, which Huff built and performed in 2016–17. The show exposes and critiques sloppy and narrow-minded anti-science arguments and bigoted attitudes. Taking audiences on a hilarious, if sometimes horrifying, march through the history of intolerance to new scientific ideas, Huff demonstrates the folly of resisting change and challenges uncritical devotion to tradition. We focus on both the subversive content of Huff's act and his engaging form of delivery, exploring how he expertly embodies the duality of being a "P.I."— meaning simultaneously "private investigator" and "public intellectual."

In this dual role, Huff investigates historically ridiculous and dangerous responses to new knowledge, in all their defensive and angry postures and frightening outcomes. As a public intellectual, Huff advocates receptivity to new ideas, prodding us to be open-minded and curious even when such ideas challenge our cherished orthodoxies. In this respect, the self-abnegation that is the currency of the stand-up genre serves his purpose well: if he, a middle-aged, straight, white southern male, can manage to open his mind to new and challenging ideas, anyone can.

1. WHO THE HELL IS STEWART HUFF?

Stewart Huff is a road comic, a professional stand-up comedian who drives himself to gigs across Middle America, sometimes playing a different venue every night. He has been performing stand-up for more than two decades, most often in front of regional audiences throughout the south-central United States.[1] Huff writes all his own material and does his own bookings.[2]

Playing regional and local circuits allows Huff to actually see his audiences and talk with them directly after his shows. This feedback loop enlivens his performances. By taking back roads in his travels, Huff gets a close look at his public in their natural habitat, their local environs. Like a private investigator engaging in reconnaissance, he is a stealth ethnographer, listening, observing, and sometimes eavesdropping as he attempts to understand the mindsets of those he meets at truck stops and greasy-spoon diners.

Huff constantly writes new material that he tries out and fine-tunes in performance. He polishes each component bit of a new set by experimenting with variations in delivery, including word choice, timing, movement, presentational style, accent, and set order. Every six to nine months Huff puts together a new show, and he has released a professionally produced CD every other year since 2011.[3] He won't be pleased with a new show until it's funny, challenging, and the right sort of cranky. After each show is "in the can" and the CD is released, he retires all that proven material and begins work on his next show.

Huff is an autodidact with a voracious intellectual appetite. His own formal education (or lack thereof) is a subject of self-mockery. He nails it: "I have a Kentucky public school education. Do you realize how dumb I am?" (January 2, 2016, Lexington, Kentucky). Huff found his first and only year of college disappointingly uninteresting, and he regularly tells audiences, "I dropped out of college to tell jokes to drunk people."

To date, Huff has never had a TV show or a cable special, or been invited to be a guest on a late-night talk show. More a storyteller than a joke-teller, Huff has long accepted that his material doesn't fit into the standard four-and-a-half-minute slot that TV talk shows allot to comedians[4] His priorities are elsewhere: Huff has mastered the long story form, which gives him time to develop ideas beyond the big-laugh-through-thin-description format that relies on quick tension/release moments and characterizes so much stand-up, as we discuss below.[5]

2. HUFF THE PERFORMER

Stewart Huff is five foot six and boyish, with thick brown hair, a short forehead (about which he is self-conscious and occasionally makes the subject of a joke), and a greying five o'clock shadow. His look pays a casual, twenty-first-century homage to a 1940s private detective's dress and grooming: plaid long-sleeve button-down shirts, mostly in the green-blue-tan range, worn with beige or brown corduroys. He's better dressed than your average slob of a stand-up comic, but not by much. He never wears a winter coat; in winter, he wears a basic nondescript dark green flight jacket with no insignia. His shirt rack occupies the back seat of his car.

Huff identifies as a southerner, something his accent discloses in the first few seconds of his act. In one show he quipped: "I'm Southern as hell. I really am. I'm a hillbilly. I'll go to LA, people go, 'How Southern are you?' and I always say, 'You mean, like, on a scale from zero to pig-fuckin'? I'd say I'm about a six. Never done it. Thought about it. . . .'" (October 27, 2011, Indianapolis, Indiana). Huff has a conflicted and complicated attitude toward his audience's reactions. Given the nature of a road comic's work, audiences are elusive targets. Even in familiar venues there is an immeasurable element of unpredictability in the composition of an audience or the mood of a club. Oscar Mandel observes that "Each person has his own repertory of aversions, and his own intensities. Because our vulnerabilities overlap, we form

Figure 1. Publicity still of Stewart Huff, 2016. Photo by Jonathan Baldizon.

a predictable public; because they differ, we are an *unreliably predictable public*."[6] Huff's response to such uncertainties is not to pander to audience preferences but to stubbornly ground his choices in what he himself deems important—and amusing. He is proud that his comedy is challenging and doesn't appeal to everyone. In truth, he tells us his goal is only secondarily to entertain: he would rather have people hate his show than be apathetic to it.[7]

3. OUR METHODOLOGY

Our analysis relies on live viewings of Huff in performance, personal communications with him, recordings of shows Huff performed between January and May 2016 as he developed *God Hates Ann* that he shared with us,[8] and reviews of several of Huff's earlier performances posted online that illustrate relevant and recurrent themes in his comedy.[9] Seizer first became familiar with this show's content through talking with Huff. Together, the authors saw Huff perform the show live at the Comedy Attic in Bloomington, Indiana, where it was part of the *Sick of Stupid Comedy Tour*, billed as "a progressive, issue driven, southern comedy tour."[10] In some of our personal communications with Huff about his aims, concerns, and craft, he shares his creative process as he struggles with the material.[11]

The authors come to Huff's work from different perspectives. Seizer is a cultural anthropologist who studies live performance in both India and the US. Her documentary film, *Road Comics: Big Work on Small Stages* (2012), features three southern comics, including Huff. Beginning with the making of this film, Seizer and Huff have enjoyed a productive ongoing work relationship and personal friendship. Orenstein, a lawyer, law professor, and novelist, is a newcomer to Huff's comedy but not to humor. In addition to seeing his new show live, her familiarity with Huff's work comes from listening to his CDs and watching videos of his earlier work.

Our analysis employs the useful distinction sociolinguists make between the narrated text (the story told) and the narrating text (its telling). The folklorist and anthropologist Richard Bauman's groundbreaking 1975 essay, "Verbal Art as Performance," first formulated a performance-centered approach to treating events themselves as the fundamental units of description and analysis.[12] Huff's performances use the stand-up comedy form as a narrating text, a genre-frame for presenting otherwise unfunny and in fact harrowing narrated texts (in this case, true histories of murdered scientists). His shows use the dialogically rich format of live stand-up, a genre that in his capable hands delivers regular laugh lines.

4. THE SHOW

God Hates Ann focuses on people's fear of science, including the deep and irrational desire not only to dismiss scientific knowledge but to kill its messengers. The show is organized around a series of historical events in which scientists, philosophers, and freethinkers alike were murdered by violent fundamentalists, hate-filled mobs, threatened guilds, and courts of law.

At the beginning of *God Hates Ann* Huff warns audiences that the topic of this show is sad, and that its theme—how often human beings are hostile to new ideas—may make them uncomfortable. Huff states his main question outright: "How does a human mind close?"

Throughout the show, Huff uses a range of communicative means to bring audiences' focus to this question. These include: enactments of the various characters he embodies; commentaries delivered either directly or as extended asides to the audience; and an affective style that constitutes his own unique performance persona.[13] Interestingly for a genre as verbal as stand-up comedy, in performance many of Huff's most effective punchlines are communicated through recurring movements that rely on wordless affect: his whole body shakes with a combination of obsessive determination, unbridled passion, and amazed disbelief. Whether he is showing us how he used to sneakily eat chocolate-covered bananas while employed at the Dairy Queen (Huff, October 26, 2011) or describing the wildly optimistic efforts of a man trying to fly with taped-on wings (Huff 2011, track 8, "The Wright Brothers"), Huff's over-the-top embodied frantic antics regularly induce a matching convulsive laughter from his audiences. Through a combination of these performative means, Huff crystallizes, orchestrates, and transmits a feeling of righteous rage at the inequalities of treatment meted out to freethinkers of every stripe and era.

In *God Hates Ann*, Huff's first historical vignette begins like this:

> Joseph Priestley, he was a scientist from England. He was also a preacher. He discovered oxygen. *Weeellll, he shouldna done that!* He shoulda known: don't you go around discoverin' shit. A church-fueled mob? Isn't that an amazing sentence? A mob fueled by church! I don't even know how you get a church-fueled mob, did they not read the book? It says in here that we should love and accept everyone "except for that asshole who says the air exists"?! Joseph basically said, "Hey guys, this [blowing air in and out] is something." Forty human beings with torches went, "the fuck it is!" They went to kill the man. He heard them coming, it's a big mob of people right? He ran out of his

back door and escaped. They were so mad they burnt his laboratory to the ground. Then they went to his home and burnt his home to the ground. Which is hilarious, 'cause for a fire, you need . . . [and here the audience fills in, "OXYGEN!" and claps and laughs.] No amount of anger will change the truth. (Huff, August 4, 2017)

Next, Huff introduces Dr. Rhazes, a tenth-century polymath from Baghdad who was beaten with his own book for attempting to compile all the medical knowledge of his age: "*Weeellll, he shouldna done that!* He shoulda known. Don't you go around compilin' shit!" comes the refrain. Huff continues his account of murders perpetrated on those whose only sin was scientific discovery or unpopular thought, each time repeating the refrain, "*Weeellll, he shouldna done that!*" to the point where the audience is chanting it with him. We observe with Huff that when a scientist or freethinker offers new ideas and evidence that challenge entrenched orthodoxies, people have a choice: "At this point you either have to humbly admit you're wrong, or kill the scientist. And I think you know which one humans prefer" (January 2, 2016, Lexington, Kentucky).

Huff is both saddened and baffled by the tenacious inclination of human beings to fear new ideas and to inflict violence on those who discover and invent things that challenge our belief systems. It wouldn't be surprising to see a shingle hung out on his office (a.k.a. his car) advertising his particular expertise in investigating this peculiar niche (see figure 2). In a brilliant, emblematic riff early in this hour-long performance, Huff reveals what prompted his idea for this show: a chance unpleasant encounter with a seatmate on an airplane. In his angry close-mindedness, the man seated beside Huff sneers at a headline about global warming and proceeds to denounce not only the science of climate change but all science. After recounting the man's excoriating rant, Huff adds these observations:

I'm thinking, WE'RE ON A PLANE! Is it me, or are my expectations of us too fuckin' high? Am I expecting too much? You can't hate science and love NASCAR! NASCAR without science is called running. Three hours I'm on a plane with a grown man who's bitching to me about science. At some point I just started giggling. It was mean of me, I know, but it was just so childish, he was so mad. I pictured him standing in front of the periodic table: [changing his posture to a slump while gesturing in a wide arc with his right arm across an imaginary drawing board]: "This is all bullshit. It's all made up by the liberals just to piss me off. Stupid: Fluorine? Uranium? Carbon? These are Dr.

Seuss words, ain't real. Potassium's bullshit." Hah! That's the nerdiest joke I've ever written right there. By far the nerdiest joke. 'Cuz Fluorine, Uranium, Carbon and Potassium? Spell "FUCK" on the periodic table. Right. I'm proud of it too!

If the guy would've said to me on the plane, if he would've said, "You know what? I've read a lot about global warming, I just don't think our behavior's affecting it." That's a conversation. That's conversation. Instead, "Science ain't never done one thing—bunch a bullshit blahblahblah." And I'm staring at him; HE'S WEARING BIFOCALS!

There's too many people that hate science, it's just ridiculous. Hating science is like yelling at a plant. How funny would it be to see a grown man yell: "Fuck you ficus!"? Are you photosynthesizin' right now? You piece o' shit. You better not be turning sunlight into sugars, I'm gonna tear you an asshole!!" Amazing. (Huff 2017, track 3, "Dr. Seuss Words")

Figure 2. An imaginary sign for Stewart Huff, P.I., advertising expertise in murders committed by church-fueled mobs, priests, sheriffs, and any other persons who respond to new ideas with fear, anger, hatred, and violence. Graphic design by SED Mitchell.

Periodic Table of the Elements

H																	He
Li	Be			NAME								B	C	C	O	F	Ne
Na	Mg		F	ATOMIC NUMBER SYMBOL RELATIVE ATOMIC MASS								Al	Si	P	S	Cl	Ar
K	Ca	Sc	Ti	V	Cr	Mn	Fe	Co	Ni	Cu	Zn	Ga	Ge	As	Se	Br	Kr
Rb	Sr	Y	Zr	Nb	Mo	Tc	Ru	Rh	Pd	Ag	Cd	In	Sn	Sb	Te	I	Xe
Cs	Ba	57-70 *	Lu	Hf	Ta	W	Re	Os	Ir	Pt	Au	Hg	Tl	Pb	Bi	Po	At	Rn
Fr	Ra	89-102 **	Lr	Rf	Db	Sg	Bh	Hs	Mt	Uun	Uuu	Uub	Uuq				

*Lanthanide series	La	Ce	Pr	Nd	Pm	Sm	Eu	Gd	Tb	Dy	Ho	Er	Tm	Yb
**Actinide series	Ac	Th	Pa	U	Np	Pu	Am	Cm	Bk	Cf	Es	Fm	Md	No

Figure 3. The nerdiest joke Huff has ever written: "Fluorine, Uranium, Carbon, and Potassium spell FUCK on the periodic table." Graphic design by SED Mitchell.

In presenting the speech of his science-hating seatmate, Huff adopts a southern accent much thicker than his own—as well as various good ol' boy postures and gestural quirks. When not imitating the voice and persona we dub "the Southern redneck," Huff talks directly to the audience about what he thinks of science-haters, employing both absurdity ("Fuck you, ficus!") and logic ("He's wearing BIFOCALS!"). Yet at the same time, he recognizes that his own pride in a silly joke about the periodic table is also ridiculous, and that like the redneck, he too is profane and in no way exempt from a good laugh at himself.

Using a repetition of tropes—especially the refrain "*Weeellll, he shouldna done that!*"—and increasing levels of audience engagement, Huff encourages audiences to think and question while they laugh. His shows encourage critical thought by modeling this very quality on stage: Huff lets the audience know that he is thinking critically about the act as he performs it, and invites the audience to join him in doing so.[14] By the end of the hour, audiences have effectively crafted the show with him, as the event progressively taps into the audience's collective capacity for thinking about scientific ideas historically and draws them in as performance co-creators.

In both message and medium, then, Huff proves a reflexive thinker who doesn't simply discuss important intellectual ideas, but also turns a critical lens on talk itself. He talks about how we talk, and thinks about how we think. The show works because Huff is frank about his personal motives and inspiration. He recognizes and acknowledges his own frustration and, even more remarkably, his own sadness.

5. HUFF'S PROCESS

Stand-up comedy is a genre that relies on the illusion of spontaneity and the frequent use of a confessional tone.[15] Huff, however, is unusually candid about the fact that his show is scripted. He shares his writing process, demonstrating that it is an ongoing experiment in which audience participation matters. Recalling the name of every town and every venue he has played, Huff remembers whether and which audiences laughed or sat in stony silence at any given line in his show. He notes whether small tweaks—such as adding a pause, or changing a posture—elicited a bigger laugh. Yet while keeping track of what succeeds, Huff is nevertheless proudly stubborn about retaining lines—and even entire bits—that *he* likes and deems important to the message of his madness, regardless of whether his audiences like it or not. This seems counterintuitive in a genre that depends so much on the audience's pleasure. Huff's only concession to the expectation that he provide entertainment is to sprinkle puns, humorous asides, and the occasional jokey-joke that he knows will garner a laugh in among those bits that he also knows will hush, and sometimes anguish, a crowd.

By letting the audience into his careful crafting—"that line rarely gets a laugh, but I love it so much!"—Huff invites audiences to witness his process. We cannot escape the fact that this is a piece of art under construction, its scaffolding visible to all. Such transparency encourages self-reflection on the part of audience members as they realize Huff is not in this business to provide trivial passive entertainment for their transient amusement.

When the act does not work—and he readily acknowledges that sometimes his reception with certain audiences is silence, resentment, or anger—Huff faces a potentially rage-filled audience that, though unlikely to actually kill him, will certainly dismiss him and may well decide to throw shoes or beer cans at his truth-telling diatribes (both have happened). By performing *God Hates Ann* in particular, Huff takes such risks to provide us the chance to not act as a hostile, threatened, close-minded mob, though he is willing to take the personal risk that we might.

Huff does not want to be pelted with cans or shoes, but he admits that he finds the danger and uncertainty of his reception enlivening and even somewhat thrilling: "I don't mind bombing. I kinda like it, to be honest. When I'm speaking about what I love, when people hate me for it, it invigorates me" (October 27, 2011, Indianapolis, Indiana).

Frequently during the show, Huff invites the audience to acknowledge and appreciate his process by treating them as confidants, employing what we think of as "meta-commentary quips." He interrupts the flow of the funny/horrifying narrative of the anti-science bigot to confide in the audience about his own process, reminding us that he writes and relentlessly interrogates this material. For instance, in Lexington, Kentucky, he began with a disclaimer that sounds suspiciously like a brag:

> Honestly right up top, all this stuff I'm about to talk about? Has been getting nothing. I don't know what's going on, because I know it's funny, 'cause I'm stubborn. But audiences have been staring at me or yelling at me, one of the two.... I was just in Canada last week and the owner told me he was never going have me back if I did it again. So I did it again. Because I know I'm right. (January 2, ,2016, Lexington, Kentucky)

6. HOW DOES HE MAKE THIS SHIT FUNNY?

How does Huff manage to turn horrifying historical realities and depressing truths into a funny hour of stand-up comedy? This is the real challenge and accomplishment of his work in *God Hates Ann*. Given his commitment to creating shows that matter, Huff's performances must succeed on multiple levels. First, the material must work for him, helping him work through something that bothers, saddens, or otherwise upsets him.[16] Second, it must work for the bookers and club owners who count on him to make people laugh and draw paying audiences into their clubs. Third, it must resonate with the audience so that they stick with him as he explores dark and sad places into which comedians do not often tread.

Of course a successful stand-up comic has to "make 'em laugh." Huff refers to this as his contract, the one mandatory requirement of a genre that is otherwise among the most wide-open platforms a solo stage artist could imagine.

> My contract between the audience—and to a lesser extent the bookers/club owners—is: I must make the audience laugh. The problem comes from me wanting to say things that aren't necessarily funny. Because I'm stubborn, I'm going to say whatever I want to say.

That means I'm going to have to figure out how to generate laughs. Sometimes this can be accomplished with set up punchline jokes. Sometimes I have to find tricks to make the audience laugh. I think of it as my stubbornness vs. their stubbornness. I'm going to win, that's not a question. The question is: How am I going to win? That's what takes time to figure out.[17]

Huff's whimsical imagination and irreverent tone help keep it light, and genre-specific with the addition of sudden swerves into profanity and crudeness. The following introduction to the material at the heart of *God Hates Ann* provides a good illustration of how he mixes whimsy with the realities of human dedication to belief: "If you know for a fact that the *aurora borealis* is a trail of pixie dust left over from a sky unicorn, and you know that because that is what your Mamaw told you, and a scientist comes along with evidence proving you're wrong . . . weeelll, you either have to humbly admit that you were wrong, or kill the scientist!" (8/4/17). In another apt illustration of this knack, Huff decries the human race's squandering of its potential with the line, "We can make glow-in-the-dark butt plugs but we can't figure out how to get enough money to fund our schools?!" He uses incongruous images that surprise us into laughter to pose the key question: why don't we use our intelligence to better purpose?

Indeed, in the tradition of such comic greats as Richard Pryor and George Carlin, Huff employs and enjoys playing profanity for a laugh, and overlays anachronistic absurdity onto his historical accounts. When recounting the story of Mary Dyer, who in 1660 was arrested in Boston for being a Quaker, Huff reports that she was marched to her death accompanied by four drummers and exclaims, "Fuck, four drummers? The Grateful Dead only had two drummers!" (January 2, 2016, Lexington, Kentucky). He moves directly from this jarring anachronism in his own voice to that of his alter ego: a southern redneck scolding Mary, "Don't you be comin' around here with yer peaceful nonviolent oatmeal ways!"

Finally, as we argue in the following sections, Huff fuses his southern identity with physical comedy to keep the audiences laughing.

7. THICK VS. THIN DESCRIPTION

A chasm exists between anthropological and comedic approaches to the use of stereotypes. Anthropologists revel in "thick description," a concept popularized by Clifford Geertz in his classic 1973 essay collection, *The*

Interpretation of Cultures. Thick description relies on detail, on the particulars of historical events and personages. The aim of thick description in anthropological research and writing is to eradicate stereotypes by placing each human action within its cultural context. Anthropologists regard even the slightest variation (or mutation) as a contribution to living history.

Comedians generally do just the opposite. They employ stereotypes to quickly evoke ideas and images of a character type, relying on flat, recognizable figures for parodic use.[18] Comedians can then readily prompt quick bursts of laughter by subverting audience expectations, taking us by surprise. Such moves rely on stereotypes to provide the necessary groundwork for subversive play, and count on flashes of self-consciousness and reflexivity to short-circuit rational thought.[19] Comedians, accordingly, generally rely on what we might call "thin description" in contradistinction to the anthropologists' thick description, precisely to facilitate quick connections and surprising reversals as necessary tricks of their trade. Huff combines these two normally distinct and opposing modes of description in his manipulation of the southern white male persona. He uses thin description to quickly conjure up familiar stereotypes of southern ignorance, bigotry, and backwardness. At the same time, through sophisticated argument and attention to ethnographic detail, Huff employs thick description as he muses on the politics of reparation and redemption, hoping audiences will be moved to challenge this stereotype. This move could seriously deflate the business of comedic stereotyping if Huff didn't also manage to make his stories hilarious by jumping back and forth over that chasm.[20] As we discuss below, he simultaneously uses and transcends his own southern roots, all the while acknowledging how both the stereotypes and the realities of being southern continue to influence his thinking and personal development.[21]

8. PLAYING SOUTHERN WHILE BEING SOUTHERN

Huff's stereotypically bigoted southern character serves as the foil to his own equally southern but openly curious mind. Huff has an identifiably southern drawl and can easily create the redneck-bigot character simply by exaggerating elements of his own voice, gesture, and posture. He manipulates the persona by deepening his voice, shifting from his own gentle lilt to full-fledged, foul-mouthed attack mode. When he senses that he's gone too long without a laugh, Huff thickens his accent and peppers it with hillbilly inflection (unconsciously, he reports).[22] All he has to do is add a bit of extra drawl to a word—as he does with "finger" (FAIN-ger) or lawyer ("LAAW-yer")—to get a laugh, particularly when such pronunciation is accompanied by an incongruously intellectual point.

Huff's slide into this recognizably redneck accent is slightly uncomfortable because he risks reinforcing the very stereotype that his own intelligence and tolerance belie. This may be less problematic for Huff than for us as academic analysts, because he accepts that he must make compromises (i.e., use thin stereotypes) to keep his shows funny. More importantly, however, his choice to play the southern bigot character is not a sellout. The ambiguity of his relationship with his southern roots keeps the act interesting and accessible. Other comics who move between distance and proximity in playing their perceived identity for laughs, such as Chris Rock and Dave Chappelle, perform similar balancing acts, challenging (in Rock's and Chappelle's case, racist) stereotypes while simultaneously invoking them.

When Huff summons the bigoted redneck stereotype, he actively resists the default mode of casting the problem simply as one of a United States North–South divide. Instead, he clarifies that his concern is about a mindset and not a locale; bigotry is not bound by geography. The opening track of Huff's 2015 CD release *Probably* is titled "Rednecks Are Everywhere." It begins as follows:

> I have done comedy in all fifty states. Here's what I've learned: [yelling] **rednecks are fuckin' everywhere!** It's so depressing. They're in every city, every state—they're in Canada, holy shit! Canadian rednecks, I was not expecting that. It's not a regional issue. It's a human disease. There's Mexican rednecks, and Australian rednecks, and Belgian rednecks, and fifteenth-century French fuckin' rednecks. North Korea is ran by a damn redneck! (Huff 2015)

Though the bit is trenchant and funny, the redneck mindset is clearly not something that amuses Huff: he invokes it in order to shout at and mock it out of existence. This is him dancing over the chasm of thin and thick description. It is also how Huff's comedy differs from the laid-back, jocular acts of Jeff Foxworthy and his mates on the Blue Collar Comedy tour. In their work, catchphrases such as "You know you're a redneck if . . ." and "Get 'er done!" accept and reinvigorate the stereotype; these familiar expressions feel like comfort food, designed to soothe audiences rather than move them to action. The Blue Collar comedians let audiences off the hook by encouraging them to take pride in the distinctive redneck lifestyle (a cool move in that it flips usual American class values, but it nevertheless keeps the southern = redneck = bigot stereotype intact). By contrast, Huff uses the stereotype to

Figure 4. Stills from Huff's performance of "Sense Ain't Common," January 2, 2016, Lexington, Kentucky. These stills demonstrate Huff's postural and gestural changes in stance and address when he summons the redneck persona, and then again when he comments to the audience. Graphic design by SED Mitchell.

get his audiences thinking about the way defensive posturing precludes open consideration of stances that might better serve oneself, as well as the larger community. Of course, the success of Huff's strategy varies widely depending on his audience, but again, he is prepared to risk failure in the service of success on his own terms.

In addition to the accent, Huff plays with his delivery, repeating tropes and presenting repetitions in recognizable verbal forms. Most notably, this takes the form of the refrain in *God Hates Ann*: after presenting the "sins" of each scientist and freethinker, "*Weeellll, he shouldna done that!*" This scolding refrain that voices convention and close-mindedness is delivered in a high-pitched voice, elongating the first word as would his southern alter ego. Aimed at murdered scientists, it blames the victim and exposes the bigotry of those doing the blaming.[23] The formulation varies only in its accusation of the crime: "He shoulda known you can't go around inventin'/ compilin'/ discoverin'/ suggestin' shit."

In live performance, the voice of the bigot is accompanied by a change in Huff's facial expression, hand gestures, and posture: he juts out his chin, waggles his cheeks, looks skyward, protrudes his gut, then rubs it in a circular fashion until his hand stops on his belly-button, as if to make a redneck genie emerge—a gestural mnemonic conjuring inner, belligerent evil. All of this creates a particular stance that signals Huff's switch into that persona.[24] For instance, when he describes how a preacher led his congregation to trample Uriel da Costa for suggesting that man does not need a church to ascend to heaven, Huff slaps his belly while intoning, "Now close your hymnals, we're gonna beat the fuck outta Uriel. Then we're gonna have some fried chicken" (May 6, 2016, Cincinnati, Ohio).

Once he has established the character, Huff can then duck out from behind—or more precisely, shift out to the side of—this burly, clumsy, oafish man. Huff doesn't just recount the bigot's words; he is in dialogue with him, reenacting a conversation. This allows Huff to comment on the ignorance and rage-filled small-mindedness of the character he has just conjured with asides to the audience. These asides are meta-commentary quips in which Huff reflects aloud about the material he has just performed, inviting the audience to let him know whether it is working for them or not. His interaction style is thus very different from the typical blustery audience polling—"Who here is from New Jersey?" "Anyone here on a first date?" etc.—that many stand-ups engage in to suss out their audiences and trigger canned responses.

Huff's meta-commentary quips are moments of great inclusivity that have a conspiratorial tone. His mordant observation, "and I think you all know which one we prefer" (regarding killing the scientist vs. changing one's mind), doesn't feel like a lecture; it feels more like a winking Socratic dialogue wherein the audience is in on the joke.

9. MULTIPLE VOICES, UNIFIED MESSAGE

Various voices coalesce in Huff's show. There is Huff the storyteller—whether he is talking about a fifteenth-century inventor or a seatmate on an airplane. There is the voice of the ignorant bigot, so terrified of new ideas that he responds to everything with anger and sometimes violence. Next, there is the intimate voice that makes winking asides to the audience, inviting us to laugh at the bigot and at humankind in general. Finally, tying all this together, there is Huff's own sadness and righteous anger. In this last voice, Huff preaches his own gospel: "Free thinker is the most dangerous thing you can do."

About halfway through the show, Huff introduces Kazimierz, a seventeenth-century Polish philosopher and freethinker, and immediately comments: "He's a dead man. Shit. That's the trifecta right there. If you're a philosopher, a free-thinker, and Polish? That's unassisted suicide!" (May

6, 2016, Cincinnati, Ohio). We learn that Kazimierz wrote "a book of his personal beliefs. In this book was this one sentence, and out of all of them, this is the one he was convicted for: 'God did not create man. Man created God.' *Weeellll, he shouldna done that!*" Huff then recounts, in painful detail, the many violent acts visited upon Kazimierz. Even after he was strangled, beheaded, and his body burnt to ashes, "You thought we were done? Have you met us? We took this man's ashes and shoved them in a cannon, lit it, and fired his ass out of the city. What the fuck? Who the hell has that much hatred in their heart? Who looks at someone's ashes and goes, 'I ain't done with you, you son of a bitch!'" (May 6, 2016, Cincinnati, Ohio). At this point Huff breaks the spell. He bends at the waist, redneck beer gut disappearing in one quick change of footing, to utter an aside to the front row audience: "Was that too much anger for you guys?" This compassionately affective voice is the voice of Huff's sadness.

He regroups. Huff-the-storyteller moves to modern-day examples: "History is horrific, that's the truth. In Texas they want to change the word 'slaves' in their history textbooks to 'workers.' Yeah, did you read about that? If we don't want to teach the truth maybe we shouldn't call it 'History.' Maybe we should just call it 'Bullshit.' Really, you could reduce human history into two lines: 'I wonder' and 'Shut the fuck up!'" (May 13, 2016, Washington, DC).

10. CONCLUSION: HUFF AS A FEARLESS PUBLIC INTELLECTUAL

By "clarifying issues . . . drawing attention to neglected issues, and vivifying public debate," Huff serves as a "critical commentator addressing a non-specialist audience on matters of broad public concern," which are, in this case, the unfounded, gut-driven anti-science arguments and bigoted attitudes that felt particularly timely in 2016–17.[25] That Huff's work provokes reflexive thought further supports his designation as a public intellectual. While self-consciously crafting his act, drafting, redrafting, and openly criticizing the wording of a bit, Huff gets us to think, and laugh, about thinking itself.[26]

Through a combination of physical comedy, ironic asides, puns, wordplay, meta-commentary quips, alluring alliterations, accent-bending riffs, first-person tall tales, and other masterful storytelling techniques, Huff keeps audiences engaged, charmed, and sufficiently aligned with him that they are willing to hear the uncomfortable truths his show conveys.[27] Huff brilliantly conveys a serious message of openness to science while still engaging an audience that came to laugh. *God Hates Ann* provides an opportunity to mock ignorance and violence, so that we as a group can grow in empathy.

In daring to annoy, offend, or even enrage his audience, Huff replays and indeed reenacts what happened to the iconoclastic scientists and thinkers whose deaths he chronicles. In challenging belief systems and orthodoxies, Huff not only describes the brave scientists—he emulates them. Huff's identification with the scientists and freethinkers who populate his narrated texts is particularly clear when he reports in his narrating text a confrontation he had with an audience member. The audience member accosted Huff after a show and said "Listen here, buddy. Jesus Christ does not believe in transgender people." He tells the story onstage this way: "I looked him dead in the eye and I said, 'With all due respect, sir, there is no way possible that you know the thoughts of Jesus Christ,' knowing full well, in my mind and heart, he was going to shoot me. And then at my funeral, one of my comedy friends would be like, '*Weeellll, he shouldna done that!*'" (May 6, 2016, Cincinnati, Ohio). The final repetition of this phrase links all the previous narrated texts in this show—and perhaps most cannily, also applies to Huff himself, a freethinker threatened by an angry audience. This recursive application of the central trope of *God Hates Ann* reinforces its life-and-death stakes. The gruesome stories told in ways that make us laugh, the amusing and animated redneck swagger, and the foul-mouthed humor are all united in this one final, funny self-application of the show's refrain.[28]

Huff's show is a meditation on anger, his own and the angry mob's. Huff displays insight and candor when he recognizes that his anger at the murderers is also, in equal measure, deep sadness, just as the anger of the mob is tinged with panic and fear. Though suffused with indignation, frustration, and sadness, Huff's show creates a feeling of genuine camaraderie. We laugh at intolerant bigots, at Huff, and at ourselves. His show creates an atmosphere of intimacy in which we can be outraged at the treatment truth-tellers receive and still have some understanding of their tormentors.

Huff also engages with the intolerant tormenters in a more personal way: he is just as stubborn as they are because he, like them, is sure that he is right. While the confidence of his convictions connects him to and invariably helps him better understand those he criticizes, Huff's vulnerability, thoughtfulness, and regard for human intelligence firmly align him with the scientists and freethinkers he admires.

This leads us to our own final, ironic observation about Huff. He criticizes the mob, which he portrays as angry, ignorant, and intolerant; but he can't help but admire the crazy tenacity of the tormenters. He observes that the horrible deaths inflicted on the scientists and freethinkers display extensive, if highly misdirected, creativity, marveling at a particularly gruesome execution: "Is anybody else noticing the same thing I am, with these? The punishments of these people are just as creative as the victims!" (May 6, 2016, Cincinnati, Ohio). In so doing, Huff recognizes the spark of human creativity even in bigots who cannot abide challenges to their worldview. Clearly, he holds out the hope that those capable of creative torture might someday put their initiative and ingenuity to better use.

Notes

1. Huff has performed in all fifty states and several foreign countries, but his most frequent appearances are in Tennessee, Kentucky, Georgia, North and South Carolina, Alabama, Florida, Indiana, Ohio, Pennsylvania, Colorado, and Canada. During his career, Huff has moved up the ranks of the comedy club circuit ladder: from being an "opening act" for other comics (a 5–10 minute slot), to appearing as a "feature act" (a 20–25 minute slot), to finally becoming a "headliner" who performs an hour-long set of original material at clubs, bars, fringe festivals, and occasionally college dorms and restaurant buffets.

2. Doing his own bookings involves communicating with club owners and sometimes with other comedians to coordinate schedules and agree on financial terms; occasionally he must engage in negotiations over the content of his show, specifically how much "language" (i.e., dirty words) will be acceptable.

3. Since he began headlining in 2008, Huff has produced four entirely new shows that have been released as CDs produced by On Tour Records. These are: *God Hates Ann* (2017); *Probably* (2015); *I Don't Think I Believe Us* (2013); and *The Pressure of Your Expectations Is Overwhelming* (2011). See http://www.ontourrecords.com/stewart-huff. Since 2017 Huff has also hosted his own podcast, *Stewart Huff's Obsessive Curiosities*, in which he and guests consider some of the stranger objects he's collected while combing through junk shops along the back roads of America. The podcast is available at https://www.perfectapodcastnetwork.com and at Huff's On Tour Records website, https://www.ontourrecords.com/stewart-huff.

4. Susan Seizer, *Road Comics: Big Work on Small Stages*, filmed 2012, YouTube video, 53:42, posted February 2014, https://www.youtube.com/watch?time_continue=4&v=d-h5vmiOX_8&feature=emb_logo.

5. Hannah Gadsby's 2018 show *Nanette* artfully discusses the drawbacks of this common stand-up style. The buildup and release of tension is also frequently discussed by humor theorists as the relief theory, one of three classical humor theories (the other two being the superiority theory and the incongruity theory). Consult *The Philosophy of Laughter and Humor*, ed. John Morreall (Albany: State University of New York Press, 1987); Frances Gray, *Women and Laughter* (Basingstoke, UK: Macmillan, 1994); and Susan Seizer, *Stigmas of the Tamil Stage: An Ethnography of Special Drama Artists in South India* (Durham, NC: Duke University Press, 2005).

6. Oscar Mandel, "What's So Funny: The Nature of the Comic," *The Antioch Review* 30, no. 1 (1970): 75.

7. Stewart Huff, personal communication to authors, February 23, 2016.

8. This show had various titles over the period of its development. Huff called it *Sense Ain't Common* in the first half of 2016, while some who posted early recordings of Huff's show on

YouTube during that same period titled it *Weird Belief Systems* or *Murdered Scientists*. Huff eventually settled on the title *God Hates Ann* when he released a CD recording of the show in spring 2017. This title refers to a bit in the show that concerns a woman named Ann who was hit by an asteroid while napping on her couch, and the various rationalizations/explanations a diverse range of people used to explain why the asteroid hit Ann. As of this writing, Huff is producing a documentary film about the fallout of the collision of Ann and asteroid.

9. We also draw on prior live viewings and recordings of earlier shows, some of which can be found on YouTube, others of which are in Seizer's previously shot video footage.

10. The touring show also featured comedians Cliff Cash and Tom Simmons.

11. For example:

> From: Stewart Huff
> To: Susan Seizer
> Subject: Cincy Show
> May 6, 2016 at 11:18 PM
> I'm sending you the latest version of this damn show I'm trying to build. Let me know your thoughts.

Or, a few weeks later on May 23, 2016, as we began work on this essay, Huff wrote, "Just sending you crap you might use for the paper. Here's a link to a video of me working on the material."

12. Richard Bauman, "Verbal Art as Performance," *American Anthropologist* 77, no. 2 (1975): 290–311.

13. See Diana Taylor, *The Archive and the Repertoire: Performing Cultural Memory in the Americas* (Durham, NC: Duke University Press, 2003); and Richard Bauman, *A World of Others' Words: Cross-cultural Perspectives on Intertextuality* (Malden, MA: Blackwell, 2004).

14. Consult Bertolt Brecht, *Brecht on Theatre: The Development of an Aesthetic*, ed. and trans. John Willett (New York: Hill and Wang, 1992).

15. Ian Brodie, *A Vulgar Art: A New Approach to Stand-up Comedy* (Jackson: University Press of Mississippi, 2014); and Susan Seizer, "On the Uses of Obscenity in Live Stand-up Comedy," *Anthropological Quarterly* 84, no. 1 (2011): 209–34.

16. Susan Seizer, "Dialogic Catharsis in Standup Comedy: Stewart Huff Plays a Bigot," *Humor* 30, no. 2 (2017): 211–37.

17. Huff, personal communication, February 23, 2016.

18. Psychologists explain that stereotypes, once established by our culture and embedded in our psyches, are cognitive tools that serve as energy-saving devices to process information. Consult C. Neil Macrae, Alan B. Milne, and Galen V. Bodenhausen, "Stereotypes as Energy-Saving Devices: A Peek Inside the Cognitive Toolbox," *Journal of Personality and Social Psychology* 66, no. 1 (1994): 37–47. Steven Pinker argues that stereotypes are not merely social constructs but have their roots in evolutionarily adaptive categories of observation, and that they serve as short cuts for making sense of the world around us, simplifying the way we process information. See Steven Pinker, *Blank Slate: The Modern Denial of Human Nature* (New York: Penguin, 2003).

19. Sigmund Freud called this comedic process "condensation" and saw it as a pleasurable way to save us psychic energy. All the processes of our mind that are usually busy making categories and divisions need no longer do that work when a joke or a punny play on words brings otherwise disparate things together in unexpected and delightfully incongruous ways. For Freud, this was a release that laughter alone provides: it frees our minds to make new connections. We see Freud's 1902 *Jokes and their Relation to the Unconscious* as bringing together all three of the classic humor theories that seek to provide explanations for why we laugh. These are generally separated into the superiority theory, the relief theory, and the incongruity theory (Morreall [ed.], *Philosophy of Laughter and Humor*; Gray, *Women and Laughter*). While Freud's is most often considered a relief theory, we prefer to see his theory of condensation, with its emphasis on the release of psychic energy, as akin to the process of "quickening" that art historian Robert Plant Armstrong describes as the appreciative human response to "works of affecting presence." See Robert Plant Armstrong, *Wellspring: On the Myth and Source of Culture* (Berkeley: University of California Press, 1975).

20. The Tasmanian comedian Hannah Gadsby discusses the limits of the joking format as having only two features, the build-up of tension and its release. She, like Huff, finds the story a much richer format and one that has real humanitarian communicative potential.

21. Seizer, "Dialogic Catharsis in Standup Comedy."

22. Huff, personal communication, February 23, 2016.

23. An animation of the track "A Church Fueled Mob" from Huff 2017 illustrates perfectly the ugly side of such bigoted attacks: https://www.youtube.com/watch?time_continue=57&v=2HwyUY5Pyhs.

24. Erving Goffman, *Frame Analysis: An Essay on the Organization of Experience* (London: Harper and Row, 1974).

25. Richard A. Posner, *Public Intellectuals: A Study of Decline* (Cambridge, MA: Harvard University Press, 2003), 5.

26. Barbara A. Babcock, "Reflexivity: Definitions and Discriminations," *Semiotica* 30, no. 1/2 (1980): 1–14.

27. Consult Bauman, *A World of Others' Words*.

28. As Huff explained in a personal communication on May 24, 2016, "I think when I bring the 'Weeeelll' line back at the end, about the Jesus Christ/transgendered guy? It all ties together like a bow."

13

LARRY THE CABLE GUY
The Anti-Political Correctness Public Intellectual

David R. Dewberry

Jean Bethke Elshtain has shown that there is much debate and concern about the decline of the public intellectual.[1] But this disagreement may have more to do with the definition of the term than with anything else.[2] This confusion noticeably appears in a 2009 *Foreign Policy* list of public intellectuals, which includes religious leaders, scholars, writers, politicians, and activists.[3] The article encouraged readers to submit their recommendations for who should be included. The top suggestion was Stephen Colbert, the former star of the faux conservative news show *The Colbert Report*.

The suggestion of Colbert's inclusion both is and is not surprising. Not only is Colbert's notoriety due to his role as a television host and satirist, quite unlike the others on the list, but he also portrays a fictional character on *The Colbert Report*. Although Colbert uses his real name, the persona he presents does not represent his true political opinions, which are decidedly liberal.[4] Nevertheless, Colbert's persona displays the essential character traits of an intellectual: he is articulate and informed, he offers pointed critiques of social and political affairs, and he has a large public audience. If we believe, as many others do, that one comedic character espousing social and political commentary is a public intellectual, then we have an opening to look at other comedic personae as potential public intellectuals.

Consequently, this chapter examines another entertainer/comedian as a public intellectual: Larry the Cable Guy. In this chapter, I answer two questions: why do some find it difficult to view Larry as an intellectual, and how can we better understand him as a public intellectual? To answer these questions, I offer a reading of Larry the Cable Guy through the lens of the sociologist Zygmunt Bauman's *Legislators and Interpreters: On Modernity,*

Post-modernity and Intellectuals.[5] Specifically, I argue that in his comedic performances, Larry the Cable Guy engages in sociopolitical criticism with a specific focus on political correctness, which some conservatives (and even some nonconservatives) believe restricts their freedom of speech. As such, we might consider Larry an example of Bauman's postmodern intellectual.

To make this argument, I first provide an overview of Bauman's conceptualizations of the modern and the postmodern intellectual as well as a review of Dan Whitney's rise to superstardom as Larry the Cable Guy. Because some readers may reject even the notion of Larry the Cable Guy as an intellectual, I then focus on why this might be. In response, I argue that these prima facie dismissals originate from viewing intellectuals exclusively from a modern point of view. Next, I address how we might better appreciate Larry as a public intellectual by examining how his anti–politically correct comedy contributes to the anti–political correctness public discourse through the lens of Bauman's postmodern intellectual. I close the chapter with an appeal to examine intellectuals and comedians from the point of view of their communities.

BAUMAN'S ARGUMENT

In *Legislators and Interpreters*, Bauman argues that the function of the intellectual has evolved from the modern to the postmodern era.[6] The conditions of the modern era defined intellectuals as legislators, those who settle controversies and disputes through the learned application of their acquired expertise. Bauman utilizes the term "legislators" because the intellectuals are involved in matters of state, though not as elected members of a legislature. On the other hand, theorists often define the postmodern era by the fragmentation of societies and beliefs. Consequently, there is a need for an intellectual who serves as an interpreter, who communicates values and ideas from one community to another so that different communities with different knowledge systems can better understand one another. While Bauman does not directly address whether comedians would be well suited to such a role, Stephanie Koziski does so in her discussion of stand-up comedians as anthropologists. She argues that the comedian is adept at serving as an "interpreter," "articulator," and "spokesperson" between cultures.[7] This assertion reveals that while the value of the modern intellectual rests in his or her social status and knowledge, the value of the postmodern intellectual lies in the individual's discursive role between communities, which makes them public intellectuals.

Bauman's postmodern intellectual stands as a public intellectual in that the communities represented and addressed are "wider audiences."[8] While Whitney's Larry the Cable Guy persona firmly situates himself within the blue-collar economic and "redneck" regional community, Rebecca Krefting finds that Larry is successful at "reach[ing] viewers outside this class based demographic."[9] Furthermore, David Gillota explains that Larry's success reaches well beyond the confines of the South and Midwest because he uses "contemporary conventions of mainstream stand-up" rather than traditional comedic styles found in the South.[10] As such, we might view Larry as a postmodern intellectual who successfully reaches beyond his own community, rather than as Bauman's modern intellectual who engages selective audiences in matters of concern through "large academic texts."[11]

To be sure, Larry did write a lengthy book—an autobiography of sorts—that includes some of his comedy bits, but it is nothing close to the abstruse tomes associated with the traditional scholars Bauman had in mind. In fact, chapter 8 of Larry's book focuses entirely on the fact that it is the halfway point in the book, and there is no actual chapter 6. Nevertheless, as the next section argues, the book gives us insight into the beginning of Larry's role as a public intellectual.

LARRY THE CABLE GUY

Daniel Lawrence Whitney created the comic persona of Larry the Cable Guy. In his 2005 book *Git-R-Done*, Whitney describes how the character emerged from his stand-up act, which he had been doing since 1985. While living in Florida in 1991, a friend at a local radio station needed help and asked Whitney to call in with some comedy. At first, Whitney tried out a number of different characters, including an old Jewish lady from Boca Raton, a gay man, and a state trooper,[12] but none of them really resonated with the listeners.

Months later, his friend grew frustrated waiting at home for the cable guy to show up. The frustration grew into inspiration: Whitney would call in to the radio station as the cable guy. He would draw on a bit from his stand-up about a cable installer, use the southern accent that he had picked up from going to school in Georgia and later living in Florida (Whitney was born and raised in Nebraska and has a fairly normal Midwestern accent), and use a truncated version of his middle name—Larry. The character stuck and became a local celebrity. He soon earned a paying gig on the radio in exchange for (as he called them) "social commentaries" as Larry the Cable Guy.[13]

As his fame grew, more professional opportunities presented themselves.[14] When Craig Hawksley, a member of Jeff Foxworthy's comedy troupe, which was filming what would become the *Blue Collar Comedy Tour: The Movie* (Harding, 2003), withdrew from the tour, Larry filled in. The result was the beginning of a comedic tour de force. Over the next few years, the troupe released two more films, but Larry was clearly the breakout success.[15] In fact, in Larry's most recent tour in 2016, Jeff Foxworthy opened for him.

Larry's solo career also skyrocketed with the release of nine major comedy albums, seven of which topped the *Billboard* Comedy Albums chart, selling millions of copies. He has also made millions of dollars selling merchandise, ranging from Git-R-Done hats to items such as cheeseburger-flavored potato chips and the Larry the Cable Guy Bar-B-Q Five-Piece Knife Set. He has starred in a number of movies, including *Delta Farce* (Harding, 2007) and the widely popular Disney/Pixar *Cars* franchise, in which he voiced the tow truck, Mater. In addition to his ongoing comedy tours, he also hosted the History Channel show *Only in America* (2011–2013), which covered such topics as moonshine and guns.

While Stephen Colbert's faux conservative persona is antithetical to his own beliefs, the Larry the Cable Guy character is not all that different from Dan Whitney. As Joanne R. Gilbert would say, Dan Whitney created a comedic character that was both Dan and not Dan.[16] His book is mostly written in the voice of Larry, but it includes sections where Whitney is clearly the one speaking, though Larry does slip in. In one such section, Whitney explains the relationship between Larry and himself:

> In some ways I'm just like my character and in others I'm not. The real "me" is first and foremost an American and proud of it. I grew up in a small town on a pig farm in Nebraska. I like country music, Iron Maiden, Lynyrd Skynyrd, four-wheelin,' and bird huntin,' I believe Alf's TV talk show is hilarious AND I do believe in Jesus. I love John Wayne and the *Andy Griffith Show* [1961–1968]. I also love this show that's on Playboy TV right now as I write this book. I love Ted Nugent, all the branches of the military and the NRA and I think at least two cast members from *The View* [1997–] have penises. My hero is Ronald Reagan. I think if ya live in America you should learn the language AND I got no problem with the rebel flag on the General Lee.[17]

We should note two interesting points in this passage. First, it is true that Whitney loves Ronald Reagan, going so far as to name his daughter Reagan. Second, Larry's trademark camouflage Git-R-Done hat used to have the

Confederate flag on it. Now the camouflage hat has the American flag on it, or a big red *N* for his home state of Nebraska. Together, these facts show that even though Larry is a character, he is more real than it might seem, allowing Whitney to espouse some of his personal political beliefs through his comic persona.

Larry the Cable Guy is open to a range of critical interpretations as a persona and a performer. Some may examine the persona with a critical hermeneutic, arguing that he is a manifestation of intolerance and ignorance toward others due to the insensitive and offensive nature of his material. Other critics suggest that he is simply parodying and/or pandering to stereotypical rednecks and blue-collar workers, who are ostensibly not smart enough to realize that they are being ridiculed and mocked. Relatedly, we can read Larry through the lens of John Limon's theory, which holds that comedians perform abjection.[18] As Limon clarifies, "what is abject is that which one wants to cleanse oneself of, but ultimately cannot. When comedians proudly perform their abjection, it becomes comic."[19] Such is the case with Larry, who proudly owns his redneck and blue-collar status, which is the cause of much denigration of him and others like him. Then there are those who read him more charitably and see him as challenging the popularity of "affluent, educated, liberal white" comedians.[20]

But these perspectives obfuscate the fact that Larry, like Colbert, has a political message couched in comedy that he seeks to communicate from his community to others. While there are those who criticize Larry, his message, and his community, I contend that by examining the Larry the Cable Guy persona from Whitney's own perspective, by taking him at his word, and by seeing him from the perspective of his community, we can better appreciate the role that he and similar comedians play in society.

A COMEDIAN? YES. AN INTELLECTUAL? NOT SO FAST.

When thinking about Dan Whitney as a public intellectual, I readily admit that even those with the most open minds, including those who are generally receptive to the idea of comedians as public intellectuals, might be a bit skeptical. And there are some good reasons for this skepticism that arise from Whitney's public persona as Larry the Cable Guy.

First, there is his public identity, his stage name: the Cable Guy. In differentiating modern intellectuals from nonintellectuals, Bauman argues that there are thinkers and there are doers. Modern intellectuals concern themselves with reflection and thinking, whereas doers primarily focus on labor. As a cable guy, Larry is a man of action, of blue-collar work carried out by a layman. As I discuss below, Larry's appearance literally embodies the roll-up-your-sleeves work ethic of the working class.

A second reason it is hard to consider Larry an intellectual is his speech. Larry speaks in southern "folk speech," which refers to "the variations in speech from the standard, formal language taught in schools."[21] These variations occur in pronunciation, vocabulary, and grammar.[22] The classic and most prominent example of folk speech is "y'all," but for Larry it is "git 'er dun!" Anyone who has heard just a small sample of Larry's comedy can quickly attest that he speaks a nonstandard version of English, without close attention to pronunciation or subject–verb agreement. While many southerners use folk speech and its many variations, nonsoutherners see it as "coarse, unsophisticated, and uncultured."[23] Ironically enough, Larry is the only member of the Blue Collar Comedy Tour who is not from the South and does not have an authentic southern accent.

Third, Larry's appearance is not what typically comes to mind when we think of an intellectual. He wears old sleeveless flannel shirts, denim work pants, and his camouflage baseball-style hat, which is sometimes adorned with a large, shiny fishhook. This appearance strays far from the stereotype of the intellectual in a tweed jacket.

Finally, the subject matter of Larry's routine makes him the antithesis of Bauman's modern intellectual. Throughout his comedy career, his bits have consistently included jokes about matters that polite society might find objectionable. No topic is more salient in this regard than the scatological, mostly of the flatulent variety. He has jokes about his grandma "gettin' the walkin' farts," where she passes gas whenever she takes a step. Larry, of course, provides the sound effects during this bit. While the wild uncultured masses might find it all funny, such jokes seem vulgar and uncouth to those intellectuals who carry themselves with "aristocratic legitimation" and "social superiority."[24]

These assessments of Larry are not theoretically grounded, and some detractors have directed much worse criticism at him. Larry's most notable and prominent critic, his fellow comedian David Cross, went a step further in an early *Rolling Stone* review of Larry, describing him as "anti-intellectual."[25] Larry responded that he is just a comedian having a good time and that Cross should lighten up. Larry went on to describe how *Rolling Stone*'s coverage made him out to be the "Antichrist of America's intellectuals."[26] Cross later replied with a lengthy open letter accusing Larry of using "second-grade grammar" and of being "somewhat proud of not appearing (or being) too intellectual."[27]

The point remains clear. It is very easy to dismiss the idea of Larry as an intellectual or, at worst, to view him as anti-intellectual. But this does not necessarily mean Larry is not a public intellectual. Thinking of Larry through Bauman's postmodern intellectual lens demonstrates that while his critics do not perceive him to be an intellectual or even an anti-intellectual, he is very much an intellectual—but one of his own community to which his critics do not necessarily belong and which they may not even understand.

THE POSTMODERN INTERPRETER/INTELLECTUAL

Bauman argues that postmodernity is the fragmentation of society into different and varying cultures, each with its own values and beliefs that other cultures do not hold. Because the legislator failed to recognize that different communities produce different meanings, there was a need for a new type of intellectual: the interpreter. The interpreter, the postmodern intellectual, recognizes that different communities have different meanings and serves as a "cultural intermediary" between those fragmented cultures.[28] This aspect of communication between communities is what makes the postmodern intellectual, the interpreter, a public intellectual. In essence, the interpreter serves as a channel, the means by which one community communicates with others. Coincidentally enough, the interpreter is much like a cable guy, who connects two communities: the source of information, entertainment, etcetera on the one hand, and viewers on the other.

This does not mean, however, that anyone who speaks between communities is an intellectual. Bauman explains that postmodern intellectuals are those who authoritatively speak on behalf of their own community (whereas modern intellectuals speak authoritatively on matters within one community, as they do not recognize the fragmentation of communities). Larry's authority comes from the comedic persona of the uber-redneck. As David Gillota explains, "No matter how much of a 'redneck' a viewer may be, he or she will not reach Larry the Cable Guy's redneck status."[29] Larry's status as the ultimate redneck qualifies him to speak to wider communities about his community.

But this uber-redneck status suggests an irony. What makes Larry seem nonintellectual or even anti-intellectual is what actually makes him an intellectual to his community. In other words, his community values him for his blue-collar redneck persona, which is the very reason audiences outside his community devalue him. In this sense, Larry is what Lawrence E. Mintz calls "a negative exemplar."[30] That is, Larry represents and embodies "conduct to be ridiculed and rejected."³¹ Mintz also argues that a negative exemplar functions as a "shaman," one who connects two worlds, which aligns with Bauman's notion of the postmodern intellectual.³²

The question that now presents itself is this: if we are to consider Larry as a postmodern intellectual, as an interpreter between his community and others, what is the community he represents? One can approach this question in a variety of ways. But, as someone interested in politics, rhetoric, and free speech, I will focus on Larry as the interpreter/intellectual for the conservative community who opposes political correctness, which has been the most prominent political theme throughout Larry's comedy career.³³

THE ANTI-POLITICAL CORRECTNESS CONSERVATIVE COMMUNITY

Political correctness became a prominent topic after the 1964 publication of Chairman Mao Zedong's *Little Red Book*, which explained that political correctness was "the disciplined acceptance of [the Chinese Communist] party line."³⁴ The book was widely translated and circulated throughout the world and quickly "became fashionable among Western students."³⁵

Shortly after the *Little Red Book* appeared, the idea of political correctness began to circulate in Leftist academic communities throughout the United States. These communities discussed the language and ideologies of various rights movements (e.g., feminism and civil rights) and how groups of people had been marginalized and silenced throughout history by virtue of their race, sex, class, and so on. For them, political correctness was about rejecting language that is offensive or discriminatory toward others, such as people of color, women, gays and lesbians, or people with disabilities.³⁶

This position was not without objection. As Wayne Batchis writes, the "widespread use [of political correctness] reflected a perception that conservatives, particularly students and faculty in the academic setting, were being muzzled."³⁷ To combat this muzzling, there arose a "conservative war on perceived political correctness, particularly on university campuses."³⁸

This war stayed primarily within academia until October 1990, when Richard Bernstein wrote an article on the hegemony of political correctness in the *New York Times*.³⁹ Bernstein's article unexpectedly became a flash point and pushed the issue of political correctness out of the small world of academia and into the larger public discourse of television interviews, public debates, news articles/opinion pieces, and public speeches.⁴⁰ It was during this same period of time that Dan Whitney became Larry, and Larry became famous for being funny while also contributing to the political correctness debate.

Larry joined a public debate that included a number of prominent public figures, including journalists, conservative media commentators, university professors, political policy advisors, feminist and legal scholars, poets, art critics, social commentators, and even President George H. W. Bush in 1991.[41] The debate has continued unabated into recent elections, prominently championed by Sarah Palin and Donald Trump.[42] It should also be noted that Larry has not been the only comedian to take on the topic. Comedians such as Chris Rock, Patton Oswalt, Gilbert Gottfried, Dennis Miller, Jerry Seinfeld, and the late George Carlin have all challenged the idea of political correctness.[43]

While many people have been involved in the public discussion of political correctness, much of the public discourse focuses on four primary arguments: political correctness is censorship/thought control, political correctness is trivial and cannot be taken seriously, political correctness advocates commit the very evil that they fight against, and political correctness advocates use "unjust means" to achieve their goal.[44] An analysis of Larry's comedy demonstrates that his jokes invoke these precise arguments.

LARRY AS A POSTMODERN INTELLECTUAL/INTERPRETER OF THE ANTI-POLITICAL CORRECTNESS CONSERVATIVE COMMUNITY

Larry contributes to the anti–political correctness discourse through a rhetorical performance of anti–political correctness in his comedy. While there is no explicit mention of the idea of political correctness in some of his jokes, the topics and word choices result in a demonstration of anti–political correctness. Instead, his subject matter focuses on groups historically associated with political correctness: women, the disabled, people of color, and homosexuals.[45] Moreover, his language makes clear that he is not worried about cultural sensitivity or respectful language, which are also important concerns among political correctness advocates.

Anti–political correctness is evident throughout his comedy. For example, he jokes about his overweight sister whose face is covered with moles, which he makes clear are not beauty marks. In one bit, he jokes that he needed to hire a rodeo clown to distract her when he brings the groceries home. Larry's focus on a female's physical appearance, specifically skin imperfections and weight, suggests to some that he is guilty of lookism, or judging others by how they compare to a certain idealized standard of beauty. When he jokes about women not related to him, the jokes are nearly exclusively about sex or feminine hygiene. These jokes suggest to some that Larry devalues women—that to him they are nothing more than sexual objects.

Larry also makes a number of jokes about those with mental disabilities. Larry undoubtedly would have an issue with my political correctness, as I prefer words other than "retard" or "waterhead," both of which he uses regularly.[46] Larry also jokes about people with physical disabilities, referring to them as "cripples."[47] And in one of his analogies, he says, "I'm madder than Ray Charles with a *Where's Waldo?* book."[48] Joking about people's disabilities suggests that he engages in ableism, the social discrimination against people based on their disability.

He also tells jokes about African Americans and Mexicans using negative stereotypes. In one bit, he acts scared when he sees his shadow and thinks, "Two black guys [are] sneaking up on me."[49] Other jokes highlight the contentiousness of race relations. For example, he says, "I'm madder than Jesse Jackson at the airport having to answer the white courtesy phone."[50] His jokes about Mexicans predominantly address illegal immigration, unskilled labor, or their lack of fluency in English. To some, these jokes suggest that Larry holds racist and xenophobic views.

Finally, Larry frequently jokes about gays and lesbians or, as he derogatorily calls them, "queers."[51] He jokes that we should let gays into the military because they would be good at redecorating war zones once the fighting is over. He adds that women should fight alongside men, but not all the time, just once every thirty days, which is another example of why some see him as misogynistic. His language about homosexuality also invokes stereotypes of gay men as being hypersexualized. For example, he says, "I'm madder than a queer with lockjaw on Valentine's Day."[52] Because he adopts effeminate voices and mannerisms when telling these jokes, it is not surprising that several critics see Larry's comedy as homophobic.[53]

Larry also addresses class issues associated with white trash and rednecks. These jokes include references to NASCAR races, flea markets, trailer homes, and the like. While some might see him as engaging in classism, this is not a popular criticism of him. The reason seems to be that his presentation of self makes him a member of the class he is disparaging. Consequently, he is engaging more in self-deprecation, which is generally more acceptable than making fun of others—especially when joking about other people's appearance, sexuality, race, nationality, or disability.[54] However, he rarely if ever jokes about heterosexuals, whites, or men, who (according to those who advocate political correctness) are the ones who have long engaged in the marginalization if not outright silencing of other groups.

To those outside his community, such as David Cross, it may seem that Larry's rhetoric is the result of lookism, sexism, racism, xenophobia, homophobia, ableism, and, given his redneck persona, a general lack of formal education. Attributing Larry's so-called offensiveness to bigotry and insensitivity, however, overlooks the issue of free expression that his community values and exercises through anti–politically correct rhetoric.

One of the major arguments of the anti–political correctness community is that any attempt, be it legislative or through social pressure, to restrict another's language is censorship.[55] Advocates of political correctness prioritize equality and antidiscrimination, but Larry and his community value freedom of expression above these ideas.[56] As he boldly declares in one of his early albums, he is "fighting for freedoms here."[57] Larry and his community believe they should be free to express their own ideas with their own words, and not be required to moderate their language based on what others believe is appropriate. And if someone is offended, his community is quick to note that the Bill of Rights protects free expression, but does not protect anyone from being offended.

Nevertheless, Larry does not necessarily believe that he or his community is demeaning others or engaging in hateful discourse about them. In an interview, he describes his community as "good, honest, hard-working Americans.... They don't hate anybody, they just want to enjoy themselves, and they're not into that PC crap."[58] Throughout his comedy career, he has explained that he loves all people, and Dan Whitney's offstage volunteerism, generosity, and health-care advocacy, which are discussed below, certainly support this idea.

In fact, Larry and his community believe that they are the ones being discriminated against. This belief is rooted in the anti–political correctness argument that political correctness advocates are committing the very evil they are resisting. This reasoning is dependent on accepting that Larry deliberately aims his comments toward combating political correctness and not at discriminating against others. And while much of Larry's enactment of anti–political correctness is performed for the audience's amusement, there are instances where he makes this position clearly known.

Larry makes his anti–political correctness philosophy absolutely clear at the end of his first major album, *Lord, I Apologize* (2001). He says:

> Remember this. You came to a Larry the Cable Guy show. It's a free country, all right, and we're Americans and we're having fun. And that's all we're doing. Telling jokes and having a good time. So, if someone here is offended about something we're doing, we're not

here to do that. We're here to make you laugh. So, if you're offended, go home and, uh, put a bullet in your head, all right? [loud applause] Seriously. End it. End your life.⁵⁹

Larry's tone and delivery of this concluding meta-commentary reflects sincerity and seriousness. As happens in his book from time to time, the delivery comes across as being more from Whitney than from Larry. His directness and delivery underscore the important fact that his anti-political correctness is about freedom and fun. He is not there to offend others, although political correctness advocates might disagree. From his and his community's point of view, the presumed point is that this is a comedy show where he can joke around as he feels is appropriate, not based on how others think he should be. The audience came to see him. He is not there to appease others with language they would prefer.

It is a comedy performance, however, so it cannot end so seriously. As the applause dies down, the voice of Larry returns after suggesting that his critics commit suicide and adds, "I mean that in a good Christian way." The irony is obvious and makes for a funny end to the show for his presumed audience. He is serious about expressing his anti-politically correct views, but he is also a comedian and needs to create laughter. Whether the last line is merely a good-natured way to bring levity after a serious meta-reflection or is supposed to be ironic by suggesting hypocrisy on the part of Larry or his fans is a question for another time.

There are other examples of Larry using this strategy of ending a serious, direct, and sincere anti-political correctness commentary with a comedic punchline. In one bit, Larry mentions with force and anger in his voice that because America is so politically correct, his grandfather was fired as a greeter at Walmart for saying "Merry Christmas" to customers. Returning to his Larry style of speaking, he then adds that his grandfather said this in August while pantless.

One can also see Larry's approach of directly stating his anti-political correctness philosophy toward comedy in a recurring bit where he reads parodies of the popular Christmas poem, Clement Clarke Moore's "A Visit from St. Nicholas." One such poem is the "Pissed Off Christmas Poem," which reflects two major arguments of the anti-political correctness community.

The poem begins with his introduction, "Here's a Christmas poem I wanna do. I writ' dis poem one night after bein' all pissed off at the news 'cause they're so dadgum politically correct at Christmas time it irritates me."⁶⁰ He starts, "'Twas the night before Christmas when all through the house not a creature was stirring because the politically correctors done made everybody have a holiday party and took the freakin' fun out of everything." Here Larry expresses clear disdain at the extensive efforts of political correctness advocates, who took the "fun out of everything." This resonates with the argument that political correctness is trivial and cannot be taken seriously. This argument focuses on the perceived slippery slope of political correctness. While political correctness may have laudable goals, critics argue that if left unchecked, it can become excessive and ridiculous, affecting every trivial part of the world.[61]

He continues the poem by suggesting that political correctness advocates would equate the exercise of one's religion, which ties into the earlier free speech argument, with two of the most horrible crimes imaginable. He reads, "We caroled to ourselves in our living room 'cause we was afraid that some anti-Jesus moron might hear us singing 'Joy to the World the Lord has Come' and might get the ACLU to sue us 'cause we singing about Jesus and that is just as bad as rape and murder in this dadgum country." Here Larry invokes the argument that political correctness advocates are "bullies, totalitarians, and fascists" who use harassment and intimidation, not rational arguments in open debate, to force acceptance of their views.[62] He concludes the poem by wishing the politically correct a Merry Christmas, clearly meant to upset them, and that they "burn in hell." Again, the irony provides a powerful and humorous end to the bit for his fans and community.

In all of these examples and in many more, Larry's discourse deliberately avoids language that might be more appeasing and less offensive to those outside his community, all in an effort to combat political correctness. His focus is not on others; it is on him and his community fighting against a politically based movement with which they legitimately disagree. To those outside his community, it is easy to see him as marginalizing, silencing, and discriminating. But to Larry and his community, they are the ones being silenced. Political correctness is discriminating against them for expressing their views. This argument posits that anti-bigotry is bigotry against the so-called bigots.

Because of this perceived discrimination, Larry popularized an expression that was more prominent early in his career: "What the hell is this, Russia?" He often invoked the phrase to highlight the attack on his community's freedom from those who have different politics. Relatedly, Larry utilizes the term "commie" to reference liberals generally and political correctness advocates specifically. In one colorful expression, he calls them "uptight, nonsmoking, anti-Jesus, anti-gun, tofu-eating, tree-hugging commies."[63] Here Larry focuses on those who are attacking not only his freedom of (offensive) speech, but also his community's free exercise of religion, and follows it up with a reference to the Second Amendment's right to bear arms (which inspired the title of his second album, *The Right to Bare Arms* (2005), the cover of which features Larry's usual sleeveless arm with the US Constitution tattooed on his bicep). The use of the word "commie" is worth noting because the modern conceptualization of political correctness, as stated earlier, has its roots in communist China. The logic appears to be that anyone who engages in political correctness is as un-American as a communist. As he sings in one comedy song, "I ain't no commie . . . I'm a bona fide American."[64]

Larry's comedy certainly engages the issue of political correctness, but there is more to being a public intellectual than entering into the public discourse on a topic of public concern. It is important to focus not only on what public intellectuals say, but also on the role they play in society.

Dan Whitney admits that his Larry persona is just a character, but he still recognizes that Larry is like a lot of real people (including himself) who believe what Larry believes and talk just like Larry talks.[65] But he also recognizes that there are people different from Larry who enjoy his show. He discusses in his book that his appeal spans red and blue states, and he claims that the states where he had the most success early on were Minnesota, Pennsylvania, and Wisconsin, all blue states at the time. In his concluding meta-commentary in *Lord, I Apologize*, Larry acknowledges that there are people in attendance who are not members of his community—people in the audience who do not share his beliefs on political correctness—by saying, "If someone here is offended. . . ." This admonition supports understanding Larry as an interpreter from one community (i.e., his) to another (i.e., people who are offended by anti-political correctness). And the inclusion of "we" language makes it clear that there are people in attendance who *are* from his community.

In 2016, I went to see Larry perform in Reading, Pennsylvania. I arrived early and talked to as many people as I could. Lots of folks were hanging around outside the arena waiting for the doors to open. To be sure, it was a small sample size and nowhere near representative, but I found that Larry reached out to a number of different communities. Of the people I talked to, some considered themselves conservatives, while others did not. Many claimed they were not political at all. Some were blue-collar workers; others were white-collar. Many claimed they were there just because he was funny. Others were there just to see Jeff Foxworthy, the opening act. What I found is that Larry's audience is not as homogeneous as the reviews of his show and his critics have suggested. And judging by his fame and success, there is little doubt that he has been or will be heard by much of the mainstream comedy audience in America, who will surely understand his position on political correctness by the end of the show.

CONCLUSION

While Larry might have critics who cannot fathom the possibility of him being an intellectual, the argument presented in this chapter is that he may not be an intellectual for his critics, but he is an intellectual for his community. Larry does not always address the topic of political correctness, but when he does, he is speaking for a community—those who feel that they are having their voices constrained—to the rest of the world.

Whether or not one enjoys his comedy, Larry remains popular and highly visible in US popular culture. Even though Larry serves as an interpreter, those individuals outside his community do not have to agree with his positions or find him funny. But for those audience members in his community, he is speaking their truth to the masses. Matthew J. Ferrence writes that Larry "speaks the truth that the audience wants to be able to utter in their daily lives."[66] But they cannot, so they let their voices be heard by others through Larry, who serves as their interpreter to the rest of the world. And for his fans, it is comedy gold.

Larry the Cable Guy is an easy target. Ferrence describes him as the champion of the "redneck resistance," whose ideology evokes "homophobia, xenophobia, ecophobia, misogyny, [and] racism."[67] But for Larry and his community, it is not necessarily that they hate others; they just do not want to have others control their language. Even though the use of politically incorrect language might equate to hate for some, the community for whom Larry speaks does not feel that way.

Although the focus of this chapter is Larry the Cable Guy, there remains a larger take-home point. While there might be a decline in the number of public intellectuals, that so-called decline may be due to the limited ways in which we define them. As scholars and students, whether we are connoisseurs of comedy or not, we should be open to exploring the various ways of understanding public intellectuals. This work provides an opportunity to understand someone as a public intellectual who might otherwise not be seen as such. Indeed, there might be many more public intellectuals than we have tended to think. It might be the old man on the park bench, or it might just be the cable guy who tells you what he thinks as he rolls up his sleeves to get the job done.

Notes

I would like to thank Ana Nguyen for serving as my research assistant for this project.

1. Jean Bethke Elshtain, "Why Public Intellectuals?" *Wilson Quarterly* 38, no. 1 (2014): 76–88.

2. David Marshall and Cassandra Atherton, "Situating Public Intellectuals," *Media International Australia* 156 (2015): 69–78.

3. Brad Amburn, "The World's Top 20 Public Intellectuals," *Foreign Policy*, October 7, 2009, accessed May 27, 2016, http://foreignpolicy.com/2009/10/07/the-worlds-top-20-public-intellectuals.

4. Chris Cillizza, "How Liberal Is Stephen Colbert?" *Washington Post*, September 8, 2015, accessed May 23, 2016, https://www.washingtonpost.com/news/the-fix/wp/2014/04/10/the-conservatism-of-stephen-colbert.

5. Richard Bellamy, *Croce, Gramsci, Bobbio and the Italian Political Tradition* (Colchester, UK: ECPR Press, 2014), 93.

6. Zygmunt Bauman, *Legislators and Interpreters: On Modernity, Post-modernity, and Intellectuals* (Ithaca, NY: Cornell University Press, 1987).

7. Stephanie Koziski, "The Standup Comedian as Anthropologist: Intentional Culture Critic," *Journal of Popular Culture* 18 (1984): 57–76, 65–66.

8. Shaun Best, *Zygmunt Bauman: Why Good People Do Bad Things* (New York: Routledge, 2013), 1.

9. Rebecca Krefting, *All Joking Aside: American Humor and Its Discontents* (Baltimore, MD: Johns Hopkins University Press, 2014), 118–19.

10. David Gillota, *Ethnic Humor in Multiethnic America* (New Brunswick, NJ: Rutgers University Press, 2013), 88–89.

11. Best, *Zygmunt Bauman*, 1.

12. Noel Murray, "Dan Whitney, a.k.a. Larry The Cable Guy," *The A.V. Club*, August 30, 2011, accessed May 23, 2016, http://www.avclub.com/article/dan-whitney-aka-larry-the-cable-guy-61071.

13. Larry the Cable Guy, *Git-R-Done* (New York: Crown, 2005), 1.

14. Loyal Jones, *Country Music Humorists and Comedians* (Urbana: University of Illinois Press, 2008), 236.

15. Matthew J. Ferrence, *All-American Redneck: Variations on an Icon, from James Fenimore Cooper to the Dixie Chicks* (Knoxville: University of Tennessee Press, 2014), 66.

16. Joanne R. Gilbert, "Performing Marginality: Comedy, Identity, and Cultural Critique," *Text and Performance Quarterly* 17 (1997): 317–30, 329.

17. Larry the Cable Guy, *Git-R-Done*, 15.

18. John Limon, *Stand-Up Comedy in Theory, or, Abjection in America* (Durham, NC: Duke University Press, 2000), 4.

19. Limon, *Stand-Up Comedy in Theory*, 79.

20. Gillota, *Ethnic Humor in Multiethnic America*, 86.

21. Charles Reagan Wilson, James G. Thomas, and Ann J. Abadie, *The New Encyclopedia of Southern Culture*, vol. 5, *Language* (Chapel Hill: University of North Carolina Press, 2006), 134.

22. Wilson, Thomas, and Abadie, *The New Encyclopedia of Southern Culture*, 5:134.

23. John B. Rehder, *Appalachian Folkways* (Baltimore, MD: Johns Hopkins University Press, 2004), 289.

24. Bauman, *Legislators and Interpreters*, 30–31.

25. Gavin Edwards, "Larry the Cable Guy Plugs into Red-State Fervor," *Rolling Stone* 973 (June 5, 2005): 35.
26. Larry the Cable Guy, *Git-R-Done*, 92.
27. David Cross, *I Drink for a Reason* (New York: Grand Central Publishing, 2009), 206.
28. Tony Blackshaw, *Zygmunt Bauman Textbook* (London: Routledge, 2005), 59.
29. Gillota, *Ethnic Humor in Multiethnic America*, 90.
30. Lawrence E. Mintz, "Stand-up Comedy as Social and Cultural Mediation," in *What's So Funny? Humor in American Culture*, ed. Nancy A. Walker (Wilmington, DE: Scholarly Resources, 1998), 196–97.
31. Mintz, "Stand-up Comedy," 196–97.
32. Mintz, "Stand-up Comedy," 197.
33. Maggie Gallagher, "The Sex Wars," *National Review*, May 15, 1995, 67; Wayne Batchis, *The Right's First Amendment: The Politics of Free Speech & the Return of Conservative Libertarianism* (Stanford, CA: Stanford University Press, 2016), 105.
34. William Safire, *Safire's Political Dictionary* (Oxford: Oxford University Press, 2008), 555.
35. Daniele Leese, "Mao the Man and the Icon," in *A Critical Introduction to Mao*, ed. Timothy Cheek (Cambridge: Cambridge University Press, 2010), 219.
36. Geoffrey Hughes, *Political Correctness: A History of Semantics and Culture* (Maldon, MA: Wiley-Blackwell, 2010), 60–68.
37. Batchis, *The Right's First Amendment*, 65–66.
38. Batchis, *The Right's First Amendment*, 65–66.
39. Richard Bernstein, "The Rising Hegemony of the Politically Correct," *New York Times*, October 28, 1990, accessed September 23, 2016, http://www.nytimes.com/1990/10/28/weekinreview/ideas-trends-the-rising-hegemony-of-the-politically-correct.html.
40. Francisco Valdes, *Crossroads, Directions and a New Critical Race Theory* (Philadelphia, PA: Temple University Press), 65; Hughes, *Political Correctness*, 65–66.
41. Paul Berman, *Debating P.C.: The Controversy over Political Correctness on College Campuses* (New York: Dell, 1992).
42. Damon Linker, "Inside America's War over Political Correctness," *The Week*, September 7, 2016, accessed September 23, 2016, http://theweek.com/articles/647135/inside-americas-war-over-political-correctness.
43. Anna Silman, "10 Famous Comedians on How Political Correctness Is Killing Comedy," *Salon*, June 10, 2015, accessed September 23, 2016, http://www.salon.com/2015/06/10/10_famous_comedians_on_how_political_correctness_is_killing_comedy_we_are_addicted_to_the_rush_of_being_offended.
44. Maryann Ayim, "Just How Correct Is Political Correctness? A Critique of the Opposition's Arguments," *Argumentation* 12 (1998): 445–80.
45. Hughes, *Political Correctness*, 60–68.
46. Larry the Cable Guy, "Dickweed," *Salutations and Flatulations* (DJT Records, 1997, CD).
47. Larry the Cable Guy, *Git-R-Done*, 11.
48. Larry the Cable Guy, "People Like My Analogies," *Lord, I Apologize* (Hip-O Records, 2001, CD).
49. Larry the Cable Guy, "WWJD," *Right to Bare Arms* (Warner Brothers, 2005, CD).
50. Larry the Cable Guy, "People Like My Analogies."

51. Larry the Cable Guy, "People Like My Analogies."
52. Larry the Cable Guy, *Git-R-Done*, 88.
53. Larry the Cable Guy, "Gay Mafia," *Morning Constitutions* (Warner Brothers, 2007, CD).
54. Alison Dagnes, *A Conservative Walks into a Bar: The Politics of Political Humor* (New York: Palgrave Macmillan, 2012), 27.
55. Ayim, "Just How Correct Is Political Correctness?"
56. Larry the Cable Guy, "Dickweed."
57. Larry the Cable Guy, "Dickweed."
58. Edwards, "Larry the Cable Guy Plugs into Red-State Fervor," 35.
59. Larry the Cable Guy, "Going in Circles for Two Hours," *Lord, I Apologize* (Hip-O Records, 2001, CD).
60. Larry the Cable Guy, "Pissed-Off Christmas Poem," *A Very Larry Christmas* (Warner Brothers, 2004, CD).
61. Ayim, "Just How Correct Is Political Correctness?"
62. Ayim, "Just How Correct Is Political Correctness?" 31.
63. Larry the Cable Guy, "Pissed-Off Christmas Poem."
64. Larry the Cable Guy, "Lord, I Apologize," *Lord, I Apologize* (Hip-O Records, 2001, CD).
65. Murray, "Dan Whitney, a.k.a. Larry The Cable Guy."
66. Ferrence, *All-American Redneck*, 68.
67. Ferrence, *All-American Redneck*, 68, 167.

"KILLER CLOSER"
Doug Stanhope and the White Libertarian Stand-Up Tradition

Thomas Clark

> The only true freedom that you find is when you realize and come to terms with the fact that you are completely and unapologetically fucked—and then you're free to float around the system.
> —Doug Stanhope[1]

Rather than reading this paper, you might just want to watch the climactic finale of Doug Stanhope's special, *Doug Stanhope: Before Turning the Gun on Himself* (Lamoureux and Lamoureux, 2012), which is readily available online.[2] Titled "Remember When I Used to Give a Shit? / Killer Closer," this fifteen-minute double bit consists of an account of his failed effort to effect change as a comedic public intellectual followed by a densely allegorical explication of the purpose and methodology of his art and the libertarian convictions that inform it. As such it is a perfect example of how stand-up comedy as a literary genre can brilliantly fuse art, political discourse, and entertainment into condensed set pieces uniquely suited to rapid diffusion and reception through social media platforms like YouTube. These sites of contemporary public discourse represent breeding spaces for today's new types of public intellectuals, from Jordan Peterson to Natalie Wynn.

In this chapter I contextualize and explicate Stanhope's routine through three connected arguments. First, I will present him as a coherent libertarian thinker in an anarcho-existentialist vein.[3] Second, I will argue that as such, he is part of a distinctive tradition of radical stand-up comedy informed both by central parameters of the genre and by the whiteness of its performers. This tradition therefore fundamentally differs from the "charged humor" that Rebecca Krefting has identified as a key comedic practice by which marginalized groups in US society claim and perform cultural citizenship.[4] Notably, both of these branches of comedy are rooted in the countercultural practices that have informed radical stand-up since the 1960s. But while charged humor works from ethnic, racial, gendered, or queer vantage points to emphasize inclusion and critique exclusion, white libertarian stand-up proceeds from a universalizing white perspective that sees the alienated and abjective comic individual as a total critic: of humanity as a failed species; of society, nation, and family as misguided and repressive forms of human organization; and of the contemporary United States as a distinctively critique-worthy manifestation of the human condition. My third point picks up on how this latter perspective corresponds with popular conceptions of the public intellectual and reinvents them through the genre of comedy for the fragmented social and media spaces of the twenty-first century. Stanhope thus emerges as an updated version of Emerson's ideal of "man thinking" as opposed to a pigeonholed academic professional, an exponent of the Thoreauvian individualism of being a majority of one whose authority is rooted in the public performance of integrity and authenticity rather than in superiority or in consensus- and majority-building skills. Stanhope represents at once the noble American tradition of standing up to majorities in the name of principles and the troubling segregation of American society into disconnected filter bubbles of closed discourses.

DOUG STANHOPE AND LIBERTARIANISM

In his recently published (auto)biography of his mother and himself, Massachusetts-born Doug Stanhope describes himself as a dark-humored, maladjusted youth with incompatible parents: a soft, self-effacing father and a hard-nosed, dissatisfied mother who leaves the family to pursue a crooked path of career tryouts, failed relationships, migrations, and substance abuse not unlike her son's, but without the jokes. After dropping out of high school, Stanhope heads west to make his fortune in Hollywood or Vegas. Working at a dreck job in the late 1980s, he imbibes the shock comedy of Andrew Dice Clay and, prodded by his boss, begins writing material, first performing at an open mic night in Las Vegas in 1990 after downing a pitcher of beer.[5] He becomes a road comic, goes on to win the San Francisco Comedy Competition in 1995, and has been releasing a steady stream of comedy albums and DVDs since 1998. He has also hosted various TV shows, written books, and is part of the podcasting community, but stand-up remains his true vocation.

The earliest surviving video of Stanhope from 1990 already presents the basic draft of his stage persona. Beer in hand, he laconically makes wry self-deprecating observations about the false promises and inevitable disappointments of life, with a heavy infusion of blue and dark material.[6] But by the time of his first DVD release, *Word of Mouth* (Booth, 2002), his opener had evolved to intertwine shock-comedy commentaries on chocolate-smeared dildos with trenchant critiques of class privilege and the national security state, culminating in the bold assessment that he didn't care about terrorist attacks on the USA because "this country is a big terrorist pig, this fucking country is a big bloated celebrity that thinks it doesn't have to pay the cover charge."[7] This wholesale rejection of American exceptionalism and nationalism is an expression of Stanhope's deeply held libertarian convictions, which are among the most politically explicit on the comedy circuit. He has clearly laid out an anarcho-libertarian critique of US (or any) society and its institutions, commenting on fundamental issues of political philosophy and policy while providing suggestions for policy and action. He has supported libertarian politicians like Ron Paul and Gary Johnson, worn a t-shirt emblazoned with the word "Libertarian" in his show *No Refunds* (Lage, 2007), and gone so far as to renounce the political altogether, believing that "every individual person should be independent of everyone else."[8]

At this point it might be useful to clarify and define the term "libertarian," which in a US context has increasingly been understood as an ideological branch of the new Right or merely a strategy of corporate lobbyism.[9] As a political philosophy, libertarianism is fundamentally concerned with minimizing the external constraints on the liberty of any individual by other individuals, groups, or institutions of any kind, especially government. Harking back to the proto-liberalism of natural rights theory as spelled out by John Locke and other seventeenth- and eighteenth-century Enlightenment thinkers, it posits the fundamental principle of individuals' full initial self-ownership and their moral power to acquire property in external objects.[10] Historically, libertarian ideas evolved in Victorian England as a conservative response to mainstream liberalism's increasing willingness to regulate society toward progressive ends in view of the increasingly untenable social, economic, civic, and political inequality of mass-industrialized Britain. Intellectuals like Herbert Spencer in England and William Graham Sumner in the US resorted to earlier models of liberal political economy to argue for the unfettered activity of individuals and its beneficial outcomes for society, based on a belief in a self-regulating, natural evolution of the social order.[11]

Stanhope clearly falls in line with key libertarian propositions, agreeing with Jean-Jacques Rousseau that "man was born free and everywhere he is in chains."[12]

> It's not a free country. You're born free. I mean you're born absolutely free except for laws of nature. Those. . . . If you drink you get drunk. If you get old you die. That's a law, too. If you sit on a tack you will bleed from the ass. These are the only laws that you're born with and any government just fucks you out of that kind of freedom. . . . They say if you give a man a fish, he'll eat for a day. But if you teach a man to fish [pause]—then he's got to get a fishing license, but he doesn't have any money, so he's gotta get a job and he has to get into the Social Security system and pay taxes and now you're gonna audit the poor cocksucker. . . . You were born free, you got fucked outta half of it and you wave a flag celebratin', heeheeheehee. . . .[13]

Consequently, Stanhope rejects the very idea of nation, society, or any other form of social organization that impinges on the natural liberty of the individual, and any belief system based on convention: "America doesn't exist, it's just dirt with lines drawn around it," and the Pledge of Allegiance is "brainwashing cult shit," "twelve years of forced advertising" for nationalist ideology.[14] When many stand-ups were ridiculing opponents of gay marriage for attacking what didn't affect their lives, Stanhope argued against the very institution of civil unions, calling the whole debate a "trick argument" because "marriage should not be a legal institution. . . . The government should have no place in your love life. . . . If you want tax breaks, incorporate!"[15]

Stanhope has said that he doesn't "know shit about the economic side of"[16] libertarian politics, and it does not feature heavily in his comedy. It is clear, however, that he considers consolidated economic power to be no less a malignant infringement of individual liberty than government, and part and parcel of the oppressive structure of US society. In a number of bits, Stanhope gives concrete advice on how to subvert the capitalist economic order: corporate employees should engage in covert sabotage; trade economies should supplant consumerism; and jury duty should be accepted to consistently vote not guilty on any tax-related issues, as well as victimless crimes like drug possession or trafficking.[17] During his special, *Beer Hall Putsch* (Karas, 2013), he lays into the Occupy Movement for camping in Central Park "slapping on drums in a drum circle," rather than doing actual damage to the banks. "If you hate the banks, don't fuck up the park, fuck up the banks," he suggests, by maxing out dead people's credit cards or clogging branch banks with frivolous loan applications, lawsuits, and other jamming practices.[18] Whether consciously or not, Stanhope is clearly tapping left-libertarian traditions in these examples. Contrary to the more visible right-wing models proposed by Murray Rothbard and others, which argue for an unrestricted and irreversible right to appropriation, left-libertarians posit an equal original right of all free individuals to property, which mandates either a consensus on, or compensations for, unilateral acquisitions of property.[19] Since Stanhope has no faith in government as a provider of such economic justice, the only alternative is organized resistance. Thus he suggests that movements like Occupy get serious and adapt the ruthless, but highly successful, strategies of Scientology to undermine capitalism.[20]

On the subject of religion, Stanhope is a virulent atheist who proclaims a libertarian rejection of any external moral authority. He points out that he "could fill three CDs worth of just the Christian bashing alone I've done over my career, I've done Mormon bashing and Muslim bashing, I'll do more Scientology bashing once I have a stronger legal team."[21] The only acceptable religion is one of the self, and one's self must be explored and nurtured by "excess in moderation":

> Don't eat a mushroom stem and see colors, eat the whole bag and see god for one time in your life. The real god, not some storybook bullshit god that's been fucking kicked into your head for the last 2000 years that you just accept with no logic whatsoever, but a fucking real god that works for you. Any time you deny your own logic, you deny your own instincts, you deny your own god, you fucking moron. [While looking into beer bottle] All this part of the bit is coming out of the bottle, which is the weirdest thing.[22]

This Nietzschean outburst shows Stanhope's libertarianism to have a strong existentialist bent. Existentialism predicates a meaningless universe in which no objective truth, norm, morality, or identity can be discovered. The individual, lost and alienated, hovers between nihilistic resignation and living radically on her own terms.[23] Stanhope veers between these extremes. As we have seen, he encourages active transformative resistance to the status quo, but he also supports anti-natalism—the belief that humans should not reproduce, because life is not worth living: "if my parents were alive today I would sue them into poverty just for having me against my will."[24] He expresses pragmatic resignation when stating that the best one can do in the present-day United States is to "realize and come to terms with the fact that you are completely and unapologetically fucked—and then you're free to float around the system."[25] This freedom, however, requires discarding all ideologies and allegiances as false and nurturing a skeptical intellectual autonomy—a stance that perfectly describes his own acrid stand-up comedy. In fact, even Stanhope's admitted alcoholism and drug use on and off stage represent both an existentialist performative aesthetic and a libertarian political statement of complete self-ownership: "You own your own meat, if you own nothing else in the world.... Do whatever you want to it!"[26]

Significantly, Stanhope holds everybody to this radical standard, rejecting any (self-)ascription of identity beyond one's singular individuality as constricting or as an invalid rationalization of one's behavior. In other words, he expects individuals to renounce and overcome any cultural socialization to "take individual responsibility for who you are," making him a sworn enemy of identity politics in any form. A marked example is his critique of Jews supposedly flaunting their Jewishness: "'I'm a Jew. We naturally carry a lot of guilt. It's a Jewish thing.' No, it's a you thing. You, that fuckhead in the chair. It's got nothing to do with Judaism. If you have guilt, maybe you're weak of character, maybe you're fucking guilty of something, I don't know ... but it has nothing to do with some ancient tribe of blablabla. That's not attached to your DNA."[27] Stanhope evidently gives short shrift to the formative powers of history and society on the individual. This is not a given in libertarian thought, which "is sensitive to what the past was like (e.g., what agreements were made and what rights violations took place)" and would be able to acknowledge historically evolved patterns of group behavior and belief, even if it does not wish to perpetuate them.[28] Stanhope's rather smug dismissal of the power and functions of identity is more likely a function of his whiteness than of his libertarianism.

CHARGED HUMOR AND WHITE LIBERTARIAN STAND-UP

There is no question that Doug Stanhope's comedy is highly political and witheringly radical, positing a fundamentally contrarian vision of existence compared to the American mainstream. Yet, it does not conform at all to Krefting's model of "charged humor," which uses the shock tactics of hard-edged stand-up to expose the inequalities and exclusionary practices of mainstream US society while claiming cultural citizenship for nonwhites, nonstraights, and nonmen. As coined by Renato Rosaldo in his study of Latino communities in California, "cultural citizenship refers to the right to be different with respect to the norms of the dominant national community, without compromising one's right to belong" and "offers the possibility of legitimizing demands made in the struggle [of Latinos] to enfranchise themselves. These demands can range from legal, political, and economic issues to matters of human dignity, well-being, and respect."[29] In Krefting's words, "charged humor reimagines a community, disrupting the stereotypes associated with various communities and how these communities are positioned in the national imagination."[30]

This model offers a convincing conceptualization of a stand-up tradition stretching from Richard Pryor to Margaret Cho, but it does not address the white libertarian strain of stand-up comedy Stanhope represents. While his humor is clearly charged, it is not at all concerned with (and indeed opposes the idea of) cultural citizenship and group identities because of its radically individualist perspective of deconstructing normative orders. I will argue that we can trace this difference to two distinct functions of comedy as well as to the situatedness of its performers in American society as non–white/male/straight and white/male/straight, respectively.

Charged humor and white libertarian stand-up have common roots in the countercultural turn stand-up comedy took in the late 1950s and the 1960s, most vividly embodied by Lenny Bruce. As George Carlin noted, when speaking about his major influences, it was this period "where comedy went from a safe thing that described everything outside of a person to where comics started talking about their feelings, about how rigid the society was, the whole rebellion against the fifties mindset. That was what had the biggest influence. And Lenny led the way."[31] Bruce transposed key elements of the humor culture of the eastern European *shtetl* into the postwar American environment. As Ioan Davies writes: "In Bakhtinian terms, then, the popular laughter of the Jewish people expresses in parodic form self-affirmation against both the hyper-rigidity of Hebraic law and the exterminating or assimilating tendencies of Gentile culture. It is to this counter-tradition . . . that we must look if we want to understand anything of Jewish popular culture and, in particular, of its political humor."[32] The Jewish humor of the Pale served as a means of resistance against the attacks, denigrations, and assimilating tendencies of the dominant society. This can be seen as analogous to the heteronormative racial order of US society, which may ascribe subject rather than citizenship status to non–white/male/straight groups. It also tolerates, endorses, or conducts violent transgressions while trying to enforce cultural assimilation. As Leon Rappoport and others have argued, humor strategies such as self-deprecation, reverse discourse, superiority, or obscenity serve to strengthen a marginalized community's resilience, sense of identity, and ability to develop counterpositions. As a result, they represent a form of articulating and claiming cultural citizenship through charged humor.[33] But *shtetl* humor also functioned as a political critique of the power hierarchies *within* the Jewish community. Pitting the ribald vernacular Yiddish against the universal discursive authority of the sacred Hebrew language, it exposed and ridiculed power in a manner concerned not with affirming community and demanding inclusion into a larger society, but with challenging and potentially overcoming community in its current state. This use of humor as a foundational critique of authority is structurally similar to the total criticism white libertarian stand-up raises against American society.

Bruce adapted this comedic tradition to expose the incongruities of American self-images and realities, mercilessly exposing the linguistic codes and power structures of a moral and racial regime in crisis and amplifying the insecurities of an initially predominantly white suburbanized nightclub crowd desiring to consume Blackness, ethnicity, sex, and drugs and simultaneously feeling guilty and disoriented about this desire.[34] Out of this relentless interrogation and deconstruction of America grew two branches of radical stand-up comedy, first clearly distinguishable in George Carlin and Richard Pryor: when Carlin dropped out of mainstream comedy into the countercultural scene, he pursued what Prakash Kona has dubbed, in a nod to Mikhail Bakhtin's notion of the carnivalesque, *Carlinesque*: "the comedy of the spade being the spade and nothing more or less"—i.e., a relentless general deconstruction of hegemonic language that was obscuring rather than representing reality.[35] Pryor, upon abandoning safe comedy, replaced Bruce's Jewish interlocution of Blackness for a white public with multi-coded performances of Blackness and whiteness that destabilized racist ascriptions. In embracing edgy stand-up comedy, Pryor's (re)negotiation of his status as a Black performer and citizen inevitably became central to his act. His work became a template for other African Americans, as well as for ethnic, feminist, and queer charged humor.

Echoing the relationship of white male heterosexual radicals in the 1960s to the various liberation movements, Carlin's countercultural stand-up, privileged by its performer's whiteness, did not have a focus on inequality and exclusion in the way that a charged act such as Pryor's inevitably and necessarily did. Its critique, which began with autobiographical examinations and had evolved into a full-scale deconstruction of American society by the 1990s, focused on the demonstration and analysis of power and repression, not a narrative of living under it. As the Black Panther Huey P. Newton put it, "The White mother-country radical, in resisting the system, becomes somewhat of an abstract thing . . . his oppression is somewhat abstract simply because he doesn't have to live in a reality of oppression."[36] While it may challenge "social inequality and cultural exclusion" from an anarcho-libertarian viewpoint, white libertarian stand-up has no political community-building agenda. Often, it either ignores or even emphatically rejects the idea of cultural citizenship in favor of the radical individualism embodied in the very persona of the relentless jester deriding the world.[37]

David Gillota has argued that stand-up comedy in the US represents a classically American negotiation of identity at the intersection of individualism, community, diversity, and conformity. White male comics in particular have been assigned the role of "cultural critic or, more romantically, as a lone individual who is unhampered by restrictive social guidelines."[38] Stanhope constitutes the purest form of this type in not just performing uncompromising rugged individuality, but explicitly proposing it as the desirable norm against the inherent repression of society. Ironically, this stance is enabled by his very embeddedness in unmarked and privileged male whiteness, which, as Gillota points out, grants him the status of "universal subject" placed "in the paradoxical position of speaking simultaneously for 'everyone' and only for themselves."[39] This explains why Stanhope demands from Jews, Blacks, or women the same de-identification from any form of group belonging that he practices with apparent ease. He refuses or is unable to acknowledge key power differentials in US society, much less the agonies of double consciousness, which lie at the heart of so much charged humor.

DOUG STANHOPE AS A FAILED (?) PUBLIC INTELLECTUAL

When considering stand-up comedians as public intellectuals, it will not suffice to measure them against a past ideal, such as the mid-century New York intellectuals lionized by Russell Jacoby.[40] It might be useful to consider instead what defines an intellectual today, what constitutes the public, and how the (white male libertarian) stand-up fits into this picture.

When reconsidering the difference between charged and libertarian comedy from this perspective, one might argue that practitioners of charged humor are examples of Gramscian organic intellectuals, who emerge from a specific social class or group and can culturally articulate the feelings and experiences of that group both back to the community and to outsiders.[41] Thus Margaret Cho stated that "I don't think what I'm doing—for some people—is just entertainment. I think it's a kind of way of feeling we belong in the world. It's a kind of inclusion and a way to feel validated."[42] In contrast, white libertarian stand-ups, understood as free-floating critics divested of all allegiances other than that of telling unbearable truths through pleasurable laughter, fit a well-established notion of the public intellectual as "a heretic" for whom "there is no such thing as holy writ," using "strong vernacular in order to mediate a public discussion between themselves and critical participants."[43] As an existentialist libertarian, Stanhope thus has nothing to offer to his audience but a deconstruction of community as an illusion. In fact, the white libertarian stand-up is likely to have an abjective relationship not just with the world, but also with his crowd. "You want to beat the audience, not each other," Stanhope writes about a comedy competition.[44] John Limon has argued that the structural relationship between the stand-up and the public is abjective because a joke only comes into existence through responsive laughter. Comedians are thus dependent on the audience for their confirmation of themselves, even as they engage in a phallic struggle of controlling and manipulating that audience through the power of their words. They are privileged by the microphone and elevated by the stage and the spotlight. Yet when they bomb, they are also utterly vulnerable in that exposed position.[45] For the male libertarian stand-up, the performative situation offers the full expression of his autonomy through his act while totally compromising that autonomy as he subjects himself to the audience's judgment. If a joke only comes into existence through the public's laughter, Stanhope's ideal that "every individual person should be independent of everyone else" comes into irreconcilable conflict with the core of his doing, comic performance. This existential paradox may explain his decision to always perform under the influence of alcohol, or why Bill Hicks would occasionally lash out hatefully at his audience.[46]

The abjective relationship to the public inevitably relates to the (self-)perception of the white libertarian stand-up as a particular type of contemporary public intellectual: the dissenter, the revealer of truth, and the thinker, as opposed to the expert, media superstar, or knowledge gatekeeper.[47] That the YouTube incarnations of Carlin, Hicks, Stanhope, and Bill Burr carry the authority of digital public intellectuals no less than pundits such as Christopher Hitchens or Sam Harris is clearly not a result of their subject matter expertise or their pandering to audiences; rather, it derives from their perceived sincerity and authenticity as they generate laughter.[48] And contrary to adjudicating gatekeepers, stand-ups diffuse and offer easy access to thought and doubt, as their work has the potential to transpose complex political and philosophical issues into accessible comedic art.

Alice Gregory observes that public discourse, especially in social media, is now humor-based and that "[g]ood comedians aren't furnishing their audiences with an escape hatch, nor are they offering it up as mere amusement. Humor gives them both permission and incentive to examine the world for its flaws, as well as a medium for reporting them back to us."[49] Stanhope is deeply aware of this function of his humor, and even more aware of its limits. This tension informs the highly reflective closer of his 2012 show, *Doug Stanhope: Before Turning the Gun on Himself*. In this brilliant exploration of his intention to impart hilarity, horror, and a genuinely cathartic message about existence, Stanhope forges a performative victory out of a narration of failure as his announced suicide is deferred, and the enthused audience is left to question itself.

"Remember When I Used to Give a Shit?" begins by self-deprecatingly reflecting on how Stanhope had widely exaggerated hopes of effecting change in the world through his politicized stand up: "In twenty years of comedy, I've probably had a dozen good points . . . but the whole changing the world thing never really kicked in. And someone will say: 'abortion is back in the news.' And you go: Why? I already solved that on a 2004 release . . . I've yelled to thousands of drunk people about that. . . . It gets frustrating as shit. "[50] Stanhope rejects and parodies the notion that stand-ups/public intellectuals can simply preach and convert the public to accepting their argument.[51] As he points out, even his own social circle may totally agree with his points, while not acting on them: they reject marriage, criticize overpopulation and drug laws, but get married, have children, and think heroin should be illegal "because that's what killed [stand-up comedian Mitch] Hedberg." Stanhope thus feels like he is living

> in a world full of starving people where occasionally you could point out food that no one else seemed to notice for a living, where you go on stage and you go: "Did you ever notice there's a plate of nachos right over there, nyaaa." And people go "Oh, he's so right, there *is* a plate of nachos over there. . . ." But instead of eating them they shove them up their noses and assholes for entertainment value and get no nutrition out of it even though they're fucking starving to death.

Contrary to Gregory's argument, Stanhope believes his work is consistently misunderstood as mere entertainment rather than as an opportunity to interrogate the meaning of life without blinders, despite its vernacular register. He is no longer willing to take the "leap of faith . . . that you have to trust the public. You have to assume that there is somebody out there listening who is susceptible to the highest common factor in the argument rather than the lowest common denominator."[52]

Stanhope claims he has given up on effecting change, and his last desire is to find a "killer closer" with which to conclude his comedy career. But as the subsequent bit shows, Stanhope does keep caring about political ideas.

He concludes with a beautifully crafted piece that frames both his work and his convictions in the narrative of a literal killer closer: the Sea World incident in which an orca closes a show by pulling its trainer into the water and chewing on her head in front of a family audience for more than half an hour. This story, Stanhope explains, contains exactly the inherent hilarity and sense of horror defining the human condition that he wishes to convey. But it is also a parable of justice reflecting his libertarian beliefs. The trainer represents a society's attempt at warping the individual's natural self into a domesticated and commodified performer. The orca trainer is not a trainer, as the whale has been previously trained by nature; she is manipulating the whales to be "fucking circus monkeys" by withholding food until the animals commit unnatural acts, just as society manipulates individuals into betraying their true selves through its disciplinary practices.

The mauling of the trainer is a true killer closer Stanhope is deeply jealous of, because "anyone who was at that live performance will never be able to enjoy live entertainment again." This, in other words, is what he wishes for his audiences—a cathartic experience so shattering that it would suffice for the rest of their lives. Art and life, however, diverge; Stanhope does not turn the gun on himself in analogy to the Sea World narrative, but instead announces that he will return for another act.

In this bit, Doug Stanhope summarizes his political philosophy of libertarian individualism and his comedic approach of politicized shock humor by displaying them through a narrative of failure and resignation that leaves him with only the hope of aesthetic perfection rather than any perspective on radical libertarian transformation of US society. But in describing this perfection of the killer closer by means of the Sea World analogy, he does recuperate a minimal amount of hope, as (at least once in a while) the whale wins and asserts its natural self. Likewise, in refraining from "turning the gun on himself," Stanhope may be acknowledging his conviction that while he cannot make his audience change its ways, or naively expect to resolve society's key issues by virtue of a comedic monologue, the "joke forces you to agree with it, or at least reckon with its truth by acknowledging that it made you smile. Laughter is pre-analyzed agreement."[53] Stanhope ultimately reconciles perfect abjection and the "anti-rite" of demanding an end to society with the rite of affirming it as a shaman creating community in shared laughter.[54] Temporary community is found in joking about the inescapable repression of society, and a moment of freedom is constituted in the pleasure of chewing on the trainer within our own heads.

Notes

1. Doug Stanhope, *Deadbeat Hero* (Los Angeles, CA: Shout! Factory, 2004).
2. Doug Stanhope, *Before Turning the Gun on Himself* (New York: Roadrunner Records, 2012).
3. In the interest of full disclosure, and since a good deal of the academic literature on libertarianism is by libertarians, I should point out that I personally enjoy Stanhope's comedy immensely while, as a Left communitarian in the tradition of Randolph Bourne, I am almost entirely at odds with his political views.
4. Rebecca Krefting, *All Joking Aside: American Humor and Its Discontents* (Baltimore, MD: Johns Hopkins University Press, 2014).
5. Doug Stanhope, *Digging Up Mother: A Love Story* (Cambridge, MA: Da Capo Press, 2016).
6. "Doug Stanhope at Carlos Murphy's in Las Vegas, 1990," https://www.youtube.com/watch?v=nHpXc19Ci0M.
7. "Journey of 1000 Miles," Doug Stanhope, *Word of Mouth* (Austin, TX: Sacred Cow Productions, 2002). Wikipedia slots Stanhope's comedy as black, blue, political satire, insult, and observational, and it lists as his subjects American culture, current events, recreational drug use, human sexuality, religion, family, libertarianism. See "Doug Stanhope," https://en.wikipedia.org/wiki/Doug_Stanhope.
8. "Interview with Doug Stanhope," *The List*, February 16, 2012, https://www.list.co.uk/article/40464-interview-doug-stanhope-on-politics/.
9. Mark Ames, *The True History of Libertarianism in America: A Phony Ideology to Promote a Corporate Agenda*, Alternet, 2013, accessed October 18, 2016, available from http://www.alternet.org/visions/true-history-libertarianism-america-phony-ideology-promote-corporate-agenda.
10. Peter Vallentyne, "Libertarianism," in *The Stanford Encyclopedia of Philosophy*, ed. Edward N. Zalta, https://plato.stanford.edu/archives/sum2014/entries/libertarianism/.
11. Michael Freeden, *Ideologies and Political Theory: A Conceptual Approach* (Oxford: Clarendon Press, 1996), 279–85.
12. Jean-Jacques Rousseau, *Discourse on Political Economy and, the Social Contract*, trans. Christopher Betts (Oxford: Oxford University Press, 1994), 45.
13. "Liberty," Stanhope, *Doug Stanhope Deadbeat Hero*.
14. Stanhope, "Prettiest Denny's Waitress," *Word of Mouth*; Stanhope, "Liberty," *Deadbeat Hero*.
15. Stanhope, "Marriage Is Gay," *Deadbeat Hero*.
16. Doug Stanhope, interview with Zach Weissmueller, *Doug Stanhope on Comedy, His Mother, Libertarians, Alcoholics, and Trump* [Audiovisual], Reason.com, 2016, accessed October 17, 2016, available from http://reason.com/reasontv/2016/06/08/doug-stanhope-on-comedy-his-mother-liber.
17. Stanhope, "Liberty," *Deadbeat Hero*.
18. Doug Stanhope, "Occupy Elsewhere," *Beer Hall Putsch* (Burbank, CA: New Wave Dynamics, 2013).
19. Vallentyne, "Libertarianism." Also see Michael Otsuka, *Libertarianism without Inequality* (Oxford: Oxford University Press, 2003).

20. Stanhope, "Occupy Elsewhere," *Beer Hall Putsch*.

21. Doug Stanhope, "Jews," *No Refunds* (Chatsworth, CA: Image Entertainment, 2007).

22. Stanhope, "Excess in Moderation," *Word of Mouth*; Stanhope, "Jew, Jew, Jew, Jew, Jew," *No Refunds* (Chatsworth, CA: Image Entertainment, 2007).

23. "The fundamental contribution of existential thought lies in the idea that one's identity is constituted neither by nature nor by culture, since to 'exist' is precisely to constitute such an identity"—Steven Crowell, "Existentialism," in *The Stanford Encyclopedia of Philosophy*, ed. Edward N. Zalta (Stanford University, 2015), accessed October 18, 2016, available from http://plato.stanford.edu/entries/existentialism/.

24. Doug Stanhope, *No Place Like Home* (2016).

25. See note 2 above.

26. Stanhope, *Before Turning the Gun on Himself*.

27. Stanhope, "Jew, Jew, Jew, Jew, Jew," *No Refunds*.

28. Vallentyne, "Libertarianism."

29. Renato Rosaldo, "Cultural Citizenship in San Jose, California," *PoLAR* 17, no. 2 (1994): 57.

30. Krefting, *All Joking Aside*, 16 ff.

31. George Carlin and Marc Cooper, "George Carlin," *The Progressive*, July 2001.

32. Ioan Davies, "Lenny Bruce: Hyperrealism and the Death of Jewish Tragic Humor," *Social Text* 22 (1989): 97.

33. Leon Rappoport, *Punchlines: The Case for Racial, Ethnic, and Gender Humor* (Westport, CT: Praeger Publishers, 2005); Simon Weaver, *The Rhetoric of Racist Humour: US, UK and Global Race Joking* (Farnham, UK: Ashgate, 2011).

34. Davies, "Lenny Bruce," 101; David Emblidge, "The Sick/Healthy Humor of Lenny Bruce," *Revue Francaise d'Études Américaines* 4 (1977): 103–14; John Limon, *Stand-up Comedy in Theory, or, Abjection in America* (Durham, NC: Duke University Press, 2000), 13–17. Bruce's central topics between 1950 and 1959 in chronological order were religion, sex, Jews, Blacks, and southerners—cf. Emblidge, "Sick/Healthy Humor," 109.

35. Prakash Kona, "Being George Carlin: Carlinesque as Performative Resistance," *Americana: The Journal of American Popular Culture* 9, no. 2 (2010): n.p.; In setting up his famous shell-shock routine, Carlin explains: "I don't like words that hide the truth. I don't like words that conceal reality. I don't like euphemisms or euphemistic language. And American English is loaded with euphemisms. 'Cause Americans have a lot of trouble dealing with reality. Americans have trouble facing the truth, so they invent the kind of a soft language to protect themselves from it, and it gets worse with every generation." George Carlin, *Doin' It Again* (United States: MPI Home Video, 2005).

36. Huey P. Newton, "To the Black Movement [1968]," in *To Die for the People: The Writings of Huey P. Newton*, ed. Toni Morrison (San Francisco, CA: City Lights Books, 2009), 93. Of course, white stand-ups may have experienced class-based repression, social exclusion, and personal alienation.

37. As coined by Julia Kristeva, "the abject refers to the human reaction . . . to a threatened breakdown in meaning caused by the loss of the distinction between subject and object or between self and other"—*Modules on Kristeva*, Purdue University, https://www.cla.purdue.edu/english/theory/psychoanalysis/kristevaabject.html.

38. David Gillota, "Stand-Up Nation: Humor and American Identity," *Journal of American Culture* 38, no. 2 (2015): 105.

39. Gillota, "Stand-Up Nation."

40. Russell Jacoby, *The Last Intellectuals: American Culture in the Age of Academe* (New York: Basic Books, 2000).

41. Antonio Gramsci, "The Intellectuals," reprinted in *An Anthology of Western Marxism*, ed. Roger S. Gottlieb (Oxford: Oxford University Press, 1989), 113–19.

42. Margaret Cho et al., *Notorious C.H.O.* (New York: Wellspring Media, 2002).

43. Alan Hudson, "Intellectuals for Our Times," in *The Changing Role of the Public Intellectual*, ed. Dolan Cummings (New York: Taylor & Francis, 2005), 34–50, 47f.

44. Stanhope, *Digging Up Mother*, e-book, position 2414.

45. Limon, *Stand-up Comedy in Theory*.

46. Hicks performed one of the most abjective rants recorded in stand-up history responding to a heckler: "Hitler had the right idea. He was just an underachiever. Kill 'em all Adolf, all of 'em—Jew, Mexican, American, White—kill 'em all! Start over, the experiment didn't work! Rain—40 days please, fuckin' rain and wash these turds off my fuckin' life—wash these human waste of flesh and bones off this planet. I pray to you God to kill these fuckin' people." See https://www.youtube.com/watch?v=Qw3z49FBYGU.

47. Duncan Jackson and John Issit, *What Does It Mean to Be a Public Intellectual?* (Higher Education Academy, 2013 [cited]), available from https://www.heacademy.ac.uk/sites/default/files/resources/12_march_presentation.pdf.

48. Alice Gregory observes that "a joke seems uncalculated in its morality; to hear a good one is to feel as though you're being told the truth. It's hard to imagine someone who is consistently funny not meaning what she says. And meaning what one says, openly, again and again, counts for more than we typically think it does." Pankaj Mishra and Alice Gregory, "Is It Still Possible to Be a Public Intellectual?" *The New York Times*, November 24, 2015, BR27.

49. Mishra and Gregory, "Is It Still Possible?".

50. Stanhope, "Remember When I Used to give a Shit? / Killer Closer."

51. Significantly, Stanhope is not endorsing the position of stand-up comedy failing as public intellectual discourse due to its pandering to audiences or its lack of intellectual rigor, as argued by Elizabeth Bruenig in "Comedians Are Funny, Not Public Intellectuals," *The New Republic*, June 3, 2015, https://newrepublic.com/article/121956/stewart-and-colbert-are-no-substitute-intellectuals; Sean McElwee, "Comedy Can't Change the World: Why Russell Brand Is Dead Wrong about Politics and Humor," *Salon*, July 6, 2014, http://www.salon.com/2014/07/06/comedy_cant_change_the_world_why_russell_brand_is_dead_wrong_about_politics_and_humor/.

52. Hudson, "Intellectuals for Our Times," 36.

53. Mishra and Gregory, "Is It Still Possible?"

54. See Lawrence E. Mintz, "Standup Comedy as Social and Cultural Mediation," *American Quarterly* 37, no. 1 (1985): 71–80.

THE COMEDIAN AS PREACHER
Bill Hicks and the Rhetoric of Fundamentalism

Rob King

In the months before his death in 1994, the thirty-two-year-old Texas stand-up Bill Hicks cowrote a script about a serial killer who preys on hack comedians. In the script, the killer is finally apprehended by the police, who demand that he explain his motivations. "Why?" the killer indignantly responds,

> You have the gall to stand here and ask me why? Let me ask you what answer must a surgeon give for cutting from the body cancers that threaten its very existence? For verily I say unto thee my mission was no less holy, my intent no less pure. A changing moment in my life came the day I first laughed. That was when life took a new form and my sad visions were cleansed by humor and from that day on I paid homage to comedy. From that day on I studied with the zeal of monks lost in religious rapture, the works of the comedy masters. For I loved comedy and I loved those who loved it. I loved those who gave their lives to find the perfect laugh, the real laugh, the gut laugh, the healing laugh. For love, I killed those comedians.[1]

There is, in the killer's soliloquy, an evident projection of Hicks himself. Even though his own surgeons were unable to cut away the cancers that eventually claimed him, Hicks's short life modeled this ideal of comedy as "holy mission." As all humorists must, he broke taboos—in his case, brutally so, pouring vituperative scorn on many of conservative America's most sacred cows (the war on drugs, the pro-life movement, the first Gulf War). As most comedians do, he told jokes, only less as the point of his act than as scaffolding for extended diatribes against the moral debasement of American life. But as very few, if any, have dared, Hicks did all this not just in a spirit of mockery and disdain but as the cauterizing edge of what he intended, in explicitly mystic terms, as a "message of love."[2]

What Hicks strove for was nothing less than a reclamation of comedy's "healing" promise and, by this, the redemption of a disenchanted world. And he pursued these ends with an intransigence that embarrasses any effort to take him at less than face value. "No one holds comedy in higher regard than myself. No *one*," he once wrote to a critic. "It is a rarefied air the great comics must breathe, who've transcended their own preconceived notions as well as the audiences [sic] at the *same time*."[3] Hicks's splenetic takedowns of American culture and politics were, in this sense, only the necessary prelude to the radical *passage à l'acte*—Lacan's term for the genuine break with an existing order—that such a utopian project implied, even as they ensured his censorship and marginalization by America's mainstream media.[4] As Hicks joked in his last complete set, following a bit that excoriated the cowardice of President Clinton's 1993 cruise missile strikes on Iraq: "This is the material by the way that's kept me virtually anonymous in America. You know, no one fucking knows me, nobody gives a fuck"—a Cassandra-like self-perception bitterly corroborated earlier that year when, in one of his career's culminating disappointments, his twelfth and final performance on David Letterman's *The Late Show* was cut from the broadcast as "unsuitable."[5] If, by contrast, we choose to keep faith with Hicks, then we will need to do so in terms of the principle of scale that orchestrates his work; we will need, in sum, a model of critique whose vantage point is that of transcendence.

It may be wondered, then, whether the methodological frameworks that have informed the analysis of stand-up will be sufficient to this task. By and large, most of that scholarship has tended to place stand-up within the metaphorical orbit of "public sphere" theory, as first developed by Jürgen Habermas to describe the emergence, in the eighteenth century, of public institutions of "rational-critical" debate.[6] The stand-up comedian has accordingly been cast as a kind of "public intellectual" (Garber) or "anthropologist" (Koziski) who makes visible tacit areas of unacknowledged social attitudes and behavior; she is an agent of "social and cultural mediation" (Mintz) who may even build "cultural citizenship" (Krefting) by affirming communities and identities—as though the comedy club inherited the mantle of those Age of Enlightenment salons and coffee houses where, on Habermas's account, an ascendant bourgeoisie first took up the social and political issues of the day.[7] Granted that such figurative extensions should not be taken too literally—nobody, surely, would dispute comedy's dependence on registers of parody, irony, and nonsense that would be preposterous in an actual anthropological paper or policy debate—still they bespeak the difficulty, against the weight of liberal-democratic tradition, in imagining models for critique that do not somehow lasso themselves to the framework of secular reason. Worse yet, these metaphors become singularly unhelpful in the case of a stand-up like Hicks who, as the theater critic John Lahr put it in an important *New Yorker* profile, sought to persuade "*not through reason* but with joy."[8] Rather than present himself in the fashion of, e.g., a Mort Sahl, who framed his interventions in resolutely worldly terms, Hicks sought for himself a more cabalistic identity. "I am a Shaman come in the guise of a comic, in order to heal perception," he once wrote. "I am a *shaman*, a *healer* and truth is my medicine."[9] What Hicks suggests is thus an alternate framework for imagining comedic critique: not that of the coffee house, but rather, I would suggest, that of the church sermon. The analogy here will be not with reasoned debate but with religious preachment; not with critical deliberation but with evangelical fervor; not with the patient effort to convince but with the moral duty to convert. As we will see, the deepest implication of Hicks's comedy may well be the proposition, *contra* Habermas, that a full diagnosis of the ills of this world cannot proceed apart from the vantage of the *other*worldly from which the rationalist withdraws.

The life and comedy of Bill Hicks were inseparable from the spiritual commitments instilled by his upbringing. His father, James Melvin Hicks, was, at the time of Bill's birth in 1961, a traveling salesman for General Motors whose career led the family across the South—from Georgia to Florida, Alabama, and eventually, when Bill was seven, Texas, where the Hicks family settled into middle-class stability in a Houston suburb. Membership in Baptist congregations was one constant during Hicks's peripatetic youth; strictly enforced church attendance, including Sunday school and summer Bible Camp, created ethical imperatives even as it soon became a target for Hicks's teenage rebellion. "We were Yuppie Baptists," Bill later joked in a 1987 *Houston Post* interview. "We worried about things like, 'If you scratch your neighbor's Subaru should you leave a note?'"[10] Comedy was the escape hatch: by the age of fourteen, Hicks was performing routines before his classmates, his jokes cribbed from *Tonight Show* (1954–) comedians like Robert Klein and Richard Lewis as well as from his early idol, Woody Allen; by sixteen, he was climbing out the bedroom window to perform late-night stand-up with his friend Dwight Slade at Houston's Comedy Workshop.

It is no coincidence that Hicks's long slog to comedic fame through the late 1970s and 1980s was contemporaneous with the resurgence of Fundamentalism as a transformational force in the American political and social landscape. At a time when pastors were joining with politicians loudly to advocate against gun control, defense-spending cuts, and abortion, Fundamentalism became both the whetstone against which Hicks sharpened his emergent style of social critique and, paradoxically, an inspiration for his own performances. By all accounts a devoted viewer of *The Jimmy Swaggart Telecast* (1971–) and Jim and Tammy Faye Bakker's *PTL [Praise the Lord] Club* (1974–1989), Hicks discovered in televangelism a declamatory mode of self-presentation he sought to make his own. "As many times as I've watched Swaggart, obviously he's a formidable adversary," he once told Slade. "That's what makes me watch him. I'm going, 'Look at that guy perform!' It's phenomenal! It's like, 'For those of you who never got to see Elvis, you're gettin' it right now.'"[11] For one of his first major group shows—the 1987 "Outlaw Comics Get Religion" in Austin—Hicks accordingly turned Fundamentalism against itself, deploying the flamboyant performativity of, say, an Oral Roberts as a vehicle for satirizing televangelist hucksterism. Taking the stage dressed as Elvis Presley to the tune of "Also Sprach Zarathustra," Hicks launched into what the *Austin American-Statesman* described as a "blistering indictment of . . . the campaign against individuality masquerading as Christianity": "I was moved by Oral Roberts," Hicks confessed to his audience, "and when he said 31 March was his deadline, I sent him a check. Dated it the first of April."[12]

Yet external appearances were deceptive. Even as Hicks used comedy to rebel against the religious dogmas of his upbringing, he never relinquished their metaphysical commitments: the quest for worldly transcendence remained his orienting perspective, albeit one to be pursued through other, nonreligious means. It makes sense, then, that Hicks's earliest stand-up endeavors at high school began in tandem with what would become a lifelong interest in Transcendental Meditation and various other belief systems (numerology, astrology, etc.) as alternate paths to spiritual development. He may have retreated from religion, in other words, but he remained a mystic. "We are facilitators of our [own] creative evolution," he claimed in John Lahr's *New Yorker* profile. "We can ignite our brains with light."[13] The important role that hallucinogenic drugs came to play in Hicks's life has to be read in this light, too. Hallucinogens became, for Hicks, express lanes to the very state of grace that organized religion had betrayed, serious tools for the exploration of a kind of cosmic consciousness. Beginning in his early twenties, Hicks and his friends would approach mushroom trips less as debauched blow-offs than as metaphysical experiments, which they prepared for by fasting and meditating in advance. ("We were having lots of breakthroughs in those days," his Houston friend David Johndrow recalled.)[14] Hicks's later reputation as a vocal critic of the US government's war on drugs followed from this faith in hallucinogens' salvific properties. "My honest-to-God belief about drugs," Hicks explained in an interview with *High Times*, is that "God let certain drugs grow naturally on this planet to help speed up our evolution. Do you think psilocybin mushrooms growing on top of cowshit was an accident? Where do you think the phrase 'that's good shit' comes from?"[15] What Hicks wanted, in effect, was to access the Kingdom of God through the exploration of inner worlds. "You see," he explained, "Jung had this idea of a Collective Unconscious which mankind shared . . . and I agree. But! I think this Collective Mind is supposed to be conscious, not unconscious! And that is our job as the Agents of Evolution . . . [to] awaken our Mind to Truth and complete the circle that was broken with the dream of our fall from Grace."[16]

Comedy, too, could play a role in that evolution. Hicks was not the only comedian to conjoin the roles of stand-up comedian and lay preacher—Sam Kinison, a friend and important influence, had actually been a Pentecostal preacher into his early twenties—but he was unique in appropriating a religious function to stand-up. "If comedy is an escape from anything, it is an escape from *illusions*," he once wrote to a critic at the *Los Angeles Times*. "The comic . . . *reminds* us of our True Reality, and in that moment of recognition, we laugh, and the reality of the daily grind is shown for what it really is—*unreal . . . a joke*. True comedy turns circles into spirals."[17]

The conflict that is implied here—between a "True Reality" and the "unreal reality" of the daily grind—pertains, of course, not to anything resembling Realpolitik, but to the realm, once again, of metaphysics; and what it grounded, in Hicks's mature comedy, was an extraordinary mode of scorched-earth cultural critique that exceeded any merely ideological combat. By the time Hicks stole the show at Montreal's Just for Laughs festival in 1991, it seemed to many as though his routines contained nothing but pure white-heat rage with no margin for real-world alternatives, an unremittingly savage takedown of early 1990s-era American complacency, from the triteness of Billy Ray Cyrus's "Achy Breaky Heart" to Fox's *Cops* show, from the hypocrisy of organized religion to the self-satisfied apathy of Hicks's own audiences. (So much so, in fact, that he would often have to reassure audiences that "there's dick jokes on the way," as though schoolyard humor would be the delayed payoff for his mordant critique.)[18] Nor, after years of excoriating the Republican culture wars, did Hicks find relief in the election of Bill Clinton in 1992; instead of relenting, he broadened his repudiation of the American political scene. "I'll show you politics in America. Here it is right here, 'I think the puppet on the right shares my beliefs.' 'I think the puppet on the left is more to my liking.' 'Hey, wait a minute, there's one guy holding out both puppets!'"[19]

Here, too, Hicks betrayed the continuing influence of Fundamentalist belief systems. It is, for example, the argument of the rhetorical theorist Jonathan J. Edwards that the Fundamentalist worldview is structured around "countersymbols" that embody the religious community's wholesale opposition to the desacralization of contemporary life. Countersymbols, Edwards suggests, establish patterns of "choric incantation" that appeal to an originary sacred unity rooted in utter difference from the secular world in which that unity is negated.[20] One countersymbol relevant to Hicks is the notion of "confederacy"—the Fundamentalist belief, dating to the foundation of the World Christian Fundamentals Association in 1919, that a new religio-political bureaucracy (the "super church confederacy") had emerged to quash religious freedoms and do the work of the Antichrist. In Hicks's hands, this rhetoric was adapted to a critique of American commercial media—the news, in particular—in which he (rightly, no doubt) perceived the emergence of a new *media*-political confederacy that similarly obstructed enlightenment. "There is no *context* for the bullshit we see on TV. There is no *center*. This country has swallowed the fucking lie hook, line, and sinker, and wallows in it like some fat swine—*proud* of its ignorance."[21] In a 1993 essay for *Scallywag* magazine, Hicks pondered why news reports on ethnic cleansing in Bosnia–Herzegovina had no effect on American attitudes: "I'd like to venture a guess here. Could it be because you, The Media—acting as the mouthpiece for the elite state power you serve, have lied about EVERY SINGLE STORY you've ever reported on?" Hicks proceeded to imagine a world in which the American military would redirect its foreign bombing campaigns against America's own television networks: "One by one, our TVs suddenly go blank. We turn them off and breathe a collective sigh of relief. Our shared nightmare has ended. Mordor has fallen. We could then turn to our friends, our neighbors, our gardens, our books, and even to our own thoughts, listening as songbirds provide the soundtrack for our reborn earth, and the dream of forgiveness dawns gently on our healing minds."[22]

Also relevant to Hicks's critique was the related charge of apostasy. As mobilized in Fundamentalist thought, apostasy relates to the ideas of defection and desertion, but it also, as Edwards notes, requires an act of naming whereby "insiders" (the religious community) blatantly exclude those who betray the path.[23] "If apostasy . . . indicated betrayal of fundamental values by spiritual leaders, 'confederacy' pointed to the institutional structure of that betrayal."[24] For Hicks, the charge of apostasy was accordingly to be laid at the door of artists who had renounced their talents to serve the media-political complex. Jay Leno, whom Hicks had once greatly admired, was one. "It all started when he did the Doritos commercial," Hicks explained in a late routine that depicts Leno's corporate shilling as a literal Faustian bargain. "'Hi everyone, I'm Jay Leno. Anyone remember when I was funny? Here, eat Doritos. They're good—' (*makes choking sound*) Satan fucking him in the ass on national TV. (*snorting and snarling*) 'They're good 'n' crispy. Here Satan, try the nacho-flavored ones.'"[25] Pop stars George Michael and Madonna drew similar ire for promoting soda, in 1989 ads for Diet Coke and Pepsi respectively: "What kind of fucking Reagan wet dream *is* this world, man? Rock stars hawking Diet Cokes! . . . You don't see the imminent danger, do you? You're staring at me like, 'Bill, they're just musicians, and they're, you know, and they're just doing their thing, and—' NO! They are DEMONS SET LOOSE ON THE EARTH TO LOWER THE STANDARDS FOR THE PERFECT AND HOLY CHILDREN OF GOD! Which is what we are."[26]

So it is that Hicks's cultural critique, one of the most brutal and thoroughgoing that stand-up has yet given us, nonetheless finds its orienting perspective in a third term of Fundamentalist thought: the principle of conversion—the possibility, however dim, of transition from dark to light, from our "shared nightmare" to our shared being as "children of God."[27] It is as though for Hicks, in an entirely venal world, the promise of comedy became quite literally millennialist, a pathway to the restoration of God's kingdom on earth and humanity's eventual perfection. For nihilism is not all there is, and if one listens closely, one finds a repeatedly voiced belief in spiritual interconnectedness—the belief, as he once put it, that "we are all one consciousness experiencing itself subjectively." And it is this belief, far beyond the realm of politics as ordinarily practiced, that constitutes Hicks's vantage point as that of the convert.[28] Nowhere is the dependency between these registers—conversion and critique—clearer than in his routines about hallucinogens, which, in his comedy as in his life, served as avenues for transcendence. Consider, for instance, the following bit as a necessary corollary to the denunciations that typically constituted his act, and note in particular the way his initially comic evocation of the sacred properties of magic mushrooms begins to shade into something seriously meant:

> Well, once again I recommend a healthy dose of psilocybin mushrooms. (*audience laughs*) Three weeks ago two of my friends and I went to a ranch in Fredericksburg, Texas, and took what Terence McKenna calls a "heroic dose." Five dried grams. Let me tell you, our third eye was squeegeed quite cleanly. (*makes squeaking noise*) Wow! And I'm glad they're against the law. 'Cause you know what happened

when I took 'em? I laid in a field of green grass for four hours going, "My God . . . I love everything." (*audience laughs*) The heavens parted, God looked down and rained gifts of forgiveness onto my being, healing me on every level, psychically, physically, emotionally. And I realized our true nature is spirit, not body, that we are eternal beings, and God's love is unconditional. And there's nothing we can ever do to change that. It is only our *illusion* that we are separate from God, or that we are alone. In fact the reality is we are one with God and he loves us. (*scattered cheers*) Now, if that isn't a hazard to this country. Do you see my point? How are we gonna keep building nuclear weapons, you know what I mean? What's gonna happen to the arms industry when we realize we're all one? Ha ha ha ha ha! It's gonna fuck up the economy! The economy that's fake anyway!²⁹

In claiming the vantage point of divine revelation, Hicks here models a supra-ideological dimension to his comedy that renders its stakes far more totalizing than what satire conventionally achieves. But there are also paradoxes to give us pause: the standpoint of the convert, after all, exists outside of reason and so cannot be attained inductively (through rational-critical debate), but only experientially (from conversion—in this case, drug-enabled); nor does the framework of revelation necessarily vouchsafe the kind of regard for the secular realm that could be translated into "real world" agency. (Why do anything to change the world when a few grams of 'shrooms will change it for you?) It is time, then, to confront the particular challenge that Hicks poses for political thought: how, against the weight of liberal tradition, are we to evaluate forms of critique that model a nonsecular inspiration?

One place to find answers is in the most unexpected, but arguably richest, phase of Hicks's career, when he briefly found the success and visibility that had eluded him—not in his home country, but in the United Kingdom. Buoyed across the Atlantic on the success of his Montreal show, Hicks visited the UK three times between the summer of 1991 and the end of 1992, beginning with a one-man show at the Edinburgh Festival, for which he won the Critics' Award, and ending with the last tour of his career, the biblically titled *Revelations*. During this period, Hicks profited from the fortuitous patronage of the London-based production firm Tiger Television. As franchise holder for Just for Laughs' UK productions, Tiger effectively lucked into the distribution of Hicks's breakthrough performance (shown in the UK as *Relentless* on January 2, 1992) and went on to support further programming initiatives with the comedian, including the TV special for *Revelations* (broadcast May 27, 1993) and an unrealized talk show, *Count of the Netherworlds*. But Hicks also found in the UK a public ready to welcome him as a caustic observer of the American social scene. "America does not take comedy seriously, social criticism seriously," he once declared. "If you look at even the careers of Mort Sahl and Lenny Bruce, you'll notice that one was basically run out of the business and the other one killed himself due to lack of work. . . . But that's why I love Public Access, [and] that's why England has opened up for me."[30] Two moments, in particular, emblematize the increasing explicitness with which he articulated political dissent within a framework of visionary experience.

The first is from *Revelations*. As the title implied, Hicks here chose to underscore the theme of conversion more than in any of his previous shows. "My act now is bigger, less specific about personalities and more about attitudes," he explained in an interview. "It's only made me get better actually."[31] A case in point is inarguably the most famous bit in Hicks's career, the very serious discussion of the "point" of his act with which he concluded his performance. Ever since his first album, *Dangerous* (1990), Hicks had often closed his shows by confessing to a "vision" in which "the money we spend on nuclear weapons and defense" is instead used for "feeding and clothing the poor of the world"; in *Revelations*, though, that bit was reworked into a larger metaphor for the limitations of human perception.[32]

> Is there a point to all this? Let's find a point. Is there a point to my act? I would say there is. I have to. The world is like a ride in an amusement park. And when you choose to go on it you think it's real because that's how powerful our minds are. And the ride goes up and down and round and round. It has thrills and chills and it's very brightly colored and it's very loud and it's fun, for a while. Some people have been on the ride for a long time and they begin to question: "Is this real? Or is this just a ride?" And other people have remembered, and they come back to us, they say, "Hey, don't worry, don't be afraid, ever, because, this is just a ride." And we *kill* those people. Ha ha ha. "Shut him up! We have a lot invested in this ride. SHUT HIM UP! Look at my furrows of worry. Look at my big bank account and my family. This just has to be real." It's just a ride. But we always kill those good guys who try and tell us that, you ever notice that? And let the demons run amok. But it doesn't matter *because*: it's just a ride. And we can change it any time we want. It's only a choice. No effort, no work, no job, no savings and money. A choice, right now, between fear and love.

> The eyes of fear want you to put bigger locks on your door, buy guns, close yourself off. The eyes of love, instead, see all of us as one. Here's what we can do to change the world, right now, to a better ride. Take all that money we spend on weapons and defense each year, and instead spend it feeding, clothing, and educating the poor of the world, which it would many times over, not one human being excluded, and we could explore space, together, both inner and outer, forever, in peace.[33]

The difficulties in what Hicks is trying to express are only too apparent, but this is because he is operating at the limits of what is available to thought. What begins with the seeming imperative of getting off the ride—with the challenge to his audience to make an immanent break with the terms of a known reality—hesitates midway through and changes tack, retreating to a different choice about how to stay within that reality, to stay on the ride but somehow to make it better, here envisioned through a redistribution of wealth, as per the original bit.

The formula of Hicks's hesitancy here can be succinctly put: how does one represent that which, for mystic belief, lies beyond representation? As Ernesto Laclau has observed, the importance of mysticism is that it registers a "beyond" of human finitude of which the mystic claims direct experience; yet its limit is encountered in the inevitable temptation to betray that "beyond" by giving it positive representational content, by identifying it, say, with this or that God or religious dogma.[34] Hicks's toggling here bespeaks the dilemma: any greater specificity to his real-world prescriptions (here, feeding and clothing the poor) would deflate mystic insight by equating God's will with a policy initiative. "If the mystic experience is really going to be the experience of an absolute *transcendans*," Laclau insists, "it has to remain indeterminate"; otherwise, it loses its dimension as "beyond" and ends up mired in the differential realm of religious and political disputation—the realm where *this* particular God but not *that* one is said to offer the one true path to spiritual fulfillment or *this* particular set of ideological commitments but not *those* are nominated as the path of society's realization.[35] What becomes significant in Hicks—and what is often mistaken for his libertarianism—is his endeavor to resist this kind of particularization; to source ethics rather in a mystic commitment to a radical "Oneness" for which no differentiation or particularization is, by definition, possible ("The eyes of love see us all as one"). What Hicks took from his upbringing is, in this sense, exactly what he sought to return to his audience: a commitment to a "beyond" of finitude, yet stripped of religious dogma; a doctrine of universality, unbound from the particularities of human ideologies. Hicks's stand-up, at its best, expresses that intention shyly, in the only way that its fragility permits.³⁶

The second noteworthy step in Hicks's transatlantic phase saw him approximate a more conventionally Habermasian conception of social critique, at least superficially. This was for *The Counts of the Netherworld* talk show, developed for Tiger by Hicks and his fellow American stand-up, Fallon Woodland. Although Hicks's illness and eventual death ensured that *Counts* never proceeded beyond planning, an existing treatment reveals a show apparently envisioned on a public sphere model, often in unwitting evocation of the argument of Habermas's *Structural Transformation*. As Hicks and Woodland put it: "The Counts' salon serves the purpose salons and their likenesses (i.e., the jazz clubs in the 50s, the coffee houses of the 60s) have served since time immemorial as bastions of free thinking, where ideas are explored that are alternative to the established belief, the party line, or popular opinion, during times of Revolution and of Renaissance."³⁷ In this setting, the Counts were to offer "enlightened and highly dangerous" takes on the topics of the day in the company of thought-provoking guests like Martin Amis and Noam Chomsky. "[T]he Counts explore the beliefs that rule our lives; celebrating ideas which free the human spirit, and skewering unmercifully those which chain us."³⁸

But despite first appearances, this is no Habermasian coffee house. Rather, it is described as a kind of "inner space ship"—as though belonging to that realm "off the ride" evoked in Hicks's *Revelations* closer—to which the Counts summon their guests by writing down names and casting them into a fireplace. "The Counts—being Awake in the Dream—are not bound by convention, linear time, nor sense of place like the 'real' world appears to be."³⁹ Conversations with guests, accordingly, were to unfold not as "rational-critical" debate, but rather as canvases for the creative and artistic evocation of the "Unconscious Collective Mind in which we share." Silent black-and-white film segments would accompany the conversations to provide "literal, cinematic, or subconscious" commentary; "surreal scenes" would unfold inside the salon ("The Counts fencing. A beautiful woman undressing. Fallon sculpting. Bill and Martin Amis playing darts," etc.) to give "evidence of the multi-dimensional consciousness the Counts believe mankind shares."⁴⁰

This is a frankly puzzling conception of a talk show in which intellectual discussion would be just one ingredient in a broader creative endeavor to, once again, evoke an always receding universality of which, consequently, one can only "give evidence." But it also allows us, finally, to lend precision to Hicks's eccentricity vis-à-vis a public sphere model of critical discourse: it is not that Hicks *rejected* a commitment to reasoned debate, but that he appropriated reason to nonsecular goals. From very early in his career, in fact, Hicks had defined his act as an expression of the "Voice of Reason" (one early persona was that of "Sane Man," a superhero whose power was the ability to defeat those guilty of "logic crimes").[41] And this self-conception carried through into *Counts*. As he put it in a poem-manifesto for the show, "The time has come to air the Voice of Reason, / In a world gone mad, adrift on banal seas, / For all who feel that lies have had their season, / And whose Hearts Cry Out, instead, for Honesty." But again, *contra* Habermas and a whole tradition of liberal political thought, Hicks conceives this "Voice of Reason" in terms of a quasi-Jungian mode of mystic divination. A couple more stanzas and Hicks concludes his manifesto, now in prose: "Behold the Counts! Beacons encouraging the spark in every mind to join them in illuminating the Netherworld of our Collective Unconscious. Sleeper Awaken to the cry of players [*sic*] as they call for the Voice of Reason in every mind to come forth in choir and sing hymns to Beauty and Truth."[42]

Here again is the schism dividing critique into two spheres or "levels" of articulation: on the one hand, a Habermasian reason that pertains to the talk-show framework within which hosts and guests debate one another; on the other, Hicks's mystic "Voice of Reason" that reaches for a radical outside of experience that cannot be symbolically mastered, but only gestured to by a series of terms that lack determinable reference—Honesty, Beauty, Truth, and ultimately Oneness. In this strange toggling between topical discussion and metaphysical aspiration, we once more detect that dual movement, tracked earlier in the "Just a Ride" bit, in which Hicks locates himself in the space of an irreducible tension between the absolute and the particular, between transcendence of the world and involvement in it. This would in fact be one definition of the space of ethical experience; for, as Laclau further suggests, "the construction of an ethical life . . . depend[s] on keeping open the two sides of [the mystic's] paradox"—which is to say that ethical life exists in the unclosable gap between a commitment to an absolute "that can only be actualized [in this world] by being something less than itself" and the pursuit of particular real-world aims and actions whose intensity derives only in relation to an absolute that they can never measure up to.[43] If Hicks exemplified this, it is because his commitment to transcendence led not, in the end, to an anchorite withdrawal—not to the temptation of getting off the ride—but ultimately, in his career's final act, to a reimagining of Habermasian critique in an arguably more radical way, with an ethical density that other comedians have lacked.

What Hicks ultimately achieved was a mode of comedic critique that surpassed the resources of secular reason to enter what contemporary philosophy has dubbed an ethics of the Real—that perspective, extending from Schopenhauer to Badiou, that derives its politics not from the normative constraints of the symbolic order (the realm of Habermas, that is), but from a radical commitment to that which exists "beyond" the terms of what any given situation allows us to imagine.[44] But he also, in so doing, bypassed the ordinary trajectories of comicality. Humor's conventional insistence on materiality and corporeality—the slapstick nobleman who slips on a banana peel, the stand-up comedian who stages their own abjection—inverts in Hicks's hands into a quest *beyond* such finitude.[45] One may wonder whether Hicks's favored strategy of teasing his audiences with the promise of deferred dick jokes was not, in this sense, a way in which his faith protected itself against the corporeal limits to which comedy, as his dominant mode of articulation, always threatened to return him. "I think humor has to ring true emotionally, coupled with justified anger at how the world is, and how you know in your heart the world can be," Hicks once explained, before limning the paradox: "In that lies humor, and the word 'fuck.'"[46] In which case, the final subject of Hicks's career would perhaps not be salvation *per se* but rather the limits of comedy as a means of imagining salvation in the first place.

Notes

1. Quoted in Cynthia True, *American Scream: The Bill Hicks Story*, revised ed. (London, UK: Pan Books, 2013), 250.

2. Jimmy O'Brien, "Interview with Funny Man Bill Hicks," November/December 1992, in Bill Hicks, *Love All the People: The Essential Bill Hicks* (Berkeley, CA: Soft Skull Press, 2004), 92.

3. Hicks to Lawrence Christon, June 1993, in Hicks, *Love All the People*, 243 (emphasis in original).

4. On the *passage à l'acte*, see Alenka Zupančič, *Ethics of the Real: Kant, Lacan* (New York: Verso, 2000).

5. Igby's Comedy Club in Hicks, *Love All the People*, 294. The Letterman incident is extensively discussed in John Lahr, "The Goat Boy Rises," *New Yorker*, November 1, 1993, 113–21.

6. Jürgen Habermas, *The Structural Transformation of the Public Sphere: An Inquiry into a Category of Bourgeois Society*, trans. Thomas Burger (Cambridge, MA: MIT Press, 1989).

7. Megan Garber, "How Comedians Became Public Intellectuals," *The Atlantic*, May 28, 2015, accessed May 16, 2016, http://www.theatlantic.com/entertainment/archive/2015/05/how-comedians-became-public-intellectuals/394277; Stephanie Koziski, "The Standup Comedian as Anthropologist: Intentional Cultural Critic," *Journal of Popular Culture* 18, no. 2 (Fall 1984): 57–76; Lawrence E. Mintz, "Standup Comedy as Social and Cultural Mediation," *American Quarterly* 37, no. 1 (Spring 1985): 71–80; Rebecca Krefting, *All Joking Aside: American Humor and Its Discontents* (Baltimore, MD: Johns Hopkins University Press, 2014).

8. Lahr, "The Goat Boy Rises," 121 (emphasis added).

9. Hicks to Christon, *Love All the People*, 245 (emphasis in original). There is admittedly an important precedent here in Lenny Bruce, who similarly presented himself as a "doctor" or "surgeon with a scalpel for false values," and whom biographer Albert Goldman esteemed as a modern-day shaman; yet it remains the case that Bruce never quite took the Hicksian step of couching his "truth" in specifically religious or mystic terms. On Bruce and Hicks, see in particular Will Kaufman's excellent study *The Comedian as Confidence Man* (Detroit, MI: Wayne State University Press, 1997), which approaches both as casualties of what Kaufman calls "irony fatigue."

10. Hicks quoted in True, *American Scream*, 10–11.

11. Hicks quoted in True, *American Scream*, 94.

12. *Austin American-Statesman* quoted in True, *American Scream*, 101.

13. Lahr, "The Goat Boy Rises," 121.

14. Johndrow quoted in True, *American Scream*, 89.

15. Cree McCree, "Bill Hicks: Comedy for the Head," *High Times*, April 1993, in Hicks, *Love All the People*, 203.

16. Treatment for *The Counts of the Netherworld*, July 1992, in Hicks, *Love All the People*, 112.

17. Hicks to Christon, in Hicks, *Love All the People*, 243 (emphasis in original).

18. Bill Hicks, *Rant in E Minor* (Rykodisc, 1997).

19. Hicks, *Rant in E Minor*.

20. Jonathan J. Edwards, *Superchurch: The Rhetoric and Politics of American Fundamentalism* (Detroit: Michigan State University Press, 2015), *passim*, esp. 49–77.

21. Hicks to Christon, in Hicks, *Love All the People*, 246 (emphasis in original).

22. Hicks, "Unresolvable Problems—Resolved!" *Scallywag*, November 1993, in Hicks, *Love All the People*, 263.

23. See Edwards, *Superchurch*, 62–66.

24. Edwards, *Superchurch*, 66.

25. Hicks, *Rant in E Minor*.

26. Bill Hicks, *Dangerous* (Invasion Records, 1990).

27. Material in this paragraph is developed from my earlier essay, "Retheorizing Comedic and Political Discourse, or What Do Jon Stewart and Charlie Chaplin Have in Common?" *Discourse* 34, nos. 2–3 (Spring/Fall, 2012): 263–89, 283.

28. Live at the Dominion Theatre, London, November 1992, in Hicks, *Love All the People*, 146.

29. Hicks, *Rant in E Minor*.

30. Interview with Hicks, *CapZeyeZ Live! With Dave Prewitt*, Austin Public Access TV, October 24, 1993, in Hicks, *Love All the People*, 260.

31. Hicks quoted in True, *American Scream*, 176.

32. Hicks, *Dangerous*.

33. Live at the Dominion Theatre in Hicks, *Love All the People*, 146.

34. Ernesto Laclau, "On the Names of God," in *The Rhetorical Foundations of Society* (London, UK: Verso, 2014), 47.

35. Laclau, "On the Names of God," 44.

36. I am here paraphrasing Theodor Adorno's reflections on utopian thought, in the section "Sur l'eau" from *Minima Moralia: Reflections on Damaged Life*, trans. E. F. N. Jephcott (London, UK: Verso, 2006 [1951]), 157. My discussion of Hicks's "Just a Ride" bit again elaborates upon points made in my "Retheorizing Comedic and Political Discourse" essay (284–86).

37. Treatment for *The Counts of the Netherworld*, in Hicks, *Love All the People*, 121.

38. Hicks, Treatment for *The Counts of the Netherworld*, 120.

39. Hicks, Treatment for *The Counts of the Netherworld*, 117.

40. Hicks, Treatment for *The Counts of the Netherworld*, 116–17.

41. On Hicks's "Sane Man" persona, see True, *American Scream*, 32.

42. Treatment for *The Counts of the Netherworld*, in Hicks, *Love All the People*, 118.

43. Laclau, "On the Names of God," 51.

44. On the "ethics of the Real," see Terry Eagleton, *Trouble with Strangers: A Study of Ethics* (Malden, MA: Wiley-Blackwell, 2009), chapters 7–10.

45. On stand-up and abjection, see John Limon, *Stand-up Comedy in Theory, or, Abjection in America* (Durham, NC: Duke University Press, 2000).

46. O'Brien, "Interview with Funny Man Bill Hicks," in Hicks, *Love All the People*, 92.

ABOUT THE CONTRIBUTORS

Jared N. Champion earned a PhD in American studies from Boston University. His research centers on gender, popular culture, humor studies, and the environment. He edited the archival project *Cliffs and Challenges: A Young Woman Explores Yosemite, 1915–1917*, and his research has appeared in the *Journal of Popular Culture* and *Studies in Popular Culture*. His current project investigates normative masculinity and stand-up comedy.

Miriam M. Chirico specializes in dramatic literature and comedy studies at Eastern Connecticut State University, where she is professor of English. She authored *The Theatre of Christopher Durang* (Methuen, 2020) and coedited *How to Teach a Play: Essential Exercises for Popular Plays*, also published by Methuen Drama. She has published on Leguizamo previously, in "Performed Authenticity: Narrating the Self in the Comic Monologues of David Sedaris, John Leguizamo and Spalding Gray" (*Studies in American Humor*, 2016), and has written articles for *Text and Presentation*, *Comparative Drama*, and *Shaw: The Annual of Bernard Shaw Studies*. She is a board member of the Comparative Drama Conference.

Thomas Clark is an Americanist and historian with an interest in all aspects of political culture. He received his PhD in American studies at Goethe University Frankfurt, Germany in 2001, and subsequently held positions at the history departments of the universities of Kassel and Münster and at the American studies departments of Frankfurt and Tübingen, completing his second dissertation in history in 2014. With roots in the political and intellectual history of the Early Republic, he has focused in recent years on transatlantic perceptions of and intellectual exchanges between Europe and the United States and the relationship of culture and democracy, studying such figures as James Fenimore Cooper and Alexis de Tocqueville. Further interests include olfactory studies, countercultures of the 1960s and beyond, and popular culture, particularly stand-up comedy. He is also the lead singer of the punk band Hope & Anger.

David R. Dewberry is a professor in the Department of Communication and Journalism at Rider University. With a PhD in rhetoric and communication ethics (University of Denver), he is primarily a political rhetorician with a focus on free expression. He is the former editor of the *Communication Law Review* and *First Amendment Studies*. His work has been recognized with the Franklyn S. Haiman Award for Distinguished Scholarship in Freedom of Expression by the National Communication Association, the James Madison Prize for Outstanding Free Speech Scholarship by the Southern States Communication Association, and the Richard S. Arnold Prize for First Amendment Scholarship. He is the author of *The American Political Scandal: Free Speech, Public Discourse, and Democracy*. In addition to teaching at Rider, he has taught at the American Samoa Community College and was a visiting fellow at Harris Manchester College at Oxford University.

Christopher J. Gilbert is assistant professor of English in communication and media at Assumption University. His work, which looks at the role of humor in cultural politics as well as comic responses to controversy and conflict. He is the author of *Caricature and National Character: The United States at War* (2021), which looks at expressions of American cultural identity in wartime editorial cartoons. His essays appear in a variety of leading journals including *Studies in American Humor, Quarterly Journal of Speech, Communication and Critical/Cultural Studies, Text & Performance Quarterly*, and more, as well as in numerous edited volumes. Beyond academia, Chris is an avid road cyclist, a leisurely guitar player, and a drawing enthusiast.

David Gillota is associate professor of English at the University of Wisconsin–Platteville. He is the author of *Ethnic Humor in Multiethnic America* (Rutgers University Press, 2013), and his essays have appeared in journals such as *Studies in Popular Culture, Journal of American Culture*, and *Journal of Popular Film and Television*. He is also the associate editor of *Studies in American Humor*.

Kathryn Kein is a lecturer in gender, women's, and sexuality studies and assistant director of Women Involved in Learning and Leadership at the University of Maryland, Baltimore County. She holds a PhD in American studies from George Washington University. She teaches courses on gender, sexuality, and popular culture. Her publications include "Recovering our

Sense of Humor: New Directions in Feminist Humor Studies," a review essay on feminism and humor in the journal *Feminist Studies* (2015); and "Domestic Failure, Comic Pleasure: Phyllis Diller and the Feminist Potential of Failure, 1955–1969" in *Studies in American Humor* (2018).

Rob King is a professor of film and media studies at Columbia University's School of the Arts. He is the author of *Hokum! The Early Sound Slapstick Short and Depression-Era Mass Culture* (2017) and the award-winning *The Fun Factory: The Keystone Film Company and the Emergence of Mass Culture* (2009). He is currently working on a study of adult filmmaker Radley Metzger and is coediting, with Charlie Keil, the *Oxford Handbook of Silent Cinema*.

Rebecca Krefting is associate professor in the American Studies Department at Skidmore College. She specializes in feminist comedy and performance studies. Her book, *All Joking Aside: American Humor and Its Discontents*, charts the history of "charged humor" or stand-up comedy aimed at social justice. She has published journal articles in *Studies in American Humor*, *Comedy Studies*, and *Journal of Cinema and Media Studies* and is a contributing author to edited collections including *The Laughing Stalk: Live Comedy and Its Audiences, Hysterical!: Women in American Comedy, Transgressive Humor of American Women Writers, The Joke Is On Us: Political Comedy in (Late) Neoliberal Times*, and *Ethics in Comedy: Essays on Crossing the Line*. She has been invited to speak about her research at colleges and universities domestically and internationally. Her current research examines the historical forces shaping the economy of stand-up comedy.

Peter C. Kunze is a visiting professor of communication at Tulane University. He holds a PhD in English from Florida State University and a PhD in media studies from the University of Texas at Austin. He edited *The Films of Wes Anderson: Critical Essays on an Indiewood Icon* and *Conversations with Maurice Sendak*, and co-edited *American–Australian Cinema: Transnational Connections*. His research on comedy has appeared in *Comedy Studies* and *Studies in American Humor*.

Linda Mizejewski is a distinguished professor of women's, gender, and sexuality studies at the Ohio State University. She is the author of five books in feminist media studies, including *Pretty/Funny: Women Comedians and Body Politics* (2015). She is also the co-editor of the anthology, *Hysterical! American Women in Comedy* (2017), winner of the Susan Koppelman Prize from the Popular Culture Association. Mizejewski has been a Fulbright lecturer in Slovakia and Romania, and her research has been awarded grants from the National Endowment for the Humanities and the American Council of Learned Societies. At Ohio State, she has won the Alumni Distinguished Teaching Award and the Harlan Hatcher Distinguished Faculty Award.

Aviva Orenstein is a professor of law at the Maurer School of Law at Indiana University. She writes and teaches about the law of evidence. Her scholarly interests concern the intersection of evidence law and culture. Orenstein was a humor columnist for her local paper, the *Herald Times*, and still runs into folks who have put laminated copies of her essays on their refrigerator. No one does this with her scholarship. In 2016, her debut novel, *Fat Chance*, was published to little acclaim but much personal delight. Orenstein is the mother of three grown sons and grandmother of two.

Raúl Pérez is an assistant professor of sociology at the University of La Verne. His current research focuses on the social, cultural, and political impact of racist humor across various social domains, ranging from the world of stand-up comedy and law enforcement to white supremacist organizations and the political arena. His research is published in various academic journals and has been awarded and supported by the American Sociological Association, the Woodrow Wilson Foundation, the University of California Center for New Racial Studies, and the Working Class Studies Association. It has also been featured in various media outlets including *Time* magazine, the *Baltimore Sun*, the *Houston Chronicle*, *The Grio*, and *Zócalo Public Square*. His first book manuscript, *The Souls of White Jokes: How Racist Humor Fuels White Supremacy*, is forthcoming from Stanford University Press.

Philip Scepanski is assistant professor of film and television at Marist College, where he studies television history, media and cultural theory, humor, and trauma, among other topics. He is the author of *Tragedy Plus Time: National Trauma and Television Comedy* (2021). Scepanski is currently working on a second book, which explores the role of temporal conflict in film and television comedy. As a change of pace, he is also working on the history of a public affairs television show called *Prospects of Mankind*, which Eleanor Roosevelt hosted in the last three years of her life. He has also published in numerous journals and anthologies including *Television and New Media*, *Studies in American Humor*, *The Comedy Studies Reader*, and *How to Watch Television*.

Susan Seizer is a professor of anthropology at Indiana University. She received her PhD in anthropology from the University of Chicago in 1997. Her research and teaching interests include humor in use, stigma and the abject, and performance as communicative practice. Her first book, *Stigmas of the Tamil Stage: An Ethnography of Special Drama Artists in South India* (Duke University Press, 2005), looks at the on- and off-stage lives of artists who perform in the popular Tamil theater genre Special Drama. The book won the prestigious A. K. Coomaraswamy Prize from the Association for Asian Studies for the best book on South Asia in 2007. Seizer's second research project focuses on American stand-up comedians who play the comedy club circuit in middle America. She produced the documentary film *Road Comics: Big Work on Small Stages* (2012) based on this research. Prior to becoming an anthropologist, Seizer was a performer of experimental dance, theater, and circus. Many of her scholarly interests follow threads she first explored as a performer: the joys of improvisation; the way comedy can be used to do just about anything; and the particular exhilaration many find in transgressing normative gender roles through public performance.

Monique Taylor is the provost and vice president of academic affairs at Champlain College in Burlington, Vermont. Most recently she was working in international higher education for more than fifteen years, with teaching and administrative positions in Asia, Latin America, and the Middle East. The author of *Harlem between Heaven and Hell* and other publications on gentrification in Harlem, Taylor's current projects explore the slippery concept of post-racialism in the United States with an eclectic focus on food, film, and popular culture. She holds a PhD and MA in sociology from Harvard and an undergraduate degree in sociology from Yale. Taylor is a past recipient of the Graves Award for Excellence in Teaching from the American Council of Learned Societies.

Ila Tyagi is a lecturer in the humanities division at Yale–NUS College in Singapore. She completed a PhD in film and media studies and American studies at Yale University in 2018. Her research and teaching interests include American cinema and television, embodiment and sensory perception, energy and the environment, and science and technology. Her work has appeared in the journals *MediaTropes* and *Synoptique*, as well as in the edited collections *Ecocriticism and the Future of Southern Studies* (Louisiana State University Press, 2019) and *Make Waves: Water in Contemporary Literature and Film* (University of Nevada Press, 2019).

Timothy J. Viator, professor emeritus at Rowan University, taught literature and drama. He has published essays in drama, theater history, humor, and dramatic criticism—from Shakespeare to *Hamilton*. His current projects include a book that surveys and applies humor theory, *Why Is Humor?*

INDEX

Abadie, Ann J., 234n
Academy Awards, 30n, 86, 87, 99, 100
Acham, Christine, 96, 101n
Achter, Paul, 48n
Adorno, Theodor, 266n
After-Hours Stand-Up Series, 75, 84n
Albrecht, Gary L., 49n
Alexander, Jeffrey C., 50n
Ali, Ayaan Hirsi, 55
Allen, Woody, 142, 254
Alone Together, 186
Always Loyal, 44
Alzate, Gastón Adolfo, 136n
Amburn, Brad, 68n, 234n
American Civil Liberties Union (ACLU), 231
Ames, Mark, 249n
Amis, Martin, 262
Amy Schumer Show, The, 3
Anderson, Crystal, 182n
Andy Griffith Show, The, 222
Angelou, Maya, 55
Angry Black Woman stereotype, 28
Ansari, Aziz, 12, 13, 184–98
Ansari, Shoukath, 193
Apatow, Judd, 52, 67n, 165, 167n
Apprentice, The, 118
Apte, Mahadev L., 120n
Aristotle, 164
Armisen, Fred, 173
Armour, Terry, 121n
Armstrong, Robert Plant, 218n
Arnaz, Desi, 136n
Arrested Development, 54

Ashe, Bertram D., 170–71, 182n
At Folsom Prison, 17
Atherton, Cassandra, 234n
At San Quentin, 17
Attitudes Toward History, 133, 135n, 138n
Auer, J. Jeffery, 48n
Au Téléphone, 194
Avery, Kevin, 182n
Awkward Black Girl, 173
Awkwardness: An Essay, 73, 84n
Ayim, Maryann, 235n, 236n

Babcock, Barbara A., 218n
Bacevich, Andrew J., 37, 49n
Back at the Barnyard, 54
Badiou, Alain, 264
Baker, Peter, 121n
Bakhtin, Mikhail, 44, 45, 243, 244
Bamford, Maria, 10, 52–69
Banfield, Ashleigh, 196, 198n
Barber, Nicholas, 119
Barreca, Regina, 6, 15n
Batchis, Wayne, 226, 235n
Batuman, Elif, 73, 84n
Bauman, Richard, 202, 217n, 218n
Bauman, Zygmunt, 13, 219–21, 223, 224, 225, 226, 234n, 235n
Baumann, Nick, 100n
Baym, Nancy K., 185, 197n
Bécue-Renard, Laurent, 41
Bee, Samantha, 82, 195, 198n
Bee Movie, 158
Beer Hall Putsch, 240, 249n, 250n
Belknap, Joanne, 17, 30n

Bell, Melissa Hudson, 182n
Bell, W. Kamau, 12, 168–83
Bellamy, Richard, 234n
Benjamin, H. Jon, 188–89
Berger, Peter L., 121n
Bergson, Henri, 73, 74, 84n
Berman, Paul, 235n
Bernstein, Carl, 48n
Bernstein, Michael André, 41
Bernstein, Richard, 226
Berteaux, Anthony, 166n
Best, Shaun, 234n
Beyale, Shamus, 136n
Big Ass Jokes, 90, 93, 97, 101n
Bigger and Blacker, 99
Billig, Michael, 119n, 120n
Black, Lewis, 42
Blackbird, 20, 30n
Black Lives Matter, 118
Black Panthers, 170, 244
Blackshaw, Tony, 235n
Blair, Elizabeth, 51n
Blue, Josh, 66
Blue Collar Comedy Tour, 211, 224
Blue Collar Comedy Tour: The Movie, 222
Bobo, Lawrence, 120n
Bodenhausen, Galen V., 217n
Bogost, Ian, 192, 193, 198n
Bonilla-Silva, Eduardo, 120n, 121n, 122n
Born Suspect, 87, 89, 90, 93, 98, 101n
Boskin, Joseph, 120n
Boss, Pauline, 51n
Bossypants, 76, 84n
Bourne, Randolph, 249n
Boyish Girl Interrupted, 11, 72, 74, 77, 79, 84n, 85n
Bracey, Christopher Alan, 97, 101n
Brantley, Ben, 121n, 128, 132, 133, 136n, 137n
Brecht, Bertolt, 217n
Bring the Pain, 86, 93, 96, 99, 101n
Broad City, 1
Brodie, Ian, 15n, 137n, 187, 197n, 217n
Bronfen, Elisabeth, 47n
Brouwer, Daniel C., 181n
Brown, Michael, 118

Brown, Michelle, 29, 31n
Brownstein, Carrie, 173
Bruce, Lenny, 59, 142, 243, 244, 260, 265n
Bruenig, Elizabeth, 7, 15n, 57, 251n
Buckley, Cara, 151n
Budd, Jeanine, 121n
Burke, Kenneth, 47n, 123, 124, 133, 134, 135n, 138n
Burning Bridges Tour, The, 67n
Burr, Bill, 155, 163, 167n, 246
Bush, George H. W., 227
Butler, Judith, 47n
Butler, Paul, 100n

Calavita, Kitty, 181n
#CancelColbert, 104
Carbado, Devon W., 151n
Carlin, George, 4, 23, 59, 107, 108, 120n, 142, 155, 209, 227, 243, 244, 246, 250n
Carlisle, Clare, 49n
Carlito's Way, 131
Carnegie, Dale, 61
carnivalesque, 45, 244
Carolla, Adam, 57
Carpio, Glenda, 30n
Carrey, Jim, 165, 167n
Carroll, Noël, 195, 198n
Carrot Top, 57
Cars franchise, 222
Cash, Cliff, 217n
Cash, Johnny, 17–18
Cassano, Christa, 136n
Casualties of War, 129, 130
CatDog, 54
CBS This Morning, 159, 167n
Champion, Jared N., 3–15
Chandrasekaran, Rajiv, 50n
Chappelle, Dave, 23, 57, 162, 167n, 181, 211
charged humor, 4, 6, 54, 55, 56, 58, 59, 60, 62, 68n, 144, 170, 172, 175, 178, 179, 237, 238, 242–45
Charles, Ray, 228
Cheech and Chong, 129, 136n
Chewed Up, 143, 148
Chico and the Man, 136n

CHiPs, 126
Chirico, Miriam M., 11–12, 123–38
Chitlin' Circuit, 23
Chittal, Nisha, 182n
Cho, Margaret, 163, 165, 167n, 243, 245, 251n
Chomsky, Noam, 22, 262
Chris Rock Show, The, 99
Christianity, 27, 29, 58, 59, 230, 241, 255, 257
Christiansen, Adrienne E., 49n
Christon, Lawrence, 264n, 265n
Chua-Eoan, Howard, 32, 47n
Cillizza, Chris, 234n
C.K., Louis, 12, 72, 139–53
Clark, Thomas, 13–14, 237–51
Clay, Andrew Dice, 238
Clinton, Bill, 253, 256
Clinton, Hillary, 4, 58, 68n
Coates, Ta-Nehisi, 22, 31n, 196n
Colbert, Stephen, 7, 21, 52, 55, 67n, 104, 119n, 180, 219, 222, 223, 234n
Colbert Report, The, 159, 219
Comedians in Cars Getting Coffee, 12, 155, 157, 158, 165, 166n, 167n
Comedians of Comedy: Live at the El Rey, The, 67n
Comedians of Comedy Tour, 54
Comedy Dynamics, 54
Comedy Warriors: Healing Through Humor, 42, 43, 50n
"Coming Back with Wes Moore," 42
Conan, 75, 76
Cooley, Charles, 125, 129, 133
Coontz, Stephanie, 184
Cooper, Evan, 136n
Cooper, Marc, 250n
Cops, 126, 256
Corbett, Sara, 65, 69n
Cosby, Bill, 181
Costa, Uriel da, 213
Coston, Bethany M., 152n
Costos, Kathie, 48n
Count of the Netherworlds, 260
COVID-19 pandemic, 54, 67
Covino, Deborah Caslav, 49n
Cowherd, Colin, 154, 157, 166n

Cox, Laverne, 174
Crenshaw, Kimberlé, 151n
Crick, Nathan, 49n
Critchley, Simon, 74, 75, 84n
Cross, David, 224, 229, 235n
Crosshairs Comedy Troupe, 49n
Crowell, Steven, 250n
Crowley, Sharon, 47n
Cyrus, Billy Ray, 256

Dagnes, Alison, 236
Dahlgren, Peter, 51n
Daily Show, The, 159, 180
Dangerous, 260, 265n
Davidson, Amy, 50n
Davies, Ioan, 243, 250n
Davis, Angela, 17, 30n, 43
Davis, D. Diane, 49n
Death and the Maiden, 126
DeGeneres, Ellen, 144, 153n
Delta Farce, 222
De Palma, Brian, 131
Descartes, René, 164
Dewberry, David R., 13, 219–36
Die Hard 2, 126
Diller, Phyllis, 3
Dion, Celine, 178
Dirty Girl: No Protection, 109, 121n
Dolmage, Jay Timothy, 49n
Dore, Jon, 77
Dorinson, Joseph, 120n
Douglas, Mary, 169
Doug Stanhope: Before Turning the Gun on Himself, 237, 247, 249n, 250n
Drezner, Daniel W., 6–7, 15n
D'Souza, Dinesh, 105
Du Bois, W. E. B., 97
Dunnigan, Kyle, 83n
Dyer, Mary, 209
Dyer, Richard, 30n, 152n

Eagleton, Terry, 266n
Eakin, Marah, 67n
Eco, Umberto, 55
Edwards, Gavin, 235n, 236n

Edwards, Jonathan J., 257, 265n
Ellin, Abby, 51n
Ellis, Trey, 170, 171, 182n
Elshtain, Jean Bethke, 219, 234n
Emblidge, David, 250n
Emerson, Ralph Waldo, 14, 238
Emmy Award, 50n, 169, 195
Enchanted Objects, 186, 197n
Ending Racism, 171
Enlightenment, the, 239, 253
Ethnic Humor in Multiethnic America, 134, 138n, 234n, 235n
Etzioni, Amitai, 182n
Everybody Hates Chris, 100, 102n
existentialism, 14, 129, 237, 241, 242, 246, 250n
Eysturoy, Annie, 137n

Faber, Judy, 121n
Facebook, 185
Face Full of Flour, 175, 182n, 183n
Fallows, James, 48n
Family Guy, 162
Fantz, Ashley, 48n
Farhi, Paul, 119n, 121n, 122n
Farmer, Ann, 113, 122n
Farrell, Thomas B., 48n
F.A.T. Chance, 19
Feagin, Joe, 105, 106, 120n
Felsenthal, Julia, 72, 83n
female trickster, 18, 24–26, 31n
Ferber, Abby L., 141, 151n, 152n
Ferrence, Matthew J., 233, 234n, 236n
Fey, Tina, 76, 82, 84n
Field Negro's Guide to Art and Culture, The, 171
Finkel, David, 50n
Finley, Jessyka, 7, 15n
Finnegan, Cara A., 35, 48n
Finney, Gail, 47n
First Amendment Comedy Troupe, 132
Foley, Erin, 67
Ford, Stephen, 120n
Foxworthy, Jeff, 211, 222, 232
Foxx, Redd, 107

Frank, Arthur W., 49n
Freak, 123, 126, 128, 129, 132,133, 135n, 136n, 137n
Freeden, Michael, 249n
Freeman, Hadley, 85n
Freud, Sigmund, 38, 218n
Frontline, 41
Full Frontal with Samantha Bee, 195, 198n
Fulton, DoVeanna S., 19, 30n
Funny or Die, 84n

Gadino, Dylan, 121n, 122n
Gadsby, Hannah, 8, 57, 62, 216n, 218n
Galifianakis, Zach, 42, 54
Gallagher, Maggie, 235n
Gallop, Jane, 37, 49n
Ganeri, Jonardon, 49n
Garber, Megan, 3–4, 6, 7, 9, 14n, 15n, 21, 22, 23, 29, 30n, 31n, 48, 71, 83, 119n, 169, 181n, 182n, 253, 264n
Garland Thomson, Rosemarie, 49n
Garofalo, Janeane, 4
Garvey, Marcus, 98
Gates, Henry Louis, 179, 180, 183n
Geek's Chihuahua, The, 192, 198n
Geertz, Clifford, 209
George, Nelson, 170, 182n
Gervais, Ricky, 158
Ghetto Klown, 123, 129, 130, 132, 133, 135n, 136n, 137n
G. I. Joe: Retaliation, 185
Gilbert, Christopher J., 10, 32–51
Gilbert, Joanne R., 9, 15n, 40, 48n, 49n, 50n, 137n, 152n, 222, 234n
Giles, Matt, 167n
Gillota, David, 12, 15n, 21, 30n, 47n, 62, 68n, 69n, 87, 94, 100n, 134, 138n, 139–53, 221, 225, 234n, 235n, 245, 251n
Git-R-Done, 221, 234n, 235n, 236n
Glazer, Ilana, 3
God Hates Ann, 199, 202, 203, 207, 208, 209, 212, 214, 215, 216n, 217n
Goffman, Erving, 218n
Goldberg, Whoopi, 23, 55
Goldman, Albert, 265

Gomez, Patrick, 69n
Good Hair, 100
Good One, 71, 75, 84n, 85n
Gopnik, Adam, 72, 73, 84n
Gore, Al, 55
Gottfried, Gilbert, 227
Grammy Award, 72
Gramsci, Antonio, 5, 9, 15n, 23, 56, 57, 68n, 245, 251n
Grateful Dead, 209
Gray, Frances, 216n
Green, Jesse, 138n
Greenbaum, Andrew, 50n
Greene, Richard, 68n
Gregory, Alice, 246, 247, 251n
Gregory, Dick, 3, 23, 49n, 58, 59, 168, 181, 183n
Griffin, Kathy, 82, 83n
Griffith, D. W., 194
Grigoriadis, Vanessa, 85n
Gross, Josh, 50n
Grown Ups, 100
Gulf War, 252
Gunn, Joshua, 47n
Gunning, Tom, 194, 198n

Habermas, Jürgen, 253, 254, 262, 263, 264
Haggins, Bambi, 7, 15, 23, 31n, 96, 101n, 120, 151n, 181, 183n
Halberstam, Judith, 51n
Hale, Mike, 146, 153n
Hall, Stuart, 163
Hanson, Jeremy J., 49n
Harding, Sandra, 68n
Harris, Cheryl I., 152n
Harris, Sam, 246
Harris-Perry, Melissa, 19, 22, 28, 30n, 31n, 172
Harvey, Steve, 156, 162, 163, 166n
Hawhee, Debra, 33, 47n
Hawksley, Craig, 222
Hawley, Willis D., 91, 101n
Head of State, 100
Healing Bobby, 41
Hellerstein, Erica, 157, 166n
Hendrix, Jimi, 171
Henline, Bobby, 10, 32–51

Hetrick, Adam, 138n
Hey Arnold!, 54
Hicks, Bill, 3, 14, 246, 251n, 252–66
Hicks, James Melvin, 254
Hitchens, Christopher, 246
Hitler, Adolf, 251n
Hobbes, Thomas, 164
Hofstadter, Richard, 15n, 48n, 59, 60, 68n
Holden, Stephen, 133, 137n
Holmes, Pete, 76, 84n
Holpuch, Amanda, 119n
House of the Spirits, The, 126
Howard Stern Show, The, 122n
Howe, Irving, 185, 196n
Hudson, Alan, 251n
Hudson, John, 119n
Huff, Stewart, 13, 199–218
Hughes, Geoffrey, 235n
Hughes, Langston, 3
Hume, Mick, 157, 166n
Huntsberger, David, 83n
Hurwitz, Mitchell, 54
Hutcheon, Linda, 152n

I Coulda Been Your Cellmate, 10, 16–31
Ideas Industry, The, 6, 15n
I Don't Think I Believe Us, 216n
I Love Lucy, 136n
I Love You, Daddy, 139
I'ma Be Me, 129, 136n
I'm Gonna Git You Sucka, 101n
I'm Just a Person, 72
Inevitable, The, 186, 197n
Instagram, 45
Interpretation of Cultures, The, 210
Involvement of Mexican Americans in Gainful Endeavors (IMAGE), 107
Iron Maiden, 222
Isherwood, Charles, 135n
Issitt, John, 155, 156, 166n
Itzkoff, Dave, 151n

Jackass, 43
Jackson, Duncan, 155, 156, 166n, 251n
Jackson, Jesse, 228

Jackson, Todd, 121n, 122n
Jacobson, Abby, 3
Jacoby, Russell, 245, 251n
Jaffe, Allyson, 113
Jaffe, Eric, 197n
James, William, 124, 127, 135n
Jay, David, 44, 51n
Jesus Christ, 29, 215, 218n, 222, 231
Jezebel stereotype, 20
Jimmy Swaggart Telecast, The, 255
Johndrow, David, 255
Johnson, Adam, 157, 167n
Johnson, Eliana, 58, 68n
Johnson, Gary, 239
Jones, Chris, 157, 166n
Jones, Leslie, 82
Jones, Loyal, 234n
Judaism, 59, 112, 142, 221, 242, 243, 244, 245, 250n, 251n
Jung, Carl, 256, 263
Jung, E. Alex, 83n
Junger, Sebastian, 50n

Kachka, Boris, 84n
Kang, Inkoo, 119n
Kang, Jay C., 119n
Kant, Immanuel, 74
Kantor, Jodi, 151n
Kardashian, Kim, 19
Katz, Emily Tess, 85n
Kaufman, Will, 265n
Keating, Susan, 49n
Kelly, Kevin, 186, 197n
Key, Keegan-Michael, 3, 31
Key and Peele, 3
Kibler, M. Alison, 120n
Kimmel, Michael, 141, 151n, 152n
Kinder, John M., 48n, 51n
King, Clare Sisco, 49n
King, Martin Luther, 170, 172
King, Rob, 14, 252–66
Kinison, Sam, 256
Kissinger, Henry, 35
Kitchen, Matthew, 67n, 69n
Klein, Robert, 254

Klinenberg, Eric, 184, 185, 196n, 197n, 198n
Kluegel, James R., 120n
Knock Knock, It's Tig Notaro, 77, 85n
Knoxville, Johnny, 43
Ko, Sharon, 49n
Kona, Prakash, 244, 250n
Kondabolu, Hari, 52, 67n
Kotsko, Adam, 73, 76, 82, 84n, 85n
Koziski, Stephanie, 9, 15n, 55, 57, 58, 64, 68n, 69n, 176, 183n, 191, 198n, 220, 234n, 253, 264n
Krefting, Rebecca, 4, 6, 9, 10, 14n, 15n, 20, 30n, 38, 47n, 49n, 50n, 51n, 52–69, 104, 119n, 144, 152n, 170, 175, 179, 182n, 183n, 221, 234n, 237, 242, 243, 249n, 250n, 253, 264n
Kristeva, Julia, 51n, 250n
Kroll, Nick, 3
Krugman, Paul, 22
Kunze, Peter C., 3–15, 152n

Lacan, Jacques, 253
Laclau, Ernesto, 261, 263, 265n, 266n
Lady Dynamite, 52, 54, 66
Lahr, John, 132, 137n, 254, 255, 264n, 265n
L.A. Law, 126
Lampanelli, Lisa, 11, 103–22
Landay, Lori, 24, 25, 26, 31n
Larry the Cable Guy, 13, 219–36
Late Night with Seth Meyers, 154, 159, 166n
Late Show with David Letterman, 162, 181, 253
Late Show with Stephen Colbert, 52, 67n
Latin History for Morons, 123, 134, 135n, 138n
Latour, Bruno, 47n
Latour, Francie, 152n
Laughter Against the Machine, 172
Laughter: An Essay on the Meaning of the Comic, 73, 84n
Lawrence, Martin, 23
Leake, Brett, 66
Lee, Benjamin, 122n
Lee, Judith Yaross, 159, 167n
Lee, Shayne, 20, 30n
Leese, Daniele, 235n

Leguizamo, John, 11, 123–38
Legum, Judd, 157, 166n
Leno, Jay, 258
Leonard, David J., 117, 119n, 122n
Letterman, David, 166n, 167n, 180, 253, 264n
Levine, Art, 69n
Levine, Max, 67n
Lewis, Richard, 254
Limbaugh, Rush, 108, 156
Limon, John, 7, 15n, 47n, 50n, 144, 153n, 223, 234n, 246, 250n, 251n, 266n
Ling, Rich, 186, 197n
Linker, Damon, 235n
Lipsyte, Robert, 183n
Lisa Lisa and Cult Jam, 131
Little Red Book, The, 226
Littlewood, Jane, 120n, 121n
Live at Madison Square Garden, 186, 187, 190, 191, 197n
Live at the Beacon Theater, 145
Living Colour, 171
Locke, John, 239
Lockyer, Sharon, 187, 197n
Lonely Villa, The, 194, 198n
Lord, I Apologize, 229, 232, 235n, 236n
Lott, Eric, 120n
Louie, 148
Lucaites, John Louis, 48n
Luis, William, 125, 135n
Lukianoff, Greg, 119n
Lynyrd Skynyrd, 222
Lyszczyński, Kazimierz, 213, 214

Mabley, Moms, 3, 10
Macrae, C. Neil, 217n
MacRury, Iain, 185, 197n
Madagascar, 100
Maddow, Rachel, 172
Madonna, 131, 258
Maher, Bill, 155, 159, 160
Mambo Mouth, 123, 126, 127, 128, 132, 133, 135n, 136n
Mandel, Oscar, 201, 216n
Mao Zedong, 226
Marc, David, 137n

Marcotte, Amanda, 157, 166n
Maria Bamford: Ask Me About My New God!, 62, 67n, 69n
Maria Bamford: How to WIN!, 63, 67n, 68n, 69n
Maria Bamford Show, The, 54
Maria Bamford: The Special Special Special!, 54, 67n, 68n
Marin, Cheech, 136n
Markert, John, 136n
Maron, Marc, 3, 57, 72, 83n, 139
Marriage, A History: How Love Conquered Marriage, 184
Marshall, David, 234n
Martin, Steve, 57, 142, 160, 162, 167n
Martin, Trayvon, 172
Martin Short Show, The, 54
Marx, Karl, 92, 101n
Mason, Jackie, 109
Master of None, 13, 184, 187, 188, 193, 194, 197n
Masterpiece Theatre, 173
Matthews, Col. Lloyd J., 48n
McCarthy, Sean L., 68n
McCarty, Mary, 30n
McCree, Cree, 265n
McDowell, Edwin, 121n
McElwee, Sean, 251n
McGee, Sherri A., 30n
McGlynn, Katla, 167n
McIntosh, Peggy, 141, 151n, 152n
McKenna, Terence, 258
Mears, Kathryn, 69n
Medjesky, Christopher A., 155, 166n
Meier, Matthew R., 5, 9, 15n, 152n, 155, 166n
Menard, Valerie, 136n
#MeToo, 8, 196
Mexican American Anti-Defamation Committee (MAADC), 107
Meyers, Seth, 154, 156, 159, 165, 166n
Miami Vice, 126, 136n
Michael, George, 258
Miller, Bernard Alan, 51n
Miller, Dennis, 4, 227
Mills, C. Wright, 38, 188, 197n

Milne, Alan B., 217n
Mintz, Lawrence E., 7, 9, 15n, 47n, 68n, 89, 101n, 104, 119n, 137n, 169, 182n, 187, 197n, 225, 226, 235n, 251n, 253, 264n
Mirman, Eugene, 54
Misery Loves Comedy, 69n
Mishra, Pankaj, 48n, 251n
Mitchell, SED, 205, 206, 212
Mizejewski, Linda, 10, 14n, 16–31, 68n, 84n
Modern Romance, 184, 185, 190, 191, 194, 195, 196, 197n, 198n
Molloy, Parker, 166n
Mo'Nique, 10, 17–31
Mo'Nique: One Night Stand, 19, 20
Monroe, Marilyn, 19
Moore, Clement Clarke, 230
Moore, Wes, 42, 44
Morales, Ed, 136n
Morello, Tom, 172
Morley, David, 163, 167n
Mormons, 241
Morreall, John, 167n, 216n, 218n
Morris, David B., 51n
Morris, David J., 41
Morrison, Toni, 250n
Muñoz, José Esteban, 47n, 49n
Murphy, Eddie, 181
Murray, Noel, 234n, 236n
Muslims, 59, 241
Musto, Michael, 30n

NAACP, 19, 107, 116
Nachman, Gerald, 23, 31n, 121n
Nanette, 8, 216n
National Association for the Advancement of Colored People, 19, 107, 116
Native Son, 175
Neal, Mark Anthony, 182n
neoliberalism, 59, 104, 105, 109, 116–19
Netflix, 52, 54, 184
New Jack City, 101n
Newton, Huey P., 244, 250n
Nguyen, Ana, 233
Nietzsche, Friedrich, 241
Night of Too Many Stars, 139

Noah, Trevor, 165, 166n, 167n
No Refunds, 239, 250n
Notaro, Tig, 10–11, 70–85
Novak, B. J., 42

Obama, Barack, 58, 100n, 174, 179, 180
O'Brien, Conan, 75
O'Brien, Jimmy, 264n, 266n
Occupy movement, 172, 240, 241
Office, The, 173
Of Men and War, 41
Oh My God, 145, 149
Old Baby, 67n
Olivier, Laurence, 128
Omi, Michael, 120n
One Mississippi, 72
One Night Only, 175, 182n, 183n
Only in America, 222
Operation Iraqi Freedom, 41
Oppliger, Patrice, 69n
Orange Is the New Black, 174
Orbey, Eren, 198n
O'Reilly, Bill, 152n, 156
O'Reilly Factor, The, 4
Orenstein, Aviva, 13, 199–218
Oscars, 30n, 86, 87, 99, 100
Oswalt, Patton, 3, 54, 227

Pacino, Al, 131, 133
Parker, Dorothy, 3
Parkers, The, 19
Parks, Rosa, 170
Parks and Recreation, 13, 173
Parsons, Talcott, 188, 189
Patton, Stacey, 117, 119n, 122n
Paul, Ron, 239
Payne, Nicki, 66
PC. *See* political correctness
Pearsall, Stacey, 44, 51n
Peele, Jordan, 3, 31n
Peirce, Charles Sanders, 145
Penn, Sean, 130, 131, 133
Perez, Danielle, 66
Pérez, Raúl, 11, 15n, 103–22
Perez Family, The, 126

Personal Connections in the Digital Age, 185, 197n
Peters, John Durham, 50n
Peterson, Jordan, 237
Phat Girlz, 16, 17, 19
Pickering, Michael, 120n, 121n
Pinker, Steven, 217n
Plan B, 67n
Plato, 164
Poehler, Amy, 82
political correctness, 12, 13, 104, 105, 107, 108, 109, 117, 154–67, 173, 219–36
Politically Incorrect, 4
Pollak, Kevin, 69n
Portlandia, 173
Posehn, Brian, 54
Posner, Richard A., 6, 15n, 181n, 218n
Poulakos, John, 49n
Powell, Colin, 93–95
Powers, Nicole, 122n
Precious, 30n
Presley, Elvis, 255
Pressure of Your Expectations Is Overwhelming, The, 216n
Pretty/Funny: Women Comedians and Body Politics, 10, 14n, 68n, 84n
Pride, Richard A., 101n
Priestley, Joseph, 203
Prince, 171
Principles of Psychology, The, 124, 135n
Prinze, Freddie, 136n
Probably, 211, 216n
Professor Blastoff, 72
Pryor, Richard, 4, 23, 31n, 58, 59, 107, 128, 142, 181, 209, 243, 244
PTL Club, 255
Public Enemy, 179

Queens of Comedy, The, 19, 20, 21

Raab, Scott, 119n
Rae, Issa, 173
Rage Against the Machine, 172
Rappoport, Leon, 243, 250n
Rather, Dan, 137n

Reagan, Ronald, 222, 258
Real Time with Bill Maher, 159, 160
Red Border Films, 41
Reddit, 161, 167n
Regarding Henry, 126
Rehder, John B., 234n
Reid, Vernon, 171
Relentless, 259
Remnick, David, 154, 156, 165
Revelations, 259, 260, 262
Revenge, 126
Reynolds, Daniel, 30n
Rhazes, 204
Richards, Michael, 103, 110, 121n, 162, 167n
Richardson, John E., 110, 121n
Rickles, Don, 108, 109
Right Now, 195, 196, 198n
Right to Bare Arms, The, 232, 235n
Rivers, Joan, 3, 10, 23
Road Comics: Big Work on Small Stages, 202, 216n
Roberts, Oral, 255
Rock, Chris, 11, 23, 86–102, 104, 144, 153n, 155, 162, 181, 211, 227
Rodriguez, Paul, 125
Rogers, Will, 3
Román, David, 135n
Romano, Nick, 198n
Rookwood, Dan, 197n
Rosaldo, Renato, 242, 250n
Rosario, José R., 137n
Rose, David, 186, 197n
Rosell, Christine, 101n
Rossing, Jonathan Paul, 49n, 119n
Rothbard, Murray, 241
Rothman, Lily, 85n
Rousseau, Jean-Jacques, 240, 249n
Rubin, Karen, 50n
Ruskin, Zack, 52, 67n
Ryzik, Melena, 151n

Safire, William, 235n
Sager, Mike, 45
Saget, Bob, 42
Sahl, Mort, 59, 254, 260

Said, Edward, 5, 15n, 57, 58, 65, 68n
Sanders, Bernie, 4
Sandler, Adam, 99
San Francisco Comedy Competition, 238
Sapphire stereotype, 28
Saraiya, Sonia, 153n
Sartre, Jean-Paul, 7
Saturday Night Live, 99, 101n, 147, 180, 181
Savali, Kristen West, 119n
Saxton, Alexander, 120n
Scarry, Elaine, 50n
Scepanski, Philip, 11, 86–102
Schmitt, Casey R., 5, 9, 15n, 152n, 155, 166n
Schopenhauer, Arthur, 264
Schüll, Natasha, 191, 192
Schumer, Amy, 3, 4, 21, 81, 82
Schwartz, Barry, 184
Scientology, 241
Sconce, Jeffrey, 94, 101n
Scott-Heron, Gil, 171
Screen Actors Guild (SAG), 136n
Second City Headlines & News, 54
Secret Life of Pets, The, 139
Seinfeld, 158, 161
Seinfeld, Jerry, 3, 12, 104, 154–67, 180, 227
Seizer, Susan, 13, 50n, 199–218
Selzer, Jack, 47n
Sengupta, Somini, 135n
Seuss, Dr., 205
Sexaholix . . . A Love Story, 123, 132
Shafer, Jessica Gantt, 122n
Sharpton, Al, 162
Sherman, Yael D., 84n
Shockley, Evie, 182n
Shouse, Eric, 69n
Silman, Anna, 119n, 120n, 235n
Silverman, Sarah, 3, 4, 21, 117–18, 139, 155, 166n
Simmons, Tom, 217n
Simpson, O. J., 93, 94, 95
Skinny Cooks Can't Be Trusted, 19
Skinny Women Are Evil, 19, 30n
Slade, Dwight, 254, 255
Smith, Anna Deavere, 123, 132, 135n
Smith, David Livingston, 48n

Smith, Mychal Denzel, 97, 98, 101n
Smith, Ryan A., 120n
SNL, 99, 101n, 147, 180, 181
Social System, The, 188
Sociological Imagination, The, 188, 197n
"Soldier's Heart, The," 41
Sontag, Susan, 22
Sotomayor, Sonia, 138n
South by Southwest, 67n
South Park, 162
Spacey, Kevin, 139
Spencer, Herbert, 239
Spic-O-Rama, 123, 128, 132, 135n, 136n, 137n
Squires, Catherine R., 181n
Standing Up, Speaking Out, 152n, 155
Stanhope, Doug, 13–14, 237–51
Stern, Howard, 160, 167n
Steve-O, 43, 51n
Stewart, Jon, 7, 21, 55, 139, 180
Stewart Huff's Obsessive Curiosities, 216n
Stokes, Michael, 44, 45
Stone, Laurie, 133, 137n
Stories of Service, 42
Strachan, Maxwell, 101n
Sumner, William Graham, 239
Sundance Film Festival, 72
Swayze, Patrick, 130
Sykes, Wanda, 57, 129, 130, 136n

Talking Funny, 158, 167n
Tandy, Jennette, 14n
Tate, Greg, 170, 171
Taylor, Diana, 217n
Taylor, John, 47n
Taylor, Melissa Floyd, 158, 167n
Taylor, Monique, 12, 168–83
Tea Partiers, 2
This American Life, 168
Thomas, James G., 234n
Thomas, Mary, 29
Thoreau, Henry David, 14, 238
TikTok, 45
Tomlin, Lily, 3
Tonight Show, The, 181, 254
Top Five, 100

Tosh, Daniel, 155
Totally Biased, 172, 173, 180, 182n
To Wong Foo, 130
Transcendental Meditation, 255
True, Cynthia, 264n
Truly Tasteless Jokes series, 109
Trump, Donald, 118, 126, 227
Tubman, Harriet, 28
Tumblr, 44
Turkle, Sherry, 186, 197n
Turner, Victor, 169
Twain, Mark, 3
20%, 67n
Twitter, 45, 157, 162
Tyagi, Ila, 13, 184–98
Tyler, Aisha, 173

United Shades of America, 12, 169
Unwanted Thoughts Syndrome, 67n

Valdes, Francisco, 235n
Vallentyne, Peter, 249n, 250n
van Agtmael, Peter, 49, 50n
Velázquez, Loreta Janeta, 138n
Veterans Portrait Project, 44
Viator, Timothy J., 12, 154–67
View, The, 222
Villa, Pablo, 51n
Vonnegut, Kurt, 133

Waithe, Lena, 187
Walker, Madam C. J., 28
War Comes Home, The, 41
Wareheim, Eric, 187
Wartorn: 1861–2010, 41
Watkins, Mel, 23, 31n
Way, Katie, 198n
Wayne, John, 222
Weakness Is the Brand, 54, 67n
Weaver, Simon, 104, 119n, 250n
Weheliye, Alexander, 182n
Weinberg, Cory, 152n
Weinstein, Harvey, 139
Welch, William M., 50n
Wells, Noël, 187

Wenger, Ian, 51n
Wenzel, John, 122n
West, Mae, 19
Where's Waldo?, 228
White, Laurel, 83n
White, Richard D., Jr., 14n
Whitlock, Kay, 17, 30n
Whitney, Dan, 13, 219–36
Wilkie, Ian, 47n
Willett, Cynthia, 84n
Willett, Julie, 84n
Williams, Robin, 10
Wilmore, Larry, 21, 31n
Wilson, Charles Reagan, 234n
Wilson, Darren, 118
Wilson, E. O., 22
Wilson, Flip, 181
Wilson, Jason, 120n
Wilson, John K., 120n
Winant, Howard, 120n
Winerman, Lea, 197n
Wise, Tim, 141, 152n
Wood, David, 41, 49n, 50n
Woodard, J. David, 101n
Woodland, Fallon, 262
Woodward, Bob, 48n
Word of Mouth, 239, 249n, 250n
World Christian Fundamental Association, 257
Wounded Warrior Project, 42
Wright, Richard, 175
Wrigley, Deborah, 50n
Writer, Rich, 68n
Wuster, Tracy, 14n
Wynn, Natalie, 237

X, Malcolm, 96, 97, 98, 101n, 170, 171

Yagoda, Ben, 73, 84n
Young, Damon, 98, 102n
YouTube, 47n, 55, 146, 217n, 237, 246
Yu, Kelvin, 188

Zayid, Maysoon, 66
Zemler, Emma, 69n

Zinoman, Jason, 119n
Zoglin, Richard, 121n
Zwagerman, Sean, 14n, 15n
Zupančič, Alenka, 264n

www.ingramcontent.com/pod-product-compliance
Lightning Source LLC
Chambersburg PA
CBHW030337240426
43661CB00052B/1656